Alfred Mainwaring

Report of the Third Decennial Missionary Conference Held at

Bombay from 1892 to 1893

Vol. 2

Alfred Mainwaring

**Report of the Third Decennial Missionary Conference Held at Bombay from 1892 to 1893**
*Vol. 2*

ISBN/EAN: 9783337429621

Printed in Europe, USA, Canada, Australia, Japan

Cover: Foto ©Suzi / pixelio.de

More available books at **www.hansebooks.com**

# REPORT

OF THE

THIRD DECENNIAL

# MISSIONARY CONFERENCE,

1892-93.

VOLUME II.

# REPORT

OF THE

## THIRD DECENNIAL

# MISSIONARY CONFERENCE

HELD AT

## BOMBAY,

### 1892-93.

VOLUME II.

Bombay:
EDUCATION SOCIETY'S STEAM PRESS, BYCULLA.

1893.

# TABLE OF CONTENTS.

## VOLUME II.

### X.—EDUCATION AS A MISSIONARY AGENCY.

| | PAGE |
|---|---|
| Speech by the Rev. Dr. Hooper | 413 |
| Paper by the Rev. W. H. Findlay | 414 |
| ,, Rev. Dr. Mackichan | 424 |
| ,, Rev. A. B. Wann | 439 |
| Speech by the Rev. Dr. Ewing | 448 |
| ,. Rev. L. B. Wolf | 454 |

#### DISCUSSION.

| | | | |
|---|---|---|---|
| Bishop Thoburn | 458 | The Rev. R. Scott | 467 |
| The Rev. W. A. Roberts | 460 | ,, J. Shillidy | 468 |
| K. C. Banurji, Esq. | 461 | ,, D. Anantam | 470 |
| The Rev. M. Phillips | 462 | ,, J. Duthie | 471 |
| ,, J. G. Hawker | 463 | ,, Dr. Miller | 472 |
| ,, W. A. Mansell | 464 | ,, Dr. Mackichan | 475 |
| ,, J. Haythornthwaite | 465 | ,, A. B. Wann | 477 |

### XI.—INDUSTRIAL WORK.

| | PAGE |
|---|---|
| Speech by J. Morris, Esq. | 478 |
| Paper by the Rev. J. Frohnmeyer | 479 |
| ,, Rev. T. Snell Smith | 492 |
| Speech by the Rev. Dr. Fairbank | 498 |
| ,, Rev. J. Small | 499 |

#### DISCUSSION.

| | | | |
|---|---|---|---|
| The Rev. Sorabjee Kharshetji | 501 | The Rev. J. Blackstock | 506 |
| ,, C. W. Lay | 503 | ,, Dr. J. Chamberlain | 507 |
| ,, W. E. Rambo | 503 | ,, Dr. Weitbrecht | 508 |
| ,, M. B. Fuller | 504 | ,, J. Duthie | 509 |
| ,, E. T. Butler | 505 | ,, J. Frohnmeyer | 509 |
| ,, N. E. Lundborg | 506 | | |

## XII.—THE OBSERVANCE OF THE LORD'S DAY IN INDIA.

|  | PAGE |
|---|---|
| Speech by J. G. Shome, Esq. ... | 511 |
| Paper by the Rev. W. D. Phillips | 511 |
| ,,  Rev. F. W. Warne | 519 |
| Speech by the Rev. A. P. Begg ... | 525 |
| ,,  Rev. J. A. D. Macdonald | 529 |

### DISCUSSION.

| The Rev. I. W. Charlton ... | 534 | K. C. Banurji, Esq. | 538 |
|---|---|---|---|
| ,,  H. C. Stuntz | 535 | The Rev. J. S. Gray | 538 |
| ,,  E. G. Elsam | 536 | ,,  A. W. Prautch ... | 538 |
| ,,  J. F. Campbell | 537 | ,,  C. G. Conklin ... | 539 |
| ,,  H. G. E. De St. Dalmas. | 538 | Miss Gordon | 540 |

## XIII.—THE SOCIAL CONDITION OF THE LOWER CLASSES.

(*a*) HOW FAR ARE MISSIONS CALLED UPON TO AMELIORATE IT. (*b*) THE OPPORTUNITIES IT AFFORDS FOR MISSION WORK. (*c*) MASS MOVEMENTS TOWARDS CHRISTIANITY MORE OR LESS ARISING FROM IT. (*d*) THE DANGERS INCIDENTAL TO SUCH MOVEMENTS AND THE RIGHT LINE OF ACTION WITH REGARD TO THEM.

| Speech by the Rev. J. Smith ... | 541 |
|---|---|
| Paper by the Rev. Dr. J. Scudder | 544 |
| ,,  Rev. Dr. L. L. Uhl | 550 |
| Speech by the Rev. J. Heinrichs | 563 |
| ,,  Rev. J. Stone | 571 |

### DISCUSSION.

| The Rev. A. Andrews | 574 | The Rev. C. B. Ward | 581 |
|---|---|---|---|
| ,,  W. H. Campbell | 575 | ,,  J. E. Padfield | 582 |
| ,,  J. E. Davies | 576 | ,,  W. B. Simpson ... | 584 |
| ,,  N. E. Lundborg | 578 | ,,  J. A. Graham | 585 |
| ,,  Dr. Weitbrecht ... | 579 | ,,  Dr. J. McLaurin | 586 |
| ,,  Dr. J. L. Phillips | 580 | ,,  Dr. L. L. Uhl | 587 |
| ,,  J. Parson | 581 | | |

## XIV.—MISSIONARY COMITY.

| Paper by the Rev. A. Clifford ... | 590 |
|---|---|
| ,,  Bishop Thoburn ... | 601 |
| Speech by the Rev. F. Ashcroft | 614 |
| ,,  Rev. H. Gulliford | 617 |
| ,,  Rev. J. Shillidy | 621 |

## CONTENTS.

### DISCUSSION.

| | PAGE | | | PAGE |
|---|---|---|---|---|
| The Rev. N. E. Lundborg | ... 624 | The Rev. J. P. Jones | ... | 629 |
| ,, Dr. L. L. Uhl ... | ... 626 | ,, Dr. Hooper | ... | 629 |
| ,, R. A. Hume ... | ... 627 | ,, G. H. Rouse | ... | 630 |
| ,, Dr. J. L. Phillips | .. 627 | ,, A. Clifford | ... | 630 |
| ,, Dr. P. S. Johnson | ... 628 | Bishop Thoburn | ... | 631 |

## XV.—WORK AMONG ANGLO-INDIANS AND EURASIANS.

| | |
|---|---|
| Speech by the Rev. Dr. T. J. Scott ... ... ... ... ... ... | 637 |
| Paper by the Rev. H. Gouldsmith ... ... ... ... ... ... | 638 |
| Speech by the Rev. D. Osborne ... ... ... ... ... ... | 645 |
| ,, Rev. I. F. Row ... ... ... ... ... ... | 652 |

### DISCUSSION.

| | | | | |
|---|---|---|---|---|
| The Rev. C. A. E. Diez ... | ... 657 | Mrs. F. L. McAfee | ... ... | 660 |
| Mrs. Sorabji ... ... | ... 658 | The Rev. J. E. Newsom ... | ... | 661 |
| The Rev. H. C. Stuntz ... | ... 658 | Miss A. M. Andrews | ... ... | 662 |
| ,, S. W. Organe ... | ... 658 | The Rev. Dr. J. L. Phillips | ... | 662 |
| ,, D. Reid ... | .. 659 | | | |

## XVI.—CHRISTIAN LITERATURE.

(*a*) VERNACULAR. (*b*) ENGLISH. (*c*) THE SCRIPTURES. (*d*) COLPORTAGE.

| | |
|---|---|
| Speech by Eugene Stock, Esq. ... ... ... ... ... ... ... | 664 |
| Paper by the Rev. H. Haigh ... ... ... ... ... ... ... | 664 |
| ,, Dr. J. Murdoch ... .. ... ... ... ... ... | 674 |
| ,, the Rev. S. W. Organe ... ... ... ... ... ... | 687 |
| ,, the Rev. G. P. Taylor ... ... ... ... ... | 701 |
| Speech by the Rev. A. W. Prautch ... ... ... ... ... | 707 |
| ,, Rev. J. A. Thomson ... ... ... ... ... | 711 |
| ,, Rev. Dr. Weitbrecht ... ... ... ... ... | 716 |
| ,, Rev. Dr. W. F. Johnson ... ... ... ... | 719 |

### DISCUSSION.

| | | | | |
|---|---|---|---|---|
| The Rev. Dr. J. L. Phillips | ... 725 | The Rev. H. J. Bruce | ... ... | 732 |
| ,, Dr. Chamberlain | ... 726 | ,, J. Duthie | ... ... | 734 |
| ,, J. A. D. J. Macdonald... | 728 | ,, W. J. Richards | ... ... | 734 |
| ,, G. H. Rouse ... | ... 729 | ,, H. Haigh | ... ... | 735 |
| ,, J. E. Padfield ... | ... 730 | Dr. J. Murdoch | ... ... | 736 |
| ,, M. Mody ... | ... 731 | The Rev. S. W. Organe | ... ... | 737 |
| ,, Dr. T. J. Scott ... | ... 732 | ,, G. P. Taylor | ... ... | 738 |

## XVII.—CLOSING MEETING AND BUSINESS ARRANGEMENTS.

| | PAGE |
|---|---|
| Speech by Bishop Thoburn ... ... ... ... ... | 741 |
| Resolutions ... ... ... ... ... ... ... | 744 |
| XVIII.—PUBLIC TEMPERANCE MEETING ... ... ... ... ... | 748 |
| XIX.—PUBLIC MISSIONARY MEETING ... ... ... ... ... | 760 |
| XX.—MEN'S MEETING ON PUBLIC MORALS ... ... ... ... ... | 771 |
| XXI.—MEETING OF THE CHRISTIAN WOMEN WORKERS' UNION ... ... | 776 |
| XXII.—LECTURE BY THE REV. DR. HOOPER ON "TRANSMIGRATION" ... | 782 |
| XXIII.—SERMON BY THE REV. G. KERRY ... ... ... ... ... | 796 |
| XXIV.—PAPER BY THE REV. J. W. THOMAS ON "STATISTICS" ... ... | 806 |
| XXV.—EXTRA PAPER BY REV. M. PHILLIPS ON "EDUCATION" ... ... | 815 |

## XXVI.—APPENDIXES.

| | |
|---|---|
| A., LIST OF SOCIETIES REPRESENTED ... ... ... ... ... | 825 |
| B., LIST OF MEMBERS PRESENT ... ... ... ... ... ... | 826 |
| C., STATEMENT OF ACCOUNTS ... ... ... ... ... ... | 840 |
| D., LIST OF SUBSCRIPTION ... ... ... ... ... ... | 841 |

# X.—EDUCATION AS A MISSIONARY AGENCY.

## FOURTH DAY.

MONDAY, 2nd January 1893.

### MORNING SESSION.

LARGE HALL, 10 A.M. TO 1 P.M.

The Rev. W. HOOPER, D.D., C. M. S., Jabalpur, in the chair.

FOURTH DAY.

A passage of Scripture was read by the Rev. J. Smith, and prayer was offered by the Rev. Dr. Weitbrecht, after which the Chairman said:

It was said by the Chairman of the Saturday morning meeting that the subject then before us was the most *important* of all that are before this Decennial Conference; and I think I may truly say that the subject *now* before us is the most *burning* one with which we have to deal in the Conference. As we are all aware it is one, on which opinion, the opinion of the truest and most earnest missionaries, has been especially divided, and on which somewhat strong feeling has been evoked, and perhaps strong language used, on either side. I hope, however, and I believe I am expressing the hope of us all present this morning, that the "Spirit of truth and love," whom we have just been invoking in the hymn which we have been singing, will so fill and animate all our hearts and minds, that in all that may be said this morning we may remember, that those who hold *both* sides in this question, however ardently they may adhere to their own sides, and even however exclusively they may advocate them, have but one common object in view, *viz.*,

A burning question.

Spirit of truth and love.

FOURTH DAY. the establishing of the Kingdom of our Lord and Saviour Jesus Christ in the minds and hearts of the people of this land. If we hold fast to this conviction, there will be no fear of anything being said this mornnig which could wound the feelings of anyone.

We have before us three excellent papers. All three are exceedingly excellent, viewing the subject from somewhat different standpoints; but, it seems to me, bringing before us unanswerable arguments for patient continuance in the good work of missionary education. There is also another paper which has been put into my hands, that by the Rev. Maurice Phillips, of Madras. I am not in the secret of the Business Committee; we do not know why it has not been set before the Conference as the others are; but it should, I think, be read by all who can get a copy of it, for it sets before us the other side of the question with what seems to me considerable convincing power.

## FIRST PAPER.

By the Rev. W. H. FINDLAY, M.A., W. M. S., Mannargudi, Tanjore.

*A wide subject.*

In a topic so wide as that of Missionary Education I should have been glad if the Provisional Committee had given some indication of the particular aspects, departments or problems of the subject which it regarded as deserving the consideration of this Conference. It would be putting the clock back a whole generation to raise in an assembly of Indian Missionaries the question whether or not Education is a proper and valuable missionary agency. This branch of Missionary labour has been approved by the hearty and authoritative declarations of successive Conferences, and adopted as an integral part of their operations by all the larger and more experienced Societies, Protestant and Romanist, English, American, and German; so that among us who are gathered here a debate whether street-preaching is a legitimate and valuable missionary method would be no more out-of-date and academic than a similar debate concerning missionary education.

But the Committee has perhaps borne in mind, in giving this subject a place in the programme, that we assemble in such Conferences as this not only to take counsel together for the great task upon which we are all engaged, but also to set forth the principles, processes and results of our work to the Church in other lands, which from afar watches, supports and in considerable measure controls, missionary operations. And although among the men who are face to face with the problems and labours of the evangelization of India there can be no serious question of the worth of an agency, the effects of which pervade and facilitate every department of missionary effort, yet it is natural that to those looking from a distance its value should not be so evident. They cannot track its manifold influences, which like all the most potent forces, work for the most part imperceptibly. Its operation proceeds, like that of the seed and the leaven, from the inward to the outward, from the hidden to the manifest, and only the skilled observer on the spot can trace the chain of cause and effect which establishes its potency. To the distant or superficial gaze, the cause, watched at work, seems to be effecting little or nothing, and the effects, when in due time and place they appear, are put down to other causes; so that it is emphatically true of educational missions that they labour and other agencies enter into their labours. It is not to be wondered at, therefore, that uneasiness in regard to this method of promoting the Kingdom of God should from time to time recur and vindication of it be needed anew.

*Fourth Day.*

*Interest in the subject "at home."*

Yet it is impossible not to feel surprised sometimes, that where ready approval is accorded to medical missions and "social" schemes, which combine in their scope soul and *body*, educational missions which similarly combine soul and *mind* should elicit grudging support or encounter positive suspicion. A sound mind is surely as desirable a preparation for the Gospel and as real a part of the Gospel blessing, as a sound body. Does it more promote the glory of God to banish disease than to banish ignorance? Is it a task remoter from the calling of the missionary to diffuse secular truth than to diffuse physical well-being? If the medical mission and the famine kitchen testify the glorious fact which our Lord's miracles so blessedly taught, that the salvation offered in Christ is a salvation of the *whole man*, is not a ministry to the mind needed to complete the testimony, by showing the power

*A sound mind as important as a sound body.*

FOURTH DAY. of Christianity to redeem the intellect from the bondage of superstition and error, and to endow it with knowledge and power? If offers of medicine and food are useful as interpreting the love of God to man and of Christian men to their fellows, does not the offer of education, at least in this land and in this era, more effectually impress these central truths of our religion upon a people who may refuse our food and suspect our dispensaries, but are eager for our schools? None can deny that it is the Gospel—the printed, preached and, above all, the *practised* Gospel—that is to save India, and that this threefold proclamation of the Gospel is the first and essential function of missions, apart from which all other methods and agencies would be as body without soul, as a foreign tongue without interpreter. But it is equally indisputable, with Christ's example before us, that this proclamation of the Gospel should be accompanied by auxiliary agencies, to prepare its way, to promote its acceptance, to exemplify and initiate its blessings. And among these auxiliary agencies it must be admitted that, where opportunity permits and even invites, as it does in India, those which seek to bless the mental and moral part of man's nature will do more to further the highest aims of Christian missions than those which seek to improve his physical condition.

Often the Truth of Christ has had to go forth to her work among the heathen, poor and solitary, "the voice of one crying in the wilderness;" and even then she has been strong and has prevailed. But when I conceive her worthily furnished for her glorious mission, with such equipment as it behoves the Churches of Europe and America to-day to endue her with, far other is the vision that rises before me. She goes forth among the sin and sorrow stricken nations erect, commanding, confident, swift. Her glad message is written over her vesture that men may read it; it is proclaimed from her lips that men may hear it; it shines from her face and all her person that men who will not read nor hear may yet feel the power of it. And on either hand she has ministers bearing gifts, on the right, gifts of light and freedom, of purifying, and quickening for the mind; on the left, gifts of succour and healing for the body. And while the threefold utterances of her message never ceases, with lavish hands she flings these gifts before her, she scatters them around her, she leaves them behind her as she goes; so that wherever she comes, not only is the acceptable year of the Lord proclaimed, but the New Year's Day has dawned.

<small>FOURTH DAY.</small>

But I cannot bring myself to spend time in apology for the use of an agency for which, the more closely it is examined, the more abundantly do reasons spring up in defence of it, reasons *á priori* and *á posteriori*, reasons from Scripture, common-sense and experience; an agency against which the only objections that can be alleged are that it is new—as every good method of work has been in its turn—and that it does not, to a short-sighted, untrained and misdirected gaze, exhibit "results" enough; an agency the abandonment of which would change the whole face and the whole future of Indian missions. I would rather, remembering that any method of Christian work will be fruitless unless pursued with a right aim and in a right spirit, attempt to suggest in this paper what view the educational worker should take of his work, and what ideal he should keep before him in prosecuting it. I need not dwell on the supreme essential of success—in this as in every other field of Christian effort—that the worker should be a whole-hearted follower of Christ, possessed by an all-controlling zeal for the glory of God and the salvation of men. Among us here, that must be a truism, though a truism that should hang in large letters in the chamber of our hearts, to be before our eyes whenever we there examine ourselves and our work in the sight of God. I shall also pass by many other conditions of the highest success in missionary educational work, that I may call attention to one principle which there is much temptation to abandon, and which must be firmly maintained by the educational worker, whether foreign or Indian, engaged in the college the primary school, the work-shop or the zenana, if he or she would use this agency most effectually for the glory of God and the establishment of His Kingdom in India.

<small>Apologies not necessary.</small>

The principle I would insist on is, the *unity* of the task laid upon the educational missionary, the principle that all parts of his work, including the so-called "secular," are truly missionary, and together form a whole of which no part is to be sacrificed to any other. In vindicating missionary education the argument is often used that the school brings within sound of the Gospel audiences more attentive, regular, and impressionable than the preacher outside the school commonly obtains,

<small>The unity of the educational missionary's task.</small>

**FOURTH DAY.** and audiences which could not be reached except through the school; that, in fact, school work is a form of preaching to the heathen, differing from other forms only in the character and condition of the congregations it addresses and in the means by which it attracts them. This line of argument is abundantly warranted by facts, and it may legitimately be used—at least I hope so, for I have often used it—in commending educational missions to those whose sole conception of the duty of missions is to "preach the Gospel," in the common and narrow sense of that phrase. But the educational missionary will come far short of his duty and privilege if he allows himself to look upon his work in this light. He has had put into his hands the plastic mind and character of heathen youths, and he is responsible, in the measure in which they are under his care, for the kind of men they shall be when they have grown up and taken their place in the world, for what they shall make of life and what life shall make of them. He is responsible to God for the impress they shall bear in their purely intellectual as well as in their spiritual features; indeed it is his high calling to work the work of Christ upon all sides of their nature that he can touch, to inform and infuse them, to the utmost of his opportunity, with all that belongs to the fulness of the blessing of the Gospel of Christ. The Hindu parent, on the one hand, may regard the Scripture lesson as waste of time, and value the school only for its secular instruction; and the Christian supporter of missions may sometimes, on the other hand, tend to depreciate the secular, and to regard the hours spent over the Bible as the object of all the educational apparatus; but the teacher himself must not be drawn aside to either of these errors. He has not done his duty to the Hindu parent unless he has with all earnestnes striven to fill his pupils' minds with that which is the most precious of all knowledge, and to mould their characters and aspirations after the Sole Pattern for men; and he has not done his duty to Christ and the Church unless, besides seeking to lead his pupils to a living faith in the Saviour, he has striven, in his many-sided contact with their mental and moral nature, to stamp the image of Christ, and pour out the gifts of Christ, upon all that is in them. If he is betrayed

"Secular" and "religious." into maintaining in his own idea and practice the current separation between the "secular" and the "religious" sides of his work, if he regards or treats five-sixths of the school curriculum as a bait to secure an audience for the Scripture lesson, if he measures the results of his work solely by the number of converts won among his pupils or by the steps they take on the road toward conversion, he comes grievously short of the right standard. Look at the parallel case of the medical missionary. Dare any one suggest that he should value his hospital and medicines, the exercise of his trained care and skill, only as an attraction to draw men within sound of the preacher's voice and within reach of the handbill? If nothing else forbade so inhuman an attitude to the medical side of his work, the vows which he took when he received authority to exercise the healing art bind him, and rightly bind him, not to degrade it into an instrument for attaining even the highest ulterior ends, but to exercise it ever as a sacred calling in the service of God and humanity; and the medical missionary feels that he is as truly following his Master and doing His work in India when he makes the lame to walk or the blind to see, as when he tells the story of the Cross or presses upon the sin-diseased the need of a Saviour. The latter may be a higher service, bringing him higher delight; but he will feel it to be not more necessary and not more truly a part of his missionary calling than the former. The calling of the teacher is as sacred, and as little to be made a mere instrument, even of the highest purposes, as that of the doctor. The state of the mind does not appeal to our senses as the state of the body does, else the spectacle of a dark, crippled, stunted mind would rouse in us stronger pity than the sight of a helpless and suffering body, and the teacher who made light of even the most "secular" part of his treatment of the mind would seem more repulsively callous than the doctor who should trade upon physical infirmities. The missionary teacher will not, of course, any more than the missionary doctor, put every part of his work on the same level. The unfolding of the truths of God's word and of the facts and meaning of the life and death of Christ, he will ever esteem the most precious service he can render to his pupils; and to render them this service will, day by day, be the most serious and the most delightful of his duties. He will feel that if this were lacking, all else in his work would be vain or worse than vain. Yet the other

*Fourth Day.*

*All teaching is sacred.*

**Fourth Day.**

studies must also be treated as ends in themselves, and not merely means to an ulterior end; though "secular," they must be held sacred, as contributing, if rightly pursued, to the glory of God in the restoration of the fallen nature of man.

*The word "secular" often misapplied.*

"Secular" is a word that in modern times has got into bad company; it frequently connotes worldliness if not wickedness. But we do great injustice to one of God's best gifts, if we attach any such signification to it when we speak of secular knowledge or secular instruction. Granted that secular teaching, divorced from the highest teaching of all, may be pernicious, that in this land it is often seen to be an instrument of evil and not of good; that is no more than can be said of any of God's good gifts. And though Hindu or Government schools and colleges of Western education may do little to further, and in some cases may do much to hinder, the Kingdom of Christ, we must, nevertheless, believe that this same instruction, when given in the name and for the sake of Christ, when presented as a product and a part of the gifts He has received for men, when associated with and permeated by religious teaching and influence, not only ceases to be pernicious but becomes a positive and substantial blessing. The secular truth that is so often contrasted disparagingly with religious truth, is it not a direct and glorious product of our Christianity? The Western knowledge that is so eagerly sought after, and that is exerting so mighty an influence in India to-day, is it not a beam from the Light of the World, whose lustre should be our joy and pride? Search for the sources of our modern culture, our science and philosophy and arts, and it will appear that the impulses, the tendencies, the qualities of mind and character to which it must be traced, are themselves directly due to the all transforming influence of Christianity. Revivals of learning have followed closely on revivals of religion; love of truth, vision to see it, perseverance and energy to pursue it, strength to grasp and hold and use it, have come where the saving knowledge of Christ has come. In Him the mind, as well as the soul, has found freedom and manhood; and Western knowledge and civilization, at their purest and best, manifest the glory of God revealed in Christ as truly, though not as splendidly, as Western virtues and graces, at their purest and best. We often hear it remarked that the loss of miraculous gifts of healing has been more than made up, to the modern Christian world, by that growth in knowledge which has led to the wonders of present-day medicine and surgery; and that these are the fulfilment, in one sphere, of our Lord's words when he said: "Greater works than these shall ye do." If that be true, it should be recognized as equally true that all developments of modern knowledge and power are superhuman in their origin, gifts from God in Christ, approaches, from many sides, toward that new earth and new mankind of which we had the promise and the foretaste when our Lord was on earth.

*Fourth Day.*

See then what missionary education, even on its secular side, has to offer to this land of India. Our religion has brought to the Western nations that have most fully yielded to its sway, mental light and power, progressive revelation of truth in all departments that the mind of man can explore, growing knowledge of the Divine laws which govern the universe, and therefore growing harmony between the mind of man and the mind of God. The Spirit of Truth has come, and in a wider sense than was foreseen, is leading the nations that will follow Him into all truth. And along with purged vision, invigorated intellectual powers, enlarged knowledge, purified and expanded imagination, have come, for Christian nations, increased wisdom in meeting the problems of a suffering and sin-stricken world, a more understanding sympathy with human need, a general and progressive amelioration; the influence of Christ pervading the whole nature of man and through his whole nature reaching and blessing all departments of his life. I need not picture the contrast to this condition of things which is presented by the intellectual, social, moral, material condition of a country like India; nor need I picture what the mind of the Indian child is by long heredity, nor what, when left to Hindu upbringing, it becomes by association and training. But these things being as we here in India know them to be, I make bold to believe that, along with him who gives a cup of cold water to one of these little ones, he who, in the name and for the sake of Christ, teaches them even their multiplication table, has blessed them with Christian blessing, and shall in no wise lose his reward.

*The Spirit of Truth permeates all.*

**Fourth Day.**

*Give India the full benefit of Christian progress.*

We of the progressive nations are wont to congratulate ourselves that each new generation enters on the accumulating inheritance of the wisdom and culture of the centuries; that in the upward climb of progress the children start, not where their fathers started but where they left off. We are born late; but we are born to a larger, richer, fuller life than our fathers knew. The nations that are born late to the new life in Christ, have they not a claim to similar compensations? They have waited long in heathen darkness and death for us to bring to them the light of life; we should bring it to them now in the full lustre which it has attained in centuries of Christian progress. Can you imagine a man sending his boy to a dame's school and forbidding him to travel by train, on the ground that dame's schools were in vogue and railways unknown when he himself was young? It would be no less monstrous if we, " in the full blaze of Gospel day," should say to heathen nations : " You shall start in your Christian course just where our ancestors started, and you shall painfully achieve for yourselves, in the slow course of centuries, the joys and graces and powers which belong to the full fruition of the Kingdom of God." Not for a moment would I suggest that we in our day have any better or fuller answer to offer than Peter and Paul had in their day, to the ever-recurring question "What must I do to be saved?" Not all the centuries of time will add anything to, as they will take nothing from, that "Gospel of Christ" which "is the power of God unto salvation to every one that believeth." When we seek to turn the sinner from the error of his ways and lead him to a saving knowledge of God in Christ, we have but the old way to point out, the old promises to rely on, the old power to use,— and, thank God, we need no other. But the Kingdom of Heaven which our Lord established here on earth is not merely the series of the saved men and women of successive generations; it is a society in which the living Christ ever dwells and which, through His indwelling, is ever growing and blossoming more and more, in all the provinces of its nature and life, into the richness and fulness of the manifold glory of God. And the question which concerns our educational work and much of our other work is this :—When we come to proclaim in a land like India that 'The Kingdom of Heaven is at hand,' are we to present and establish that Kingdom as it was in its first beginnings, or as it is after the illuminating and energizing Spirit has wrought His work within it for nineteen centuries? Laggards, shameful laggards, have we been in bringing the Gospel abroad to heathen lands; let us at least bring it now glowing with its fairest blossoms, laden with its ripest fruits.

*Fourth Day.*

It would be easy to urge many other considerations enforcing the principle that the educational worker, in the highest or the humblest sphere, should combine the "religious" and the "secular" departments of his work in one sacred calling. I might dwell on the intricate connection between body, mind, character and will, which makes it well-nigh impossible to influence one without influencing the rest, or to separate the effects of one from the effects of the others. In our Lord's miracles of healing we find His ministrations to the body and to the soul so combined that it is sometimes hard to draw any demarcating line between the physical and the spiritual cure; and in school work, rightly done, there should be the same happy blending of operation upon soul and character and mind. But without enlarging upon this, I will only point out, in conclusion, how effectually the principle I have insisted on is calculated to shield the educational worker from that very danger which the critics of missionary education most often allege against it. We hear it declared that the present-day multiplication of University and Government examinations, of regulations raising the standard and enlarging the area of the secular instruction given in our schools, tends to diminish their religious influence and missionary value and to seduce the missionary teacher into making pass-lists and grants, rather than souls, his prime concern. Every form of mission work has its peculiar temptations; and nothing but a close and constant walk with God, a humble and watchful dependence on His grace, will save the missionary in any sphere from lowering his aims, swerving from his principles and deceiving himself by false standards of success. I do not, for my part, think that the temptations to such declension which beset the preacher of the Gospel are less formidable, though they may be more subtle and of a character less easily appreciated at the present day, than those which assail the educational worker. But be this as it may, it is surely plain that the safeguard for the mission teacher against the risk which he runs through the present-day aggrandizement of the

*Every branch of work has its temptation.*

**Fourth Day.**

*Let all our teaching be of the best.*

secular side of his work is, not to dispense with the secular, for that is impossible and would be un-Christian, not, by severing connection with Government or University, to seek licence to lower the efficiency of the secular side of his work, but heartily to recognize its solemn and sacred importance, its vital relation to the highest ends which Christian missions pursue. University and Government regulations, and all helps that will prompt and guide us in improving to the highest possible efficiency the secular instruction in our schools, are good. It depends on our own missionary spirit to see to it that the religious instruction shall share in the improvement; and this will be best secured by recognizing that both have the one aim of imparting to the pupil, in his whole nature, the manifold blessing of Christ. While the secular and the religious are treated as independent or opposing interests, the one aiming at the wordly welfare of the pupils and the prosperity and prestige of the school, the other aiming at the salvation of souls and the fulfilment of missionary purposes, it is natural that, whenever one scale rises, the other must fall, and that the teacher in yielding to the pressure of the secular should feel himself unfaithful to his highest ideal. But let the religious and the secular be regarded as allies instead of opponents, let them be as the vessel of gold and the vessel of brass both sacred to the service of the sanctuary, and then the benefit of either is the benefit of both. Let the educational missionary recognize that the task assigned him by Christ is to transform, by all the means the school affords, the whole nature of the pupils committed to his care, and let the same lesson be impressed on all workers in the educational field, down to the humblest teacher in the Primary School, and then, in the day when the history of the Christianization of India comes to be written, it will be manifest beyond a doubt that in that great process missionary education has rendered splendid and invaluable service.

---

## SECOND PAPER.

By The Rev. D. MACKICHAN, D.D., F. C. M., Principal, Wilson College, Bombay.

In laying this statement before this Decennial Conference I feel placed under a two-fold disadvantage. The invitation, to which

I have the honour to respond, reached me only when I was preparing to start on my return voyage to India, and the nature of the discussion to which I was asked to contribute was not communicated to me till my arrival, and then only in the general form indicated in the title of this paper. The subject, however, is one which I count it a privilege to be invited to discuss in any of its aspects, and I shall endeavour to turn the disadvantage to which I have referred to my own profit, and I hope also to the profit of our Conference by confining myself to certain outstanding features of the questions which have become so prominent in the missionary thought and discussion of the present time.

To those who are engaged in this department of missionary labour it is neither a surprise nor a discouragement that this question has become so prominent. Other forms of missionary agency have had their turn in the process of review which is a feature of the present missionary period, and from such inquiry missionary education has no wish to escape. I look upon it as a testimony to the development of this agency and a tribute to its importance that it should be so placed under review. Agencies which are still in their comparative infancy and which have a great future before them, as for example that of zenana missions and the education of women in India, have only to reach the point of development already attained by this department of missionary education to be subjected to a similar process of criticism. The day of their trial and of their triumphant vindication will come. The surprise and discouragement only begin when such discussions issue in rivalries and antagonisms between methods which are organically united and as little opposed to each other as the members of the same living body. It is this perverse tendency, in some measure the result of the very intensity of the life and work in which it manifests itself, that has imparted an element of acrimony into such discussions from which it is hoped that this Conference under the guidance of the Spirit of truth and holiness and peace will be entirely preserved.

There is an *à priori* difficulty present to the minds of some of the best of men and the most devoted of workers to which at the outset reference must be made, for, I believe, it lies at the root of more than one-half of the criticism with

*Fourth Day.*

Criticism a sign of development.

Is higher education an unscriptural departure?

**Fourth Day.** which we have to deal. Missionary education in the developed and highly organized form in which it comes before them is to such minds so different from the ordinary, the normal forms of agency, that they are disposed to regard it as an unwarrantable departure from Apostolic simplicity and New Testament precept. To them it is at best a very roundabout way of fulfilling the Saviour's command: "Disciple the nations," and they impatiently demand that it should give place to some of those other activities which have secured for themselves a conventional claim to the character of Apostolic and missionary. But if we start with the assumption that the Scriptures enunciate a missionary policy in the manner of a stereotyped injunction, we need not discuss this or any other method of Indian evangelization, for we shall not find it there. Nay, we shall not find there rules for the details of the evangelization of any land. But if we take a deeper and broader view, if we look at the whole record of God's dealings with men culminating in the life and work of our Lord and Saviour, if we take Him to be our life and His Spirit our guide, we shall be prepared for every variety of Christian operation and ready to recognise in the growth of each the guidance of the Spirit which He has promised, the outworking of His life in its many-sided activity. I venture to say that no missionary has entered the field of labour in India or Africa or China with preconceived ideals (and who can be without them?), who has not had to ask himself regarding many of his most important duties whether they are compatible with these his first conceptions of the missionary life. David Livingstone, in the depths of untrodden Africa, had to ask himself this question. His robust Christian sense enabled him under heavenly guidance to penetrate the depths of Africa's needs and to transform by his sanctified touch what seemed unministerial and secular into sacred and devoted service. Not less true is it that in India the Christian mind must be prepared to take this broad view of Christian problems. Our mission is the establishment of the Kingdom of God in this land, and we must be prepared to place ourselves in contact with every part of the life of the nation that comes within the scope of this broad conception. In whichever region of the people's life and thought Christ is needed, there we must be ready to go with His life-giving message and supply

*Our work to establish God's Kingdom.*

the healing ministration of His Word. I am familiar both by experience and otherwise with the routine of missionary life on several of its sides, and I have no hesitation in affirming that the missionary who is evangelizing in a district has his time as much engaged in what to a superficial view is purely secular, as the missionary who has been called to evangelize in school or college. His work is no less sacred on that account, and it is all the more devoted, because it is often in this very region of work that the strength of his faith and patience and hope is called into highest exercise. What work is held in more honour than that of the women who visit their sisters in Indian homes, bringing with them the light of Christian sympathy and love, and yet how much of their activity would it not be difficult to bring within our narrower definitions of evangelization? In a non-Christian land everything that is animated by Christ's Spirit is evangelistic, is missionary.

Let us dismiss then from our minds these prepossessions which really foreclose all consideration of the question, and observe further in this view of our subject that the development of Christian education in India is a great fact in the Providential guidance which the Head of the Church has vouchsafed to His servants. It would seem that much of the discussion of this question is conducted on the assumption that such guidance has been withdrawn from the Church, and that missionary policy, as it is called, is simply the result of man's ingenuity and device. I do not mean that Christ's servants are entitled to claim His authority for everything they are led to do; the principles of all their policy and procedure must be tested by the clearly enunciated principles of God's Word; but in dealing with the large question before us we have to face the fact that, not by accident but in obedience to Christ's Spirit, working through so many independent channels, churches separated in their government and organization, and differing even in some of their doctrines have, during a period of more than half a century, moved onward in the midst of varying success and manifold discouragement to the present development of the methods now under consideration. I have a profound distrust of missionary theories; we dare not say that India must only thus and thus be converted; but I have an equally profound faith in the over-ruling guidance of Him Who is our

*We still have Christ's guidance.*

**Fourth Day.**

Leader and Commander in this service. Step by step have the churches moved onwards in the work of Christian education. They have been ever surrounded by difficulties in the prosecution of this mission; but one after another these have been, in the wonderful Providence of God, removed, varied tokens of His approval have been vouchsafed to the work; and although the difficulties of to-day are no less numerous than in the past, they are new problems, they are to-day's difficulties, and faith can rise beyond them to anticipate an onward movement in this department of the Lord's work. And the testimony of those who are engaged in this work corroborates this evidence of divine guidance. They have come to this land with the same objects as other labourers; they have entered the field which God in His providence has opened up for their efforts, and many will be prepared to join in the testimony that there is no desire for Christian opportunity, no longing for means of spiritual usefulness which cannot find its highest fulfilment within the sphere which the mission school or college opens up to every one who seeks it. With them there is no question regarding this work. So deep is their conviction that it is difficult for them to be patient in the presence of the superficial criticisms which they encounter, and which to them at least must often appear as little short of profanity in view of the felt sacredness of their own calling.

*Testimony of the workers.*

Leaving these preliminary considerations we advance a step further, and consider the special circumstances in the condition of India which render this form of work so important and so necessary. I think it will be admitted by all who have thoughtfully considered the problem of Indian evangelization that the strength and influence of Hinduism are to be found in that great *socio-religious* organization which is conveniently described as the system of caste. The records of each Decennial Conference have shewn how possible it is by the presentation of the Gospel to the masses who lie outside this system to attract large numbers of individuals to the profession of Christianity; but they reveal with equal clearness the fact that such methods have achieved comparatively little in the way of distinct Christian accessions from the great religious system which dominates the land. This is not a fact that can be set aside by referring us to the Apostolic dictum that "not many wise men after the flesh,

*Caste not affected by the "mass movements."*

not many mighty, not many noble, are called," for within the system of which we speak there are myriads of the poorest and weakest whose attitude towards the Gospel is as full of resistance as that of the mighty and wise amongst them; it is the result of the natural working of that system to which all these classes, the noble and the poor, the mighty and the weak, the wise and the unwise, alike belong. They are parts of a system which has crushed out the individual life, has swallowed up the sense of responsibility and the demands of conscience in the overpowering claims of caste. So far as the relation of the different parts of this community to the Gospel is concerned, they are all alike, and the demands which the Gospel makes upon the social life of all are practically the same. Now it has been abundantly demonstrated that there has been no visible Christian progress amongst such classes, except upon the foundation that has been laid by Christian education, and those who have been called to work amongst them do not need to be reminded of the fact. It is not implied in this statement that the power of the Divine Spirit is not able to break down every obstacle that can rear itself within the human heart. Such exceptional manifestations of God's gracious power may be looked for everywhere, but it is not the exceptional but the ordinary methods of divine procedure that should furnish the law of the church's life, and these point unmistakably to the necessity of that preparation which comes mainly through Christian education. It may be said by some that secular education will furnish all the human aid that is needed. It is with no desire to disparage the work of men who are carrying out with ability and with zeal the programme of secular education that the Christian educationist maintains another view. He is only too conscious of the smallness of his own achievement to depreciate that of others. But the testimony is borne in from all quarters of the land that secular education, apart from the inculcation of the principles of Christianity, has proved a very doubtful blessing so far as the religious condition of the people is concerned. The Government itself which presides over this system is profoundly conscious of its failure, and seems to shrink with some alarm from the consequences of its own action. It turns for help to all who can supply the influences which it must exclude from its own system. Surely this appeal is a

*Fourth Day.*

*Secular education not sufficient.*

**Fourth Day.**

*Caste not a system of rules.*

*A living organism.*

*Educational progress.*

testimony of authority and weight. Nor does any one require a very intimate knowledge of the scope and nature of such education to enable him to corroborate this testimony. You hear it said that railways and commerce and education are undermining and destroying the caste system of India. There could not be a greater misconception. The caste system is not a body of rules—it is a spirit, a life. Those external modifications which lie on the surface have little to do with the spirit of the system. The adaptation of caste to the changing circumstances which mark the progress of education and commerce is an evidence not of its weakness but of its strength. It is a living thing which can adapt itself to its environment. Were it only a rigid lifeless mass, it would soon be shivered into fragments under the mighty tread of general progress. But it is not this rigid thing, but a living organism, and nothing can uproot it but the power of a new life. It is Christianity and the spirit of Christianity, by whatsoever channel it is brought, that can alone uproot this mighty growth. Education may modify, but Christianity alone can destroy this spirit. A merely negative system of instruction may bring about disorganization, but Christianity alone can furnish the new principle, without which the old will continue to live on in all its strength. It will not do to point to individual instances of success or failure on either side. We must look at the broad facts of the case, and ask whether it is secular education or education imbued with the spirit and teaching of Christ that will work out this change. The question then arises—Shall we or shall we not address ourselves to the task of meeting the demands of this the central portion of our missionary task? An important section of the people of India, that which constitutes the real centre of the nation's life, has entered upon a new development. Its traditions and its aims unite in urging it forward in the path of educational progress. We cannot stay this movement even should we desire it. We have no interest in any attempt to do so, for our strongest sympathies are with it. But we ask— Shall Christianity stand aside while this development moves onward to consequences which bode no good to religion or to morality, or shall it throw itself into close contact with those classes which are affected by it, and, taking hold of the movement, seek to guide it to a higher result? If we understand aright our mission to India, we can give only one answer, and that without misgiving or hesitation. It is our duty thus to endeavour to bring under the influence of the Gospel those mighty forces which are moulding, with results so rapid, the future of the people of this land.

*Fourth Day.*

In judging of the results of the efforts which are being made in this direction, two considerations must be clearly kept in view. We are in danger both of under-rating this influence and of magnifying the extent of this agency. It is difficult for those who are living in the midst of these results to estimate their real value. The very existence of Christian education in India has a moral effect beyond the limits of those who are immediately affected by it. It is not possible for us to appreciate the changes effected, because we have no means of comparing the present condition with that which would have taken its place had this influence been withdrawn from the entire field. The place which Christian education has asserted for itself has given a tone and direction to the whole movement quite out of proportion to the area over which it extends. The effect of the whole is modified by the features of the part. Again, the extent of Christian education, the amount of strength which the Christian world has thrown into it, is after all a very little thing. We have scarcely began to realize the scale on which such things must be attempted and done. How often are Christian colleges and schools left undermanned and unprovided with the means of efficient and successful working? What a demand is left to be made on the energy and devotion of the few who are entrusted with the work of many, and who, if they did not every day feel themselves upheld by their conviction of the urgency of the claims of this work, would utterly sink under its burdens! I can imagine only one object for which a Conference like this can assemble to discuss this question, namely, that it may be able to represent to the churches concerned in this enterprise the smallness of their conceptions and their efforts in relation to the great problems and great opportunities which have been set before them. I trust that by the manner in which as a Conference we shall unite in setting forth the claims of this work, we shall be able to call upon the churches to rally to the more effective maintenance and extension of this work.

*Two dangers.*

FOURTH DAY.

*Comparisons misleading.*

*Zeal not abated.*

*The area covered.*

Comparisons have sometimes been made between the present conditions of missionary education and those of the past. It has sometimes been urged that the Christian result of missionary institutions is less now than it was in the former days. Those who maintain that it is not less but greater have no difficulty in admitting that there is a difference. It is conceded on all hands that relatively the number of accessions to Christianity is smaller, but the conclusions deduced from this are untenable. First of all, I do not believe that the zeal with which in the former days the message of Christianity was addressed to the young men of this land was different from that which animates the workers in the same field now. It is possible (and this is my own conviction) that the smallness of the area in which they had to work, and the selected character of the material, rendered a more intensive Christian work possible, a greater concentration of effort on individual cases. But if we admit this difference, what is the inference to be drawn from it? Surely, not an argument against the method, but the conviction that Christian education has not been maintained in a degree commensurate with the expansion of the field. The Christian institutions in India are undermanned and their influence is curtailed by this circumstance. Then let us man them and equip them better.

But in all our thoughts on this subject let us not lose sight of the fact that a larger Christian work is being accomplished. The largeness of the area over which the work has extended is a fact full of encouragement and grounds for hope, when rightly interpreted. The Word of God is more widely known, the principles of our religion are more widely inculcated, and the eye of faith that can look beyond results, which reach their full development in the present, can discern in this the guarantee of a more rapid extension of the Kingdom which we proclaim, the steadily growing preparation of a nation for a higher faith. The Christianization of India is a bigger fact than some are disposed to imagine, and it will require every kind of effort and every form of agency which the most advanced Christian life of our time can devise. We are dealing with a problem which is in many respects unique. The whole problem of the Government of this land is a unique problem requiring special methods and impatient of stereotyped theories. Not less is the Christian problem beset with special difficulties and special necessities. These difficulties are being met and wisely met by Christian education, and amongst these necessities is that of a wide outlook, a far-seeing vision and a deep sympathy with the aspirations and wants of the people. Lord Bacon reminds us that there is a quality of mind (he suggests that it might be called *longanimity*) required in certain kinds of undertakings, and if this longmindedness, this power to look ahead to the far-reaching consequences of present plans, is needed anywhere, surely it is needed in the work of engrafting a new civilization and a new religion on peoples of a complex and highly organized life like those which meet us in this land. To such a far-seeing view the results of to-day are great and beyond the measure of the rough and unskilful tests which many are wont to apply. There are many influences at work which tend to mask and hide this Christian result. In older days there was no choice open to the enlightened mind, but the choice between Christianity and grossest superstition. The Christian conviction that brought men then to the vestibule of the Christian Church may not achieve so much in a condition of religious opinion which has provided other resting places, only temporary, for such minds. The circumstances of the time are also less favourable to religious enquiry. Many other interests help to fill the void in the Indian mind and to absorb activities which in other days would have been turned into the channels of earnest religious thought. These are facts to which no one who is in contact with the life of educated India can shut his eyes. They are part of the conditions under which Christian work must be carried on, but no hindrance which they present to immediate visible Christian result should for a moment discourage us or cause us to relax our efforts on behalf of the special class amongst which our labours are carried on. After all, in every department of mission work, education in some form or other is the great instrument. Elementary education has been the great instrument in the hand of missionaries whose work calls them specially to certain classes of the people (George Bowen used to say that the majority of all the converts in Western India were the fruits of education), and education in the form in which we advocate its use has been the great instrument of progress in all the Christian work which has been carried on amongst those classes with which higher

*Fourth Day.*

Longanimity.

Changed conditions.

Education the instrument of progress.

**FOURTH DAY.**

*The Bombay Government impartial.*

education has to deal, and which cannot be omitted or overlooked in any effort to reach the centre of life and power in India.

But we shall be further told that the connection of this education with the Government which aids it, and the Universities which guide it, has brought about a deterioration of its Christian quality. I think that we in Bombay are entitled to be heard on the question of the relation of missionary education to Government. We have had the fullest experience of all that can be involved in such a connection. We had a time of discouragement, amounting almost to opposition, and this has been succeeded by a period of justice which places the Bombay Government in the front rank of impartial educational administration. Examining our experience during both these periods, I am unable to see that missionary education has been influenced in any injurious manner by this connection or deflected by it from its highest purpose. The temptation to secure passes at the cost of the character of the education imparted is one by which, so far as I am aware, missionary education in this Presidency has not suffered itself to be influenced. We are now under a system which takes little account of such passes, which places all educational institutions on their honour, and I am bound to say that this trustful administration has not seen any diminution of true educational efficiency, nor has it produced any changes in the arrangement of the work of religious instruction. These have, from the beginning, been unaffected by the form or extent of Government connection. I cannot help feeling that there is much injustice and not a little ingratitude in the language that is often held on this subject by those who forget that Government has, under the conditions which it has found it necessary to impose, been an important factor in the development of this as of all other educational work. Neither this connection, nor the fact that it places religious instruction outside the ordinary school or college curriculum, need interfere with the strength of the religious influence of a missionary institution. The religious lesson may, under all these conditions, be so conducted as to overcome the effect of any such restriction. Everything depends upon the instructor. If he rises to the full height of his spiritual responsibility, his Bible hour may be as great a reality as any part of his work, and success in this will secure for him similar success in the real work of every other class. There is a good side as well as a bad in this so called examination pressure. There is a positive benefit in anything that tends to efficiency and the maintenance of a high standard. The Christianity of an institution can be manifested in connection with efficiency much more than by laxity or inefficiency, and provided the standards laid down are reasonable and suitable, there is much to be grateful for in any stimulus to vigorous and efficient work.

*Fourth Day.*

Before I pass from the subject let me allude to a misconception which appears to be very prevalent with respect to the connection of colleges with the universities. The members of the Bombay University would be surprised to hear themselves spoken of as if they were a department of Government. Indian universities are not Government institutions. The colleges which are affiliated to them form an essential part of the university system, and the Christian colleges have their share in the administration of the university like every other class of similar institutions. It is absurd to speak of the university connection as if it implied a subjection to Government control. Whatever may be the defects of our Indian universities, it is too late in the day to think of any withdrawal from this connection. Higher education is bound up with them, and to separate from them would mean the renunciation of all connection with the higher education of the country. More than this, the connection is one which gives missionary education its own part to play in the development of these universities to which it thus stands related, an influence which it should never allow itself thoughtlessly to surrender. Let us dismiss the entirely erroneous supposition that our relation to the university is but a new form of Government control, and all the impressions which grow out of this supposition, and understanding its real character let us rather recognize in it a new obligation to be faithful to the responsibilities which it lays upon us.

*Indian Universities not Government institutions.*

There is a claim put forth, one which has been in the air for some years and in these latter times has found in some quarters articulate expression, that the work of missionary institutions should be confined to the Christian community, and that the money which is spent on missionary institutions should be devoted to the education of Christians and the fitting of them to occupy important positions in the church and in

*Education of Native Christians.*

**Fourth Day.** the world. I know that the advocacy of such a claim as this is one which secures an easy popularity with the Indian Christian who imagines that his true interests are being thus safeguarded, and with the Christian at home who has never been in real contact with the problem. As a friend of the Indian Christian, concerned for his true interests and his highest usefulness, I advise him to beware of being seduced from his true manliness by any such plausible programme. To him I say— Christian education is already yours in a very special sense. You have not only the general advantages which belong to you in common with all others, but already special help and special encouragement according to your need is offered to you. There is not a Christian young man in Western India (and I am sure that this holds good in at least an equal degree in many parts of India) with any ability and any aspiration after higher education, for whom the door of admission does not stand wide open in the form of special accommodation in Christian colleges, and the aid of special scholarships. Every encouragement that can be legitimately given is offered, and when I look back upon the record of the education of the Christians in Western India, I find rising up before my recollection not merely the few who have attained to university distinctions, but a still greater number who, with all the advantages that we were able to offer them, failed to persevere. It is quite possible that missionaries not engaged in education have failed to sufficiently encourage in the Christian youth the desire for education or to sympathize with his just ambitions, but complaints on the score of want of help in Christian institutions, when help is needed, and of failure by reason of the absence of due encouragement are groundless; and they are not the truest friends of the Indian Christian who encourage him to think that this complaint is well founded. I can speak freely on this subject because I have no fear of being misunderstood by those who are mainly concerned in this statement. I state now what I have often said to them individually and collectively in the spirit of affectionate sympathy. We have too much respect for the character of Indian Christianity to treat it in any other fashion. These helps will be most heartily given to a community which is entitled to special encouragement from us, and should the need arise for a wider extension of such help I should be the first to plead for it, but always under this condition that we do nothing to impair the feeling of self-reliance in those whom we seek to encourage. This is of more value than any form of education, and such extravagant demands as those to which I have alluded would purchase the object sought for at a cost too dear.

Further, it is no part of our principles that Indian Christians should grow up in isolation from their Indian fellow-countrymen. The presence of Christians among Hindus, Parsis, and Musalmans, sitting side by side with them on the same college benches and competing with them for the same university and college honours is not a thing which we shall ever desire to prevent. We long to see it year by year in an increasing degree, and deprecate anything what would detach in the smallest measure the sympathies of the Christian from the non-Christian in India. Christian colleges, as they now exist, are fitted to meet the highest requirements of the Christian community. There are many of us who would be thankful if, in our own land, we could find educational institutions for our own children in which we could feel the same satisfaction in regard to the whole tone of the instruction and the influence of the instructors.

*Indian Christians should not be isolated.*

There is yet another point of view from which the demand must be considered. The challenge—'maintain your colleges for Christians'—means 'close them.' A slight knowledge of the finances of these colleges and of the financial plans of mission boards ought to be sufficient to add to what has been already pointed out, the additional condemnation of such a suggestion that it is utterly impracticable. It would mean either to increase three-fold or four-fold the expense of the maintenance of the colleges or the placing of such higher education altogether beyond the resources of the Indian Christian. Surely, this is not a prospect which can bring much comfort to Christians in India, or any satisfaction to missionaries who desire their advancement.

*Colleges for Christians only.*

But let no one imagine that we hold that there are no real wants in the Christian educational system of India. There are wants, and these are deeply felt by those who are engaged in the work. They run up, most of them, into this, that missionary education is everywhere undermanned and too feebly

FOURTH DAY.

**The missionary overburdened.**

supported. The missionary occupied with this work is so overburdened that he cannot attain without enormous effort to even a moderate realization of the ideal which he has set before him. He is surrounded by opportunities that many might envy, and yet to avail himself of more than a mere fraction of them is beyond his power. An increased staff throughout the field is one of the first necessities. Some are inclined to the view that this increase should take the form of men set apart for special work outside the ordinary curriculum; others maintain the view, and the traditions of our mission, as well as my own convictions, support it, that a fuller equipment of the ordinary staff is the best means of coping with this problem. This is a subject which may well admit of different opinions and perhaps also of a varying practice in different localities, but the need of such reinforcement dare not be overlooked.

**Knowledge of the vernacular.**

I should also be disposed to urge that the missionary engaged in education should have a larger personal contact with every side of the work. Amongst his qualifications should be, if possible, a thorough acquaintance with the languages of the people. It is his function to enter into closest relation with the people of the land. A first-hand knowledge of the people and their condition is necessary for the full discharge of such a function, and for this a knowledge of the language in which their life and character are enveloped is requisite. Such an equipment, would, I believe, help to prevent the growth of one-sidedness in interest and sympathy which is always a misfortune in any department of missionary labour. The best evangelistic missionaries, like the late George Bowen, a life-long friend and advocate of missionary education, have been wide enough in their sympathies to appreciate the importance of educational work, both higher and lower. In like manner the missionary engaged in education should be identified with forms of work different from his own, and should be prepared, when opportunity offers or necessity arises, to take part in them. Thus it might be hoped that the true unity of the work might be more fully manifested in the mutual co-operation of all its parts.

**Study of religious systems.**

Following out a little further the same line of thought, I would add that the times demand on the part of all missionaries who are in contact with the great religious systems of India, and especially of missionaries who are engaged in educational work, a patient and scholarly study of these systems. For this, as for many other things, there was more leisure in the earlier days: but in these times of reaction, marked by numerous attempts to rehabilitate decaying faiths, the need is as great as it was in any former period of missionary effort. But I shall not dwell upon this because it does not concern exclusively any one form of missionary effort.

*Fourth Day.*

It is a large programme which is thus assigned to missionary education, and yet it leaves out much that might well be added. In view of it, surely it behoves us not to burden the missionary with the additional task of a defence of methods which have established themselves by almost universal consent in the missionary practice of so many of the Christian churches that are represented in the evangelization of India. The missionary will never grow weary of his work, but he may well grow weary of discussing it. The question is surely past the stage of discussion; it has reached the higher stage of imperative demands. Some of these demands I have placed before you. Be it your privilege as a Conference to place them before the mind of the Christian church, and thus to render a becoming service to a work which is laying a foundation deep and solid for the Christian future for which all our labours are preparing.

*Defence of methods a burden.*

## THIRD PAPER.

By Rev. A. B. WANN, B.D., E. C. S., General Assembly's Institution, Calcutta.

I. ITS PLACE DEFINED.—The place of education as a missionary agency can only be settled after a consideration of the aims of Mission work in general, and of special nature of the Indian mission field in particular. The aim of mission work is to fulfil the command of Christ to preach the Gospel to every creature, making disciples of all nations, preaching repentance and remission of sins in His Name, baptizing them and teaching them to observe all His precepts. Its aim is not to produce merely a general good influence, nor yet to convert individuals here and there, but to bring all nations under professed and real obedience to Christ. It is a common-place of Biblical Theology

*The place of education.*

FOURTH DAY.

that the true evangelical expression for the aim of Christ, and consequently of Christians, is the "Kingdom of God," and the inspired vision of the Apostle John shewed him the kingdoms of this world at last become the kingdoms of our Lord and of His Christ. The aim of missions is to bring about this change, to set forth Christ as King, and to bring men to honour Him and serve Him as such, not only in their private thoughts, but in their whole lives, and in all their relations with other men. It is plain then that any agency which tends, on the whole, to promote the observance of Christ's precepts, to spread His teachings, or even to remove hostility and prejudice, is, in a wide sense, a missionary agency.

But there is another truth, not less prominently set forth in Scripture, which must be borne in mind ere we can accurately define a missionary agency. The Gospel is the declaration of the redeeming grace of God. It is a message to every individual calling him to reconciliation with God through Jesus Christ by the Holy Spirit. It is not a scheme of mere improvement and reformation for the race, but a power of regeneration for the individual. It brings each man face to face with God for a personal acceptance of His grace, without which there is no true entrance into His Kingdom. Hence the chief and central aim of missionaries must be to set Christ before men for their individual acceptance, or in the words of the Lord Himself, to be His witnesses. Wherever, then, we have a man whose life is lived in personal fellowship with Christ, whose household, business, and social life is ruled by His commands, who exerts on those about him a purifying and uplifting influence, and who seeks to bring others to the same obedience by testifying to them what Christ is to him, we have a true missionary, and his whole activity is a missionary agency.

The missionary.

But for the purposes of this Conference we must limit the name of missionary to those whose whole time is given to the setting up of the Kingdom of God and bringing men to reconciliation with Him, without having to think of, and labour for, a provision for themselves and their families, and we must limit the term missionary agency to those modes of life and work which they freely choose as most conducive to the success of their aim. How then are missionaries to proceed? Naturally, the first thought must be, to go wherever men are found, and proclaim to them in their own tongue the wonderful works of God in the Gospel of His Son. "The foolishness of preaching" is the central Missionary Agency. It was so in the Apostolic age, and must be so till the earth is evangelized. But the work must be done methodically and systematically, if it is to be thorough. There are preliminary difficulties to be overcome ere the Word can be preached. Again, men do not often hear the Gospel willingly, and prejudices have to be removed. Yet, again, the modern Missionary finds himself a pioneer of civilization, and the heir of a vast number of blessings which the Gospel has brought in its train, and he cannot but seek to make men partakers of them, especially as the beneficence of them is an effectual witness to the truth of the good news of God's love. And the infant Church and its workers must be watched over. Hence arise the Pastor Missionary, the Translator-Missionary, the Author-Missionary, the Traveller-Missionary, the Doctor-Missionary, the Engineer-Missionary, the Artisan-Missionary, the Gardener-Missionary, nay, even the Secretary Missionary and the Editor-Missionary. I venture to say, that among the one thousand male Missionaries in India, there are not a hundred solely preaching Missionaries. Those who are generally looked upon as such are much employed in other work, and even those who come nearest to the simple Preaching Missionary are often very largely employed as bishops, or overseers, of their catechists and other workers. The existence of the Educator-Missionary is justified by the same arguments that make it right for a man to turn aside from preaching pure and simple into any of the lines of activity indicated above. Christian education is one of the highest boons that can be bestowed upon any people; it removes prejudices and conciliates the affections; it furnishes an opportunity for the daily direct preaching of the Gospel, and it brings the Missionary into heart-to-heart contact with the people with whom he has to deal.

II. ITS SPECIAL ADAPTION TO INDIA.—Now, turning to the Indian Mission field, do we find any special circumstances which indicate that educational work should, or should not, find a prominent place among our Missionary Agencies?

And, since there is practically no difference of opinion as to the value and place of Elementary Education alongside of

*Fourth Day.*

*His many-sided occupation.*

*Higher Education a necessary part of Missionary work.*

**Fourth Day.**

preaching work, I confine myself to the question of Higher Education. There are, in my opinion, two special features in the circumstances of India which make the Higher Education not only a legitimate, but also a necessary and important factor in the evangelization of the country. The first is the social constitution of the country, based upon the caste system, which renders it necessary that the various classes should be dealt with separately. The second is the educational position of the country, which is drawing its intellectual and moral light from the West, and is thus laid open for the reception of the Gospel along with and through the stores of Western literature. On each of these points it is necessary to expatiate a little.

*Spirit of caste unbroken.*

Though the caste system is slowly crumbling away, its spirit is unbroken. No Missionary of any experience is ignorant that the educated classes are not reached by the ordinary methods of preaching, and must be dealt with separately, if at all. The method of the Higher Education is the only one which, as yet, does reach them in any numbers. We have no warrant to pass them by, or to decline to make the patience and long-suffering of God our example in dealing with them. Further, when we consider that Hindu Society is an organism, and that the educated men must not be looked upon merely as so many souls, but as the brain of the organism, possessing an enormous and disproportionate influence over the other members, it is evident that Missionary work, if intelligently conducted, must devote, even for the sake of the mass of the people, a considerable part of its energy to the propagation of the Gospel among the educated classes. Every student of Hinduism has been struck by the wonderfully mingled flexibility and tenacity which enable it to retain its hold over its members. Every worker among Hindus has realized how dependent each individual is on his own section of society, and how difficult it is to stir up a sense of individual responsibility. A statesmanlike Mission policy will not ignore this fact, but will seek so to influence the whole organism, that it may be drawn towards Christ, and while to the ignorant poor the Gospel is preached, the educated often poor enough—shall also be evangelized. And the most effective means to that end has hitherto been the Higher Education.

Again, we see a flood of ideas and influence pouring in from the West, and taking possession of the minds of the men who are the social and religious rulers of the people. These ideas are coming in by the channel of reading and education. And while we can thank God that the great names of English Literature are those of men whose work is clean and wholesome and permeated with a Christian spirit and saturated with Christian thought, it is not their books that are found most frequently in the hands of Indian readers, but books of a far lower and more degrading kind. Again, in Government and Hindu Colleges, education is generally conducted without reference to that fear of the Lord which is the beginning of wisdom, and the old religion gets swept out of the convictions of the students, carrying away with it such sanctions of morality as it possessed. I cannot refer here to anything which may be done in the way of directly supplanting the debasing and irreligious literature which finds its way into India; but I can point to the Mission Colleges as the standing witness of the compatibility of religion with, and the domination of religion over, secular enlightenment. Their influence extends not merely to their own students, but through these students over all the others, and through the University over the whole course of Higher Education in India. If India is to become one of the kingdoms of our Lord, its education must be sanctified, and that, under present circumstances, can only be by Missionary effort. The cessation, or even the slackening of such effort, must be looked upon by every true friend of India with dismay.

<small>Fourth Day.</small>
<small>Western influences.</small>

These considerations were felt in their full strength by the Duffs and Wilsons of two generations since. They saw that an English education was the most powerful factor in destructive work upon the fabric of Hindu superstition; they saw that such an education would be welcomed by the keener minds of India; they saw in this their opportunity for a constructive work going on alongside; and they deliberately became the pioneers of Higher Education, conducted throughout with a reference to religion, and crowned by direct religious teaching, in the hope that thereby they might not only win converts from classes untouched before, but make an effectual assault upon Hinduism in central stronghold.

<small>The effects of an English Education.</small>

III. PRESENT DAY DIFFICULTIES.—The Decennial Missionary Conference is a fitting time and place from which to look back to see how the work has succeeded in the past, and what is the outlook for the future. And as there is in some quarters a disposition to believe that while at the outset this work was really successful, it has gradually ceased to be so to a very great extent, I would ask the members of the Conference to consider the bearing of the two following movements on the question.

*First*, the enormous expansion of the Higher Education by the direct action and indirect countenance of Government. Mission High Schools and Colleges contain a smaller *proportion* of those under instruction than formerly. Consequently, their influence is less directly felt. Moreover, the abundant provision of the means of education outside of Mission Institutions takes away from the prestige which they formerly had, and so tends to diminish their influence. Nevertheless, as I have already indicated, there is reaction as well as action; and the presence of Mission Institutions alongside of others produces, I believe, a very different tone in education from that which would exist were there none. In view of this fact, the way to make Mission Institutions more spiritually efficient is to make them more educationally efficient, to man them with such an ample staff, and so thoroughly to equip them that, aided by that Christian zeal which no Government salary can buy, they may stand unapproachable in efficiency. It is impossible that they can supply all the Higher Education, but they might be made such, that the flower of the Indian Youth would eagerly enter, and receptively hear the truth.

The question has been raised whether Mission Colleges could not work better apart from the Universities. It has been supposed that the whole routine of work might thus be made more Christian, and special Christian teaching more prominent, and that the Colleges would escape from the great educational pressure that weighs upon them at present. But it must be borne in mind that a Mission College standing alone, or under a Christian University, would have to work its students just as hard as at present. Not even Christians would attend it unless its certificate or degree were educationally equal to any other. Moreover the text-books prescribed at present are by no means anti-Christian; indeed, they are many of them truly Christian. It is true that the curriculum of the Universities at present demands excessive cram, and so stunts independent thought. But that is an educational, not a religious defect, and will soon, perhaps, be remedied by the general sense of educationists. We hope to see the Colleges given a freer hand in their method of preparation. In the meantime, it would be a pity, for the sake of a little more liberty, to diminish the general value of our training, and to forego the great reflex influence which Christian educationalists exert on the whole University.

*Second*, the changed attitude of educated Hindus in respect of religious thought. I believe this more than any other fact is the cause of the decrease in the number of baptisms of students in the Missionary Colleges. Time was when the earnest-minded Hindu lad, brought up in crass superstition, and set face to face with the truth as it is in Jesus, found himself compelled to make his decision between them, and so a comparatively large number were baptized. Now a kind of *via media* has been found. A vast number simply accept Hinduism as a social system, and to a great extent adopt Christian conceptions of God and religion. The compliances to idolatry are reduced to a minimum and explained away. From one point of view, the change is a gain. It indicates an advancement of thought, a desire to live a higher moral and spiritual life. Such men honour Jesus, and observe many of His precepts. It is a sign that the Kingdom of God is extending its sway. And we may say, though it seems inconsistent, that the present slight success of Mission Institutions in proselytising is due to the great and good influence they have exerted in the past. But, on the other hand, such a state of mind is an attitude of compromise with sin; it keeps back men who feel the power of the Gospel from the open confession which Christ requires; it stifles the heart's craving for a true and complete Saviour from sin. Such an inconsistent and comprising condition cannot long co-exist with a keen sense of sin and desire for deliverance; and Educational Missionaries should, I think, aim above all at convincing each pupil of his personal responsibility in view of Christ's claim on him. These men have been driven from their old orthodox position, and they have now entrenched themselves in this modern liberal camp. They have borrowed Christian thought,

*Fourth Day.*

Changed attitude towards religion.

though many repudiate the debt. They are trying to defend Hinduism with weapons taken from the armoury of Christianity. We look with confidence for another stage of the conflict, when this second barrier will be thrown down, and surrender will be made to Christ.

IV. THE WORK HOPEFUL AND REAL.—These considerations seem to call for increased effort on the part of the Home Churches to strengthen their Educational Institutions, increased effort on the part of the Missionaries to make clear the spiritual issues of the Gospel to their students, increased patience, and prayerfulness, and expectancy on the part of all interested in the work. And it may not be out of place to entreat those who are apt to judge hastily to have confidence in the men who know the subject best, *viz.*, the Educational Missionaries themselves. We are not men who will spend our lives in doing work which is excellent only in theory. We *know* our institutions are doing good. But the amount of the good, the real part played by the Mission Schools and Colleges of India, will not be realised in general till India is Christian, and men come to write the new chapter of Church History.

In reading the history of Missions we praise the men who, in spite of discouragement and apparent want of success, stuck to their work, and, it may be, died without seeing it come to fruition. But in estimating the value of the work of living men, the work round ourselves, another rule is often applied, and " How many have you baptised?" is the test of work. It is strange to find men who repudiate any high sacramental view of baptism applying this test. For baptism, to the man who receives it, may mean everything or it may mean nothing. It may simply indicate a vague hope of somehow improving one's condition by putting oneself under the Missionary's care. It may indicate a genuine surrender to the service of Christ of a chastened heart and an ennobled life, after a deep and searching work of the Spirit of God. Such cases we should all like to see, and sometimes do see,—but how many? Unless we are prepared to say that the rite of baptism has saving efficacy apart from the spiritual apprehension of Christ, it can only be one out of many indications that the kingdom of God is extending. Much as I personally wish to see and pray for thorough conversion and open confession of Christ among our students, I cannot but feel that the moral and spiritual influence exerted on our students who remain unbaptized is as genuine Christian work as the work of baptizing men whose moral and spiritual education has to be begun after baptism. There is an intensive view of Christian work as well as an extensive. There is a real preparation for the Gospel which is more valuable than an unreal profession of it. The history of the "conversion" of our European nations and of the baptised savagery of the Middle Ages might teach us thankfulness that we have, in India, a great class of educated men to whom we may give, be the cost what it may, a firm hold of the morality and spirituality of the Gospel.

*Fourth Day.*

V. EDUCATION IN THE CHRISTIAN CHURCH.—Looking forward to the future of our Institutions, we see that they will play an important part in the development, as well as in the formation of the Christian Church in India. The Christian Community is rapidly advancing in numbers, and more rapidly advancing in influence and education. It is the duty of the Missionary Churches to aid the poorer lads of really good abilities to obtain a good education; and it is a question whether our existing Institutions could not be more utilized in this way. Three remarks may be made in this connection. It is the duty of all Missions to co-operate with the Educational Missions in this work, not making both the education and the support of Christian lads fall upon the latter. Further, it is only really capable lads who should be helped in this way; nothing but harm can come from forcing a dull lad through the mill of college education, just because he is a Christian. For such, as well as for others, Technical education should be provided. Lastly, the Christian Community is still so small, comparatively speaking, that the small number of Christians in our Institutions at present is not to be charged to the indifference of the Missionaries, but to the fact that there are no more fit to be sent. The same remark applies to the employment of Non-Christian teachers. There is not material enough to furnish Christian teachers; and such as are fit for the work are often unwilling to enter it, looking for more lucrative employment elsewhere. But this is a difficulty which time will solve; and we may look for a period when the Christian High Schools and Colleges will do for India as much as they have done for Britain and the United States. The future Church of

*Effect of education on the Church.*

**Fourth Day.**

India, the daughter of the Church of the Reformation, will, like its Mother-Church, welcome enlightenment, and through its Colleges, maintain the sovereignty of the Gospel over the proudest achievements of the human intellect.

**Recapitulation.**

To recapitulate what has been said:—

There is a wider and a narrow view of Mission work, both Scriptural. Missionary Educational work, like many another Missionary Agency, justifies itself from either point of view. Moreover, the peculiar social and educational position of India seems to indicate it as an agency specially fitted for use in this land. The results it has already achieved are great and lasting: and its present meagre success as a proselytising agency is largely due to the enormous increase of education outside of Missionary enterprize and to the improved moral and religious feeling of the educated classes. Increased educational efficiency and more intense spirituality ought to bring about more direct and apparent results. And, lastly, special attention should now be given to the educational needs of the Christian Community.

## FIRST SPEECH.

By the Rev. J. C. R. EWING, D.D., A. P. M., Lahore.

**No other work so important in the Evangelization of India.**

If in our discussion of Educational Mission work, we include all that has been done in schools of every grade, there will possibly be entire unanimity of opinion amongst us as to the very decisive results which have accrued from this form of labour. That the village and the bazaar Mission school has by its fruits justified its right to exist, we possibly all agree in believing. That the Mission High School and College are equally important and indispensible, some have dared to doubt.

Side by side, however, with these honest doubters, there is to be found a great, and I believe, increasing number of men and women who, after all that has been and can be said against higher education, as an evangelizing agency has had its utterance, are profoundly convinced that amongst all the forms of work which the great Head of the church has guided us in undertaking for Him in India, there is no one that bears a more important and apparently necessary relation to the evangelization of the entire people dwelling in this land than does this.

It is this distinct conviction that has made many willing to undergo the incessant toil of the class room, and has given them the grace hopefully to continue the concentration of their energies upon the field furnished by the school or the college.

*Fourth Day.*

That all such effort has proven distinctly successful, is claimed, I suppose, by none; that some of it has produced but little in the way of tangible results will be sorrowfully admitted by all.

The same may with perfect truthfulness be said of every form of evangelistic agency. How often has the apparent paucity of visible and immediate fruit of the work done by the bazaar preacher, the zenana teacher and the tract writer saddened our hearts and tried our faith!

The educational missionary, who with heart and soul believes in his work, and who has an intelligent grasp of the situation in India, has the utmost confidence in the coming of the harvest. It may be delayed, but if so the fact should not surprise nor overwhelm us. He works in a soil distinct in some of its characteristics from all others. True it is only the human heart after all with its sin and weakness and unbelief, and yet it is the heart subjected to a host of special and subtle influences which are calculated to keep it back from the unreserved acceptance of the truth as it is in Christ Jesus.

*The soil in which the educationalist works.*

That these influences may be effectively resisted and more of the boys and young men of our educational institutions brought to the position of definitely deciding for Christ there are certain things which seem to me of essential importance.

The first of these is that the college or school be permeated by Christian influence. As necessary to this I would urge first of all that definite Scripture teaching have a prominent place in the work of every day. I have somewhere heard that the greatest of all educational missionaries testified that of all those who were brought to Christ through his instrumentality every one traced his conversion to the impression made by some particular passage of Scripture. It is the Gospel of the Old and New Testaments, and not our thoughts about it that should be given the place of prominence. It is a Bible in which we thoroughly believe that we are to teach, and if men are to be saved by the power of Jesus of Nazareth, it is surely of the utmost importance that He be held up before them not merely

*Give the Bible prominence.*

**Fourth Day.** as a Teacher of the highest possible type of morality, but also as one who is able to deliver from the guilt and the power and the pollution of sin.

Nothing in this connection is more trite than the remark that Scripture teaching is not in all of our schools in the hands of those who are duly qualified for it.. The man, who through mental, or it may be moral, weakness, has failed to pass his trials for licensure and ordination, sometimes has been thought fit for the work of a Bible teacher. We do not dream of sending him forth to preach in the villages, but we set him down as our substitute, to teach and to live Christianity in the presence of the wideawake young minds of the classroom. This practice may not be so prevalent as some would lead us to believe, but wherever it or anything like it prevails at all, can we wonder that there should be the report, at the end of each year, no baptisms!

*Christians for Bible teaching.* Such a view will possibly be condemned as extreme by some, yet I venture to think that it is *always* a mistake to allow a non-Christian, and usually such to allow a merely nominal Christian, to undertake the teaching of the Word of God.

The mere perfunctory memorizing of Scripture, where there is the absence of the personality and warm words of one, who having himself passed from death unto life, commands the Gospel of the Son of God, is, I fear, often worse than useless.

If missionary education is to be what it certainly may be, God's Word should, I venture to think, be the most prominent book, and the one to which the best time and best teaching at our disposal should be given. "But," it will be urged, "easier said than done," and right true it is that an adequate supply of duly qualified Christian teachers is hard to secure. Let us then have fewer schools and colleges until such time as we can provide for the sympathetic loving thorough study of the Bible, for where that is non-existent the school or college might as well and perhaps better be so also.

*Avoid perfunctoriness.* Those who have personal experience of this work do not require to be reminded of the well-nigh irresistible tendency to perfunctoriness in our Bible teaching. After an hour-and-a-half given to English or mathematics or philosophy, and before later periods to be given to other secular subjects, comes, in our college, the period for Bible study.

This, for various reasons, we regard as the best time. It **Fourth Day.** requires, I assure you, the most careful previous preparation and the constant remembrance that this is indeed Divine truth that we teach, and that these are needy souls before us, to enable one at all to even approach his ideal of the way in which the Truth of God should be presented to an audience like that.

The school-room is the educational missionary's preaching *An audience* place. Where has any missionary ever found a better audience? *that listens* The objection that his audience cannot from the very nature of *intelligently* the case be in a receptive frame of mind is not a strictly valid *every day.* one, since the student has voluntarily entered the class knowing that Christian teaching formed a part of the curriculum. Here the preacher has a most respectful, and usually an attentive audience every day, and if he is to thoroughly influence that audience he will never for a moment forget that he is a preacher, and that what he sows is living seed in the hearts of his hearers, and that it is destined to spring up and blossom and bear fruit, to all eternity. I do not think that the ordained missionary is out of place in school work. Here he has to preach at least once every day, and he might not be able to do more than this were he not a teacher, and whatever of theological training he has enjoyed, is of the greatest value, perhaps in no sphere more essential—in aiding the accomplishment of what should be the paramount aim in all that he does, namely to win men to God.

In so far as may be possible intimate personal relations with *Follow up the* students ought to be established and maintained. It is simply *work out of* wonderful how this affects his attitude toward the message we *school.* have to put before him in class. It opens the way too, to numberless opportunities of finding what is going on in his heart, and in so far as the spirit of Christ governs the missionary revealing to him that spirit. Every hour spent by the missionary with his boys outside the class room may be of the greatest value—more peradventure from his own point of view, than many hours spent within it.

This is not the place for, nor would time admit of, any attempt *Higher* to justify the existence of what is technically known as higher *education* education, as a missionary agency. Such argument is, I venture *compulsory to* to believe, not necessary. The very circumstances in which we *the Christian.* are placed, the condition in which we find the country, compel us

**Fourth Day.** to undertake the task—and it is by no means a hopeless one—of bringing the influences of the blessed Gospel to bear upon the rapidly increasing numbers of those who are receiving Western education. This education they will have whether we take part in it or no. The question is—are we prepared deliberately to leave those who are destined to be the leaders of social and political life in this country untouched and uninfluenced by the faith we have been sent to preach, or shall we continue as we have begun—only God grant that it be with still more grace and wisdom—to gather one here and another there into the Kingdom from out of the multitude and to impress the truths of the Gospel upon the many until such time as the seed thus sown shall ripen into a far richer harvest than we have yet seen, or it may be expected?

*The far reaching effects of education.* We are all more or less familiar with the difficulties attendant upon any effort to influence the student class by means of bazaar or chapel preaching or by the press. I cannot of course speak with authority as to other large cities in India, but in Lahore we certainly find that the audiences at English lectures and sermons, are very largely made up of those who have learned something howsoever little of the Gospel in the mission schools and colleges of the province. Others go their way unheeding and inaccessible to all effort made to secure from them a patient hearing of the claims of Christianity. Are we then to let all the youth thus go away? A thousand times, no!

*More results than generally imagined.* Many more of the educated are impressed with the truths of Christianity as a system than we perhaps imagine. Two months ago, a student of the B. A. class in our college, believing himself to be seriously ill, made in my presence and in the presence of a number of his fellow-students the declaration that for more than a year he had been fully convinced of the truth of the Gospel, acknowledged his personal sinfulness, and his entire acceptance of Jesus as his personal Saviour.

The numerous half-way houses which have in these latter days sprung up between old Hinduism and Christianity, constitute the greatest hindrance to the natural and legitimate outworking of the plan of missionary education. It is hardly to be expected that a thoughtful youth should pass any of them by in his progress upward from old Hinduism; indeed, some pause for a while at all, and very many, as we know, permanently remain in one or in another. This, while it does add tremendously to the difficulties of our task, is still by no means a reason for the relaxation of effort. We are filling the *Somájes*, and whatever of odium there is in that, let us cheerfully bear our share. The very fact is in itself a proof of the efficacy of the agency through which we work, and we have reason, and analogy and revelation—all to assure us that this process in which Mission education has borne so large a part is to end in the final acceptance of Him Who was crucified, by many who are now fain to be satisfied with the mere husks and fragments of truth.

*Fourth Day.*

As we compare the present with the past, and note how that within a decade or two great changes have taken place in the attitude of educated non-Christians toward the Gospel; when we see hundreds of intelligent well-educated people, evening after evening for weeks together, eagerly listening to the most uncompromising Christian addresses, the conviction comes to us, that in this all those who are giving their lives to educational Mission work may find abundant cause for thanksgiving and rejoicing. When we inquire whence have come very many of the most efficient of the preachers and teachers in our Missions, and whence many of those Indian Christians in business or professional life, who are by their lives commending the Faith of Christ, we discover in answer to our question a proof of the most decisive character that the work of the school and the college has been by no means in vain.

*Change of attitude.*

If our schools have not shown the results we desired to see, the reason is probably to be found in the fact that our work has not been as well done as it ought to have been. But because we may have toiled clumsily or even carelessly, shall we despise and condemn the instrument which even in spite of our inefficiency has wrought such wonders in the land?

Fathers and Brethren, fair and candid criticism let us warmly welcome, defects in our methods let us be ready to recognize and remove, and with unshaken confidence in the power of the Truth committed unto us, why should we not share more largely in the promised enduement of power from on High, and even from this time forth enter upon the reaping of an abundant harvest?

FOURTH DAY.

## SECOND SPEECH.

By the Rev. L. B. WOLF, M.A.,

Principal, A. L. M. College, Guntur, Madras.

*Light wanted, not heat.*

There are two considerations which should be borne in mind in such a discussion. They are—(*a*) That the whole matter should be considered with all the light at our command, while there should be generated, paradoxical though it may seem, as small an amount of *heat* as possible. All want light; heat no one desires in such matters. (*b*) That we clearly deal with education as a Missionary agency, and leave institutions and persons alone; the system, and not persons, is up for discussion. Such a course cannot but help us to get free from all heated controversy, and will produce the clearest evidence as to the legitimate claims of this arm of the Mission service.

*The system, not persons, to be discussed.*

The Conference can do no better than to deliberately weigh the able papers which have been prepared by those whose experience enables them to speak, and whose devotion and consecration entitles them to be heard. A *résumé* of these becomes our first duty then.

*One of the best Mission Agencies.*

I. All are practically agreed that this agency is one of the strongest, which, under God, and the guidance of the Spirit, is to produce the evangelization of this great land. That no more excellent place can be found, in which to preach Christ, than the Schools and Colleges of the land.

*Especially for reaching Hindus.*

II. That this agency is especially well calculated to reach Hinduism in its home—its caste system. And this they maintain for the following considerations :—

*Reaches the unformed mind.*

(*a*) Because through this agency the mind of the nation is reached and influenced during the formative and most critical period of its development, before it has been caught in the toils of the Hindu communial life ;

*Fills a gap.*

(*b*) Because it fills up the gap between the Church's physical ministry by her Industrial schools and hospitals, and the purely evangelistic and spiritual work, by dealing with the *mind* in its course of development and preparation for life ;

*Introduces a new principle.*

(*c*) But more than this, because through it there is introduced into the Hindu system a new principle of life, spiritual and divine, which must be found in this Hindu body, with its caste and hoary custom, before it will receive any material change from without. The change must be *implanted*, the truth must be brought to work; the school and college are the natural and appropriate arena for this implantation of truth;

(*d*) But this agency is especially fitted to accomplish this, because it supplements the place of the purely negative influence of the Government school and college by the positive teaching and holy faith of the holiest life known among men. And, in addition to this, it meets the antagonism to Christianity of the Hindu school, as well as the attacks which Western science of a certain school is only too fond of making. It also furnishes an excellent ground on which to meet the infidel and sceptical notions, which are only too apt to manifest themselves in the course of such a transformation as must take place before this land is lifted out of its mythical and superstitious past into the full enjoyment of the light and civilisation of the lands of the West;

(*e*) Because it furnishes a common ground where Hindu and Christian youths may meet, and by actual life and conduct enables the former to see those who have embraced Christianity; and finally

(*f*) Because through this agency the Hindu educated youth has revealed unto him the character of Christian thought, as against the agnostic, materialistic, and infidel tendencies of the West, and this both by the practical faith of his Christian teacher, as well as by the opportunity which it gives to combat those theories so hurtful to Christian thought and life.

III.—The principal objections are next considered; that it is cried down as *secular* work; that it is not in accordance with New Testament methods of work: that this yoking together of Missionary effort with the Government and University destroys its efficiency, and is unwarranted by the spirit of Missions; that its small results condemn it as an evangelistic agency; that it, as a system, neglects the instruction of the Christian youths of the church. That it should be more efficient, no one denies. but the reason for its inefficiency is found not so much in the system as such, as in the way the work is *manned*, or rather *undermanned* so as to cripple its usefulness. It should most surely be more strongly supported by an agency that takes up its work—a special agency—to follow the young men into their homes and at their business. Many impressions are completely

*Fourth Day.*

Supplies positive teaching.

Furnishes a common ground.

Reveals Christian thought.

Objections.

FOURTH DAY. effaced through not following up the good work begun in the school. It is too much to lay the blame of small results to the charge of this agency, without bringing into contrast the character of the work to be done, as well as the actual advance made against the Hindu unit by all methods of Missionary work.

From all this, the conclusion, which we should logically draw from the situation, seems plain. Evidently it is not that which is referred to by Dr. Mackichan, *viz.*, that we should close our schools to all, but Christian youths. Such a course would close most of our schools and colleges, and stop the regular preaching of the Gospel to thousands of youths who are now being made acquainted with the holy Scriptures, and with the Life of Christ. It would divorce the growing Hindu community of Christians from their fellow-students of other faiths, which would be a great hinderance to the cause of truth in its practical development. It would without fail look like a confession that Christian schools have failed to make Christian truth a reality in the minds of this growing young India; and it would look, as if Christian thought were not able to cope with the practical issues of life. All of this would be a great loss to the cause of truth in the Hindu nation. That it can influence the life and mould the character, under all circumstances, the Christian Church must ever maintain, and nowhere should we insist on its prominence, as of such supreme moment, as in all our schools for the young. Surely it would not be a wise conclusion, that because so small results have accrued, we should give up the agency. Why should our objector see only the few conversions here, and fail to grasp the whole situation, that we have just passed the threshold of this great task of bringing the Hindu nation to Christ. We are entering the court of temple, and if we believe God's promises, then surely the end will be the entire filling of this Hindu temple with the glory of the Lord of Hosts. And the work is not slow after all. To men, no doubt, it may seem so, but to God who looketh not on affairs as men, and in the light of history, the process is *fast.* A thousand and one influences are at work.

*Educate not only Christian, but all youths.*

*Those who know the work believe in it.*

There is only one conclusion, then, in view of the facts; that this agency is an eminently legitimate one for the preaching of the Gospel and the enlightenment of

the nature, along Christian lines of thought. It should **Fourth Day.**
count for much, dear friends, that those who are engaged
in this work are most deeply convinced of its value as a
Missionary agency. Christian men and women are willing that
this work shall stand or fall by their convictions concerning
it. They want others to allow them to work along those lines,
without the hindrance of adverse criticism. They desire
their faith in their work to stand as the best argument for its
usefulness.

But it may be that we have greatly magnified the opposition
which this agency has to contend against from Christian
friends. Our objector may not exist in such force as to render
so much defence necessary. It is devoutly to be hoped that
such is the case. If it be so, all we want to obtain here is more
light, so as to enable us to do our work better, and win
young India more powerfully and quickly to Christ. We *Christ our*
have only one weapon on which we place our supreme reliance *Hope.*
—one Gospel, one faith, one life, one hope. Christ is that
Gospel, He is our only hope. If any one has another and surer
way to accomplish India's evangelisation and Christianisation,
we should be glad to know and embrace that plan. If our
schools and colleges do not hold up Christ Jesus and Him
crucified, for young India's acceptance, then we should be told
of it; and when those at the heads of educational institutions
present a Gospel of morals, or culture, or civilisation, then it
becomes the duty of those who control such schools to call
a halt. All such teaching is disloyal to Christ; and we
have no sympathy with it. But it is not for this Conference to
find fault with those who preach an emasculated Gospel. That
is the duty of those who support the work of such institutions,
if any there be, which we very much doubt.

If we have not found the best way, let this Conference point
us out the way, and we will walk therein. But you will certainly excuse us, if we cannot agree that the best way lies along *Plans not*
the lines of a Christian university for all India; or of schools *advisable.*
for Christians only, either of which plans does not strike us as
meeting the great needs of this land or of the Christian Church,
whose duty to the heathen youths is real and binding, and can,
as we have tried to show, be fulfilled by the present plant
to an eminent degree.

**Fourth Day.**

If we have made mistakes, correct us in love, and we will not repeat them. But do not meet us and compel us to defend the smallness of our results in any agency, where Christ is honoured, loved, and adored, where the Holy Ghost is sought for guidance and help by devout men and women, and Christ and His truth is presented with all earnestness and faith.

Results will take care of themselves, if we preach the kingdom, and Christ will be believed on and accepted not according to our plans or wishes, but according to God's gracious purposes in Christ Jesus.

*Noble educationalists.*

And now, Christian friends, I see a long roll of names, men and women, who were worthy to suffer and die for India, whom God called, in His providence, to undertake great things for His Son among these peoples. At the head of the list, you will find that of Anderson, noble example of faith and piety, whose labours Madras can never forget; passing down you will read the name of one of princely intellect—chief in great things undertaken for this land—standing head and shoulders above his fellows, yet humble and patient at his work—Duff of Calcutta; and lower down, your eye will rest on the name of that saint and Christian hero who gathered around him Indian youths like a father,—Noble of Masulipatam; and at the end, that eminent Christian scholar and Sanscritist—friend of culture, but more than this, friend of God—Wilson of Bombay: and the vision rises, and with these, many others in humble places, who counted not their life dear unto themselves, unite with common accord in earnestly urging us to press on, assuring us that the Lord of Hosts fighteth for us; and in due season we shall reap if we faint not.

But above the encouragement of these noble sons and daughters, you can see Him standing, Whose Leadership all those acknowledged, and hear His clear command,—" Go ye"; and His blessed promise.—" And I, if I be lifted up from the earth, will draw all men unto Me." Our work is plain. May the Lord guide us in it to His honour. Amen.

*Oh for a hundred Wilson Colleges.*

The meeting being now open for discussion, Bishop Thoburn, d.d., M. E. C., Calcutta, said :—Lest what I am about to say may possibly be misunderstood, I shall begin by expressing the wish that we had one hundred more colleges in India like the one, the hospitality of which, we are enjoying this morning. It is the greatest possible mistake to assume that the things which we accept as the best makes it impossible for anyone else to have that which is good. The best does not exclude the good, nor is it always true that that which is best for one place is best in every place. I regard this institution, and all similar institutions in India or elsewhere, as valuable auxiliaries to the great Missionary work in which we are all engaged. I will venture to add that I fear we waste much valuable time in attacking one another's methods and in interminable discussions over questions of policy which can never be settled by any hard and fast rule. I rise to advocate Christian schools as a Missionary agency, and my definition of the word Christian in this connection is a school in which the pupils, the teachers, and the teaching are all thoroughly Christian. A mistaken notion prevails that as soon as a school is made up of converts and becomes Christian in this sense, it ceases to be a Missionary agency. The idea of many seems to be that we must bring in non-Christians in order to influence them by our teaching, but in a country like India the school which is thoroughly Christian must, in the nature of the case, be also thoroughly Missionary. I would not exclude the non-Christian, but say to every Brahman and every respectable Muhammadan youth, "You are welcome to the advantages of our school if you wish to enter it." This changes the attitude of both the Missionary and the non-Christian pupil. The latter is a party placed under obligation, and he must accept the school as a privilege, and not enter it with demands which at once place the Missionary in the position of an obligated party. With regard to the amount of Bible-teaching given in a school, I attach little importance to it as a matter of routine. That which makes a school Christian is not the quantity of so-called religious teaching given, but rather the intangible something which for want of a better name I shall call the *atmosphere* of an institution. It should be made so thoroughly Christian that every pupil who enters it will feel at once that he breathes a purer and brighter atmosphere than he finds without. He should be kept constantly under an active Christian influence, and it is impossible to conduct a school of this kind in a country like India without powerfully affecting all the pupils. With regard to the character of our colleges, we should bear in mind that the ideal college has not yet been realized in any country—at least in my humble opinion it has not. I cannot speak for England from observation, but in America I have looked in vain for my ideal of a Christian college, and I am sorry to say that some of the institutions which are distinctively recognized as Christian colleges in that country, have less claim to the title than these great Mission colleges in India which are sometimes freely criticized for their defects in that respect. I have been astounded since

*Fourth Day.*

Christian schools.

The ideal College does not exist.

**Fourth Day.**

*The M. E. C. not opposed to education.*

coming to Bombay to hear that a general impression prevails that the Mission which I represent this morning is opposed to education as a Missionary agency. A greater mistake could not prevail. On the contrary, from the village school held under a village tree, up through all grades to our eleven high schools and our two colleges at Lucknow, we employ every educational agency which we can press into the service; but we make all Christian. We exclude no non-Christian pupils, but each one must enter the school with a full knowledge that he comes into a Christian school in the fullest sense of the word. Some of you cannot work on our present lines, simply because you have not the environment which makes it possible. Here, for instance, in Bombay the principal of this college cannot find the Christian pupils with whom to fill his hall, and hence it is absurd to

*A uniform policy impossible.*

talk about imposing a uniform policy upon all schools. Let us, however, work toward this ideal, and before I take my seat I will add that the ultimate ideal of all Christian educators in India ought to be the creation of a great Christian university in India. Ever since I first read Sir Charles Bernard's remarks upon this subject, I have been unable to resist the conviction that this is the ultimate goal to which we must direct our efforts. We must have a Christian university which shall provide a Christian curriculum for all its students, thoroughly Christian in character and adapted to the actual wants of our Christian youths. It may be too soon to create it to-day, but we should keep it in view constantly, and I trust the time will come when it shall be created, and become the great overshadowing university of this empire.

The Rev. W. A. Roberts, M.A., C. M. S., Nasik, said:—"The child is father of the man." "Give us the children and we will influence the destiny of the nation." "What is young learnt is not old forgotten." We use these platitudes, but do we really appreciate them? Not only in connection with the high schools and Anglo-Vernacular schools, but also in the case of the elementary schools, *there is a tendency on the part of*

*Tendency to prefer Evangelistic work.*

*some of our Native brethren to leave this work for the Evangelistic branch of Mission work.* ( I prefer the word "Native." If the word is changed now, the substitute will be changed in ten years' time; our Native friends need to exercise some of our Western common sense in this matter.) A few reasons may be assigned for this tendency:—(*a*) We have

*It leads to a Divinity school.*

started Divinity schools in some of our Missions and these have a captivating name. (*b*) In many cases Evangelistic

*Ensures more pay.*

agents are better paid than School agents. (*c*) And in the next place, though not altogether the fault of the agents, but also of the working of the Missions, in some instances Evan-

*It is easier.*

gelistic work is easier work than school work. To go for a

hort distance in the morning and speak for ten or fifteen minutes, return and spend the whole of the day in household matters, and perhaps repeat the work of the morning in the evening, is far easier than to bear 'the burden and heat of the day' in school-teaching. [At this point there were some expressions of disapproval, but Mr. Roberts said that he had stated nothing that he was not prepared to prove.] This tendency has perhaps been fostered by some Societies. They look to statistics and seem to forget that it is not meteoric blazes, but the steady starlight and moonlight that influence the darkness of the night. I know one Mission where, in the monthly abstracts, evangelistic agents are termed "Spiritual" agents, and school teachers simply "School" agents. In some of their uses there is danger that the word "Spiritual-mindedness" may become a synonym for "exclusive-spiritedness," and the word "Gospel" a synonym for "emasculation." What is the remedy for this state of things? (1) I would let those who are engaged in school work keep to it with tenacity. Do not let us, who are not so directly engaged, talk against school teachers, rave against them, and pray against them; but rather let us honour them, admire them, and strengthen them in every possible manner. (2) Many of our errors, errors in doctrine, errors in action, errors in organization, are attributed to the fact that we do not, in our measure, realize the comprehensiveness of God. Although we may act with our seventy years with short-sightedness, He will continue to act on the principles that guide Him as being eternal. Nearly all His great works are slow in progress. (3) Let us learn from Nature. The mushroom comes up in a night, but the oak takes years to come to perfection, but the oak remains when millions of mushrooms have passed away. The mushroom often panders to a vitiated taste, while the oak has effected the destiny of nations.

Kali Charan BANURJI, Esq., M.A., B.L., Calcutta, said, in substance, that as a fruit of Missionary education himself, as one who had had some experience in the giving as well as in receiving of it, and had taken a part in the conduct of education generally, his testimony emphatically was, that it would be disastrous to retire from education work as a Missionary agency. Of late expression had often been given to the opinion, that no educated person was likely to become a Christian. Any step, indicative of loss of confidence in educational Missions, would help only to crystallise the mischievous opinion. Believing as he did, that the legitimate outcome of education must be Christianity, he had no hesitation in pronouncing the opinion to be absolutely false. The function of Christian colleges was to make it perfectly clear that the best mind was bound to be a Christian mind. The contact of Christian and non-Christian students in those colleges was calculated to produce most

*Fourth Day.*

*Meteoric blazes.*

*The remedies.*

*Perseverance.*

*Avoid short-sightedness.*

*Learn from Nature.*

*Testimony of an educated Indian.*

**Fourth Day.**

*One's mother-tongue.*

*Blessings of Christian education.*

salutary results. He well remembered how, when he was yet a non-Christian, a Christian fellow-student of his used almost daily to put himself out, for the purpose of accompanying him home, on the classes breaking up, and instilling into his mind, all the way along, the truths of Christianity. As to the suggestion of a Christian university, he believed that under existing circumstances, it would defeat the very object it was expected to accomplish. It would lead to the withdrawal of non-Christian students from Christian colleges, and to the effacement of the Missionary factor in the control over non-Christian education, now exercised by the universities. He would also add that the Missionaries who wielded most influence outside the Christian colleges were just the Missionaries who had made their usefulness felt within the colleges.

The Rev. M. PHILLIPS, L. M. S., Madras, said :—I have read the three papers on this subject with very great interest. I am acquainted, of course, with the fourth paper referred to by the Chairman, for I am the author of it. I rejoice to find that I agree with the papers in many things. For instance, it is urged in one of them that Missionaries engaged in educational work should acquire a knowledge of the language of the people among whom they labour. I say "Amen" to that with all my heart, for depend upon it the mother-tongue of every man is the best way to open his heart. This I know by experience, for I am a Welshman, and no music is so sweet to my ears as the music of that divine language. I also agree with the papers that Christian education is good, that its influence is elevating, and that it shows the beneficence of the Christian religion. I am not aware that any one doubts this. It has been said a hundred times, and the same may be said of many other things introduced by the English into India. Above all I am glad to find that I am one with the papers as to the "barrenness of the results of our educational work," *i.e.*, results in the higher sense—results for the production of which our educational work is carried on, *viz., bringing the Hindus into a living knowledge of Christ.* I stated in my paper that as "a matter of fact our colleges are the means of producing scarcely any converts *now*." I am glad to find that the three papers written by educational Missionaries confirm this. Here, then, is an acknowledged fact, a startling fact, for it means nothing less than that our 'Missionary Education as an evangelistic agency' is a failure! This is a fact which this Conference and the Home Churches should earnestly consider. And the question must be asked sooner or later—How can this state of things be remedied? What is to be done? The papers say, 'Let us go on on the old lines, but with greater vigour and zeal. Now it is true that I differ from the papers. I say,—*Reconstruct our educational work; carry it on, on a different principle.*

The principles on which it is carried on at present is to give education to the heathens in order to evangelise them; Native Christians being allowed to participate in the education given. I suggest that we reverse this order and carry on our educational work chiefly in order to elevate the Christian community; heathens being allowed to share in it as far as practicable. I maintain that this is the principle on which we should carry on our schools and colleges. What does it involve? It involves the necessity of *increasing* the number of primary schools and of *decreasing* the number of high schools and colleges. It involves also the exclusion of heathen teachers from, and the employment of only Christian teachers in, our schools and colleges. If this principle were adopted, I submit that our educational work would be placed on such a basis as to command more respect from the people of this land, inspire more confidence in the Home Churches, and be a far more powerful factor in the Christianization of India than at present. It would also be the means of setting at liberty a good number of Missionaries to preach the Gospel who now spend most of their time in secular teaching; for the great want of India to-day is preachers, preachers, preachers.

The Rev. J. G. HAWKER, L. M. S., Belgaum, said:—We cannot afford to neglect those at the head of society. We want to reach and to influence the whole Hindu community; and our best means of influencing the official and professional classes, and those who are to be the leaders of the people, is to connect ourselves with the most intelligent youths in the country, and during the five, six or seven years of their school course to do all we can to help them in their educational efforts to form mutual friendship with them, and to instil into their minds sound and high principles of morality, and the more satisfying and farther-reaching principles of religion. The differences in the conditions of educational work in India, now and forty years ago, are undoubtedly great. Forty years ago there were no universities to control the work, and the Missionaries could go leisurely on their course in their own way. Now high schools and colleges must fulfil the universities' requirements, and the consequent high pressure and cram much interfere with the serious and thorough consideration of religious subjects which Missionaries strive to induce in their pupils. The refusal to receive Government inspection and aid would not help us in the least. I was once working in a school which did not take the Government grant, and the result was that we could not employ a competent staff of assistant masters, and had to do more of the secular teaching ourselves. I have not found our connection with Government interfere with the religious instruction I wished to give, but working for the university examinations has sometimes pressed me rather hard. This difficulty is unavoidable. We *must* work for the university examinations, or we shall get but very few, and very inferior boys to attend our schools. We must accept the necessary conditions of work among this interesting class of the people, and do our best in them. And I do not despair of the result. Government officers have spoken to me with pleasure of the higher morality of Mission school students. I have known young men in our schools to be unconfessed disciples of the Lord Jesus. I have seen masters and boys take a deep interest in the daily devotional exercises of the school, and have been asked to recommend books of prayer to help the students to pray for themselves. And I believe it possible by daily teaching, and daily influence, and daily prayer, to lead many of our lads and teachers a long way into the kingdom of God, and hope that the day will declare more numerous and more joyous results than we have known in the day of our toil.

The Rev. W. A. MANSELL, M.A., B.D., M. E. C., Principal, Christian College, Lucknow, said :—We who are in the providence of God called to this work have need to be thankful that the times have so changed that Christian education needs no longer any excuse or apology to the students in our Mission schools. The youth of India understand our position, and they appreciate it. In the little experience I have had in this line, I have found no difficulty in preaching anywhere to any body of students, a simple, distinct, and uncompromising Gospel. This attitude on the part of the students makes it possible to emphasize what has already been referred to, the *devotional spirit* in our colleges and schools, and to preach not only a formal doctrinal Christianity, but to instil a living Gospel into the hearts of those with whom we have to do. And the rapid increase in the number of our Christian students makes it not only possible, but imperative, that the Christians should be the centre of influence in every Christian college. That is to say, there may be, and there should be, in every school a nucleus of Christian students, who themselves may become a direct evangelizing agency, and earnestly labour for the conversion of their fellow-students. The testimony of Mr. Banurji on this point is of immense importance. And this is not a vain dream. The Christians are coming. When we note that in a single Mission there are more than ten thousand Christian children in the schools, who can say that the time is not soon coming when our colleges will be filled with Christian students, and those who are not Christian will come to look upon it as a foregone conclusion that they too must join the community of Christians? This, then, is the opportunity which God has given us. This is the responsibility which we must meet. Our own Christian students must be educated, and well educaated and make a strong and effective evangelizing agency. It may, be of interest to note that the conservative Bishop of our conservative Mission is arranging to place during the coming year 500 Christian boys and 500 Christian girls into our Anglo-Vernacular schools with a view of making them efficient evangelists among their own people. These Christian students, however, must be trained for the widest usefulness, and there is therefore a place for all kinds of education in our schools. Business, and the fine arts, as well as law and medicine, should have their place, and fill their place in our educational plans. The typical school must be able to turn out not only accomplished Christian scholars, but also skilful men of the world fitted to succeed in life. But above all, and in all, and through all, should be seen and felt the power of the living Christ. Let our Christian colleges here be like our Church colleges at home. Let us deal with these young men as we would deal with young men at home, struggling to find a basis for their faith. Let it be known that every influence, every power, every effort, in these colleges is Christian, and we need not fear about their success. Those who are engaged in this work may well feel that they are called to bring the youth of this land to the feet of Jesus Christ. And I believe that before all of us there is this ideal, and that we may work together heart to heart and hand to hand in the interests of vital Christianity.

*Fourth Day.*

*Give students a useful education.*

*Let every influence be Christian.*

The Rev. JOHN HATHORNTHWAITE, M.A., C. M. S., Principal of St. John's College, Agra, said:—If there be one encouragement which we, as Missionaries, receive from a Conference like this, it is in learning the manifold varieties of work which are here represented, and in seeing how little does our own field of individual labour comprise the sum-total of earnest effort that is being put forth. May God give us grace to appreciate each other's work more, and to pray for His blessing upon every department of Missionary work. (1) The first point to which I would direct attention is that Missionary educationalists have already forced, I think, the Government Educational Department of this country to acknowledge that Muhammadan and Hindu students are something more than merely physical and mental beings, and to recognize the fact that a purely secular education is radically defective. For example, during the present year I have been engaged in teaching—as the prescribed curriculum of the B. A. course in the University of Allahabad—such subjects as these: Flint's Theism, Calderwood's Moral Philosophy, Butler's Sermons, and Milton's Paradise Lost. In the hands of the devout Missionary such books form a splendid supplement to the Scripture-teaching, for which we cannot be too thankful; but wherever they may be read, in every non-Christian college, they have a Christianizing and spiritual force of their own, which cannot but be productive in

*Moral subjects now recognized necessary.*

FOURTH DAY. — influencing character and thought. (2) I desire to say a word in favour of Hindu Boarding Houses attached to our Christian Colleges. As time goes on, experience teaches us that new departures may be desirable, with a view to more effective dealing with non-Christian students. Two years ago the Church Missionary Society was led to open a Hindu Boarding House in the compound in which I live, and I think the experiment has proved successful, so much so that I hope to open a second in the near future. These hostels are practically self-supporting, and provided they do not extend to such proportions as to render it impossible for each boarder to be in constant contact with the Missionaries, they seem to me to constitute that "missing link," so often found wanting in the past, whereby the daily Scriptural lessons may be still further enforced by personal intercourse, example and sympathy. I do not say I can point to any definite result in the way of baptisms, though many I believe to be "not far from the Kingdom of God." I think we, in educational work, need to cultivate a large spirit of hopefulness and patience. At a previous meeting Dr. Ewing of Lahore told us of a Hindu Bible Class. A similar one was held regularly last year for a while in our hostel. I was told—not being present, as the idea was purely spontaneous on the part of certain students—that these meetings were always begun and ended with prayers to God through Jesus Christ. I have myself frequently heard one member of this little band—a Muhammadan—pray in public, closing with "through Jesus Christ our Lord." These are little indications which speak for themselves as to the desirability of such establishments. (3) In conclusion, I wish to read a letter which I consider a most valuable testimony to the value of Missionary educational work. It is not written by one of ourselves, though by one who is in the fullest sympathy with us, by a gentleman who is at the head of one of the largest Government Colleges in India—I mean Mr. Thomson of Agra College, one of the most successful educationalists of our times. He writes:—"St. John's College has lately undergone a great change, and is now starting on a new course. Hitherto the aim of the college has been chiefly the conversion of non-Christians, though the training of Christians was not neglected. But now the Christian community in Upper India has become so numerous that their education must be your first care. As a means of conversion, I believe the college will, in future, be more efficient than it has been in the past, for the increasing proportion of Christian students will give the whole place a Christian tone, such as it could not have before. But I think the Christian students should be your first consideration. In these provinces the number of Christians is now considerable, and it remains to make them

Hindu hostels.

Weighty words of a non-Missionary.

influential by their intelligence and attainments. As a matter of fact, St. John's is becoming a Christian College in a new sense. To an old Indian like me the change is probably more striking than it can be to yourself, and therefore I have urged you to get a good staff of teachers, and maintain a first class college, primarily for Christian students, but admitting any non-Christians who may choose to attend. For this you will require in the College Department at least three Europeans as Professors, and in the School Department one, who might be called Chaplain (to Christian Hostel), though he would do some teaching also. The door is now open, and if you enter with a force like that, you will do great things. But if you miss this opportunity and let the Christian students wander away to better-manned but non-Christian Colleges, the loss to the cause you have at heart will be serious." These, you will agree with me, are weighty words, and all the more so as proceeding from a non-Missionary and a lay-man.

*Fourth Day.*

The Rev. R. SCOTT, F. C. M., Wilson College, Bombay, said:—Notwithstanding your enthusiasm, education is a somewhat wearisome word and work, and it is one of the things that like the poor we have with us always. Yet a philosopher who had a keen vision of the higher trend of things described human history in its inner meaning and purpose as the education of the race. Some indeed depreciate or deny its place as a Missionary agency on account of the slowness of its working and the quietness of its results, contrasting it with what is deemed the instantaneous and perfect illumination of the Spirit. But such contrast is (we think) foreign to the mind and economy of God. The real opposite is impulse; and in the slow and silent processes of instruction God works not less, but rather more surely than in the sudden movements of mind feeling which we often too readily regard as Divine. What raised the Jews above the other nations of the world? Not the flame of the burning bush, not the thunders and lightnings of the Mount, but the inculcation —line upon line and precept upon precept— of that law of Sinai and the lessons of that wondrous story, until through a thousand devices and an unwearied discipline they were engraven on the minds and hearts and memories of the people. And it will be found to be attested by all history that in proportion as peoples receive a true and real education—not cleverness of speech and superficiality of knowledge, but the educing and edification of mind and character—will they ascend in the scale of nations. I shall occupy my few minutes with two remarks. The first concerns methods, and is this: that higher education bears to work among the educated and higher classes the same relation as the girls' school bears to work amongst women—as the primary school bears to work amongst the depressed. These are the

*God works slowly and silently.*

*Methods.*

**Fourth Day.** three divisions of the people that have been specially before this Conference. The girls' school was described by one speaker as the central part of woman's work; and we know that our Methodist friends of the North-West owe their success largely to their numerous elementary schools. Similarly, it is to the high school and the college that Missionaries owe their influence amongst —without them they would lose touch with—the active members of the Aryan and intellectual races. The same relation, I say, requiring as in the other cases to be supplemented by work that follows the student in his after-days, that reaches other members of his family and other families of his community, and that brings other kinds of influence to bear on life and its decisions. My second remark regards results.

*Results.* Here also, I maintain, that of our various kinds of work and in the various spheres the effect is the same in kind or similar, differing chiefly in degree. Conversion, regeneration or renewal is the work of God. The work of man is educational, that is to say, it is elevating, enlightening, refining ; bringing help for the guidance of thought and will, of character and conduct.

*Mass baptisms.* What is the justification of the baptism of masses? Not a conviction that the men and women are individually regenerate, but the fact that new communities are being formed in subjection to Christian influence—communities out of which Christian peoples may arise. Amongst them, as amongst the more educated, the good we do is largely in the imparting of a higher or finer intelligence, a truer or worthier idea of life. But there is this striking difference, that in the one case baptisms are numerous, in the other case rare. And why? What is the secret reason of this obvious fact? It is this : in the one case, baptism means social deliverance and elevation and improvement ; in the other, social ostracism and injury. How the difference will stand after a century or two—whether in the former case India escapes the danger of a lowered and semi-pagan Christianity, whether in the latter there will be mass movements of communities of the higher ranks (a result confidently to be expected in the day of Him in Whose power are the times and the seasons), we need not presume to foresee. For the present the voices of duty are distinct and many-toned. And we who bear the brunt of men's judgments need not hesitate to believe and to affirm that our work is supremely necessary, that in the region of mind and spirit, in respect of higher thoughts and aims, in the reform of private and of social life, the influence of our work on the Hindu has been greater, ay, perhaps tenfold greater than that of any one of the less-questioned methods.

*Opinion of an Evangelistic Missionary.* The Rev. J. SHILLIDY, M.A., I. M. P., Surat, said :—I am not an Educational Missionary, but I have had sufficient experience during the last eighteen years to enable me to form an opinion on the subject. I do not come here prejudiced for or against educational work as a Mission Agency. I am pleased to see that the subject before the Conference to-day has been put in this way— "Education as a Missionary Agency,"—for I don't believe we can draw distinctions between primary, secondary or higher education as Mission Agencies; they stand together or they fall together. In discussing this subject there are certain facts which should never be lost sight of. One is, that whatever our mission work be, its principal aim ever must be to lead the non-Christian to Christ. Another only too patent fact is that whether our work be Bazaar Preaching, Bible and Tract Distribution, District Touring, Lectures to the Educated, Medical Zenana or Educational, much of it is very unfruitful, so far as we can judge. There are missionaries I believe in this Conference who have worked steadily as Bazaar preachers for years, and who could not point to as many converts as they have worked years. Should Bazaar preaching be given up because frequently little or no results can be shown ? No one would say so. And, again, what is meant by results ? A definite number of reported conversions, or baptisms, or what ? I have known cases where hundreds of conversions were telegraphed all over India, and, I believe, even to England, and these so-called converts attended the Christian service on the Sunday, and idolatrous ceremonies on the Monday, and this work was lauded by many as producing grand results ! On the other hand, I have known Zenana ladies working faithfully and zealously for many years, and to this day they cannot point to a single woman who, as the result of their teaching, came out and professed Christ publicly in baptism. But should this work be given up because it is without numerical results ? Not so, for, in the particular case we have in view, we happen to know that, although there have been no baptisms, many women have been influenced by Christian teaching—women who Nicodemus-like come to Jesus by night. There are results and results then, and this should not be forgotten when discussing education as a Missionary Agency. Occasionally Missionaries are blamed for not employing Christian teachers only in their schools. All agree that other things being equal Christian teachers would be preferable, but the difficulty is how to get them. In our own Mission we made determined efforts to get some, and with this end in view helped five young men to a college education, but as soon as they were ready for work, three of them got at once good Government appointments and never served us for an hour. I don't blame them for this, but our experience, which is a not uncommon one in India, I think, indicates a very real difficulty that missionaries have to contend with. If they don't educate their Christian youths, they are held up to derision as doing more for the heathen than for Christians, and when they do educate them well they frequently defeat the very object that, as missionaries, they had in view.

*Fourth Day.*

*Results.*

*Difficulty of getting Christian teachers.*

**FOURTH DAY.**

**A Wednesday Sabbath School.**

A great deal was said in praise of Sabbath schools at a previous meeting, with all of which I heartily concur. I have been myself a Sabbath school *teacher* for years, but my best Sabbath school by far is, if you will excuse the Irishism, the one that meets on Wednesdays, when I myself examine the boys of the upper classes belonging to our vernacular day schools in the Scripture lessons learnt by them during the previous week. We can't as missionaries afford to give up the work of the Christian education of as many of the young of India as we can possibly reach.

The Rev. D. ANANTAM, C. M. S., Bezwada, Kistna District, said:—After hearing such able advocates as my brother Kali Charan Banurji and others, I feel the cause of Missionary education does not require advocates like me; and I am rather sorry I sent in my name to speak this morning, as I am sure there are others who can better employ my five minutes than myself.

**The blessings of Mission Schools.**

I stand here, not as a man of great culture or learning, which I am not, but simply to testify to the blessings of missionary schools. Missionary education has done great things for India; it has produced great men, and its triumphs are untold. But I stand here, I say, to bear my testimony to the saving influence it has had over hundreds, I wish I might say thousands and hundreds of thousands of young men and lads. I am not a prominent figure in the mission field, but I thank God, I stand before you a rejoicing Christian, one who has been taught the saving power of Jesus. These twenty-five years or more I have loved Him, and long to love Him more. If this is anything towards advocating Missionary education, I have done my duty this morning. It is sometimes said that so much money is being spent on education by Missionary societies, and very few become Christians now-a-days through its instrumentality. With reference to this, let us remind ourselves that, weighed in heaven's balances, a single soul brought to the saving knowledge of Christ in a Missionary institution, is worth all the money and men spent in that cause. I was a pupil of that great Missionary College, the Noble College, where a goodly number of Brahman and other Hindu youths have been brought to Christ; and for a period of seventeen years I was a master in the same college, seeking to lead others to the Saviour. But for the last few years I have been a renegade, as my friend Mr. Roberts would perhaps have it! I have not turned my back upon educational work, because I thought that itinerating was easier and more comfortable, but because I thought I was needed in that work more than in the college then. I confess that at one time I used to think that village work was much easier than school work; and in talking to the late Rev. Mr. Bhushanam of our Mission (he was indeed an *ornament* to our little community, as his name implied), I used to say to him, "You

**A pupil of the Noble College.**

have a very comfortable work, Sir; you go about the villages and enjoy yourself!" He would simply smile; of course, I was not worth arguing with. But I have changed my mind; I hope I have grown wiser since. If I were asked to choose for the *easiness* of the work, I should at once say, "Give me back my work in the Noble College." Of course, teaching in a school is wearisome work, but then you have home comforts; you have many advantages which you cannot have in village work.

*Fourth Day.*

The Rev. J. DUTHIE, L. M. S., Nagercoil, Travancore, said:— A good deal is being said this morning about results. In dealing with *results* of missions we need to be very careful. There are results and results. In my district I have read in the newspapers lately of very extraordinary results, viz., 4,186 "conversions" in one year. The L. M. S. has been working a good many years in the district in Travancore referred to, but we can show only about 9,000 people who have abandoned idolatry and become Christians. I wish to observe with respect to these 4,186 "conversions" that some 67 of them, at least, in a village known to me, while reported in August last as being 'soldiers of Christ,' were on the 16th December engaged in a "Devil Dance." Untruthful reports may do little harm here; but they work much mischief at home. I believe in Educational work. I have worked hard in this line for thirty-six years; and yet, if you were to ask me how many converts I have made, I should feel much puzzled to know how to answer such a question. But for all that, I claim to be a Missionary. We (Educational Missionaries) have, it seems to me, three things to do—(1) We must let it be clearly understood by the people that our schools and colleges are truly *Missionary* institutions. Let us nail that flag to the mast. (2) We must deal honestly with the youths, who come to us for education. We must be true educators and teach what we profess to teach honestly and well. And (3), especially we must teach the Bible. Let there be no mistake about this either; and it seems to me we ought not only to teach the facts of Scripture, but do our work very much on the principle on which the Negro preacher constructed his sermons. When asked about his preaching, he replied, 'Well, first I *splains*; second I *spounds*, and third I put in the *rousements.*' We must not fear to put in 'the *rousements*,' and to tell every individual student in our school plainly and faithfully and often how he can obtain the salvation of his soul. As I have just said, I thoroughly believe in education as a Mission Agency. At present I do not see how any material modification of our methods can be made. I am persuaded that, if there be failure, the failure is not in our methods but in ourselves. As one connected with the Educational Department of the Mission to which I belong, I cannot but feel that I have come short in many ways, and would desire that I may be more earnest in

*Misleading "results."*

*Three important duties.*

FOURTH DAY.

*Leave results to the Lord.*

*Thankfulness for unanimity.*

*Differences about details.*

*No ideal College yet found.*

*Improvement always desirable.*

future for the salvation of the boys under my care. Let us speak out straightly to our students on the all-important question, and urge them to embrace salvation through the Lord Jesus Christ—leaving all *results* to Him.

The Rev. W. MILLER, L.L.D., (C. I. E.), F.C.M., Christian College, Madras, said:—Now at the close of the discussion I feel little inclined to say anything, unless it be that I am most thankful to find how completely the subject of higher Missionary Education has got out of the number of controverted questions. It was not so twenty years ago at Allahabad. Perhaps it was not perfectly, though very nearly so, even ten years ago at Calcutta. But the tone of every speech to-day puts it beyond a doubt that the Missionary body is practically unanimous as to everything in the matter about which it is important that we should be unanimous. Evidently there is now no difference of opinion as to the place of Christian Colleges in the whole round of the church's work being a place that must be filled. There is no one who any longer doubts that the disappearance of these colleges would be in every point of view a great calamity. Of course, to the end of time there will be, and there ought to be, differences, as to many questions of detail. I daresay we are not quite in agreement as to many subordinate points bearing on the equipment and the management of Missionary institutions. But the main point is that there is entire unanimity as to Christian Colleges to fill the place, which those we already have do their best to fill; but better ones than we have if we can see our way to make them so—being an absolute necessity. Undoubtedly, there is room for improvement in every such college that exists. We have been told by Bishop Thoburn that even in America, that land of wonders, the ideal Christian college has not yet appeared. If the ideal of the thing has not been realized either in America or in any other Christian land, little wonder that it has not yet been realized in India. I do not suppose that there is a single educational missionary who imagines the college he may represent to be anything like so good or so powerful as he would like, thankful as he may be that in some feeble measure it is doing a real part of Christ's work on earth. Even with Mr. Phillips I am at one on this point. And I am glad to find that at the bottom all Mr. Phillips means to say seems to resolve itself into this—Not that we ought to be abolished, but that in this point and that point we may be improved. Now I trust I have never conveyed the impression that I regard the Madras Christian College as standing in no need of any improvement. At all events, I do not so regard it. I am well aware of many improvements that are desirable, and I am labouring to effect them. And any suggestions towards the improvement of that college, which may come from any critic will be thankfully received and carefully considered. But with all the unanimity which so plainly exists as to the only vital matter, viz., the absolute need there is, as a part of the whole missionary scheme, for Colleges as Christian and as efficient in every way as we have grace, and wisdom, and means to make them,—with all this unanimity, for which I am so deeply thankful, I do not know that a time will ever come when there will be no need for the principles on which our educational work proceeds being restated and explained. In matters of this kind there may long, if not for ever, be some need for our turning back to first principles. There will be need that we should do so for the sake of those who look at our labours from far away, and for the sake of those who have but lately come to join in them, even though there be no longer any need of it so far as those are concerned who have appreciated the full truth upon the point through the experience and observation of many years. I rather think there will always be a tendency among those who are inexperienced in the Church's work and who look mainly at the surface of affairs to say strong things against this form of missionary labour. You know that such a tendency exists around us, and that it prevails not with those alone who are opposed to all Christian effort, but with some also who are in a real enough sense its friends. It is worth our while to ask what the cause of this antagonism to the work of educational missions is. The fact appears to be that of all forms of mission effort, ours is the most open and striking testimony to the plan on which all God's real work is done, and the most unlike the idea on which it is natural for men to think that great work must be done. God works silently, and if not always slowly, yet always step by step. In all His works of nature there is a preparation, there is a process, there is a passing upwards from a lower to a higher stage. And the whole sacred history is a testimony that the general method in which God does His works of grace is just the same. Meanwhile, man's natural idea is that things should be done suddenly and in a moment. God's light comes step by step each morning. There is the first faint streak and the growing brightness of the dawn long before the sun shines in majesty. Man, if he had his way, would have the sun appear with the startling suddenness of the lighting of a gas lamp. Now, even men who have been converted and are being sanctified, do not easily lay aside the natural human mode of judging or at once fall in with the divine methods. It is not wonderful, therefore, that they should dislike that which makes those methods very prominent. Yet these methods are Christ's methods, and Christ took infinite pains, though with only qualified success, to make His immediate followers understand that it was along the divine lines of work alone that His Kingdom

*Fourth Day.*

*Reiteration of first principles.*

*God's ways not our ways.*

| | |
|---|---|
| Fourth Day. | was to be set up. I need hardly remind you of how in all the parables in which the nature of that kingdom is expressly taught, this idea of a process, of a preparation, of a growth, of a passage step by step to higher stages, is made as prominent as possible. There is the sowing of the seed, there is the growing of the corn, the working of the leaven, the gathering of fish into a net which a previous process has made ready. In every figure that He used, our Master showed that it was by one thing after another and growing out of another that His Kingdom *must* come. Nevertheless, the very men whom He taught so carefully could not free their minds from expectations of great and sudden and unprepared-for changes that would win the praise of the world. They were the same men who, in spite of all His teaching, asked, " Wilt Thou at this time restore the kingdom to Israel?" There can be no doubt as to what Christ's central thought about the method of His Kingdom's coming was. There can be no doubt that this central thought had great difficulty in getting fully lodged in the minds of His truest followers, and did not get lodged in them at all until the Spirit had fully come. There need, therefore, be little wonder if there is the same reluctance on the part of good men now to appreciate work, especially when it is done by very feeble hands in which this central thought is set in the very forefront. Perhaps it is not more really, but it is certainly more obviously true, of educational than of other forms of genuine Christian endeavour that Christ's central thought about the way in which His Kingdom comes regulates it all. In the very nature of the case, we who are engaged in education cannot do those great and startling things which suit man's natural tendency and win his praise. The very idea of our work obviously is to lay ourselves along God's mighty plan, to be simple and little-regarded instruments in God's hands, to do this small thing to-day and that to-morrow, confident that God's ends are being wrought out, whether men see the bearing of what is done or not. It is ground for rejoicing that the speeches of to-day have shown to how large an extent the missionary body has entered into the mind of Christ on this point—to how large an extent it has passed beyond the stage at which the disciples still were until the Spirit came. And if, in spite of this advance, there still are those who speak against the work of education, we may rightly take the comfort that the real reason of the charges, and the enmity which produces them, is that we prefer Christ's methods and the practical application of Christ's principles to those methods and principles of action which it is natural for man to praise. In this, as in all things, let us learn to ' Count the reproach of Christ greater riches than the treasures of Egypt.' Let me close by heartily thanking you for the intelligent sympathy which you have this day shown for us in that difficult |
| Slow to understand | |
| We seek God's approval not man's. | |

part of the common work to which we in particular have been called.  *Fourth Day.*

The Rev. D. MACKICHAN, D D., F. C. M., Bombay, writer of one of the papers, said in reply:—I feel that the spirit which has characterized our discussion to-day of a subject that has often been somewhat keenly debated is an answer to the prayers that have gone up from the Decennial Conference—a fulfilment of the hopes which found expression in our opening meeting. Instead of replying to the discussion I feel disposed to invite you to join in thanksgiving. It has been a matter of great encouragement and delight that deep down in the hearts of all our Christian friends and fellow-workers there is the conviction that educational missionary work is a force which is being felt throughout this land. The speech of Mr. Maurice Phillips forms no exception to this general agreement. We recognize in him a friend and ally. The main difference between us is that he is working out his scheme on paper; we are trying to work it out in fact. The education of Christians is an object that is dear to the hearts of all missionaries engaged in the work of education. Nothing in my own work has given me greater joy than to find Native Christians sitting side by side with their non-Christian fellow-countrymen, taking rank with them in all the work of the College and in the honours of the University, and to see friendships springing up among them which may prove deep and lasting. That is the kind of Christian education we want to see in this country. Our ideal is not one which would separate Christians from the great body of their fellow-countrymen, but one which aims at keeping them in touch with all their people in a position in which they may exert a sympathetic permeating Christian influence on the educated classes to which they belong. I am prepared to admit that the circumstances of all parts of India are not the same, and that in certain portions of the field the requirements, and consequently the methods to be pursued, may be different. We all feel free to admit these, and we rejoice in the success of every other method; but we maintain that with regard to the Christian Colleges which we represent and the field in which they are working, the method which we employ is the best suited to advance the interests of Christ's Kingdom. It is an entirely mistaken impression that where there is not a large body of Christian students there is not a Christian atmosphere. The atmosphere of all the Christian Colleges with which I have any acquaintance is a Christian atmosphere in the truest sense of the term. To this every one who has any real contact with the work of Mission Schools and Colleges will be prepared to testify. It surprises some of us that the existence of a prayerful spirit amongst the pupils of such institutions should be alluded to as a matter of note. I know School and College

*An answer to prayer.*

*Educational work a power in the land.*

*The Education of Native Christians.*

| | |
|---|---|
| Fourth Day. | classes in which the omission of prayer would be both noted and regretted by large numbers of the pupils. Reference has been made in the course of this discussion to the proposal for a Christian University. That proposal has been made in the interests of Christian education and with the best intention. But what would it mean? It would involve the withdrawal of large numbers from Christian influences, and it would mean still more—the loss of the very class in whose interests the proposal has been made. Do you not think that the Christians are as intelligent in regard to their academical interests as the non-Christians? Do you imagine that they will separate themselves from the educational life of their country and retire to a separate University? You do not understand them if you suppose that they will readily consent to such a separation. They will go where their countrymen are: they will not consent to be divorced from the body of their educated countrymen. It is not for us to encourage any such withdrawal, but to strive more strenuously than ever to make those institutions, in which they and their educated non-Christian brethren share the same instruction, what they should be as instruments of a truly Christian education. We all have our views with regard to Government education in India. We all know that under the limitations which are imposed upon it, it is not able to do the work which an education which recognizes the spiritual needs of the people should accomplish for the people of India. But while we thus judge of the system, we ought to beware of using expressions which would throw a suspicion on the men who are engaged in it. Amongst them are to be found Christian men who are conscientiously and ably discharging the duties of their position who would naturally feel pained by any unjust reflections. It is the defects of the system with which we have to deal, and of these defects increasing experience brings increasing evidence. The Government itself recognizes the truth of the position. They have in fact appealed to others to take up a work which, from the necessary limitations imposed upon them, as a Government they cannot themselves hope to accomplish. Let me, in conclusion, express my own conviction, based upon a long experience of the work done in this College, that I do not believe that you will find in any department of missionary labour, work that is more spiritual in its aim and character than the work of Missionary Institutions. Every hour spent amongst the young men of these Schools and Colleges may be an hour of Christian service—a service that is fitted to call forth the highest spiritual sympathies of every Christian worker who knows his high privilege and his great opportunity. I thank God for the time and spirit of this discussion; I believe that all of us who are engaged in this work will have occasion to thank God for its results. As I have said in my paper, the question |
| A Christian University. | |
| Distinguish between the system and the men. | |
| No more spiritual work than this. | |

has now advanced beyond the stage of discussion; it has reached the higher stage of imperative demand.

The Rev. A. B. WANN, B.D., E. C. S., Calcutta, writer of one of the papers, said in reply:—If I were to consult my own feelings, I should prefer to say nothing now. I have already had my say in the paper which is in your hands. And though I confess I came to the Hall this morning, priming myself to answer objections made against the papers, yet now I find my occupation gone. I do not wish to do more than simply second Dr. Miller and Dr. Mackichan. Let me simply say, as being in some measure a representative of the Christian Educationists of Bengal, that we who have come here from that province are going back to our work with renewed zeal and hopefulness, knowing that we have the confidence and sympathy of our fellow-missionaries. The whole work is one; and success in any department does not depend solely upon the men who are engaged in it. We who are working among educated young men feel that the work is too great for us. We meet men who are our equals in intellect; it is solely our experience which enables us to teach them. We desire and aim at the conversion of individuals, but we believe that there is a great movement in the whole class, which it was beyond our power to create, and will be almost beyond our power to control. And this is the work of the Spirit of God, in answer to the prayers of the whole Church. Knowing that the work is one, we must strive to know and understand each other's work better. Perhaps we educationists have been narrow, and shut ourselves off too much. It would be well if we all had to acquire the vernacular of the province we work in. I was for three years a preaching missionary in this city, and would go back to that work with pleasure, if I were not needed where I am. And I am thankful that I have learned the work and difficulties of those who labour among the less educated classes. On the other hand, it would be well if all missionaries took a livelier interest in our college work. The doors are open; we welcome you to come and see it. For I am certain that the opposition to our work is based on ignorance. Once let a man come face to face with these young students in our colleges, and speak to them, and he will never cease to be interested in them, and in the work done for them. As has been said, to-day's discussion seems to indicate a step in advance with regard to the appreciation of our work; and I can only repeat that it sends back to our homes with new cheerfulness and zeal, and with a strengthened resolve to bring all our teaching to bear on the turning of our students to God.

*Fourth Day.*

*Encouraged to renewed zeal.*

*All engaged in one work.*

*More knowledge needed.*

*Opposition the result of ignorance.*

# XI.—INDUSTRIAL WORK.

## AFTERNOON SESSION.
### LARGE HALL—2 to 4-30 P.M.

FOURTH DAY.

J. MORRIS, Esq., Bombay, *in the Chair.*

*Industrial work should be extended.*

The Chairman said:—We have for our consideration this afternoon—"Industrial work." I believe this is a subject which has often occupied the attention of Missionary Conferences; but it is a question of great interest and importance, because it has such a practical bearing upon the well-being of the Native Christian community, and is therefore bound to press itself to the front on an occasion like this. If one may express an opinion, I venture to think that Industrial work should occupy a more prominent position on this missionary programme, and should be looked upon as a part of educational work; and that any general movement for the establishment, on a practical basis, of industrial work in connection with Christian missions, by educating the Indian Church to look forward to such a work, will be a great step in advance, and will go a very long way towards helping the Indian Christian community into an honourable position of prosperity and true independence, and therefore relieve the missionary from many of the difficulties which he now experiences in the care of his converts. In this connection is it too much to hope that the missionary societies might be induced to stretch out a helping hand to that large and increasing community of domiciled Europeans and Eurasians, and by assisting them in such a scheme provide a body of trained men who, by the circumstances of their lives, are the most fitted to succeed in such a work under missionary supervision?

Might not such an union tend to popularise the movement and raise up in India a great tradeguild which would eventually contribute to the prosperity of this vast community? I speak with diffidence, as my experience is confined to this city; but, as a practical man, whose business has for many years brought him into contact with native artisans, I think there is an ever-increasing demand for skilled workmen; and I believe, generally speaking, that if an Indian Christian is a master at his trade, his religion will not be a bar to his employment, but that he may stand shoulder to shoulder with his Hindu and Muhammadan brothers in our labour markets, and I think that this applies not only to the arts, but to manufactures, and perhaps to agriculture.

*Fourth Day.*

*Demand for skilled labour.*

## FIRST PAPER.

By the Rev. L. J. FROHNMEYER, Basel Mission, Tellichery, Malabar :—

I must begin with a *testimonium paupertatis*. The topic of Industrial Mission has been dealt with almost at every Mission Conference under different designations. In most cases it has been the Basel Mission which was selected to plead for mission tiles and towels; and looking over all these papers and the discussions attached to them, it seems that the ground is rather well trodden. It is somewhat humiliating besides to see, now and then, that in compliance with the word of our Lord, "By their fruits ye shall know them," such who know something of the existence of a Basel Mission, know it only by its industrial productions. As I am Principal of a Theological Seminary and of a Normal School, besides Pastor of a congregation, one may imagine the amount of satisfaction it gives me when I receive an order from Mysore or Calcutta to send half a dozen table-cloths. Should there be any want of enthusiasm for the matter on my side, the post-scriptum "Please, be sharp" ought to make my heart beat high. Some Muhammadan firm at Madras also never tires of asking me how much

*Jack of all trades.*

**Fourth Day.** commission I should be prepared to give for selling my cloths at the capital of the Presidency. I should feel sorry, if the impression in missionary circles were, that Basel missionaries cannot, and like not, to speak about anything else but of the centre and crown of their work—the Industrial Establishments. We are so far from boasting of our Industrial Mission that, as often as we are called to the platform, we appear there fully prepared, that objections will be raised against our Industrial Mission. We do not say: "Be our imitators!" We shall be satisfied, if our cause is fully understood amongst our fellow-workers, to whose sympathies we cannot be indifferent; perhaps our experience may also be of some use to those who work under difficulties similar to ours.

**Missionary principles.** As to missionary *principles* in this connexion, I should think there is on the main no difference of opinion between us. That we have come out to India to win souls for Christ and to preach the Gospel to all nations of this vast empire, none of us will deny. We may go a step further and say: what we consider to be not only one of many results we should like to achieve, but the deciding fruit of our work out here is the *spiritual* regeneration to be effected by the Gospel. If any missionary could do purely spiritual work without being encumbered by anything like cares for the earthly subsistence of his converts, I should think him happy. Where these outward things can be settled by the people themselves; where the social surroundings are in perfect order, I am sure no missionary will care to mingle with the tremendous question; how man's soul and body should be kept together? On the other hand, I fail to understand how missionary work can be looked upon as a mere spiritual matter. Quite apart from the care for the existence of converts, there is so much of earthly and secular business necessarily connected with, and preparing for, the spiritual work, that to ignore this would do away with mission-work altogether? mission-work carried on in this world cannot shun the conditions and tasks of this earthly life. Even Christ did not restrict himself to purely spiritual work. He was followed by people who sought first of all for bread, and he did not send them away.

**Examples of our Lord and St. Paul.** St. Paul and the other apostles made it their common bond to remember the poor, and St. Paul travelled about not only as the great ideal of every missionary in general, but as the first representative of Industrial Missions. It would be against the spirit of Christianity itself to assist probationers up to the day of baptism and then to send them away with the cheap consolation that the Lord will provide for them. In most cases such a procedure would undo even the spiritual work accomplished before. The kingdom of God is not eating and drinking, but as long as we belong to the *ecclesia militans* we cannot do without it. I think it is mere duty and a duty of love for a missionary to try his utmost that such, who by their conversion have lost the means of livelihood, may earn their daily bread by some good and useful work. How could converts believe in the sincerity of our Christian love, if the whole of our Christianity were to consist of spirit and words without any manifestation of what is called " practical Christianity ? " Quite true: "The base things of the world, and the things that are despised did God choose," but this does not mean, that having become spiritually rich in Christ, they must remain henceforth in bodily poverty and misery. Besides, wheresoever Christianity has been implanted and nourished in a people, it has been conducive to the development of culture and to a transformation of all conditions of life. Such a result is something perfectly natural. I am very far from recommending a mission by the means of culture; the Basel Mission has kept clear of this modern idea, and we have always been anxious to give Mary prominence before Martha. On the other hand, as the parable of the leaven indicates, the outward conditions of our people will not remain unaffected by Christianity. There is besides the direct preaching of the Gospel, the power of example, which will manifest itself in the practical conditions of life, *viz.*, mission-work done by the introduction of Christian diligence, Christian integrity and respectability, a mission-work which intends to prove by evidence, as far as possible, that godliness is profitable for all things, having promise not only for the life which is to come, but also for the life which *now is*. It is this prominence given to the universal character of Christianity that in addition to practical difficulties has given rise to our Industrial Mission. So much as to principles.

Still the Basel Mission did not commence work with a fixed set of theories, *a priori* deciding, that there must be an Industrial mission. It is not a favourable idea of the Basel Mission

*Fourth Day.*

*The power of example.*

**Fourth Day.**

*Only a temporal make-shift.*

to have industrial establishments, neither is it a national inclination of German Missionaries to introduce industrial mission-work. On the contrary, the opinion amongst our own missionaries has always been very much divided as to the merits and demerits of such work, not to speak of the public opinion amongst the Christians contributing to our mission at home. Without touching in any way the principles laid down as to practical Christianity and the inseparable connexion between what is spiritual and what is outward in Christianity, I do not hesitate to say that our mission looks upon this Industrial Mission as a temporal make-shift forced upon us by circumstances, and we hope that it belongs but to a transition state and will lead over to something more permanent, more reliable and more natural.

*Why the work was undertaken.*

*What first of all led to the establishment* of an industrial institution, were the immense difficulties we met with in opening for *our converts* a way to lead a life becoming a Christian. The real difficulty in this respect begins *after* baptism. In that part of India, whither we have been sent to work, some native customs make things really worse than they usually are. There is the " Marumakkattayam" or the inheritance in the female line, in consequence of which even converts, who were in possession of something, will in most cases be deprived of everything. Very often the former way of living is out of question, if it was really heathenish, so some new way must be found out. Outside of the mission the difficulties are almost insurmountable. The caste-feeling, still very strong in those parts of India, prevents them from working amongst non-Christians. A great many handicrafts are in the hands of certain castes, and as long as the Christian community is not strong enough to give sufficient employment to its own members, to enter into competition with non-Christian artisans would be a hopeless undertaking. I cannot deny that now and then the difficulty lies also with the converts themselves, some of whom lack all energy, and either have never been accustomed to work or else are under the impression that Christianity will not only give rest to their souls but also to their bodies. It is Christianity which has sanctified labour; whilst in Hinduism exertion is looked upon as an evil which is undergone only as far as it is absolutely necessary. The majority of the people we have to deal

*Converts' views of work.*

with would prefer to commence life's work by taking a pension. This is a fact to be reckoned with, and the circumstances of our converts will not be improved by ignoring this fact. For many of our new Christians it is a new lesson, and not an easy one, that it is God's will that a Christian shall work with his hands the thing that is good. In addition to this there is the other obstacle that some useful and good occupations are looked upon to be degrading and not becoming an honorable man. We cannot expect that our converts and new Christians will, by baptism, at once get rid of such prejudice, howsoever foolish they may appear to Europeans or Americans. Time must be given to the leaven of the Gospel until such remnants of the former life have gone. To give our converts this lesson, we did not begin with establishments, but with something that now is considered a novelty, a kind of industrial school in connexion with our boarding school at Mangalore. In 1846, two book-binders, two lock-smiths, and two weavers were trained in this way. Finding this training impracticable in connexion with an ordinary school, some boys were apprenticed with native artisans, some were sent to Bombay, others to military stations in order to learn some trade. In this way book-binding, tanning, shoe-making, weaving, tailoring, a baking and other handicrafts were learnt by them, but not sufficiently well to be of any use. This led to the sending out of European artisans, first of all of a lock-smith and a clock-maker. These two experiments failed, and so a weaver was sent out. Improving the original looms and implements of Indian weavers and gradually bringing them up to a more European standard, the first weaving establishment came into existence. Without proceeding farther in this history of our Industrial Mission, I may add that, after many experiments, our Mission finally settled to the weaving industry at Mangalore, Cannanore and Calicut, with branches at Tellicherry, Chombala and Codacal. Moreover, there is a mechanical establishment and a press at Mangalore, carpentry and some tailoring in connexion with the Mission shop at Calicut. The work was commenced merely with the intention to teach our converts some handicrafts, and with the hope that something like house-industry would be the outcome of it. How far we have succeeded in this will be shown below. On the other hand, we cannot deny that the character of our establishments has changed altogether.

*Fourth Day.*

*A beginning.*

**Fourth Day.**

**Co-operation.**

Mr. Pfleiderer, who has been for many years the head of our Industrial Mission, explains this in the following manner: "We were gradually convinced that we had to reckon with facts, and that, as in other countries, so in India, the days of the small tradesmen were numbered. The single individual can not go ahead against the general competition, and it was only the system of improved machinery and combined labour by which success could be attained." What Mr. Hudson of the Wesleyan Mission pointed out at the Bangalore Conference as *their* great difficulty, you will see has been experienced by us too as a real difficulty; namely, that such industries as are likely to be of any use to an individual for getting an independent livelihood are not self-supporting but entail considerable loss, while, on the other hand, such industries as our mission carries on chiefly, though self-supporting, seem to keep our Christians always depending on the mission. As to the production of native articles a competition seems to be impossible. An establishment dealing with such articles never could flourish, and even if the mission were prepared to sustain loss in order to make our Christians independent, single individuals could stand the competition still less. Our Christians cannot live on the wages of indigenous labourers, who are not wholly dependent on their handicraft. A Christian family has also necessaries unknown to a Hindu family. I do not refer to luxuries, but to needs which are the beneficial consequences of Christianity. Even Native industry in many branches (for instance in weaving) struggles for existence and is dying away gradually. This is chiefly due to the English colonial system, at the bottom of which we see the anxiety that English productions should have a great run in the colonies. The country is overflown with cheap English weaving, all formerly done by Native industry. Not only the Mission industry, even the Native industry must reckon with these changed circumstances. Going through the bazaar of Tellicherry one can see Moplah-tailors by dozens busy at the sewing-machine, and if a Christian tailor wants to compete with them, he must needs have a sewing-machine too. So after all as a temporal measure we considered our industrial establishments to be the best way to serve our poor Christians.

**Drawbacks.**

We are, however, not unaware of *the drawbacks* and the manifold deficiencies adhering to this particular mission agency. A friend of mission-work, passing through some of our stations, told me, that the whole looks like one great establishment kept up for the maintenance of our Christians. Others say, that our Christians, if dependent on us for their livelihood, will remain dependent on the missionaries in every respect, and they compare them to plants in a glass-house, carefully looked after and guarded against cold and wind. They prognosticate, of course, that once exposed to the struggle of life and the temptations of this world, they necessarily must discredit our mission. There is some truth in all this criticism. Although a state of dependency may be very natural and wholesome at the beginning of mission-work, it is true the majority of those people who get employment in our establishments are still entirely dependent on the mission. They live comparatively easy, they need not go about and look for work, being assured that every day there will be some work prepared for them, but in proportion to this the feeling of responsibility has become deplorably weak in some of the house-fathers. In spite of very good wages, a good many of our people, leading a careless life and even not exerting themselves to make both ends meet, remain poor and run into debts. Some are even not satisfied with getting their work from the mission; in case of any emergency they rush to the missionary expecting him to help them. Even if employed by the mission a state of relative self-dependency could be arrived at; it is, however, seldom that we meet with signs betokening a craving in this direction. There are social drawbacks in addition to this. The first indications of calamities invariably connected with big manufactories cannot be denied. Family life and happiness must suffer, if father and mother must go for work and leave the little ones in care of an elder sister or a non-Christian servant. Now, the necessity of what Germans call "interior mission" has been felt, and Infant Schools in connection with our establishments have arisen. In a place where so many people live together, naturally also something like an *esprit de corps* will spring up, and the spirit is not always of the best kind, reminding one of the proletarian spirit rising under similar conditions at home. The more some get the more they will expect, and often it seems, as if the Christians who have received almost no temporal benefits from the mission, prove to be more thankful and more devoted to their

*Fourth Day.*

*Social drawbacks.*

**Fourth Day.**

**Pastoral drawbacks.**

mission than such as are entirely depending on it. There is also danger that the real aim of mission-work may be totally misunderstood, and the pastoral work in such a congregation may become a very dissatisfactory business. If Christians, not spiritually minded, look upon the establishments as being the most important part of missionary work, if not the sole aim of the mission, such a view may even prove detrimental to the spiritual life of our congregations. If the pastor himself is in charge of industrial work, he will first of all be considered to be the employer, and eye-service and a time-serving spirit will easily manifest themselves. If a lay-missionary is the head of the establishment, there will be the danger that the majority of people look upon the manager of the establishment as upon the head of the congregation too, and treat the pastor and his office with indifference; even a renewal of the old dissension between Cæsar and Pope is not quite beyond apprehension. Another drawback is further, that a Christian congregation, kept together as a separate body by some establishment, can scarcely be expected to exert such a Christianizing influence upon the non-Christian population, as real Christians would do, if living amongst the people to whom they belonged before their conversion. Thus congregations, in which the Industrial Mission predominates, may lack in missionary spirit, if great care be not taken to stimulate them. Another great difficulty cannot be kept secret. As to giving occupation to new converts and other Christians these establishments are only a palliative; if they are full, we shall be placed before the old problem again and again. The establishments cannot be increased *ad infinitum*, and thus also Societies which have such, must continually be on the look-out for something which will really meet the case and make their people stand on their own legs. There remains finally a fearful apprehension not to be lost sight of. Industrial work remains depending on the oscillations of the world's emporium. What if by some unfortunate combinations, by competition from outside, by a great European war, some catastrophe should take place and we should be compelled to shut our establishments? Such a prospect is dreadful in the extreme. Thinking about all this, we also made trials with agriculture. The question is such a complex one that I cannot enter upon it here. All I can say is this, that the difficulties with which such undertakings are beset, are even more puzzling than what we have experienced in our Industrial Mission. Agricultural work is done in connexion with our Orphanages at Mooldy and Paraperi, but up to this without any result of getting a self-dependent livelihood for our Christians.

<small>Fourth Day.</small>

In spite of all these drawbacks, I must admit, that in our mission we cannot do without these establishments for the present. Some of our most flourishing congregations would scarcely exist without the aid of them. The argument that by such institutions we hold out worldly advantages, does not greatly exercise my mind. First of all, we do not begin the establishment, fill it with non-Christians, and then wait for conversions. It is true, not only the spiritual and eternal blessings of Christianity attract a good many of the people, they also expect deliverance from all the miseries of their outward life, corresponding to the two-fold misery in Hinduism. If such look upon Christianity with the expectation that they will be redeemed from everything that burdens, maltreats, frets and worries them, they do but the same that those poor sufferers did who looked upon Christ. Where the Spirit of God after indefatigable preaching of the Gospel has wrought upon the hearts, these establishments may be an additional help to attract people. In some places this will not take place at all. And even if they do attract, there are many ways by which God may attract a man's heart. Also in Europe conversions take place in consequence of bodily ailments, poverty and other miseries. Besides admittance to the establishments and to instruction does not mean baptism. I consider it to be one of the great advantages of these institutions that they do offer an opportunity to test the sincerity of probationers. "Help is only given under condition of persevering work, and "hypocrites seldom like to work," as Mr. Lechler remarks in a paper on Industrial Institutions. But not only for new converts or poor catechumens our establishments have become quite indispensable, they have also preserved their original designation as industrial schools. For a real industrial school the circumstances are not favourable; the handicrafts accessible for Christian youths are but few, and for a small mission as ours the establishment would be too costly for several reasons. However, all our establishments are also places of apprenticeship for some young men. To send them to heathen masters would be a

<small>Necessary at present.</small>

<small>A test of sincerity.</small>

FOURTH DAY. very dangerous experiment. The question what to do with all the boys of a Christian congregation is a real problem, and the system of public instruction is but increasing the difficulty. We have no real primary education, an education not aiming at a literary career, but containing the elements of knowledge necessary for everybody. What is called primary education with us are 4 or 5 standards of a curriculum laid down for a course of instruction ending with the B. A. degree. Having reached a 5th or 6th standard, either want of money or of ability prevents most of our boys from going further on; but having got a smattering of English education, they come to know that it is below their dignity to take to manual work, and so some of them will turn out to be good-for-nothings. For a good many of these the establishments have become a real refuge. These establishments further help us a good deal in keeping our Christians together; having them a lengthened period of time under Christian influence, we are enabled to plant amongst them and to fasten Christian manners and morals. Most of our people are mere saplings and in need of special care and anxious supervision. I need not say that regular and persevering work in itself is an educational factor. We try to escape the dilemma either: first *ora*, and afterwards *labora*, or: first *labora* and then *ora*, but keep to the old *ora et labora*. Each day's work begins and ends with prayer, and I am sure, also, that preaching and pastoral work, if the establishments are what they ought to be, must have more effect amongst people who earn their daily bread by regular work than amongst people embittered and pining away under the burden of poverty. It is a fact that a vast number of our Christians have been enabled by these establishments to lead a Christian life in happiness and comfort. Their houses being clean, orderly and comfortable, may be distinguished at first sight from the houses of non-Christians. These establishments have also enabled them to get a better education for their children, and the progress in this respect from one generation to the other is quite remarkable. If these establishments have not become a blessing to every single individual—as I have admitted before, those institutions cannot be blamed for it altogether. Besides the firm position our mission has taken in the caste-question, our establishments have been instrumental too in settling this difficulty. Caste-feeling amongst

*Misuse of education.*

*Ora et labora.*

Christians is a thing perfectly unknown amongst us. In such establishments, where non-Christians have been admitted, a great many of them have in course of time become inquirers and after all believers in Christ. Another advantage is, that the staff of missionaries is increased without an additional expense for the Society; much care and work for the outward concerns of our Christians has been taken off the hand of the ordained missionaries. The Missionary Society itself does not undergo any pecuniary risk in keeping such establishments, as no mission funds are taken for this agency. On the other hand, the shareholders get only 5 per cent. interest on their invested capital, whereas the remaining surplus goes to the mission as a free contribution. Many a station could not have been founded but for the Industrial Mission. One-tenth of our Indian Christians, who get employment in these establishments, may have in addition to the personal benefit derived from these institutions, the gratifying satisfaction of knowing that by their work the great cause of evangelizing the people of their own soil is promoted.

*[margin: Fourth Day. Caste feeling unknown. Helps to extend the work.]*

To be sure, if Industrial Mission is expected to be accompanied by all the results mentioned above, different *conditions* must be fulfilled. First of all, the manager of such an establishment must be an European expert. It is a great mistake to think that for doing this work effectually not so much capacity is needed as for ordinary mission-work. A narrow-minded lay-missionary, not qualified for his work, is a misfortune to any mission-station. He must be capable to pay regard to quite different circumstances and materials. It has happened that a carpenter, who at home was accustomed to work with tender wood, merely by finding the wood in India to be hard, lost courage altogether and went home. Such an artisan must know his craft more thoroughly than one at home. A weaver ought to know the art of dyeing, too, as well as other auxiliary arts, and every artisan must be prepared, if necessary, to repair his own implements. If his establishment is meant to be a mission agency, he must be a real Christian and inspired with the enthusiasm of a true missionary. In our mission the lay-missionaries are put on an equal footing with the ordained missionaries in every respect; they are members as well of the Presbytery as the Station-Conference, an

*[margin: Manager's qualifications.]*

| | |
|---|---|
| Fourth Day. | arrangement which perhaps is capable of improvement. There must be strict order in these establishments, else such manufactories will become a real nuisance. Idleness, filthy language, drunkenness and the like cannot be tolerated. Altogether a Christian spirit must prevail. The manager must give the impression that the spritual and temporal welfare of his people affects him more than anything else. Any considerable number of non-Christians in these establishments ought to be avoided; if they are not inquirers, their influence on the Christians will in most cases be pernicious; however, a small number, properly supervised, will do no harm. An excellent manager of our weaving establishment in Mangalore exerted such a beneficial influence upon his people, that almost all the non-Christians desired to become Christians. |
| Only preparatory. | If, in conclusion, the question is raised, how far we have succeeded in training by means of such institutions for a *state of self-dependency*, the answer will be, that these institutions can do only preparatory work. The training to industrious habits in itself is the first step. The wages in most of our establishments are so liberal that parsimonious people easily may lay up something either for days of special need or for getting gradually houses and compounds of their own. A great many of our people have succeeded in this, and every encouragement possible is given by our establishments in cases where Christians show themselves anxious to arrive at a more solid basis for their earthly subsistence. There are savings-banks with a view to old age and days of sickness in connection with the establishments. To save our Christians from the hands of usurious Moplahs in time of famine, rice is bought by the establishments and sold to the workmen there. I need not say that such establishments must be self-support- |
| Hopeful results. | ing, else they should not be kept up, because finally they would prove to be only a particular kind of charity. Some hopeful signs of real self-dependency I cannot leave unmentioned. One carpenter-shop at Calicut was not self-supporting as long as the manager was an European, owing to the higher salary we had to give him; still you will find on every station of our mission one or two carpenters independent from the mission, earning their livelihood by the craft learnt at Calicut. There was a boys' home attached to the carpentry-shop, and the |

manager took care of the boys. He even succeeded in training a man (his name is Amos), whom he could trust so far as to make over the whole of this work to his management. Knowing his trade perfectly well, and being an earnest experienced Christian, the establishment is flourishing under his management in every respect. As he continues to take apprentices, in addition to his own self-dependency, this establishment has not ceased to be a mission agency. Of course, what could be done with the carpentry-shop, carpentering being not so different from what it is at home, could not be done with other establishments. Still, also these are not altogether without success in the way of making Christians self-dependent. The mechanical establishment at Mangalore has been instrumental in training a good number of youths who, independent of the mission, now earn their bread. There is a considerable number of tailors outside of the establishments, but they do not get on very well for the present. If they can do only what hundreds of Moplahs and Hindus at the same locality can do as well, they will not get regular work. To make them really self-dependent by training them in superior kind of work, an European expert will be wanted for some time. At Mangalore, I hear, some of our Christians have opened a workshop for tailors. Should they get a qualified manager for this establishment, it might become a training institution for tailors sent there from our different stations. There are some weavers, too, who have disconnected themselves from our establishments and have taken to house-industry, and last year one of them went to the East as a maistry of some missionary industrial school. As a matter of course, self-dependency for a cooly working in a tile-making establishment is an absolute impossibility. But these establishments have the great advantage, that everybody, men, women and boys can be employed there. Without previous training they may earn something at once. There are new-comers too old and too stiff to be trained for some new occupation. Simply to feed them would be demoralizing.

I presume even such as cannot approve of our industrial mission will be reconciled to our work on hearing that we ourselves hope that such establishments, similar to the work of education in general, will gradually make themselves superfluous. It is but natural that such a process wants time, accord-

*Fourth Day.*

*Tile-making.*

ing to circumstances a shorter or longer time; but by-and-bye these establishments as missionary agencies must give way to something better. The congregations do increase; by means of our establishments, the industrial habits and the general wealth of the Christians are gradually improving, and so we hope by-and-bye to lay a solid foundation for independent work, for home-industry, and perhaps also for the introduction of agriculture. Like all missionary work it is a work of patience. We are satisfied and thankful in seeing the first signs of what by God's help and blessing in the days to come will be the fruit of our labour. Dr. Grundemann, in a recent criticism on our industrial mission as an eye-witness, writes: "The opponent of industrial mission reminds me of a gardener who would say: What do I care for leaves, I want the blossom and the fruit, and hence prematurely by artificial means the appearence of some blossom is enforced, whilst the leaves must decay. He deludes himself. The premature fruit he succeeded in will decay too. But he who waits in patience will gather in the mature fruit in due season." Also in this work, as in other work done for the furtherance of God's kingdom, the law laid down by our Lord and Master will stand firm in spite of all human impatience: "First the blade, then the ear, after that the full corn in the ear."

*Patience needed.*

## SECOND PAPER.

By the Rev. T. SNELL SMITH, A.B.F.M., Jaffna, Ceylon.

*Jaffna.*

The problem probably in the mind of the Committee, who prepared the programme, and which meets the Indian missionary, of providing new means of livelihood for masses of indigent Native Christians is not a practical one in Jaffna. We have no territorially separate Christian community, nor Christian villages, nor Christian quarters in other villages. Our Native Christians as a rule are prosperous individual members of a dense homogeneous agricultural community. Comparatively few of them are still agriculturists, because their superior intelligence and education have made them the teachers, inspectors, clerks, proctors, advocates, notaries, physicians, merchants and Government employés of the whole community, of which they form a constituent and most influential, though still numerically insignificant, part.

*Fourth Day.*

The average Jaffna Christian boy does not expect nor need to become an artizan; he can do better at something else, and the hereditary artizan can do better at that. There are exceptions, poor orphans, boys with merely mechanical aptitudes, though by no means dullards, sons of hereditary artizans, who have awakened to the possibility, the need or the advantage of education for themselves; but at present there are not enough of these among the Native Christians, or even in the whole community, to justify the establishment of purely industrial schools in Jaffna, as missionary institutions.

*Exceptions*

An institution, in which the industrial training is subsidiary to higher education in the vernacular, may not be an ideal industrial school; but it is a type of school which has important merits of its own. It may be called an Anglo-Vernacular *Normal* or *Training* or *High* School with an *Industrial Department* or *Annex*. The primary object of such a school should be the training of Christian teachers for vernacular village schools or the providing of secondary education, chiefly in the vernacular, for those who cannot afford or do not wish an English education.

*A training Institution.*

An Industrial Department will grow quite naturally out of such a school. To provide each embryo teacher with text-books of his own, *i. e.*, with the necessary tools of his trade, to help the boys to pay their own fees, to train the mind by training the hand and the eye, to teach the dignity of manual labour and self-help, and, finally, to provide an alternative means of livelihood in the event of lack of fitness or of chance for teaching, these are the appropriate aims of such an institution.

The peculiar subsidiary aim of the industrial training in such a school must be borne in mind in judging its results. Such a school may not turn out many artizans, for its typical product will not be an artizan, but an artistic teacher, *i. e.*, a Christian teacher with intelligent tastes and Christian sympathies for all honest labor and a fair practical knowledge of at least one useful mechanical art. Such a result is at least as valuable as a mere bread-winning mechanic, and the mechanical or industrial part of the result is only ennobled and enhanced in value by its subordination to the higher work of training the young idea.

**Fourth Day.**

*Advantages of industrial knowledge.*

That the village schoolmaster can give points to the village mason or carpenter or blacksmith, that he can build his own well-curb or house or make a chair or desk or explain the mysteries of printing or bind a book and show others how to do so too, is a good thing, all the better it may be, sometimes at least, because it is his accomplishment, not his hereditary, fated, acquired, or sole means of livelihood at which he must grub or die. "The poet is born not made," says the old saw, and the Hindu bigot answers " just so the artizan," and so say we. for the " born artizan," in the anti-Hindu but truly Christian sense of the word, is an important product of such industrial training. The mechanical aptitude is an innate gift and not a bit of caste heredity. This method of industrial training helps to the discovery of the natural bent of every boy and to the selection for special training of those true sons of Bezaleel whom " God has made wise hearted and filled with the spirit of God in wisdom and in understanding and in knowledge and in all manner of workmanship to devise cunning works, to work in gold and in silver and in brass and in cutting of stones, to set them, and in carving of timber, to work in all manner of workmanship."

There are boys who can never shine as scholars, to whom every examination is a veritable *pons asinorum*, but who have a special aptitude for some useful manual art and the occasional discovery and development of these "twice-born" masters of art is one of the happiest results of this subsidiary method of industrial training in an Anglo-Vernacular Normal, Training, or High School, with an Industrial Annex.

These other features of such an institution are important. It should give secondary education, *i. e.*, its pupils should be comparatively mature and for the most part resident boarders, though not necessarily aiming to become merely school teachers. Prosperous farmers, traders, surveyors, village notaries, dispensers, accountants, &c., &c., might well be trained in such a school.

*The vernacular should be taught.*

It should be Anglo-Vernacular with special emphasis on the *vernacular*, *i. e.*, the vernacular should be intelligently, thoroughly and practically taught, not a dead classic dialect, not mere colloquial vulgarisms, but the pure idiomatically spoken vernacular enriched by such transliterations and coinages as may be really needed to make it a suitable medium for impart-

ing Western knowledge. It is preposterous to expect that  **Fourth Day.**
English will become the vernacular of India. The vast majority
even of intelligent men can never get even a smattering of
English, and it ought to be made possible for them to get something more than the three Rs. in their own tongue. What
they get in their own tongue will be really gotten and can be
given again, which is not true of the crammed parrot lessons in
science and history which are so characteristic of the average
English-taught Hindu lad.

But English must be taught, too, not with a speaking but a  *English must*
reading vocabulary, as Latin and Greek are taught at home,  *be taught.*
with the definite aim of fitting the future teacher or master
mechanic to make intelligent use of books of reference, improved
text-books, professional and other periodicals, &c., in English,
and thus making it possible for him to keep out of the ruts, to
grow himself and to enrich the written and unwritten store of
knowledge in his own tongue. By teaching English in this
way the temptation to seek English employment will be minimized, while the vernacular will be freed, conserved and
ennobled; and at the same time the chance will be given for the
development of any special talent for English such as would
justify the building of a practical English education upon the
solid Anglo-Vernacular foundation already laid.

Men with this bi-lingual training are especially valuable in
missionary work of every kind and are the fittest beneficiaries
of bursaries and scholarships in Missionary Colleges.

We have still to consider the industries to be attempted and  *Financial*
the method and extent of training to be given, and to refer  *aspects.*
briefly to the financial aspects of the problem.

The latter conditions all the rest. It is possible perhaps to
conduct such an enterprise on a self-supporting basis in a
very small and rather commercial way, but grants-in-aid from
Government, from a missionary society, from individual patrons
or from the poor missionary manager himself are most necessary; and the more abundantly liberal these grants can be
made, the more satisfactorily and efficiently can the work be
done. The ideal basis is an endowment fund sufficient for the
efficient equipment of the school with the needed plant of
shops, tools, machinery, and raw materials, the support of a lay
missionary superintendent trained in normal and technical schools

**Fourth Day.** at home and a native superintendent or foreman. No matter how direct and large the Evangelistic and Christianizing power of the school, it does not seem right to use for its support any more than for higher English education, money given for the preaching of the Gospel to the heathen. Failing an endowment or grants-in-aid from Government, funds given for this work can be used.

**Selection of industries.** The selection of industries, and still more the method and extent of the training to be given, must be determined by the financial resources of the school. If self-support has to be cultivated productive work must be done and a market must be sought or created. Too often an industrial school or department is denied all aid from abroad and then is reproached for trying to earn money by its work.

The progressive training of the pupils as in technical work at home is very desirable; but it is expensive in itself and comparatively unproductive of income. Still a variety of training in orderly sequence should be the constant aim in every work room. This requires a staff of skilled workmen to act as instructors, and these, in turn, in a country school at least, must be provided with remunerative employment, and so the commercial feature must come in.

The local environment must guide the selection of industries. Carpentry, blacksmithing, tinkering, including tin-work, glazing and painting under that term, masonry, gardening, shoemaking, are all important industries and likely to be of use in after life. Printing and book-binding are peculiarly germane to the kind of school advocated in this paper, because helpful to the preparation of vernacular text-books, especially those greatly needed for higher education in the vernacular. These books are costly to prepare. Their circulation is so small that only small editions can be printed and this in turn enhances the cost of every copy.

**Taxidermy.** What might be called fancy or show industries like taxidermy or photography may sometimes be easily self-supporting and even profitable to the school, and boys well trained in them may easily find profitable employment. They also afford an attractive advertisement to the school. This is especially true of

**Photography.** photography. The missionary cannot take the time to prepare all the prints he would like to use, but an Industrial School

Studio will solve the problem of inexpensive prints for many missionaries and Native Christians besides earning a fair income for the school. It may help to bring the luxury of portrait photography within the means of Native Christian families and individuals; so that indulgence in a family group or a picture of the baby may no longer be an almost sinful extravagance, but a commendable evidence of advance in Christian culture.

*Fourth Day.*

There are innumerable minor practical questions of detail, but we can only refer to a few.

The pupils should be paid a nominal wage per hour to promote their interest and ambition and to help their self-support, and when possible they should be offered employment on such wages as they can fairly earn in the shops of the school during a part of their holidays.

*Wages.*

The foremen and other journeymen or skilled workmen in the shops should be chosen as far as possible from those trained in the school. If practicable they should be paid by piece-work and extra payment should be given for the successful training of the boys. They should be allowed some benefit in their piece-work from the work of the boys in official industrial hours, that it may be for their own interest to bring them forward as rapidly as possible. Piece-work is practicable in the bindery, the cabinet shop, the foundry. It is practicable, but with honest workmen hardly profitable, in the printing-room. The boys should be watched carefully and strictly, though kindly discipline must be enforced, and wilful shirking promptly punished by a change to a harder or less agreeable industry.

*Overseers to be chosen from the school.*

Fines must be inflicted at times, and prizes for good work or marked improvement are often very helpful. An occasional prize competition and public exhibition will help to encourage pupils and awaken interest among the friends of the school. The foreman of each room should be required to record the hours and the work done, the faults and the merits of all the boys working in his room.

*Fines.*

Neatness, order, cleanliness, system, are all important, and are all most difficult to secure. Carelessness in handling, lending or borrowing tools is a besetting and most trying fault. "Broken," "lost," "strayed" or "stolen," too often the last I fear, is the ultimate and often the too early epitaph of every tool.

**Fourth Day.**
**Honesty.**

There is a real danger of temptation to dishonesty in appropriating material or the proceeds of labour or in conniving at such dishonesty in others. The boys must be watched and yet they must be trusted. Honesty and faithfulness are most necessary in the foremen and the superintendent. The effort must be unceasing to make the work-room a school of training in honesty and faithfulness, and not the reverse. The industrial hours should be made attractive to each boy. The desire to excel in whatever he undertakes, to bring credit to the school as well as to himself, must be awakened. To a certain extent it is well to indulge each boy's preference in designating his industry, but real aptitudes must be carefully studied. A boy who is always blundering and spoiling tools in the cabinet-shop may soon become the best mason in the school.

## FIRST SPEECH.

By the Rev. S. B. Fairbank, D. D., A. B. F. M., Bombay.

**An example.**

He spoke in favour of Industrial Work in Missions. It is useful for the missionary as well as for the scholars in his schools. It is good for him to set an example and to honour industry by working with his own hands. And work with his spade or his axe will be as good or better for his liver than the exercise got in tennis courts. God's first law, referred to in the Bible, organizes the family. The second demands labour to subdue the ground. The apostles were from the labouring classes, and Jesus worked at his trade. When proclaiming the Gospel, He and they continued their active life, going afoot from place to place. The Jews were wise in requiring every boy, even the son of the king, to learn and to practice a trade. David retained the vigour he gained in his laborious youth as long as he led his armies in person. When he indolently stayed at home and sent Joab to lead the battle, he fell into his great sin. Elijah kept the strength he had as a farmer, by his hardy life in the desert. After many years of itineracy and evangelistic work, he ran before Ahab as he drove his chariot from Carmel to Jezreel, and then he hurried on to far off Beersheba. Solomon was well taught and gave excellent instruction on this subject. But he did not practice it himself. His many servants and many wives spoiled him. He found much study a weariness to his flesh. He must have had a bad liver, for he came to hate life and to call it all vanity and vexation of spirit. Another wise man of later age, also of Israel and a dweller in palaces, but of active life, well said that Solomon should have used another letter when he wrote *vanitas vanitatum, etc.*, and should have written *sanitas sanitatum totum sanitas*. Bodily health seems a primal requisite for a missionary, although some have done admirable work without it. Insomnia, indigestion, fear of the sun and dislike of hard work in the open air, are largely due to the lack of physical exercise. James Brainerd Taylor's good rules were to take care : firstly, of the spirit ; secondly, of the body ; and thirdly, of study. We need physical training ourselves and in all our schools to fit us for spiritual and intellectual good.

Fourth Day.

Bodily health.

The missionary must set the example and make labour fashionable. In Chicago an idle man or one without some useful occupation, though he be a millionaire, is regarded as a dude or a tramp. Labour is not honoured in India. The Buddhist idea that it is better to walk than run, better to stand than walk, better to sit than stand, better to lie down than sit, better to doze than lie awake, and better to sleep soundly than doze, is thoroughly Hindu. It is in harmony with the modern idea held by the boys when in our schools and when they become teachers as to the proper thing for a gentleman and a scholar.

Buddhist idea.

The speaker was going on to say something about the help that industry and industrial teaching in our schools would give to remedy these false and harmful notions and habits, and to refer to the improvement in the requirements as to physical culture demanded in Government examinations ; and also to speak of the admirable results attained by the industrial schools which have been established by some of our missionaries, when the bell reminded him that his allotted time was spent, and with another sentence demanding that industry should be honoured, he left the platform,

## SECOND SPEECH.

By the Rev. J. SMALL, F. C. M., Poona.

Who said that any right he had to address the Conference on this subject was grounded on his connection with an Orphanage Mission Press in Poona. The work arose out of the famine of

| | |
|---|---|
| Fourth Day. | 1876-77, when a lady offered support for destitute boys, and an anonymous gift of money was left one evening on the missionary's table with the words, "For a Printing Press," on the wrapper. The work had begun with a single small Press, but on its being made known to the children of the Sabbath schools of the Free Church of Scotland, they had given an Annual and also other offerings, amounting to about £1,000 sterling, which had been laid out in Presses, type, &c. The Press was thus also an illustration of the power of "littles," a mere collection of pence |
| Printing. | having set up a considerable printing establishment. Mr. Small went on to say that boys in the Orphanage School were apprenticed when their age allowed, and they served in this capacity for four years. Government had recognized the institution as an Industrial school, and allowed a grant of Rs. 20 per head to boys who passed in an annual examination, which embraced both the ordinary vernacular subjects and progress in knowledge of printing and compositor's work. Many boys had passed through the course and had found employment, some in Government offices, like the Photomecographic, some in Presses, like the Education Society's Press at Byculla, and others in private Presses. But undoubtedly it had been one of the difficulties of the institution to find suitable openings for the lads who had finished their course. It was found that they preferred staying on in their own Press, even on less pay, but of course it was impossible that all could be kept on. The religious training of these boys had never been lost sight of, and as a rule they had themselves, as they grew up, asked for baptism, as it was not the custom of the mission to baptize them, even though brought to school very young, until a personal profession of faith could be made. Religious training brought with it a difficulty |
| Sunday work. | in finding suitable situations for the lads, as it was not desirable that they should go where Sunday work was required, or other work of questionable character. With exceptions, such as one might always expect, the lads had done well, both in their stay at school and in their subsequent employment. |
| Independence a boon. | Mr. Small desired to add that the importance of industrial training in the native community could not be exaggerated. There were two great evils before them in India—one, the economic one of the enormous excess of agricultural employment, which in our measure we were lessening by every attempt, how- |

ever humble, to encourage trades and industries; and the other, *Forward Dev* the dependence of our people on our missions for employment and support, which could only be checked by opening independent lines, into which our youths might be led by stages. He had no doubt that instead of missions having to excuse themselves for recognizing the situation, they were simply bound to do so, if they would secure their highest end—a right-thinking, a well-ordered, and an independent Christian community.

The meeting being now open for discussion,

The Rev. SORABJI KARSHETJI, C. M. S., Poona, said:—We have gathered a large proportion of our Native Christians from among the depressed classes in India, and we wish to elevate them, and build them up into respectable communities, in order that, ere long, they may be able to support their own churches and pastors, and even to send missionaries to their brethren who have not had the opportunity of hearing the blessed Gospel. Now, how can they do all this, unless we make them capable and put them in the way of becoming independent? In my opinion, no plan is better suited to carry out our purpose than that of training those at least of the rising generation to some sort of industrial work. Among the heathen a carpenter or blacksmith has his own social position in the caste in which he is born, and he earns a comfortable living by his trade, which he believes to be *his* by divine right. I think, therefore, that it is the imperative duty of every Christian mission and missionary to raise this depressed or Sudra class from the degradation to which the lordly Brahmans have consigned them. The idea was first worked out by the Rev. W. S. Price, the present incumbent of Wingfield Vicarage, Harleston, and an honoured missionary of the Church Missionary Society in 1851. I had the good fortune to be associated with him as his fellow-labourer for some years. A plan for establishing a Christian village near Nasik, with an Orphanage for boys and girls, and an Industrial institution for training, not only orphan boys, but the sons of Native Christians, was begun with due thought and prayer, and soon carried into effect by the indefatigable energy and business-like ability of Mr. Price. By the beginning of 1855 we were in regular working order. We began with carpentry, and as the need arose, we found the necessity of adding blacksmithing, painting and weaving. But before we put a boy to any mechanical work, we taught him to read, write and cipher in our primary school. As soon as the boys finished their school course, we drafted them one by one into the Industrial school, with the exception of a few who had superior intellectual abilities

*Social position of artisans.*

*Nasik*

| | |
|---|---|
| Fourth Day. | and were trained for evangelistic work. In the Industrial school the boys were allowed to choose an industry, according to their individual tastes and inclinations. Our institution was subsequently increased by the transfer to our mission by the Government of a number of African youths rescued from slavery; and, to their honour be it said, that a considerable number of them returned afterwards to their own country, as qualified tradesmen, and lived honourable Christian lives in the Christian settlement there. I may add that six of these youths formed the gallant band that accompanied Dr. Livingstone on his last expedition in that difficult and unknown land! |
| Plan of work. | Our plan was this: As soon as a boy was apprenticed to a trade, half a rupee a month was saved for him for the first year, a rupee a month for the second, two rupees for the third, and so on, till he completed his apprenticeship, when he was paid full wages according to his skill, and the value of his work, just as we should have paid a heathen workman from the bazaar. Whatever money was saved for a boy was laid out for him in building a little cottage and furnishing it with necessary articles, so that, if he got married, he had no burden of debt weighing upon him. He lived respectably on his earnings, and even able to support his own church and pastor. If properly managed, an Industrial school need not become a burden to a mission. In fact, it is a help, as it provides work for inquirers and converts. The Sharanpur institution, of which I now speak, |
| Self-supporting. | where more than 40 boys were taught various trades, supported itself in a few years—of course, after the original outlay on the purchase of plant and tools, &c. When once we got on working lines, we received plenty of orders for work from the outside public as well as from Government. I believe we executed Rs. 30,000 worth of work for Government in building and repairing transport carts, and Rs. 20,000 worth for Messrs. Nicol & Co., of Bombay, for building their farm, &c., at a village called Jalalpur, near Nasik. We charged the exact cost for work done in our institution, plus 20 per cent. for our direction and supervision; and people gladly sent their work to us, as they found we did it better and cheaper than they could get it in the bazaar. I cannot too strongly deprecate the custom of |
| Building and repairing. | turning this class of people into domestic servants. An isolated Christian servant, among half-a-dozen heathen ones, is certain to be ruined. He is either taught some bad habit by his companions, or is maligned by them to the master, and then dismissed with a bad character: I therefore humbly urge upon every mission throughout India the advisability of having an industrial institution attached to their district. This I believe is the only feasible means of raising this class of poor Christians, and building them up into respectable, independent communities. |

The Rev. C. W. LAY, A. B. F. M., Ahmednagar, said:—The *Fourth Day.* two papers before us give two different kinds of industrial work. Mr. Frohnmeyer shows us the mission manufactory and speaks of its drawbacks. Mr. Smith represents industrial training as helping to give *vernacular* teachers or preachers versatility and more influence. I wish to speak of a new and different phase represented by our work at Ahmednagar, namely, *manual training* in the English High School. This department was projected about two years ago. Its aim is education, education of the head through the hand—" The skilful hand the cultured mind." We teach cabinet work with the same purpose as algebra or geometry, to educate. The procedure is this—A drawing of a joint or a small scale is given to a boy. He copies the drawing and then produces the idea in wood. During the first year about fifteen of these models are to be made, embracing the different cabinet joints, as mortise and tenon-right and oblique angled,—dovetail, scarpt, &c. Our young man who has finished his first year is making a set of models for the drawing-master, as nicely as they could be made in Bombay, where Rs. 2 each was demanded. Of this Rs. 2, three annas is wood and the rest represents skill. Although the aim is not to turn out cabinet-makers, yet some, no doubt, will incline to that for a lifework. Although the aim is not immediate self-support, yet it fits for support with better pay than, as a rule, does the *apprentice* course of the usual industrial school. Government is very kindly disposed toward this manual training idea in the English High School. Let me mention one great need of to-day in our up-country Christian communities, I mean Christian contractors. Hindu maistries are slow to employ any but Hindu workmen. But as the number of Christian mechanics of moderate skill is increasing, employers are needed. May some of our best Christian young men find their way from lower schools of manual training or industrial training into " The Victoria Technical Institute" here in Bombay.

*Manual training.*

*Drawing.*

*Cabinet-makers.*

The Rev. W. E. RAMBO, Christian Mission, Bilaspur, C. P., said: When I tell you that I have been in India twenty-five days more than a year, you will expect me to settle this question at once. An old missionary said to me, "If you have anything to say, you had better say it soon; for the longer you stay in India, the less capable you will feel to express an opinion." I make haste, therefore, to speak while I have something to say. In my judgment the question of industrial training lies at the very foundation of our educational work. The great difficulty with native preachers and teachers is that they live away up in the air; they regard all work as degrading, and look upon the worker with contempt. This crops out where they least think of it. I discovered one of my servants carrying water for

*Young Missionary's view.*

**Fourth Day.**

*Trade no degradation.*

some native preachers living near the mission compound. On inquiry I found they had told him it was his business to carry water for them. On another occasion the same servant was appropriated by another family to milk their cow. This went on till a young man of the family—an excellent lad too—came and asked me to let my servant leave some work he was doing for me to go to milk the cow. I said, "Can't you milk a cow?" He replied, "O, now, I couldn't milk a cow." I said, "You will never be able to learn younger: when I was your age, I could, and did, often milk half-a-dozen a day." Ladies and gentlemen, I wouldn't give much for a man who can't milk a cow! I speak of the barrenness of a *merely* intellectual train-

*Barrenness of mere intellectual training.*

ing. There is a dignity about work which such a training never imparts, and which, if a man do not understand, he cannot be a true man. Our Native Christians need something to take them out of this ethereal, intangible mode of living, and to bring them into contact with the every-day practical questions of this world. Most men whom we seek to win live in this world, and walk on the ground, and have to contend with stubborn facts of poverty and hardship that meet men of practical life. How shall a man who hates work, and revels only in the intellectual and theoretical, sympathize with him who in the fight for life has to earn his bread by "honest sweat?" or how can he influence him? The industrial training will correct this evil. But the question goes deeper than this. It goes to the very source of spirituality itself. Nothing is farther

*Industrial training co-operative with spiritual.*

from the essence of the Gospel than to consider that spiritual life can exist independently without practical usefulness. Spirituality is measured by action. "Pure and undefiled religion" is a thing to be wrought out, not to be thought out. "To visit the fatherless and widows in their affliction" implies both the ability and the willingness, both to sympathize with and to do for them. An intellectual training does not by itself furnish these. An industrial training does. Hence it is a chief stone in the foundation of spiritual character.

The Rev. M. B. FULLER, I. M. A., Akola, Berar, said:— When I came to India eleven years ago, I was disgusted at the feeling toward manual labour that I saw manifested on every side.

*Manual labour derogatory.*

I found that our catechist would pay a pice or two to a coolie to carry a little bundle that I would carry in my hand with no thought of burden. I saw that a clerk who could read and write English fairly could be had for Rs. 10 or Rs. 12 per month, while a good carpenter could command Rs. 20 or Rs. 25; I therefore began to question what could be done to make manual labour respectable in the eyes of our Native Christians. Only a few of the boys could compete with Brahmans for Government employment, and the rest must be put in the way of earning a livelihood and also of supporting their own churches.

We opened our Industrial School in January 1889, with a lay-missionary who came from America for that special work in charge, and he has had charge ever since. A faithful, godly man, a true missionary and a practical mechanic who works nine hours a day and earns more than enough to support himself, so that he is no financial burden to the mission. We began with a Government grant for the support of the school, but after a little more than a year we felt that we could not continue to receive it on account of the liquor and opium revenues, and we returned to Government Rs. 1,000 which we had received, and since then the school has been entirely supported by the mission. I believe that God always has money enough to carry on His work, and when His work needs money we go to Him to supply it and He never fails. We have in our school at present carpentering and smithing taught regularly, and the boys are doing very well. We hope that the boys trained to earn an honest livelihood will preach the Gospel on Sundays and other days as they have leisure, not for pay, but for love of the work. Some already do so very acceptably, and younger ones are coming on. The spiritual training of our boys is our first care, and we hope that they will be the pillars of our churches, both spiritually and financially. It costs much less to teach an orphan boy a good trade in connection with his studies for five or six years from the time he is twelve years old, studying four hours each day and working in the workshop five hours, than it does to teach him in school alone, for after the first year his work becomes of some value, and for the last year or two he more than pays for his food and clothes. So that for the whole term together, he is but little expense to the mission.

The Rev. E. T. BUTLER, C. M. S., Krishnagar, Bengal, said: —Firstly, I am anxious to plead for the support of old industrial institutions. Let us as a missionary body send to the Basel Mission in Madras for our cloth stuffs. The cloth is of a most excellent quality as I can personally testify; also not far from Krishnagar there is a Christian community which weaves dusters, purdahs, table-cloths and table napkins. Some years back when this community came into the Christian Church it was found necessary for them to change their work, so the Rev. James Vaughan had them taught the art of weaving. We want you to take a practical interest in this work and to send your orders for these articles to Calcutta. Mrs. Parsons, of 33, Amherst Street, Calcutta, would be glad to supply you with any quantity. Last year more than Rs. 1,000 worth were sold. Our Zenana ladies at Krishnagar have also had their converts taught the art of lace-making. I should recommend this to those of you who are anxious to find employment for your female converts. This mission cloth, these mission dusters and mission lace are worth their money, because made by those who love the Lord.

**Fourth Day.**

**Work at Krishnagar.**

Secondly, I wish to tell you how a little Industrial School is springing up in our Normal School at Krishnagar. An account of this may give an idea to some. In connection with this school is a department, the boys in which spend their daytime in various workshops in the town, they attend all the spiritual exercises of the Normal School, and also a night school in the evening. In this way at present we have lads learning tailoring, carpentry, blacksmithing, and mason's work. The Christian tailor, carpenter, blacksmith and mason will yet have his part in bringing India to Christ; let us see that we endeavour to send him forth converted and equipped in the Christian armour.

**Trades for Christian workers.**

The Rev. N. E. LUNDBORG, Secretary, S. E. L. M., Saugor, C. P., said:—I think it would be very well if all Christian workers in the mission work knew a trade on which they, in spare time and time of need, could fall back. But I tell you that I have come here to learn something in this respect. I am at present the guardian of about 3 dozen orphan children, some of whom are nearly grown up; but I am not quite sure what kind of trade would be the most suitable at present in our place. I think that nearly all trades in India are much depressed, because things can be had so cheap from Europe. I think that if India is to be successful in this way there ought to be a protection of the trade by heavy duty on imported articles. By this the Indian industry would, I think, flourish much better than it does at present.

**160 Boys.**

The Rev. J. BLACKSTOCK, M. E. C., Boys' Orphanage, Shahjanpore, said:—There are about 160 boys in the Orphanage of which I have charge. Their ages vary from five to thirty years old. Of this number above 100 are in our day school and between 30 or 40 in the Industrial School. The custom has been, and indeed still is, to only place in the Industrial School those boys who cannot succeed or at least have not succeeded in the day school. This as is natural creates a prejudice against industrial work. The aim to overcome this opposition by impressing upon them the dignity of labour; that mechanical knowledge is just as valuable, honourable and as necessary as the knowledge acquired from books—shoemaking, carpentry, smithing, tile-making, tailoring, gardening and farming are taught with more or less success. All the vegetables, and most of the *dál* necessary for the Orphanage, are furnished from our garden and fields. They have also begun the manufacture of wire-spring mattresses. We also, by way of encouragement, give small amounts in scholarship for proficiency in learning; boys by this means contract the habit of saving. In this way one boy upon leaving the workshop and going to do for himself had about Rs. 30 in the Post Office Savings Bank.

**Dignity of labour.**

**Scholarships.**

There seems to be a very strong amount of opposition on the part of Native Christians to have their youths learn any trade or engage in any kind of manual labour. Frequently imperti- Fourth Day. nent letters came to us, telling us, that they did not send their brothers or cousins, as the case may be, to work, but to be taught, and if we would not do that to send them home. This prejudice is due, in part, to the low estimation in which any kind of physical labour is held by the people of India, and also, in part, to the circumstances connected with the early history of mission work. We aim to make every boy in the Orphanage, who is old enough to work, do something every day, so far as we have work to do, in the garden and field. This is good, both for their moral and physical development. In field-work we generally take them out ourselves and work with them; this encourages the boys to work, and removes from their minds at least, much of the shame attached to this kind of work.

The Rev. Jacob CHAMBERLAIN, M.D., D.D., A. A. M., Madanapalle, Madras, said:—No German Emperor ever ascends the throne until he has mastered some trade by which he could, if needs be, earn his own living. It is thus that the German Emperors teach their people the dignity of labour. Dignity of It has been said just now, by one of the speakers, that manual labour. labour is looked down upon here in India, and that this prejudice stands in the way of the success of our industrial schools. There is no way in which we can teach the dignity of labour as effectually as by taking hold ourselves. In this matter are we not in danger of imitating the twelve Brahmans, Count your- as told in a very old Telugu book who, going on a pilgrimage self. and being swept away by a river flood, gathered on the bank, and as each one counted to see if all had gained the shore and could count only eleven, were in great anxiety, and thought one of them must have been drowned, *for each one forgot to count himself!* We must not forget each to count himself in inculcating the dignity of labour, and off with our coats and at it! It is not the farmer who says, "Go, boys, and reap the Example harvest," but the farmer that, with his coat off, says, "Come, boys, and reap the harvest," that will succeed, and make farming pay. I never can be sufficiently thankful to my father for training us, his sons, or rather allowing us to train ourselves, in all sorts of trades. He used to say to us, in effect: "Boys, I will furnish you with all the material you need, and with all the tools you will learn to use." What slaughter we made in his piles of choice timber, and in the leather closet in the garret! Carpentering we went into, and fairly mastered cabinet-making; we learned enough to make some nice secretaries and desks. How proud we were when we hitched the farm oxen into our completed row boat and hauled it down to the water. The cats, the dog, the goat, all had to submit to the indignity of wearing the harnesses we had made, and drawing the vehicles we had manufactured, and the bricklayers' trade had to suffer

FOURTH DAY.

violence at our hands, and not a farm implement had then been invented but what we were trained to use and use well. My father little knew that he was training a missionary to open a new station among the Telugus. For when I laid the foundation at Madanapalle 30 years ago, my best carpenters learned to do better and more rapid work from me. I took the trowel from the bricklayer's hands and taught them to do a better job; and when I wished to put up a lath and plaster ceiling to keep out the power of the sun, it was only after I had mounted the staging and myself nailed on the lath and put up the first square yard of plaster and made it stick, that they would believe that plaster would stick on the underside of strips of board with cracks between; and when I had made the first American pump, they followed on. But I had to stand a severer test, for once while on a journey both my ponies lost shoes. There was not a horse-shoer within twenty-six miles, so I put on a big apron and went to work and shod my own ponies, and then, lest such a thing should happen again, I went to work and trained my own syce or groom, and he became the best horse-shoer of all that region. None of my native assistants think their dignity is damaged if they dig their own gardens or repair the broken-down carts on a journey or pitch their own tents or carry their own bundles, as they see me do mine. Yes, sir, like the German Emperors, we must teach the dignity and the usefulness of labour by example, at least doing what we can, if we cannot do every kind of work. In our mission we are teaching every young man in our training school for native assistants, some useful trade. We have eighty students now in our industrial and lower secondary school at Arni, who study one half the day and are trained in our workshops the other half, and not until they have each well learned one of the trades we teach—carpentry, blacksmithing, tailoring, rug-weaving or printing—are they admitted into the High School department, from which those mentally and spiritually fitted are allowed to go on into our Theological Seminary. When each of our Catechists and village Pastors can teach their villagers a trade, a long step will have been taken towards self-support.

A trade for native assistants.

The Rev. H. U. WEITBRECHT, PH.D., C. M. S., Batala, Panjab, said:—The admirable paper by Mr. Frohnmeyer has shown both the strength and the weakness of Industrial Missions, how much may be and has been done, and what dangers are incurred. We have to recognize that on the temporal side of missionary work our converts come under the laws of political economy. As Christians they will and must in some way contract new wants, which will bring about a more expensive sca'e of living than that of their heathen neighbours. But if so, it is absolutely necessary that man for man the Christian should be able to

Needs of Christians greater than non-Christians

produce by his labour a higher value than the non-Christian; otherwise he will infallibly fall behind in the great social race. This greater effectiveness of Christian labour can only be brought about by industrial training. But in our efforts to teach handicaps we are only touching the fringe of the question. The staple industry of India, which absorbs at least nine-tenths of its labour, is agriculture. To solve the industrial problem, the Christian community must be attached to the soil, or rather must attach the soil to itself. How is this to be done? Here I confess to the feeling of standing before a blank wall. Our missionary experiment in the way of Christian settlements have not yet been successful. They lack economical independence, and therewith stability and the power of self-propagation. The only hopeful method that I see is to enlist the help and sympathy of our higher class Christians. There are many who have amassed considerable means; and in some instances having invested these in land, they have made it their business to let out this land to Christian tenants. If this practice were greatly extended it would go far towards a solution of the industrial difficulty which presses on the poor Indian Christian, and I earnestly appeal to our Indian brethren who are men of substance to help thus to consolidate our nascent community. *(Fourth Day. Agriculture. Help of high class Christians.)*

The Rev. J. DUTHIE, L. M. S., Nagercoil, said:—I beg permission to say a word in reference to the Industrial work carried on in the Travancore Mission, viz., lace, at my own station; and embroidery, at Neyoor. The lace-work was begun many years ago by Mrs. Mauet—the embroidery by Mrs. Baylis. These branches of work are of great value to the Christian women employed, and help also to provide funds for the female work carried on by the mission. Mrs. Duthie has 150 workers in the Lace Department at the Head station, Nagercoil; and as many more are employed in the surrounding villages. A beautiful box of lace has just been sent to the Chicago Exhibition. As showing in how many ways mission work bears fruit, I may mention the case of a lace worker who was sent from Travancore to the C. M. S. Mission in Benares. That woman was of the humblest origin and had a little daughter who accompanied her to Benares. The missionaries in Benares cared for the child and educated her. In due time she was entered as a medical pupil in a Government College, had a most successful career as a student, carried off the gold medal in her college, which she received from the hand of the Viceroy, and is now at the head of one of the Lady Dufferin hospitals in a large city in North India. I may remark that I have never known a more remarkable illustration of the power of the Gospel to uplift and ennoble even the humblest in this land. *(Lace and embroidery. Result of industry.)*

The Rev. L. J. FROHNMEYER, Basel Mission, Tellicherry, Malabar, writer of one of the papers, said:—I should feel exceed-

**Fourth Day.**

*An erroneous opinion.*

ingly glad if I could speak in my own divine language; I cannot do so, and so I shall be brief in order not to commit too many sins against English pronounciation and grammar. In speaking about industrial mission I feel almost like a fish out of water, and I hope to stand here as the last sacrifice of the erroneous opinion amounting to a real superstition, that any Basel German Missionary must be competent to deal with the question of industrial mission. As my paper really did not come under discussion, I may refer perhaps to another erroneous opinion prevailing amongst English friends on the field of our labour. Some point at the high chimneys of our tiling-works and at the large establishments of our industrial mission and say:— "This Basel Mission must be immensely rich," and consequently they stop their donations. Some even seem to think that the missionaries at a station carrying on industrial work are at liberty to divide the profit of such establishments amongst themselves. Now, I need not say that, whenever there is a profit it will cover only a small fraction of our mission work carried on in Africa, China and India. Others think that it is not nice in a mission at all to make money. I myself have been once exercised in my mind about this, and I asked one of our greatest missionaries out here, old Dr. Gundert, about it, and he told me: "Look here! there are two brothers, one called John and the other James. Both of them are full of zeal to work for the Lord in some mission field. John is eloquent, James cannot speak so well, but he has got a business-head, and so he says to John: 'Well, John, you do the preaching, and I shall establish some shop or industry to support you.' So the two brothers went out to India, John as the preaching Missionary, James as the industrial missionary. In our mission even James took to preaching at many a station; souls have been won for Christ also through the agency of our industrial missionaries. It has been stated this morning that the educational work done by a real missionary should be spiritual work. We consider even the industrial work of our mission not to be altogether secular, but if done in a missionary spirit—a Spiritual work too. Any kind of mission work done by a spiritual man will prove to be spiritual work. On this account we have been disappointed somewhat to see that our industrial brethren have been omitted in the statistic tables prepared for this Conference. After all, we are in a fortunate position. Should we meet with your approval and with your sympathies, it will greatly cheer us, and I shall not fail to communicate this to our industrial missionaries, especially I shall not forget the kind recommendation given by the friend of the C. M. Society to our clothings. However, if you do not approve of our industrial mission, and object to it, well, there is even a consolation in this: we need not be afraid of your competition then.

*Spiritual industrial work.*

*A fortunate position.*

# XII.—THE OBSERVANCE OF THE LORD'S DAY IN INDIA.

## AFTERNOON SESSION.
### Small Hall, 2 to 4-30 p.m.

J. G. Shome, Esq., M.A., B.L., Calcutta, *in the chair.*

A passage of Scripture was read by J. E. Cooke, Esq., and prayer was offered by the Rev. W. R. LeQuesne.

The Chairman said:—The subject is one on which there cannot be two opinions in regard to the principle that it is the duty of all Christians to observe one day in the week and to devote themselves entirely to God's service, but there may be difference of opinion as to the way the day should be observed. "The sabbath was made for man and not man for the sabbath." We should bear that in mind in all our discussion, and if these words apply to the sabbath they apply much more to the Lord's Day. It is our duty and pleasure and privilege to rejoice in the day which the Lord hath made; this is the day when the Lord rose from the dead and obtained victory. let us rejoice and be glad in it.

*The observance of Sunday.*

## FIRST PAPER.

By the Rev. W. B. Phillips, Union Chapel, Calcutta.

This paper will aim to be suggestive rather than exhaustive. The object is to help towards the discussion of a momentous question. The general principles of Lord's Day observance need not engage our attention. We are practically agreed on all main points. But the special circumstances in which we find ourselves in India may well claim the most serious thought of the Decennial Conference. By the churches at home some of those circumstances are little known, and but faintly understood.

It would be well that the churches shou'd both know and understand. They might then sympathise with our difficulties and help forward our objects. I shall now state certain general positions and try to enforce them.

I. There are special reasons for renewed attention to this subject by missionaries.

*Increased interest.*
(1) The power of the church and of missionaries in India is increasing. Without some consciousness of power prudent men refrain from effort. It is humiliating and even injurious to push questions under some circumstances. There was a time when the feeling of hopelessness might well paralyse men in reference to the Lord's Day question. But that time is passing away. Both Government officials, merchants and planters are likely to pay more heed to the principles of Christ in the future than they have done in the past.

*Repeal of Lord's Day Act.*
(2) The repeal of the Lord's Day Act by Lord Lytton has created a current of feeling which is gradually gaining volume. This action was a reckless piece of legislation, in full keeping with much else during his régime. Public opinion in India was too weak to do anything effective; and England could not be stirred in those days of the Afghan war. I remember the hopeless feeling many at that time had, although they were filled with indignation at the reckless nature of the legislation.

*New proposal.*
(3) An actual effort has been made to move Government towards passing a Lord's Day Act which shall be suitable to Indian conditions. The Memorial from the Calcutta Missionary Conference has been sent up to the Viceroy, and copies of it have been circulated throughout India, and also sent to England and Scotland. A reply has also come, to which we shall refer later on. And although the reply is an evasion, yet the Memorial itself marks an onward stage in the movement.

*Laxity of the Native Church.*
(4) The question is becoming one of growing importance to our Native Church. We all know that there is an amount of laxity among the Native Christian community upon Lord's Day observance which is decidedly unhealthy and needs to be checked. With their heathen traditions and surroundings, and in full view of the European neglect and desecration of the day, we cannot pretend to be surprised at any laxity on the part of the Native Church. But we must deplore such laxity and recognise its growing importance.

II. Present attitude of European Christians towards Lord's Day observance.

*Fourth Day.*

Fifteen years of itinerancy in Moorshedabad, Bengal, made me acquainted with the usual treatment of the Sabbath by Government officials, and silk and indigo manufacturers. The Public Works Department paid almost no regard to the day, and took shelter behind the fallacy that native contractors *must* be allowed to do as they like. You would see the Government Engineer going to church in one part of a building, and his contractors plastering and whitewashing the other. A magistrate, who would afterwards figure in Calcutta as chairman of a missionary meeting, would allow any amount of removal of office furniture and other unnecessary work to be done on the Lord's Day. Subordinate officials were allowed to pile up work upon clerks to be taken home and done on Sunday. As it was then, so I believe it is now, with no change for the better.

*And among Europeans.*

Silk manufacturers used to run their factories without any regard to Sabbath rest for their employees. The skeins were whirling on the wheels as usual, and the tale was weighed and counted in the evening as on other days. A *few* of the English and Scotch managers would make some sort of difference in the day for themselves, but even they could not escape from the inquiries and anxieties inseparable from the rush of work.

Indigo factories were equally indifferent to the day. Often have the men in charge said to me: "We lose count altogether, and really do not know which is Sunday." Crops are sown; inspection goes on; indigo is cut and carried; and soaking, beating, pressing, continues just as usual. No wonder that men lose all count of days! To superintend work like this young fellows come out from the pious influences of many a Scotch and English home. And let us not be severe in our judgment of them. *The battle is too hard.* Many would far rather keep an easy conscience and have a Sabbath's rest: but the traditions of the service, the iron grip of interested shareholders, the laxity of Government, the indifference of the heathen, the ready abuse of the day by many reputed Christians, all these things are against them. It needs a man of very high Christian principle to fight successfully for Sabbath observance amid the mercantile and planting commu-

*Desecration of the Lord's Day.*

**Fourth Day.** nity of India. It is time that Christian missionaries and churches came forward and tried to make it somewhat more easy for men to honour their God in this land.

It is two years since I was in Moorshedabad, and I cannot say whether the Factory Act of 1891 has made any difference. The district itself may well serve as a typical one. Its connexion with British commerce dates back to the days of Oliver Cromwell; in its Cossim Bazaar, Warren Hastings began his Indian career; from its chief city Souraj-ad-dowlah went down to perpetrate the crime of the Black Hole of Calcutta; and on its battlefield of Plassey Clive laid the foundations of the Indian Empire. The present rules of the mercantile service are probably substantially the same as have prevailed for the last two hundred years. It is time there was a change.

*Europeans are responsible.*

III. English and Scotch capitalists are responsible for much of the Lord's Day desecration in India.

The capital that works most of the silk, indigo, jute, pottery and other industries in India comes from England and Scotland. Many of the shareholders and directors of these companies are deacons, and elders and leading men in the churches at home. They are accustomed to observe their own Sabbath, and would feel much scandalized if asked to keep open and inspect their offices and factories. Yet their money and system is keeping silk, indigo and jute assistants, and engineers doing just that very thing in many parts of India. There needs a shaking among certain dry bones in Dundee and London. Many a pious elder, and even missionary director, should ask himself a few unpleasant questions and come to a few new resolves about his capital and influence in India. Methinks a vast deal of our hope for the lessening of Sunday work out here depends upon the action of men in England and Scotland.

*Municipalities.*

IV. Municipalities are allowed to disregard the Lord's Day. Frequently in the mufassal (country districts) meetings of the Municipality are purposely arranged on the Lord's Day. This is directly contrary to the spirit of religious neutrality in which such institutions should be carried on. A Municipality, both in its Commissioners and subordinates, is open to the whole community. It should be worked on lines that will be consistent with the religious scruples of all sections of the public. Both Commissioners and employees may be, and often are, Christians. A style of work, therefore, which ignores the FOURTH DAY. sacredness of the Lord's Day is a direct breach of the principles of religious neutrality.

The ordinary work of municipalities is carried on with almost utter disregard for the Lord's Day. Some kinds of work must be done, but they should be limited to what is absolutely necessary. As it is, road-mending, building, tank cleaning and much other unnecessary work is carried on just the same every day. This presses very heavily in many places upon both European, Eurasian and Native Christian, and demands the serious attention of Government. The Viceroy of India is responsible for safe-guarding the rights of the public conscience. Municipalities should not be allowed to run upon lines that are inconsistent with the principles of religious neutrality.

V. Government has degenerated in its attitude towards the Lord's Day. *Attitude of Government.*

Time was, in the days of Lord William Bentinck (1827-1837) and Lord Hastings (1844-48), when more vigorous measures were taken to protect Sabbath privileges. The following circular will speak for itself:—

"Home Department, Camp Bhurniah, 12th January 1847."

"The Governor-General is pleased to direct that all public "works, carried on by order of Government, whether under the "direction of its own officers, or through the agency of contractors, "shall be discontinued on Sunday.

(2) "Cases of urgent necessity, in which delay would be detri-"mental to the public service, are to be considered as cases of "exception, and all such shall be immediately reported to the "Military Board for their special orders, and for the information "of Government. The officer in charge of the work will act on "his own discretion, where delay in waiting for the sanction of "the Board would be attended with injurious consequences.

(3) "The cessation of work on the Sunday shall be an under-"stood condition in all future contracts for public work, whether "an express provision to that effect be inserted in the deed of "contract or not. No claim therefore of addition to the amount "of the contract, on account of the suspension of the labour on "Sunday, shall be admitted."

We ground a claim for Government action upon *physical* and not religious considerations. We respect true religious neutra-

**Fourth Day.**

lity on the part of the Indian Government as the attitude in keeping with its position. But we believe that every Government is bound to safe-guard at least the *physical* well-being of its subjects. It is quite sufficiently established that human brains and bodies need more rest than is gained by mere nightly sleep. The human organism requires a seventh day of cessation from toil, if it is to have a fair chance of healthy, vigorous life. From this point of view Government has a duty to its Hindu and Muhammadan, as well as to its Christian subjects. It should protect them from the greed of capital, and encourage the establishment of Sabbath observance.

**Holidays.**

At present an undoubted and strong obstacle in the way of Sabbath observance in India are the numerous holidays arising from the religions of the country. Those holidays among Hindus cover 23 days, and among Muhammadans six days, making a total of 29. But these may be thrown in to represent the extra wear upon life in an Indian climate; and to count for the English and American annual holiday. Moreover, the pressure of commercial life is driving some of these holidays into very close quarters; and is likely to succeed in this more and more as the power of Hinduism wanes. Nor must we forget that the English Saturday afternoon is practically unknown outside of a city like Calcutta.

**Sunday kept by some Hindus.**

Government might get some help towards encouraging a seventh day's rest from an argument supplied spontaneously by some of their Hindu subjects. In two of the busiest bazaars of Calcutta, for a considerable time, a number of shop-keepers have steadily refrained from all Sunday business. This is a most marked testimony to the value put upon an English custom, for its own sake, and without any regard to the religious questions involved. We may reasonably expect that this practice will grow. And as it grows the task of Government in encouraging a seventh day's rest will become increasingly easy.

VI. Reply of Government to the Memorial of the Calcutta Missionary Conference.

**How not to do it.**

The gist of that reply may be summed up in these words. "We have been skilfully advised how *not to do it*; and we intend sheltering ourselves behind that advice until compelled by some greater pressure to give more earnest heed." Under these circumstances our reply to Government should be somewhat as follows : — "We much regret the need for further action on our part ; but we are quite determined to mature the needful amount of pressure to compel the Government of this country to go back somewhat upon its reckless legislation of 1877."

The word "reckless" may appear strong in view of Government statements as to previous inquiries. But we do not believe that it is any stronger than is warranted by the facts of the case. We need not question that inquiries were made, nor that Government had worked up an apparently good case. But we are dealing with a question involving the moral sentiments of many thousands of British subjects, who have no voice in that part of the British Empire where their lot is cast. Yet they are descendents of a nation that has been educated at least for 230 years to regard the Sabbath as a *Dies non*. Yet Government asks these British subjects to accept as sound the following summing up of the question at issue. In reply to a Memorial of the Calcutta Missionary Conference in 1883 Government said :—

"I am to inform you that the authorities who have from time to time given their opinions on the general question of the applicability of the Lord's Day Act to India have been unanimous in holding that none of the provisions of that Act, except those which relate to the execution of process, have ever been in force in any part of India, and most of those authorities have further held that even those latter provisions have never been in force here, and that accordingly the repeal of the Act by the Code of Civil Procedure *had no practical effect whatever.*"

This reply ignores completely one of the most powerful factors of the case. The educating and restraining force of such an Act is not so much in its power to punish, as in the moral conviction that it fosters. Penalties for breach of the Lord's Day Act in England have been almost non-existent for generations ; but the moral impression produced has been enormous. And the majority of British subjects come out to India under the sway of those moral convictions. The existence of the law in India was a similar fosterer of convictions. The repeal of that Act was a distinct removal of a most valuable moral influence ; an influence which was on the side of Government ; an influence ready to be increasingly used in promoting the physical well-being of two

*Fourth Day.*

*The Government view.*

**Fourth Day.** hundred and eighty millions of its Indian subjects. To say that "the repeal of that Act" by the Indian Government "had no practical effect whatever" is to ignore the mighty force of the almost universal previous conviction that Indian Law was on the side of Lord's Day observance; and such a reply is not worthy of a great Government.

But the latest reply of Government to the Memorial of the Calcutta Missionary Conference requires a more lengthy and searching consideration than is possible in this paper. And the subject will doubtless be taken up vigorously by the Conference concerned.

*Practical suggestions.*

VII. PRACTICAL SUGGESTIONS.—(1) Let this question of Lord's Day observance have a more prominent place in the attention of every Indian Missionary and Conference. Its place in God's Word demands such prominence.

(2) Let no opportunity be lost of urging the question upon the mercantile community, both in India and Britain. The present state of things proves a great snare and hardship to many lives.

(3) Let the press be used freely both here and at home to awaken the public conscience, and to create that pressure without which the Indian Government will not act.

(4) Let facts be collected to prove the utter fallacy of the Government contention that the "repeal of the Act has had no practical effect whatever." I am certain, from personal observation, that it has had a very widespread and a very marked effect, both among Natives and Europeans. It has greatly encouraged loose treatment of the day. And surely such treatment needed no encouragement in India.

(5) Let the Calcutta Memorial, together with the reply of Government, and a well-prepared criticism of that reply, be printed and widely circulated both in India and at home.

(6) Let an effort be made to prepare a Memorial for signature by the Christian professional and business-men of India. It is believed by some that there are a good number of such men who would willingly support such a movement.

## SECOND PAPER.

FOURTH DAY.

By the Rev. F. W. WARNE, M. E. C., Calcutta.

I have freely conferred with Rev. W. B. Phillips, the writer of the first paper. He has very ably put before the Conference many of the special reasons why this subject should have the careful and prayerful attention of this Conference, and has given a number of very practical suggestions. My purpose is to supplement the first paper, to state some of the Scriptural truths on this question, and make but one suggestion, which I hope will be acted upon by this Conference.

I. THE SABBATH WAS INSTITUTED IN PARADISE.—The Sabbath is but one day younger than man. God made man on the sixth day, "And God blessed the seventh day and hallowed it: because that in it He rested from all His works which God had created and made." Gen. 2, 3. It is peculiarly suggestive that man's first day, in his uprightness, innocence, and with all his faculties pronounced "very good" should be a Sabbath day. There is after this no full statement of the Sabbatic law until the giving of the commandments, but we have enough to show that from the first the national reckoning of the Jews was by weeks. Noah reckoned by seven days in sending out birds from the Ark. Gen. 8, 12. Laban and Jacob also reckoned by weeks. Gen. 29, 27. In Joseph's time also the Hebrews reckoned by sevens in the division of time. Perfect proof that the Sabbath was prior to the giving of the commandments is found in the full record of the manna, in the sixteenth chapter of Exodus; how on the sixth day "they gathered twice as much," and Moses explained: "This is that which the Lord hath spoken. To-morrow is a solemn rest, a holy Sabbath unto the Lord." "And it came to pass on the seventh day that there went out some of the people to gather, and they found none." This divinely given object lesson was before the commandments were given, and proves that a Sabbath was a merciful provision from the first, suited to the needs of the human race.

*Scriptural Sabbath.*

II. THE GIVING OF THE COMMANDMENT.—The finger of the Lord writing the fourth commandment on a tablet of stone was but a fuller statement of a divine merciful institution which God considered necessary for man even in paradise. In this

*The 4th Commandment.*

**Fourth Day.** commandment God has condescended to use three cogent arguments to press its observance upon us. The first is taken from his own example. "The Lord ... rested the seventh day." The second from the bountiful and liberal portion of time allowed for our temporal interests. "Six days shalt thou labor and do all thy work." The third from the dedication of this day to his own immediate worship and service. "The Lord blessed the Sabbath day, and hallowed it." It is therefore a sin, a sacrilege and a theft of, that which is holy, to use any part of this day for unnecessary secular pleasure or work. The fourth commandment is as binding in its line as the first against idolatry, as the sixth against murder, as the eighth against stealing. Between the authority of these commandments there is no difference. The introducing into this commandment the words "nor thy cattle" gives a peculiar emphasis to the physical side of this question. It is impossible to state or comprehend the significance of this commandment, which is the longest, and is placed in the middle between those which relate to God and those which relate to man. It is a merciful provision for the moral and spiritual wants of man, and the physical wants of both man and beast, providing alike a weekly day of rest for man, whether good or bad, and also for the animals which serve him.

The Lord's Day.

III. Sunday, or the Lord's Day.—The transition from remembering or observing the seventh day, to that of the first day of the week, need not be discussed. We agree in believing that the Son of Man is Lord even of the Sabbath, that the Jewish Sabbath was a part of the law which our Lord came, not to destroy, but to fulfil, that we are now under a new covenant, and in it on our day of holy rest we remember not a finished creation, but a completed redemption. When we remember the Lord's Day, if we look backward, we are reminded of His Resurrection, and if we look forward, of the general resurrection and the Sabbath of eternal rest beyond.

How we in India shall remember the Lord's Day and keep it, not as a business day, or as a holiday, but as a holy day, is our concern. Even in Christian lands this seems to be a time when the best efforts of the united church are required to save this divinely given day of rest for the purpose for which it was given. If united efforts on the part of all the churches are needed in

Christian lands to preserve this day, how much more do we need to be united in this land, where the many millions of India have yet to be taught the nature and purpose of the Lord's Day.

*Fourth Day.*

IV. AN INDIA LORD'S DAY UNION RECOMMENDED.—The chief purpose of the writer of this paper is to recommend that this Decennial Conference take steps toward forming a Union Society which shall unite the Christians, and so far as possible all the people of India on this question. I suggest this because these societies have had such a mission in other countries, and a quotation or two from their objects and work will suggest some of the work such a Union could do in India. In England the "Society for Promoting the due observance of the Lord's Day" has for its objects:—"To diffuse information on the subject by the publication of books and tracts on the Divine Authority of the Institution. To adopt such measures as may appear best adapted to lead to due observance of the Lord's Day in the metropolis and throughout the Empire. To open correspondence for the purpose of forming local associations. To promote petitions to the Legislature for the enactment of laws repressing the open violation of the Lord's Day."

*A Union recommended.*

The "Working-Men's Lord's Day Rest Association" also in England, was established in 1857, and its object is "To secure to the people their natural and scriptural right to the rest of the Lord's Day." Some of the work done by this Society is worthy of our notice, such as the resistance to the schemes for opening museums, &c., on Sundays. About 6,000,000 publications have been issued. Many working men have been enrolled as members of the Association. All parliamentary operations effecting the Sabbath are watched, and opposed or supported, as the case may require. The "American Sabbath Union" aims to lead public opinion in the United States regarding the civil and religious observance of the Sabbath, and the violation of the Sunday laws of the land. It looks after national and local legislation for the protection of the public peace and order, and for the rights of all classes of people to their weekly rest-day.

V. SOME REASONS FOR HAVING A LORD'S DAY UNION IN INDIA.—(*a*) The foregoing quotations from the objects and operations of societies in other countries, similar to the one

*Reasons.*

**Fourth Day.**

proposed for India, teach us that such a Society can do many kinds of work in India and enlist a great variety of agencies, and unite on this question people of widely different views on other questions. It is believed that when such a society is organized in India, that not only can the Christian communions be united, but in many places peoples of other religions will unite in this work of securing a day of rest for the many millions of overworked people in this land.

(b) There are special reasons for united effort. The Native Church is growing rapidly and requires much teaching and literature on the Sabbath question. European Christians become very careless about the observance of the Lord's Day in India. The Government has degenerated in its attitude on this question, and Municipalities are also indifferent or opposed. The greed for gain in some cases, both of the employer and the employee, leads to the neglect of the Lord's Day, and in many cases Europeans employed are indirectly compelled to violate conscience. The rights of British subjects to the Lord's Day are very indifferently protected in India. The Statute Book of India which is the national conscience, just as the Executive Government is the national will, is a blank on this question, as is seen from a Government letter to the Calcutta Missionary Conference, dated 27th September 1883.

The position was summed up in paragraph 4 of that letter, which is as follows:—" I am to inform you that the authorities who have from time to time given their opinions on the general question of the applicability of the Lord's Day Act to India have been unanimous in holding that none of the provisions of that Act, except those which relate to the execution of process, have ever been in force in any part of India, and most of those authorities have further held that even these latter provisions have never been in force here, and that accordingly the repeal of the Act by the Code of Civil Procedure had no practical effect whatever." Note carefully the whole Act has been repealed. These and many other considerations seem to make united effort a present duty.

**Public sentiment.**

(c) The success of other Union Organizations in India should encourage a united effort on this work. I wrote to a high Government official for suggestions before writing my paper, and, among others, received this one, " If the Conference can arrange to set apart some one to go about India to create public sentiment on the Sunday question, good would come of it." The success of the Bible and Tract Societies, the "Young Men's Christian Association" during the three years of a resident Secretary in India and the "Christian Literature Society for India," may well be quoted as encouraging examples. [margin: Fourth Day.]

(*d*) Conventions would be held in various parts of India and local interest could be awakened, the public conscience educated, the spiritual life of the church improved, a better state of Sabbath observance secured, and thereby every interest of all missions would receive help.

(*e*) The Sabbath question in India has many complications peculiar to this country. Their solution will require the united wisdom of the churches and the creating of a literature suited to the situation in India. [margin: The laity.]

(*f*) Several efforts have been made by the Calcutta Missionary Conference and perhaps others, but no one Conference can represent all India, for it is estimated that two-thirds of the missionaries working in India are not in any Missionary Conference, and there would be a smaller proportion of the laity, and they are a much more important factor in this question than the missionaries.

(*g*) Isolated Europeans in India require the help such a union could afford. Through it they could make their grievances known. A brief quotation from a well-known Bengal missionary working in a jute district will tell its own story:—" The physical and economical phases of the question have been well put by " the Jute Wallahs" themselves. The experience of the ages is on their side, when they say that they would enjoy better health and do better work if allowed to rest one day in seven. The morality of the question must not be lost sight of, I mean we must not forget to consider the effect of Sunday labour upon the moral nature of these men. Many of them come out with good recommendations from their ministers and with a settled determination not to disgrace their Christian profession or the old people who taught them to "Remember the Sabbath day to keep it holy." They are engaged by Christian men at home, and as a matter of course expect as much Christian consideration in India as draught cattle get in Scotland. But if they are unfortunate enough to arrive when the mills are running seven days a week, [margin: Moral side of the question.]

**Fourth Day.**

*Sabbath breakers claim our sympathy.*

they have to violate conscience by breaking the Sabbath, or run the risk of being sent home as failures. It is all very well to say they should adopt the latter course; so they should. We all ought to do many things we do not; but most of them are young fellows whose principles have never previously been put to any great strain, and they are quite unprepared for such a severe test of character. Then there is the fact that the older hands have knuckled down, and these older ones assure them that, although they do not like it, they must do it. A yielding to such pressure may show the absence of the grand old covenanter's spirit; but we must remember that these men fight their battles one by one and not altogether. I do not wish to minimise their weakness, but to show that they have a strong claim on Christian sympathy. Whatever Sabbath breaking may be to other people, it is sinful, yes, exceeding sinful, to a Scotchman. This being so, it is impossible for him to work in the forenoon and delight in the service of God in the afternoon. The Sabbath becomes a day of condemnation instead of comfort. The memory of better days torments the man, the climate adds its depressing influence, and older men who have already succumbed, invite him to 'peg' and tennis. The weary body and jaded mind crave excitement and company, and too frequently the temptation is yielded to and moral ruin is the result."

*A. M. E. C. Memorial.*

VI. HOW CAN THE ORGANIZATION BE EFFECTED IN INDIA? I will cite a case which I trust is to the point. Just a little above four years ago, a Memorial was sent to the General Conference of the American Methodist Episcopal Church. This memorial asked that body "to take the initiative in forming a National Sabbath Committee by appointing several persons to serve on such Committee, with instructions to ask other religious bodies to appoint representatives in order that the invasion of our day of rest and worship may be successfully resisted by the united forces of American Christianity, in the interest alike of the Church and of the Nation."

On May 15th, 1888, the following resolution was passed:—"In view of the important interests involved in the above Memorial, your Committee recommends that the General Conference take the initiative in forming a National Sabbath Committee, and that all other evangelical denominations be invited to appoint representatives to serve on this Committee."

Almost immediately following this preliminary action the response from the other churches was prompt and hearty. And within two months from that time fifty-five representatives of the leading denominations of the United States had been officially appointed by these bodies to serve on the National Committee. This National Committee assembled in November of the same year. Shortly after, a Constitution for a National Sabbath Organization was prepared and plans of work outlined. The Union began to work, and its auxiliaries were formed, and they were ready to work just in time to meet the combined efforts to open the Worlds' Fair on the Lord's Day, and thus working with the churches, a petition, with over twenty-four million signatures, pleading for the closing of the Worlds' Fair on the Lord's Day, was sent to the Government and a great victory has been won. There will be steady and increasing work for such a society in India. *Fourth Day. The World's Fair.*

I plead earnestly that the Decennial Conference may go just as far as its prerogatives will permit it, in casting its representative influence on the side of united effort to save the Sabbath in India. I plead for this, because I believe that every interest, religious, social, moral, political and physical will be advanced by obeying this law of God. May God through you greatly promote the Sabbath cause in India. In conclusion, I suggest that this Decennial Conference appoint a Committee with instructions to invite all missions in India to appoint representatives, and to take the necessary steps towards forming a Union Society suited to this country. *A proposal.*

## FIRST SPEECH.

By the Rev. A. Paton Begg, b. a., L. M. S., Calcutta.

A subject like this, involving matters of conscience and valued rights, requires and will repay your most careful and sympathetic attention. As an English pastor in India for six years, I have found my people with but rare exceptions (and these only such as one meets with in England also) in undisturbed possession of the Lord's Day as a day of rest from the work of the week. As a missionary in constant contact with the native community, I have had many opportunities during the past eight

FOURTH DAY. years of observing how the Sunday has become an established institution as a day of rest among the upper or educated classes, those that come most within the range of English influence—official, educational or mercantile. The position of the Sunday as a standing official holiday in the Government calendar accounts for this latter to a large extent.

*An official holiday.*

Anything, therefore, that would interfere with the Lord's Day as a standing holiday from the office and business work of the week would be widely felt as a grievance, and if it were not that the encroachments now and again made on the Lord's Day are generally of a local and temporary character, they would be keenly resented by the most enlightened portion of the community, including that growing section of the native community that looks to the Government to preserve and extend the rights and privileges of British citizenship in India.

The two papers before us deal with the subject in a comprehensive way, but the wording of the subject and the limited treatment and time that this Conference can give to it, leave much yet to be overtaken when the practical suggestions put forward by the writers are adopted, as I trust they will be. Neither of the papers deal with the history of the Lord's Day and of legislation in connection with it in the different countries where it has been legislated for.

*History of the Lord's Day.*

A knowledge of this history would be useful to us in dealing with the problem before us in India, and would do much to remove misconception and prejudice from the minds of many around us who are indifferent to, or failing in their duty towards, Lord's Day observance.

*The Assyrian idea of the Sabbath.*

There has been a remarkable development in the conception of Sabbath observance since that of the early Assyrians. Their idea seems to have been that of cessation from all work, sacred as well as secular, on the seventh day; such cessation being regarded as in itself a form of worship. This was a remarkable instance of the observing of a day in the most literal sense of the term; the day was hallowed or considered as a holy day.

*Bible teaching.*

In the Bible we find an immense improvement on this conception from the very first. There the day is a gift from God to man—a great charter of human freedom—placing for one day in the seven, or at the end of each week, the slave and his lord, the servant and his master, on an equal footing as sons and subjects of one great Father and Lord, and the main idea of the observance of the day was that of making the day one of holy convocation and worship. No doubt there were misconceptions of the day amongst the Jews erring on the one side in Pharisaical strictness and on the other in wordly laxness, but the main idea of the nature of the observance proper to the day is clear, and its position and authority in the Old Testament are equally clear. When, however, we come to New Testament times, we find a wonderful change.  *Fourth Day.*

Our Saviour warned men against breaking or minimising the least of God's commandments, and expressly extended the scope and deepened the significance of almost every commandment in the Decalogue. We see this in the case of *the third* commandment, where He speaks of taking solemn oaths or swearing; *the fifth*, where He speaks of the devoting of things as corban; *the sixth*, where He speaks of hate; and *the seventh*, where He speaks of modesty. In the case of *the fourth* commandment, however, there is this noticeable feature that His words and deeds made Him appear more to the Jews as a breaker than as an expounder of the law, and He does not appear to have been desirous to avoid giving this shock to them.  *Our Lord's teaching.*

The transition from the Old Testament Sabbath to the Christian Lord's Day, when we look at it in the light of our Lord's action and teaching in the Sabbath Day incidents of the plucking of ears of corn by the disciples, the healing of the man who had a withered hand, and of the woman who had an infirmity, the man who had dropsy, and lastly, the man who was infirm and who was sent off carrying his bed, involves much for reflection, and especially the words in John v. 17: "My Father worketh even until now, and I work," and the comment on them in v. 18.

It seems as if we had there new legislation for Sabbath observance like that which we find in Isaiah lviii. 6-7, where it is written: "Is not this the fast that I have chosen? to loose the bonds of wickedness, to undo the bands of the yoke, and to let the oppressed go free, and that ye brake every yoke. Is it not to deal thy bread to the hungry, and that thou bring the poor that are cast out to thy house?"

It is not strange, therefore, when we turn to those three places where the Apostle Paul treats of Sabbath observance to find

FOURTH DAY.
St. Paul's view.

that the sanctions that clung to the day and the conscientious regard for the day, as a day set apart or holy are recognised, but are not regarded as an essential element in the economy of the Gospel. "One man esteemeth one day above another: another esteemeth every day alike. Let each man be fully assured in his own mind. He that regardeth the day regardeth it to the Lord." Romans xiv. 5-6. "How turn ye back again to the weak and beggarly rudiments whereunto ye desire to be in bondage over again? Ye observe days, and months, and seasons, and years. I am afraid of you lest by any means I have bestowed labour upon you in vain." Galatians iv. 9-11. "Let no man, therefore, judge you in meat or in drink or in respect of a feast day or a new moon or a Sabbath Day: which are a shadow of the things to come, but the body is Christ's. Colossians ii. 16-17.

It is not for us, but for history to pronounce on the bearing of the teaching of our Lord and of the Apostle Paul here on the Sabbath. We find that the Sabbath gradually ceased to be generally or even largely observed, and that it has now practically ceased to be observed in the Christian Church, and another day, the Lord's Day, has gradually taken its place, and has been viewed as possessed of many, perhaps in some cases all, the sanctions that previously belonged to the Old Testament Sabbath. Thus we find Justin Martyr speaking of the day in terms that resemble the sanction for the Sabbath (given in Exodus xx. 11):

Justin Martyr.

"We assemble in common on Sunday, because this is the first day on which God created the world and light, and because Jesus Christ our Saviour on the same day rose from the dead and appeared to His disciples." Then, later on, we find Con-

Constantine.

stantine in 321 A.D. legislating for the Lord's Day as a Sabbath, forbidding work on that day in the towns, but allowing work in the country to be done on that day, owing to such work being more liable to interruptions from the state of the weather than that of the towns and to its being limited by the seasons. From that time onwards there has been legislation in the different countries under Christian Government enacting the Lord's

The Puritan times.

Day observance with various degrees of strictness. At one time the legislation was much more strict in England than in Scotland, but in the Puritan times legislation, requiring a more rigid observance of the day, was adopted also in Scotland, and that sentiment regarding the day which is often thought to be peculiarly Scottish, had been already prevalent in England before it began to develop in Scotland. We have not to do at present with the general question of Government Legislation for Lord's Day observance, but with conditions resulting from the legislation in the past, and it is our duty to help those who are made to suffer by uncalled for and unexpected changes in the legislation, and to claim to be heard when past legislation is to be modified or repealed and long established religious rights and privileges are imperilled. The New Testament teaching sets before us a greater task and a noble duty in place of the old Sabbath observance, and on the simple principle that the greater includes the less, we may say that it is our duty as Christians and as philanthropists to do all we can to secure the Lord's Day as a day of rest and to hallow it according to the example and teaching of our Lord Himself.

Fourth Day.

## SECOND SPEECH.

By the Rev. A. D. J. Macdonald, Christian Literature Society, Calcutta.

A Sabbath map of the world, published in 1884, shows Sabbathless lands in darkness, while the degree of observance attained elsewhere is represented by various lighter shades. India appears as semi-illuminated, regarding the Sabbath to some extent by custom, while yet there is no Sunday law. Japan, on the contrary, is described as an unchristian Government, which distinguishes the Lord's Day by law. It is plain, therefore, that the repeal of the Lord's Day Act, by which British and Indian Christians are deprived of their legal *dies non*, will give little satisfaction to those who go no further than to compare the action of these two Asiatic Governments; but there are more and weightier reasons which will induce this Decennial gathering to support the action taken by the Calcutta Conference in its late memorial.

Sabbath map.

I shall remark first, on the *degree of observance already attained:*—The weekly rest-day is an institution already well known in some parts of India. There is little difficulty in explaining to the Hindu children, who are taught in primary

Already partially observed.

FOURTH DAY.

schools near our large towns and European centres, the meaning of this enactment of God's law. "*Which is the Rest-day?*" "*On what day are the mills and the offices closed?*" "*On what day do the Babus come home from the city?*" are questions which are speedily answered by the cry, "*On Sunday.*" Thus the example of Christians has already diffused a wide practical acquaintance with the benefits of the Dominical Institution. We may say that an unorganised but powerful Sabbath Union already exists in the Christians who are, with various degrees of earnestness, showing to India by the most powerful of all teaching—that of example—the value of the Lord's Day. Every Christian wields an influence which is working either for or against the extension of Sabbath observance. This was impressed upon me the other day when I was looking at the stock of a Muhammadan bookseller in one of our large cities. The hour was late on Saturday afternoon, and the failing light made me say that I should have to come another day. The shopkeeper at once asked whether I meant to come on the morrow, in which case, said he, "*I will open my shop.*" I then saw, as never before, how the influence of one individual may tell either for or against the maintenance of this divine ordinance.

Starting from the undoubted fact that a large number of the people of India are in favour of a periodical day of release from toil, we may enquire, apart from theological opinions, as to what is the *most attainable system of rest-days for India*. Mr. Phillips has shewn that the number of days sanctioned as holidays amount to 29, or little more than the time bestowed on the Saturday half holiday observed in England. These festivals are, however, very unequally distributed, and considering the extra wear upon life in the Indian climate, we may well join with Mr. Phillips in urging that Indian toilers require more relief than the holidays allow. The testimony of Proudhon, one of the ablest of French Socialists and Atheists, may well be quoted to prove the advantage of the seventh-day rest from a secular stand-point. "Shorten the week by a single day," says he, "and the labour bears too small a proportion to the rest; lengthen the week to the same extent, and labour becomes excessive. Establish every three days a half-day of rest, and you increase by a fraction the loss of time, while in severing the

Testimony of a Socialist.

natural unity of the day, you break the numerical harmony of things. Accord, on the other hand, forty-eight hours of rest, after twelve consecutive days of toil, and you kill the man with inertia after having exhausted him with fatigue."

*Fourth Day.*

The famous radical, Louis Blanc, in his vain effort to save the Sabbath law of France, said: "The diminution of the hours of labour does not involve any diminution of production. In England a workman produces in fifty-six hours as much as a French workman in seventy-two hours, because his forces are better husbanded."

*Louis Blanc's theory.*

To the same effect might be quoted the words of Alexander Von Humboldt, with regard to what he called the "dry, wretched, decimal system," which in the French Revolution was substituted for the seventh-day system of repose. But I will only add the testimony of our present Prime Minister, who shows by his activity in advanced age, the practical benefits to be obtained by that periodical cessation from toil which he thus advocates:

*A. Von Humboldt.*

"Believing in the authority of the Lord's Day as a religious institution," says Mr. Gladstone, "I must, as a matter of course, desire the recognition of that authority by others. But over and above this, I have myself, in the course of a laborious life, signally experienced both its mental and physical benefits. I can hardly overstate its value in this view, and for the interest of the working men of this country, alike in these and in other yet higher respects, there is nothing I more anxiously desire than that they should more and more highly appreciate the Christian day of rest."

*Mr. Gladstone.*

It is plain, then, that we may say with Michel Chevalier, the eminent French political economist—"Let us observe Sunday in the name of hygiene, if not in the name of religion." Considering that many Hindus and Muhammadans do already observe this day for their own advantage; and further, that the great body of Christians in this country regard the possession of this day as a right, it is evident that this is the most available of all times for the purpose of affording to the people a periodical release from toil. These 'fifty-two springs,' as Coleridge has called them, evenly distributed over the whole year, are the most available of all expedients known to the world of politics for relieving the pressures, strains, and concussions of human

*M. Chevalier.*

FOURTH DAY.

Earl Cairns.

A Lord's Day Union.

toil. It is earnestly to be desired that the action of Lord Lytton will speedily be revoked, and the boon of a Sunday rest secured, as far as legislation can justly secure it, to the people of this great country.

THE FORMATION OF A LORD'S DAY UNION FOR INDIA.— Earl Cairns, however, truly said: "The institution of Sunday is only maintained because the vast majority of the people of this country, altogether irrespective of churches and denominations, are convinced that it depends, not on human law, but upon a higher and greater law, which we are all bound in conscience to obey."

Apart, therefore, from all attempts to influence the legislature, there is a duty which we owe to the people of India. It is that of informing them as to the reasons, chronological, hygienic, social, and above all religious, which have determined the foremost nations of the world to observe the Sunday as a day of rest. This information should be addressed in the first place to the Hindus and Muhammadans who have already to some extent shown their appreciation of the institution. We must also revive the Christian sentiment in the minds of our own fellow-countrymen, who in this country are so apt to forget the reasons which have determined their fathers in the observance of the Lord's Day. For this reason I welcome the proposal of the Rev. F. W. Warne, that a Lord's Day Union should be at once formed to enlighten the uninformed, and to appeal to the indifferent, as well as to strengthen those who, amid discouragement and difficulties, are contending for their Sabbath privileges. I trust that one immediate outcome of this Conference will be the formation of such a Union.

I well remember some years ago one Sunday morning, on my way to preach, seeing an Englishman accompanied by a number of native assistants busily engaged in the task of land surveying. A little further on I came to some rude little huts, the encampment of a number of Dhangars, or low caste men from Chota Nagpur, who were employed in digging drains and repairing roads. Though the majority had gone forth to work, some half-dozen of them were sitting in the encampment. On asking them the reason why, they replied that they were Christians, and that they could not work on Sunday. Though far from their land and their own people, they had not forgotten their faith. A young Englishman, brought up in this country, once complained to me that when out snipe shooting on a Sunday, he had come to a village with a church, and that the people of this place refused to provide him with a canoe and ferry him over the swamps because it was the Lord's Day. He is now a constant attendant at Divine worship, and I feel sure can sympathise with the refusal which then so much surprised him. There is little doubt that many require enlightenment as to the obligations and the privileges of the commandment regarding a holy day. The Mission House at Dum Dum has always enjoyed the sense of Sabbath rest, which is in many parts of India so difficult to obtain. The Small Arms Ammunition Factory, which supplies the Indian Army with cartridges, resounds with activity during the whole week, and the musical note of the steam saws, the roll of the machinery, and the reports of the guns which test the cartridges are to be heard without cessation, until Sunday brings a day of respite to the swarm of toilers who throng the factory on the other days of the week. Thus the contrast has brought, every Sunday morning, that sense of the Sabbath in the very air which is so potent a means of blessing in the manufacturing centres of our native land. But latterly we have had an unwelcome disturbance in the establishment of a Golf Club by our side. The early Sunday morning brings from Calcutta a number of English gentlemen who spend their day in this sport, and drive away again to the metropolis as the church bells are calling the people to Evening Prayer. I cannot conceal my sorrow that so many of our countrymen in India, in this and similar methods, should show a practical contempt for the day which is consecrated to the service of their Saviour, and I do not doubt that if they were acquainted with the reasons which have made ours a Sabbath-keeping land, many of them would shrink from assisting to desecrate its sanctities and destroy its benefits. Let us therefore do what we can to enlighten those who are ignorant, and plead with those who are irresolute as to the observance of the Lord's Day in India.

It is here that we find the highest sanction for the Sabbath. "It is one of the three Dominical Institutes," says Dr. Pope. The Lord's Supper, the Lord's House, and the Lord's Day are all standing witnesses to the claims of the Redeemer.

*Fourth Day.*
*Result of Example.*

*Games on Sunday.*

*The 3 Dominical Institutes.*

FOURTH DAY. And here I would go even further than Mr. Warne, regarding as I do the Sabbath, not only as a memorial of Christ in Redemption, but also of Christ in Creation. For the very first word in the Hebrew scripture sets forth Christ as the Creator. "The word BRESHITH *in the beginning*—I quote my honoured father—refers not only to time but to Him who is "*the Beginning of the Creation of God.*" The word RESHITH is applied to princes, to first-fruits, to sacrifices, to the first-born; and everywhere denotes that which is "first in the sense of being principal or chief." The Jerusalem Targum very significantly renders RESHITH here by "*Wisdom*," suggesting the MESSIAH, and for this the Targumist appears to have the highest sanction; for the Messiah Himself as the impersonation of "Wisdom," discoursing of the creation, says: "*Jehovah possessed me*"—mark, not *in* the beginning of his ways, but "*the Beginning*"—First, Head, Chief or Leader, "*of his ways, before his works of old*" (Prov. viii. 22), with this agrees the Gospel of St. John, where the word "*Arche*" expresses the idea of the FIRST in order or Prominence, while the "WORD" or *logos* is kindred to the WISDOM of the Book of Proverbs. This subject can only be glanced at here, but it is clear that if Christ be the Beginning of Creation, then the Sabbath which commemorated that creation was already the LORD'S DAY. Redemption has stamped the Day with a more glorious import, but we shall err if we think that this institute had not from the beginning that direct connection with the Second person of the Blessed Trinity which has become more manifest in the Resurrection of our Lord from the dead. It is this relation of the Day to CHRIST Himself which, above all minor considerations, makes it imperative upon every Christian missionary to pray and to labour for its fullest recognition in this land where we find ourselves the ambassadors of JESUS.

The meeting being now open for discussion,

Our Lord and the Sabbath. The Rev. I. W. CHARLTON, M.A., C.M.S., Nuddea, Bengal, said:—I cannot agree with what seems to be the opinion of some that our Lord intended to do away with the Sabbath, for if He had so intended He would hardly have taken so much trouble to reform it. We, as missionaries, owe a great deal to our Christian brethren here in India as, consciously or unconsciously, our actions are to a large extent moulding their future, and influencing for good or bad their position with regard to such questions as Sunday observance, and I do not hesitate to say that, in the evangelistic work which I have always done in conjunction with, and through the instrumentality of, Native Christians, the looseness of some missionaries with regard to the observance of the Lord's Day has proved one of the most serious stumbling-blocks. Only a short time ago, when staying with some voluntary helpers in a village in the south of Calcutta for the purpose of evangelistic work, I was astonished one Sunday to find that some of the leading workers had sent a boy to the bazaar to buy some refreshment. Some was offered to me, and when I refused on the ground that it was bought on Sunday, they seemed utterly unable to enter into my feelings. I proceeded to explain, but after a long talk the only answer I got was that other sahibs thought differently, so it could only be a "matter of opinion" after all. It was the example of of "the other sahibs," whose habit it is to use Sunday trains, which made it easy for them to lightly visit the bazaar on the Sabbath! I once asked a Sabbath-breaking carpenter why he worked on Sunday, and he immediately threw in my face the fact that such and such a sahib always travelled by train on Sunday. The connection between the two may not be easy to trace from our point of view, but I venture to assert that our appeal to such a man is almost incurably weakened and an unnecessary stumbling put in his way by want of care on the part of the missionary to whom he referred. When in work in London it was my rule never to enter a public conveyance on Sunday; and about 10 years ago I proposed never to do so unless under the most urgent necessity. I may add that under the good providence of God such necessity has never arisen. They told me that in India things were different, and that here Sunday travelling could not be avoided, but as yet I see no necessity for more laxity in this respect. You can get to most places in India from first thing Monday morning to last thing Saturday night; and, if not, after having travelled six days, its time you rested one! I don't believe Sunday trains are a necessary part of God's plan for the conversion of India. On the contrary, I believe it would be a great help to our work if every Christian worker would promise, excepting under the most urgent necessity, never to use public conveyances of any kind on the Lord's Day.

*Fourth Day.*
*Missionary example imperative.*
*Bazaar supplies.*
*Sunday travelling.*

The Rev. H. C. STUNTZ, M. A., M. E. C., Naini Tal, N.-W. P., said:—We shall make a great mistake if we attempt to enforce Sabbath observance apart from the whole commandment with which God originally bound it up. The Sabbath portion of that commandment is but one-seventh of the whole. We often forget this, and think of the fourth commandment as concerned only with keeping one day sacred, whereas its original purpose was *to secure six days of honest industry*, followed by one day of rest and worship. "Six days shalt thou labour" is as binding as that portion which we often regard as the whole of the

*Six days' labour.*

*Fourth Day.*

*Example.*

*Religious toleration.*

*The 4th Commandment.*

*Example of Christ.*

commandment. Society butterflies and easy idlers of all sorts will break the Sabbath in their quest of pleasure so long as they continue to violate the divinely ordained law of toil. Neither the idle nor the lazy know how to rest. We need to remember, also, that in this matter of Sabbath desecration, it is not the Government alone, nor the large employers of labour, who are to blame. We ourselves break down the barriers by Sunday travelling, Sunday buying at the door, in the bazaar, &c., &c. We must have the Sabbath Union for which Mr. Warne pleads. I am ready to join it here and now. But in asking Government for legislation relief, we must remember two things : *first*, the peculiar and trying position in which the Government of India is placed ; and *second*, that we must base our request for help on grounds of which a Civil Government can take cognizance. It is profitless and unkind to blink the difficulties which confront this Government. A mere handful of people ruling one-fifth the world's population with their bigotry and superstition. We believe in religious toleration. We would none of us advocate the compulsory observance of the Lord's Day by Hindus and Muhammadans. The difficulties of framing a law on this question are neither few nor easily overcome. What we have a right to ask is that all Government servants, all Europeans and Native Christians, should have a day of rest, and that no man shall suffer for observance of the day. Pleas for this legislation, to get a hearing in the Legislative Council, must be based, not on the Decalogue, but on the economic and humanitarian aspects of the question.

The Rev. E. G. Elsam, M. E. C., Kampti, said :—I would like to ask the question : "Is the fourth commandment still in force or has it been abrogated?" It seems to me the whole question of Sabbath observance hinges on this. If the command is still in force, then we Christians are bound to obey it by abstaining from all work on Sunday except such as is absolutely necessary. If it has been abrogated, then I do not see on what grounds we continue to observe a Sabbath at all. Now, it seems to me that the Lord Jesus never did anything to show that He did not intend the command in the Decalogue to remain in full force. I do not believe He ever broke the Sabbath. There had grown up around this command of God a great many human traditions, and all our Lord did was to clear away these man-made excrescencies; but he never did anything forbidden by the law of God itself. It has been said that He broke the fourth commandment when He defended His disciples for plucking and eating the ears of corn on the Sabbath-day and when He performed works of healing on that day. But the act of His disciples was no breakage of the original law, anymore than cutting off a slice of bread on the Sabbath would be. It was fully justified by the *necessity* they were under. So that all our Lord did was to justify works of necessity and of mercy on the Sabbath. In the 24th of Matthew, and the 20th verse, Jesus says, when talking of the destruction of Jerusalem, "Pray ye that your flight be not .... on the Sabbath-day." Here, it seems to me, we have a clear intimation from the Lord that at the time of this destruction there should be a Sabbath-day;" and He evidently sanctions and enforces its observance; otherwise, why should He tell them to pray against having to flee from Jerusalem on that day? But the destruction of Jerusalem did not take place till many years after Christ's crucifixion, and the establishment of His church; and by that time the church observed the first day of the week instead of the seventh as the Sabbath. All this our Lord fully foresaw; and, foreseeing it, He speaks of the day then observed by the Christian church as the Sabbath-day, and thus carries over to it all the sanctions of the ancient Sabbath. Now, this being the case, it seems quite clear that we are bound by God's law to keep the Sabbath. We must observe it thoroughly, avoiding all unnecessary work both for ourselves and our cattle, &c., according to the terms of the fourth commandment. It seems inconsistent to teach the command regarding the Sabbath as part of God's law, to profess to believe it is still binding, and then to pare it down to suit our own convenience. I am glad Mr. Macdonald spoke of not employing hired vehicles on the Sabbath. This seems to me to be a thing we should be careful about. *Fourth Day* — *Avoid unnecessary work.*

The Rev. J. F. CAMPBELL, C. P. M., Rutlam, C. I., replying to what a former speaker had been understood to say, showed that Christ had not broken the Sabbath law; for it was indisputably in force during His life, and had He broken it He would not have been sinless, and therefore could not have been our Saviour. He had interpreted it, and observed it in its full meaning. The way to relieve the 'troubled consciences' is not to take away God's ordinance, but to relieve men from unfair pressure towards breaking it. "The Sabbath was made for man." The great Artificer who made us knew our need and ordained this weekly Sabbath accordingly. He knew our beasts of burden would require it and He commanded that they should rest on it also. It has been proved in London that horses, which work only six days in the week, can do more than those which work seven days. Why are France and Germany coming back to the observance of the Sabbath? Because experience has taught them their need of it. Similarly, when it was proposed to change the mail day, so that the mail steamer should leave Bombay on Sunday, the Parsees, Hindoos, and Muhammadans objected, because they found they needed the day of rest. Public safety requires the observance of the day of rest. Railway servants often have to work 14 or 16, or some *Necessity of one day's rest.*

**Fourth Day.**

**Law on the Sabbath.**

times even 24 hours on a stretch, and also on Sunday, and accidents result.

The Rev. H. G. E. DE ST. DALMAS, N. Z. B. M., Brahmanbaria, Tippera, asked if it was legal to summon a witness in a court of law on Sunday? A case had occurred in Bengal where a mission servant had been taken up by the police and examined by torture; the doctor had afterwards seen him and a complaint was made to the magistrate. The magistrate, police superintendent and doctor were all Bengalis. The magistrate tried and dismissed the case at his own house on a Sunday morning, the Zenana Missionary having to appear as a witness, not knowing if she could legally refuse to attend on the Lord's Day.

KALI CHARAN BANURJI, Esq., M. A., B. L., Calcutta, said:— It was not legal, unless it was a police case requiring investigation, on the ground of Sunday being a holiday. He remembered a case which happened last August: a European judge had come from one district to hold his court in another district, and a case remaining unfinished on Saturday, it was suggested to the judge that the case might be taken up on Sunday as the parties were not Christians. Mr. Banurji, who was representing one of the parties, objected to this, upon which the judge said, "Certainly;" and instead of conducting the case, the judge presided at a lecture given by Mr. Banurji on the Sunday.

**Sunday evening entertainment.**

The Rev. J. Sewell GRAY, B. A., C. M. S., Lucknow, said:— I wish to call your attention to two things: these are not in connection with the observance of the Sunday by the Indian Christians, but by our fellow-countrymen. In Lucknow, the station in which I live, during the Moharam, the great buildings of the Muhammadans are illuminated; one special evening is set apart for the Europeans. A notice was circulated that this particular evening would be the Sunday evening during the festival. If the Europeans turn their Sunday into a day of pleasure by accepting these invitations, how can we expect the Indian Christians to keep their Sunday holy. The second thing is cricket matches are played on Sundays by the soldiers, and those men who believe on keeping God's day holy find it very difficult to refuse the officers' invitation to play on that day. Let us, who are sometimes brought in contact with these men, do all we can to encourage them to stick to their principles and show those living around us that we still regard the fourth commandment as binding.

**Sports.**

The Rev. A. W. PRAUTCH, M. E. C., Thannah, Bombay, said:—I desire to speak a few words by way of testimony to keeping the Lord's Day. It is so easy to fall into doubtful, careless and questionable courses that we must constantly be on our guard, or we shall confirm the ungodly by our inconsistent actions. Regarding the matter of Sunday travel, some justify themselves on the plea that they must use the railway in order to reach their preaching appointment: this is not God's way. Either the person ought to go on Saturday, and stay over Sunday, or not go at all. A lady once travelling on a Sunday gave the guard a tract; he politely returned it, stating that he was there because he had to work, and she had better keep the tract for herself as she was travelling from choice. In the Eastern part of America a Camp Meeting Committee conceived the plan of having Sunday trains bring the sinners to the Camp grounds, and they waited on the railway manager, who granted it. After a little the sinners found they could have excursions by trains, without the Camp meeting, or religion mixed in, so they had them, and of course the Christians could not protest, as they originated the confusion, and now the Sunday excursion train is an established thing. We must, therefore, keep our testimony clear, especially for the sake of our Native Christians. If they see us slack they get the impression that the keeping is only a matter of convenience, and get indifferent, whereas if they see our carefulness regarding it they will be helped, certainly not hurt by our example. In order to be consistent, I wrote to the non-Christian postmaster, asking that my mail be kept till Monday, as I believed the Post Office ought to be closed on Sunday and the clerks have rest. The man evidently had never heard of such a thing among Christians before, so he wrote and asked if it was a fact: I said, "yes," and I have no doubt if he ever hears me preach he will think of this consistency with God's will; at least he can't bring up my Sabbath breaking as a reason for rejecting the Gospel. In some of the out-stations Saturday's paper arrives on Sunday, and people take the keen edge off their spiritual appetite by filling their minds with worldly matters: the only safe plan is to be very careful in this matter, and rather err on the right side for the sake of our example, and even refuse to do the things we don't feel condemned about, because we may offend some weaker one, we shall then be sure of God's blessing.

The Rev C. G. CONKLIN, M. E. C., Calcutta, said:—The Calcutta Missionary Conference took steps a few months ago to have a rule passed preventing work on the shipping in the Hooghli. Upon the memorial of the Missionary Conference the matter was investigated, and a rule was made by the Lieutenant-Governor forbidding labour on the river on Sunday, except on the payment of a large sum for the privilege. I mention this as a note of encouragement. I believe if a representative body of Christians move in this matter, that soon we will have a Lord's Day Act for India. I am sorry it is thought that this Conference has not the power to pass resolutions upon this or any other matter. We need a Lord's Day Union to strengthen ourselves and to protect and educate our native church;

FOURTH DAY.

Sunday travelling.

Consistency.

Lord's Day Act.

FOURTH DAY.

4th Commandment.

and as the Government professes to be Christian, we might expect them to recognise the first day of the week as a day of rest.

Miss GORDON, Bombay, said:—The Lord gave the fourth commandment, written by His own hand on the table of stone. God's greatest blessing will rest upon that day which He has sanctified. It is not a Jewish institution, because it was given before the Jewish race began.

The *Rev. A. Paton Begg* proposed that the Business Committee of the Decennial Conference be requested to appoint some one to confer with the various Missionary Conferences about the formation of a union for the observance of the Lord's Day.

The proposal was duly seconded and carried.

## XIII.—THE SOCIAL CONDITION OF THE LOWER CLASSES.

(A) HOW FAR ARE MISSIONS CALLED UPON TO AMELIORATE IT. (B) THE OPPORTUNITIES IT AFFORDS FOR MISSION WORK. (C) MASS MOVEMENTS TOWARDS CHRISTIANITY MORE OR LESS ARISING FROM IT. (D) THE DANGERS INCIDENTAL TO SUCH MOVEMENTS AND THE RIGHT LINE OF ACTION WITH REGARD TO THEM.

Fifth Day.

## FIFTH DAY.

Tuesday, 3rd January 1893.

### MORNING SESSION.
Large Hall.—10 A.M. to 1 P.M.

The Rev. J. Smith, B.M.S., Delhi, *in the chair.*

After prayer had been offered by the Rev. Mr. Ward, the Chairman said:—

I have been struck by the minute description given in the Word of God as to the construction of His Kingdom on earth, the means for its extension and edification. The first thing is the unity of the body, of which we have just been reading (*Eph.* 4 c.). We all know that its great characteristic is that of harmony among its members. God hath given to His Church every variety of talent needful for its extension and edification. There is no competition between preaching and teaching: both are needful and have their proper place: both are provided for and approved by the sacred writer. "He gave some to be Apostles, and some Prophets, and some Evangelists, and some Pastors and Teachers." Now, I strongly feel that we ought to go back to first principles, and setting aside human wisdom, rest solely in God's Word. Our

The unity of the body.

**Fifth Day.** peculiar adaptations fit us for different kinds of work in the Lord's vineyard, and He has need of us all. Indian missions find plans for every description of talent; we want translators, medical workers, Zenana workers, teachers of the young, and above all preachers. The first thing for a young missionary is to ascertain what the Lord has fitted him for, and then do it with all his might, suffering nothing to move him from his straight path. Some brethren have peculiar fitness for teaching and training, but no gift for public preaching and disputation: let everyone be fully persuaded in his own mind and follow fully the teaching and guidance of God's Spirit.

**To the poor the Gospel is preached.** I wish to call attention to several things connected with the subject of this morning's Session. Christianity has always commended itself to the poor: "To the poor the Gospel is preached," and they receive it most readily. In all ages of the Church's history conversions to Christianity have commenced at the lowest strata of society, and, as Spurgeon once said, gradually risen to the scum. The work is not what some think it to be. Going to a village of untaught people for the first time and baptizing a number of them before you leave it, will not materially help on the real work of conversion. I began my life's work in a large mission school in 1842, where I remained four years: since that time I have spent nearly fifty years **Fifty years' work.** in the bazaars and villages of Northern India. My happiest days have been spent in preaching the Gospel to the lower castes, and I commend the work with all my heart and understanding to my missionary brethren. The task requires no ordinary faith and perseverance. The people are ready to hear, but ages of body and soul slavery have blunted their capacity for understanding to such an extent that "line upon line" is necessary before they will be able to give an intelligent account of the hope that is in them. They, however, soon appreciate the superiority of the Gospel, and see in it the only means of ameliorating their condition and delivering them from the thraldom that has weighed on their race for ages past. In order to success in this work among the labouring classes, two things are needful, viz., thorough organization and continuity of work on the same lines. In Delhi at one time there were forty Busti and other meetings weekly, with an aggregate attendance of 2,000 people. Every meeting had a sprinkling of Native Christians, but the majority were non-Christian residents of the Bustees in which they lived, and where the meetings were held in the open-air. Our Native brethren will not work effectually, unless their day's work is fixed, according to a regular organized plan, and then a weekly review of work done is needful in order to secure regularity and perseverance. The next thing is continuity. First impressions are weak; the Natives of India are a most conservative people in matters of religion; it often takes a long time before they understand anything spiritual, and hence the necessity of our work being continuous and persevering. I have often known a field worked until it was ready for harvesting, and then the work was given up and the opportunity of reaping lost. It is most important also that great care should be taken in keeping up a succession of workers of the same mind. It has often happened that a worker has succeeded in a work long cultivated with success, and want of sympathy with the kind of operation, or mode of labour, has led to its disorganization and temporary ruin. Thus one man may overturn, if not destroy, the work of his predecessor.

In conclusion, I would say a word on the subject of failures. Some painful remarks were made yesterday on this subject. Let us not forget that on one occasion so many left following the Lord Himself that he said to His disciples: "Will ye also go away." The Apostle Paul suffered more from the failing of converts than he experienced in the care of all the churches. He said, "All they of Asia have forsaken me," and when he stood at the Romish tribunal, he said, "No man stood by me." Under

*Fifth Day.*

*Continuity.*

*Failures.*

**Fifth Day.** no circumstances does the missionary need our sympathy more than when those for whom he has laboured and prayed cease from following the Lord, still the labour spent on such is not lost; they take back with them more than they brought. All through the history of the church, these apparently receding waves have been visible; but after a time they have advanced again with renewed force.

## FIRST PAPER.

By the Rev. J. Scudder, m.d., A.A.M., Vellore, Madras.
"The social condition of the lower classes."

*Pariahs.* My remarks will refer exclusively to the Pariahs of Southern India, among whom I have laboured for more than 30 years, but doubtless will be more or less equally applicable to the lower classes in the whole of India.

Our first inquiry will be what is this social condition.

*No social standing.* Volumes have been written on this subject. The papers and periodicals of the past few years have contained many articles on this question, both from Christian and Hindu friends, representing their deplorable state. So full and extensive has been the discussion, that those who are in any way interested in their welfare, must be fully aware of their pitiable position, and I might dismiss the subject by merely saying that they have *no social standing.*

*Outcasts.* They are outcasts from society in the full meaning of that term, without any rights or privileges which are to be respected by the community. Despised, abused, abhorred and shunned by all, they do not receive the consideration allowed to the cattle and dogs of the land. Their touch, yea, their shadow also is considered pollution. Even money will not be received from their hands, but must be placed on the ground before it can be accepted by another. If they meet a casteman in the streets, no matter how heavy a burden they may be carrying, they must drop it, and retire till he has passed by; they are hardly allowed to enter a village, much less to live there, but are compelled to build their miserable huts, often in a more miserable situation, apart by themselves, where there may be no possibility of their contaminating others. Under no circumstances, though they may be perishing from thirst, are they permitted to draw water from the village tank or well. Any animal, though covered with filth, may descend into the tank, slake its thirst and wash itself, but no Pariah would dare to do this, even though he were the cleanest of the clean.

The schools of the land are virtually closed to them, and it is an exception to find a Pariah in any school, save those sustained by missionaries. When admitted, they are compelled like culprits to occupy the furthermost corner.

*Their disabilities.*

Many Chuttrams are built for the convenience of the Hindu while travelling, but no shelter is offered to the poor Pariah.

They are not usually permitted to enter the courts presided over by native magistrates, but must stand without and give their evidence.

Not a temple in the land is open to them, but they have to content themselves with a few unsheltered shapeless stones for their gods, and appoint their own ignorant priests to administer their religious rites. They literally have no standing in society.

Their financial condition is, if possible, still worse. All of them are poor, very poor. If possessed of a little land, they are often robbed of it. If allowed to retain its nominal possession, this is almost worse than robbery, as there would be benefactors who would usually cheat them out of the greater share of the produce, though *they* do all the work, and every obstacle possible is thrown in the way of others to prevent them from becoming landholders. Many of them do not know where to-morrow's food is to come from—half-starved, poorly clad, abused and cruelly treated by their masters, their condition is one of abject slavery, from which it is impossible for them ever to free themselves. Pages might be written in depicting their wrongs, but I have time for no more.

*Their financial condition.*

Morally, their condition is most pitiable. There is hardly a command in the Decalogue, which they do not transgress every day. And what else can be expected of a class who are so fearfully treated.

*Their moral condition.*

Such in brief is their condition. Are we not then right in saying that those who are thus loathed and shunned, oppressed, impoverished and enslaved, who are saluted with a curse, and often cruelly beaten, whose clothing is rags, and whose only luxury are the dead cattle and carrion of the land, have no social standing? Can a more deplorable condition be imagined?

**Fifth Day.**

I.—*How are missions called upon to ameliorate it.*—They certainly need help. Their sad condition appeals to the heart of every philanthropist. Rivers of blood and millions of money were given to free the slaves of America. England has long been noted for her magnanimous efforts on behalf of the slave, but who is there to come to the aid of these poor people? Are they to be left for ever in their present position? Even the heart of the Hindu has been moved with compassion for them, and a society was formed some years ago to ameliorate their condition, but thus far with no practical results, and now they admit that there is no hope for the Pariah inside of Hinduism. Even though they may become learned and wealthy, refined and cultivated, they say that the Pariah can never be received to any social standing among them as long as they remain heathen, and that their only hope is in a change of religion.

How to help them.

For a time hopes were entertained that the Government of Madras might be induced to aid them, but these hopes have been dashed to the ground by its recent action.

Mr. Tremenheere, the Collector of Chingleput, having acquainted himself by a personal inspection of their villages and houses, sent a vivid description of their distressing and hopeless condition to the Government, with a suggestion that something should be done for their relief. He did not paint the picture in too high colours. There is not a statement of his to which every missionary who has had any experience with them, would not say aloud "Amen," and could add still more harrowing details. But his efforts have been of no avail.

A Government servant.

The Madras Missionary Conference presented a Memorial to the Governor, in which they pointed out the disabilities of the Pariah and their wretched condition, and requested that a Commission should be appointed to enquire into the facts of the case in order that some way might be found to ameliorate it. This also has been useless, and the only hope held out is that something may be done for them in the educational line.

The Madras Conference.

I will not permit myself to express any opinion on this action, as being a missionary interested in the welfare of these down-trodden people, it may be considered as "biassed," but will content myself by quoting an article on the subject from the *Times of India.*

FIFTH DAY.

The *Times of India.*

"Governments have at times a way of dealing with important questions which is calculated to perplex—we had almost said to dismay—even the most tolerant of citizens. Such an instance has just cropped up in Madras over the Pariah question. The position of these unfortunate people has occupied for some years the attention of officials and missionaries alike. It is practically beyond dispute that a system which can only be adequately described as slavery obtains among the Madras Pariahs, and it is no less certain that they are only too frequently oppressed and tyrannised over by the higher castes, with little or no protection against manifest acts of injustice. The Pariah finds it difficult, if not impossible, however hard he may struggle for an independent existence, to hold a plot of land, and even the humble cot which shelters him is no longer his own if it should unfortunately happen to take the fancy of some covetous and scornful village *mirasidar*. The Pariah, in short, begins life on the down grade; and even if he does not pursue the downward part of his own accord, or by reason rather of the hopeless helplessness of his position, he seems to be thrust downwards by the sheer force of caste tyranny. Apart from a series of careful inquiries undertaken by the missionaries, the Collector of Chingleput, Mr. Trenenheere, has concerned himself to make a careful investigation of the whole matter, and to embody the result of his enquiry in a Report to Government. His reward is an official 'wigging.' He is told by the Government of Madras that his statements are 'sensational,' and his proposals 'utterly impracticable' as being 'based on the fallacy' that the direct conferring of land upon the Pariah is the main lever by which his material condition can be raised; and he is censured for his 'thoughtlessness' in dealing with so important a matter in a 'hasty generalisation.' The Commission of Inquiry, which was so largely asked for, is curtly refused, and the whole subject is dismissed in a manner which, but for the intimation that the Director of Public Instruction is 'considering' the question of benefiting the Pariah by educating him, could only be described as little short of contemptuous. Most of the statements in the memorial presented by the missionaries are dismissed with a flat denial, despite the fact that they are

Fifth Day

the outcome of personal investigation and observation, and the Government even goes so far as to roundly assert that the condition of the Pariah is 'improving, though slowly.' They admit, however, that by social custom 'which it is impossible to control' these harassed and oppressed people are 'hustled' out of the schools, and thus do not reap their share of benefit from the educational operations of the State; but, on the other hand, 'if the Pariahs are cajoled and cheated owing to their ignorance and folly, Government cannot prevent it.' The only saving clause in this remarkable Resolution is a promise that Government will 'give what facilities it can' to Pariahs and non-*mirasidars* generally for obtaining cultivable land by making small allotments out of areas freed from preferential sites by purchase at sales for arrears of revenue, and thus at the absolute disposal of Government; and this despite the Government's own dictum that 'any attempt to bolster up the Pariah or any other of the labouring classes in the way proposed by Mr. Tremenheere could only lead to an increase of pauper holdings without any advantage to the cultivator or Government.' We trust that the last has not yet been heard of this very singular Resolution."—*Times of India.*

I think all of us will agree with the sentiment of the last sentence, and "trust that the last has not been heard of this singular Resolution," but that the subject will be ventilated and public opinion aroused till something be done for their help. It remains for this Conference to decide whether they consider it worth while to take any notice of the matter.

As the Hindus cannot, and Government does not consider it necessary to help them, who then can, if not the missionary? Are they to be left to go on for generations in their present state? I think we are bound by every law, human and divine, to render them all the assistance in our power and, if possible, raise them from their low state to a higher plane. But how, and to what extent that aid should be given, are questions that are not so easily decided.

Are all to be helped.

Is it to be extended to all, whether they become Christians or not? Undoubtedly all would be glad to do so were it in their power. I should like to see a Christian school opened in every Pariachery, with sufficient inducements offered to the scholars, to enable them to attend regularly. Were we able to do this, I believe it would be successful, and we would see a great transformation in the people in the course of a few years. But as the resources of most missions are limited, I fear, unless Government aids us most liberally, we shall have to confine our labours almost entirely to those who join us.

These we must help, and we can do so in three ways—(*a*) We must thoroughly instruct them in spiritual things. Of this there can be no doubt, if we desire them to become true Christians. (*b*) We must educate them, as there is very little hope of their ever rising as long as they remain in their present ignorance. (*c*) We can aid them in their worldly affairs. How far this aid should be carried is a question that gives the missionary more trouble and anxiety than almost any other part of his work.

Much has been written on this subject. So I need not repeat even though time would permit what has already been so well said, but only remark that I think aid should never be given where it encourages laziness or a dependent spirit. Our aim is to make them energetic and independent men, and if the aid rendered does not accomplish this it is worse than thrown away.

But there are cases where I think we should aid them. Poor as they are, they lose many things important in their eyes by becoming Christians. Under no circumstances will their former masters help them, but, on the other hand, use all their power to render their state still more miserable. In such cases, we must stand by them, and often by a little judicious pecuniary assistance may enable them to earn an independent living. It is impossible to lay down any law on this subject, but it must be left to the decision of the individual missionary.

In these three ways we must and can aid them, with the assurance that their social status will be raised and their condition vastly improved. Every mission can show many noble Christian men and women who have been rescued from the lowest depths of society by these means, and we hope the time is not far distant when all will be thus benefited.

II.—*The opportunities it affords for mission work.*—Little need be said on this head. It undoubtedly opens the way for the missionary. They are friendless and helpless, without any to take an interest in either their temporal or spiritual welfare.

**Fifth Day.**

The missionary goes to them as a friend, pities their condition, and shows them that he is anxious to be their friend and to help them in every way possible. If assured of this, they become ready listeners to the Gospel message.

**They will all become Christians.**

III.—*Mass movements towards Christianity more or less arising from it.*—The success of missions has thus far come mostly from this class. They have little to lose and much to gain by becoming Christians. Many of them are becoming convinced that there is no hope for them or their children, and that they will never rise to a respectable standing in the community as long as they remain heathen. They have no caste to lose, and they are so raised by Christianity that they fear not to stand on a level with the proud Brahman. When fully convinced of all this, I feel assured that they will come over in still larger numbers than in the past.

**No danger.**

IV.—*The dangers incident to such movements and the right line of action with regard to them.*—I do not anticipate any great danger, if the people are rightly handled after they come. There would be danger of lowering the standing and spirituality of the church by admitting them to full membership, while ignorant of the cardinal doctrines of religion. Indiscriminate baptisms should be avoided. They should be kept on probation until thoroughly instructed in the great truths of Christianity, and until they show by their walk and conversation that they are new men in Christ Jesus. If this course be followed, I think we need not apprehend any evil result from a mass movement towards Christianity. My only fear is that the churches at home may not be able to furnish the men and means for their proper instruction. If these are forthcoming, the greater the movement the greater will be our joy, and the greater will be the prosperity of the Church of God.

---

## SECOND PAPER.

By the Rev. L. L. Uhl, ph.d., A. L. M., Guntur, Madras.

**Who are the lower classes.**

I.—The first inquiry may well be, Who are the Lower Classes? In the Telugu country they are the Málas, Mádigas, Rellu and Dakkulu, forming the great cooly population of this country, as well as the weavers, leather workers and sweepers. For South India they compose the out-of-caste classes and are made up of Pariahs and Hill Tribes. The local names are many, for the whole of India, wherein the general term Chandala is applicable, while the frightful term Rakshasa was used in Sanskrit writings. This paper deals with those lower classes known as Málas and Mádigas.

*Fifth Day.*

II.—The second inquiry is, What is the social condition of these people? The reply is given at some length, as the inquiry lies at the foundation of this whole discussion. As all the conditions of a class interblend and appear together, the social can only be best seen in its various related phases. All mistakes of meaning may be avoided and statements definitely understood if, instead of theoretical investigation, actual concrete results be given. These two principles will govern this discussion.

*Their social condition.*

(1) Five-fold is the social condition of the lower classes. From the civil point of view the position of out-castes deprives these people of all rights among their Indian fellow-citizens. The acquisition of lands is out of the question, except to a very few. These people are at the mercy of merciless creditors who can at any time possess themselves of house, cattle, loom and tools in a civil action, but who do not constantly do so because of that prudence which preserves the goose of the golden egg, for almost every Pariah is in debt. These classes are the least cared for, if cared for at all, by hospitals and dispensaries having caste men in charge who cannot make full examination of the patient. They are deprived of the privileges of vaccination in the majority of cases, for even if the vaccinator himself is willing to go among them he is restrained from doing so by the pressure from the villagers' social prejudice. The Local Union Panchayat does not look after their welfare and provide them with any share of road and light in their isolated hamlet. Their persons are without protection, so that creditors, plunderers and foes from the castes beat, wound and even kill these people, escaping punishment through the aid of false evidence, the village authorities and the lower magistrates. It is notorious, in the writer's district, how the villagers league together against a poor fellow in a case, and how justice miscarries often in the petty courts. Moreover, though the Police Department is thoroughly orga-

*No rights.*

**Fifth Day.**

nized, the lower class man stands small chance of getting protection at the police station, because he has no influence there and because he cannot at all avail himself of the evidence of higher class witnesses to events.

*No sanitary helps.*

(2) From the hygienic point of view the condition is the worst possible. This shows itself in their sites for residence, which are always the refuse and insanitary part of a village; it shows itself in their houses, which are small, wretched and closely packed together, becoming a congested mass with the increase of population; it appears in their water-supply, which is ever something else than the good wells and ample tanks of the caste people—more often a pit of muddy water fouled all around the entrance; and it is finally and touchingly shown in the absence or the wretchedness of the burial ground.

*Poor food.*

(3) From the physical standpoint, they are driven to subsist on the meanest fare, for they are prevented in all attempts to get a better livelihood. This results in the tendency with vast numbers to dropsy from anæmia, it fruits in the readiness with which they fall victims to cholera and die in numbers from the same, its harvest is the greater liability to fever and fatal results therefrom; while, in combination with their bad situation sanitarily, these people are exclusively attacked with the guinea-worm through their shallow and marshy water pits. Notwithstanding that they are the labourers of the country, they are reduced in their power of continued physical endurance.

*No instruction.*

(4) From the intellectual side they are denied all instruction. As the result of this they cannot think systematically, if most of them can think at all in the higher sense, they have been unprovided with the forms and methods of thought, they are dull of apprehension, they cling to one idea and request almost like a mono-maniac, their mind is the proverbial frog in a deep well with narrow opening, and their conscious reaction to new stimulus is painfully slow.

*No moral restraint.*

(5) In the view from character, they are impelled to every means to get for themselves their only four necessities—food, clothes, house and partner. Here they are at the confines of immorality, so that lying, stealing and adultery are good or bad according only as the poor fellow gains his ends or not, and that without discovery. Even the punishments awarded by their tribunals are incentives to low life in the general feasting

and drinking to which all fines are applied, in adjudicable cases. **Fifth Day.**
Nowhere, it seems to the writer, have promises so little value, has honesty so few votaries, licentiousness so unchecked a sway, or foul words so current a usage, as among these lower classes. He believes this to be true for the class all over India.

This, then, is the substance of the results from the social status of the lower class man. He is civilly disabled, hygienically unprotected, physically victimized, intellectually dwarfed, and morally debased. There are exceptions to each and every point taken, and this is illustrated, in one feature, by the exclamation of a Sub-Collector in the Krishna District, "What strong, fat-looking fellows the Pariahs of your district are!" This better physical condition is, however, only the case with a relatively small number, and that in the rice-growing taluks of the district. All betterment of these people in any way has been through English laws coupled with English enforcement of the same and against the wishes of the other classes; while moral improvement has also set in, in single instances, through individuals having had duties with worthy Europeans. The description heretofore given stands for the condition of the lower classes under the social system of native India.

III.—In the next inquiry, the first on the Programme, *viz.*,— how far are missions called upon to ameliorate the conditions described—a word should be said about the term 'Missions.' The writer takes it that the appropriate word here is Missionary Societies, and that the efforts made for betterment refers to what the missionaries can or should do. The reply, then, is: the missionary should make efforts to improve the social condition of these people in all the features and phases herein above described. *What can be done?*

(1) In one direction, he should teach these classes their rights and privileges as well as their responsibilities under the law; he should arbitrate in cases of debt and, in prudent instances, give loans where he can; he should take pains to inquire into cases of hurt and murder; give every information to the police; use proper influence to strengthen the back-bone of the lower magistrates and co-operate in so far as it is not meddlesome in bringing matters before the superior magistrates. He should even do all he can in endorsements of petitions *Take interest in them.*

by these people for fields, in the case of the industrious; while he should agitate with the Board of Revenue for such changes of the land *darkhast* rules as give owners of adjacent property a prior right to all vacant lands, and such as require all lands applied for by two or more parties to be put up for sale at public auction. In these ways the poor people will be led to feel they are not brutes to be abused and destroyed at the owner's behest, they will have something more of manhood awakened, and will have new avenues of livelihood thrown open to them.

(2) In another direction, the missionary should use his influence with Local Fund Boards, and other departments concerned, to secure a good water-supply in wells or tanks, and he should do what he can to obtain better hamlet and house sites for these people. Aids of this character will better the sanitary condition, guard against the ravages of disease and improve the physical condition which, after all, bears so powerfully on the intellectual and the moral.

(3) In still another direction, the missionary should do what he can to open schools for these classes, train teachers, utilize the assistance of Government and spread education among them: in this way the brutalizing effects of ages of oppression and low life will be somewhat modified and some impetus be given to higher aspirations.

(4) From the moral side the missionary should do all he can to introduce Christianity as the only means for the establishment of conscience and a sense of duty. He should also see to it that real offenders are rebuked, or punished by law in cognizable cases; he should agitate for such changes of the Native Christian Marriage Acts as will make divorce more easy to an impecunious people in case of the continued infidelity of one of the parties: he should move for the insertion of a clause in the Penal Code, declaring it a crime to make engagements of marriage for parties under marriageable age; and he should also agitate for another clause, in the Penal Code or elsewhere, removing the privilege of the 'convert' to put away the other party by becoming a 'pervert' and making such an action a punishable offence. With regard to the latter proposition it is to be said that all approach towards the Christian religion is accompanied with better marriage rules, while worse ones go with all departure from Christianity. These and other means

*Marginal notes:*
FIFTH DAY.
Use influence.
Open schools.
Preach Christ.

will help to make character and remove the present many incentives to the violation of marital duties and sexual relations.

In all the methods proposed, the missionary would do better by aiding the Christian communities alone, as the pagan community is too large for him either to undertake any line or lines of help or to acquaint himself with the facts and come to know the real deserving parties. Even among Christians he should remember he will generally be imposed upon, so that he should make thorough investigations and then proceed with caution. It need only be mentioned that the utmost deference and respect should be shown in bringing all matters before the authorities. With these provisions, the writer emphasizes each and every aid described, on behalf of Christians, and has in his incompetent way himself been working on these lines. No money aid should be given by the Societies, except in cases of schools and legitimate evangelistic work, and except, perhaps, in the establishment of some well planned loan fund, which should in time, as payments are made, itself become self-perpetuating.

*Fifth Day.*

*Aid Christians only.*

IV. The second inquiry of the Programme, *viz.*,—what opportunities for mission work does the social condition of the lower classes afford—is answered by the words *immense opportunities*. The oppression of the ages has made these people ready for at least an earthly helper. Vast sense of some sort of want has been developed, and this leads to where wants may be met. Pessimistic conditions and feelings in a sinner will more surely lead him to Christ than optimistic ones. Of all people, these have no fulness, but are utterly empty in the midst of surrounding power, wealth and abuse. The missionary can be a friend to them, his friendship will be accepted in time, and he can, without let or hindrance, pursue evangelical methods adapted to the situation. But right here there are two sides of the question. There is no doubt 'immense opportunity' for mission work; the people accessible form one-fifth of the community, constituting thousands for each taluk, and hundreds of thousands for each zillah or district; they are at once willing hearers when interested, and do not waste time with odd theories and strange objections; they are docile and obedient, as a rule; and their children offer such a scope for work as pains the labourer who sees but cannot utilize the field. It is,

*Immense opportunities.*

**Fifth Day.**

however, true that the opportunity for work is at the same time very small. The religious feeling is debased, the mind is undeveloped, and the motive is wrong. The correction of motives is filled with all difficulty, because of the poverty of mind, the introduction of new thoughts is slow, and the religious feeling can hardly be purified by the new currents from Christ. From this view of the little intellect, the little capacity, the little religious feeling, as well as the small round of life of the lower class man, the opportunity for mission work with him is exceedingly small. It requires one to take in the future as well as the present, the second century as well as the first, to preserve the real value of this opportunity for mission work, and then, not by imagination or by empty faith, but by clear perception and wise method, the view shows opportunity great and large.

V. The next inquiry concerns mass movements of these lower classes towards Christianity, and here, too, the term used needs be considered.

**Mass movements.** (1) Mass movements may be such for an extended area of country, or may simply affect one or a few villages. In the writer's mission field we have had all the various movements of the people towards the Gospel, almost in regular procession, and with the intervals between the stages marked by the lapse of years, viz:—first and earliest the accession of an individual here and there, then a few individuals in occasional instances, again a family coming together, than accessions of a number of families at one time, after many years the movement of a large portion of single villages, and finally a succession of large accessions from each of many villages. Mass movements over wide areas are illustrated by the ingathering of the Mádigas, as if by some sudden impulse, in the American Baptist and the General Synod Lutheran Mission for about the years 1870-1880, and to which movement the great Madras famine of 1877-79 was a stimulus, but of which it was not the origin. The mass movements of the Málas in the writer's district also began before the famine times and is another instance in point. Scientific social and religious writers will study in future times, with interest and for varied purposes, that great movement of the Mádigas, and all records of the event should be carefully preserved. The writer understands that this is the first mass movement among the lower classes in India, and he has often **FIFTH DAY.** pondered over the fact that in the Palnad, the part of the Lutheran Mission most distant from the Baptist head-quarters at Ongole, there had been accessions of single individuals from the Mádiga class years before the now well-known decision of the missionaries at Ongole to receive this class and work more for them. The conclusion is that there are natural precursors to mass movements. A recent instance of this movement of the lower classes in masses has occurred among the American Methodist Episcopal Missions in Oude and the North-West Provinces, giving even larger results in numbers than the similar movement in the South, for the first few years.

(2) It should not be understood, however, that these movements include the whole of the community or even of a village. At the village of U—where over 125 persons were baptized some years ago, there were recently seven inquirers; in the village of T—where it was reported every house was Christian, one pagan is discovered who remains pagan; the writer has found heathen Mádigas among the Christian pálems in his visits in the Nellore District. The wisdom or the will of these poor people would still keep up connection with their heathen neighbours who abound somewhere, and this fact once more emphasizes the peculiar nature of the minds to be dealt with.

(3) Under the writer's own observation, wherein he has worked with each individual, there has been a general movement in as many as a score of villages, while several score of other congregations in his charge were established, as far as numbers go, under such movements. Space and time forbid more than a mere summary of the reasons which have influenced these movements. Those reasons are:—Famine and scarcity, lack of tanks and wells or deficient water-supply, troubles arising from water-supply, need of house sites, desire for fields, cases in the civil or criminal courts, sickness, misfortunes, wish for schools, marriage alliances to be made, vetty lands to be protected, property to be preserved, hope of employment, better paying labour, a desire to have children supported in the mission boarding schools, quarrels with the lower classes or disputes with the upper classes, and a large number of cases with some undefined expectation of better physical things. The majority of the lower

*Reasons for such movements.*

FIFTH DAY.

classes are so lacking in energy and get up, that even any and all the reasons given would not, to the individual, constitute a wherefore for the trouble of embracing Christianity, but there are always energetic fellows who are leaders in a village, these are carried by any strong reason as above, and where several chief men have common interests they combine and influence the mass to follow. Thus local mass movements have been generated, and then the movement never stops with the originating village, but sweeps on, often making no impression on the nearer, to neighbouring villages connected with family bonds, and under the laws of mental contagion. Lest the writer be misunderstood as naturalistic and not acknowledging the work of the Holy Spirit in these movements towards Christianity, he desires at this point to express his conviction that the Spirit uses and over-rules these means, and further to add that he has followed only the human currents for these, and these alone he can measure and describe to some extent.

Dangers.

VI. The sixth inquiry of this paper, the fourth of the Programme, deals with the dangers incident to mass movements, and this inquiry stands only second in importance among all the topics. Even missionary workers may overlook the dangers from these mass movements, hence it is no wonder the outside Christian world is often carried away with the reports of vast additions to the church. The heart swells at the sight of great numbers knocking at the gateways for admission and enthusiasm leaps to the walls of Zion to shout the multitudes in. The missionary who daily goes among these multitudes, spiritually and mentally hearing, feeling, tasting and smelling them, has his heart swelled with pain and his enthusiasm decidedly quenched.

Mistaken notions.

(1) The greatest danger is that these multitudes will mistake what Christianity is and miss it, and will go on through their lives with these mistaken notions—this will prevent growth and development. This evil is heightened when the accessions are larger and the missionaries and teachers fewer.

Unworthy motives.

(2) The unworthy motive is a most insidious danger, warping and twisting even the best and most thorough system of instruction, and which, in untaught multitudes, keeps the individual soul out of the kingdom.

(3) Another great danger is that caste and pagan usages will be introduced and perpetuated, for even in individual cases

these cannot be at once corrected, let alone in the case of mul- *Fifth Day.*
titudes to whom old customs are as the bone and marrow in the
body. The missionary may issue specific orders, he may print
and circulate rules to be read, he may even himself repeat and
re-repeat at the head of his columns of disciples the usages to be
avoided, but he will find at the end, if he is a philosopher, that
instinct and usage, unaccompanied with enlightened intellect,
are blind following their own way as surely as the dog returns
to his vomit, and that the mere taking on and the mere repeating
of the name Jesus effects no exorcism over low-class caste and
pagan usages. Here are laws of a psychological and social
nature which should be kept in mind.

(4) A special great danger from these mass movements is *Women*
the omission to gather in the women or the overlooking of all *neglected.*
instruction for them, and this is felt, for an indefinite number of
years, by these women either keeping out of church or avoiding
all instruction and thus maintaining the heathen status of the
wife and mother.

(5) A further danger from the movements under discussion *Individuals*
is that the missionary and his workers will trust to general *not reached.*
efforts, large meetings and such like labours, much as a Professor
would have to do with five hundred boys on his hands in one
class. The Professor's 500 boys *can* be handled as a body for all
the purposes concerned, but the missionary's 500 can never be
managed in a mass, having due regard to the end desired. If
advice in school, college and university, to Ministers, S. S.
Teachers and every class of Christian workers is that each
individual must be reached and influenced, then these movements are fraught with danger and present one of the problems
of the age.

(6) There are also other dangers. The lower classes *Ingratitude.*
look much upon the missionaries and their work as if all
were somehow endowed with more than human power; this
prevents the cultivation of gratitude which is most entirely a
non-indigenous product to these people, and it at once also
throws vast obstacles in the way of Christian and church
development. The ingratitude of this people wrings the heart
of the missionary with pain. Worse than this : they receive
the help for which they come, like the hungry shark they take
it as their right—is it not their nature the stoic might say—

Fifth Day.

Vanity.

they wait for more, while as to benevolence and giving, they were not constituted for these. Worse then this: cupidity and greed are excited which always heighten disappointment and foment discontent.

(7) Another evil is the inevitable result of sudden transitions, in a silly but leavening vanity and self-assertion. With new or imagined champions, impudence to the villagers and to their superiors often possesses them, and they not only omit courtesy but push themselves forward to offensiveness and insult, with a whole train of results following in quarrels with villagers, revenges, destruction of property and actions in criminal courts.

Dangers! These stand thick and big in the mass movements as trees in the virgin forests. First and last, and which cannot be repeated too often, is the fact that the masses will fail to learn Christianity; dull and obtuse, wrongly motivated, they will be baptized, and they will commune without being Christians; vast numbers will not become Christians in years, multitudes will not become so in their lifetime, many will not be so in the second and third generation. As to these people generally being converts in any sense of having turned from the world to Christ and from sin to holiness, the writer believes the thing impossible under the orderly constitution of the intellectual universe. The word *convert* is an abused term when applied to these accessions. The root of change is not in the soul; but in the stomach, in the eye, but not in the heart. The writer calls these people brethren, he seeks to be brotherly towards them, but he confesses that the use of the word and the application of the manner is as yet almost entirely with a pedagogical heart. That feature of this whole question most liable to imperil mission endeavour is the dissemination far and wide among the home churches that these thousands and scores of thousands are converts. The very foundation of missionary endeavour and hope in the churches will be shaken, decades hence, when the true state of affairs is apprehended while, worse yet, the workers themselves will be lulled to quiet and deluded into songs of victory instead of being excited to utmost effort and consumed with deepest care for the incoming multitudes. The churches will be wiser and more missionary from a foresight than from an aftersight of the situation.

In no sense converts.

VII. The last inquiry is the most important one—what is the right line of action to be pursued in these mass movements? The writer would be presumptuous in the extreme were he to even hint that this question is answered in this paper. The best he can do is to express his own convictions and give some conclusions from experience. In the Lutheran Mission of the General Synod we are on the watch for better methods, while every few years we modify our system of work and improve it, or at least hope we do.

*Fifth Day. What methods to follow.*

A study of the dangers from mass movements shows them to be five-sourced in pagan usage—impoverished mind, debased motive, wrong expectation and lack of moral courage.

*Pagan usage.*

(1) The introduction of entirely new customs in every point tainted with heathenism is imperative, so that it should be seen to that feasts, marriages and burials are put on a new basis. Some features of the old might be allowed to remain with respect to music, but not with respect to song or story. We in the Lutheran Mission, at our stage of the work, cannot change those social customs of our people based on caste, and are only hoping for enlightenment to do this; we try to keep caste out of the Lord's Supper, the Church and Christian work, but, if we were to begin again, the writer would make thorough renouncement of caste in all social life also to be indispensable to church membership. However, the place to begin work in a mass movement is not at the customs of the people.

(2) Firstly, candidates should be taught as much as possible before baptism, and advantage should be taken of the motive, to impel the inquirers to learn chief truths about Jesus, salvation and the church. They will better persevere and learn before baptism, and if they do not then learn they will never do so, for at baptism their ends will have been accomplished, and then they will have, as they suppose, every reason for every claim they wish to make.

*Teach before baptism.*

(3) Again, discrimination should be made among inquirers; they should be dealt with as individuals, never as a body, and they should be tested before baptism is administered. Many will not continue even to attend church, much less to learn, and many will revert to former pagan usages in any case, so that it is infinitely better to give the most unworthy, time to withdraw before taking on the Christian name rather than after that event.

*Individuals.*

**Fifth Day.**
**Instruction.**

(4) Once more, not a soul should be baptized until he can be provided for with regular instruction and worship—if there be no teacher available, then let the baptism be postponed, for ignorance and heathen customs will not abandon these people because they have received baptism. None of us yet know the exact nature of Christian-heathen still following heathenism and perverting any precious Christian truth spread among them and their community.

**Duty of giving.**

(5) Further, the duty and the pleasure of giving should be inculcated from the first. While yet their wants are urgent they will contribute, and this contributing should be developed—lack here is death to the incipient church. The writer has many a time seen proportionately larger giving by the inquirer than by the Christians. They should therefore at the outset be taught to contribute for teachers, for houses of worship, for the mission, for the Bible and other Societies, and for every good cause.

**Renewal of promises.**

(6) Again, these people should be required to present themselves in public in stated meetings, at fitting times and as frequently as possible, to renew old promises and make new ones. This will kindle a sense of responsibility and develop courage. The writer has found it helpful to so use the time when the new candidate first promises to learn the Gospel—the time of tonsure, for we have uniformity as much as possible in the wearing of the hair,—the reason of baptism and the time to admission to communion; moreover, he would rather increase these stages if he could, for all the church, her institutions and her workings are markedly pedagogical in the case of these people, cultivating them slowly into the Kingdom of Christ.

**Worship.**

(7) In another direction, the usual form of worship ought sometimes to be varied, no matter what that form may be, and this will prevent to some extent the perpetuation of formality which broods like the night-mare over these masses as well as over India.

**Schools.**

(8) In another respect, this whole subject of mass movements, touches heavily on the educational work of missions, which work should be pressed and pushed to supply needed teachers for schools and congregations. Even for the raw, untaught, undisciplined multitudes of inquirers, the more advanced teacher or catechist is the more to be desired, and the upper secondary student does infinitely better work than the upper primary

man, while with the better teachers the sooner and the surer will those multitudes become Christ's children. *Fifth Day.*

(9) Once more, there is the matter of discipline. Slight *Discipline.* nothing. Do all things with dignity. Make no haste. Rebuke every case, study individuals, in successive steps shame, warn, fine, increase fines, send individual letters, call before the church, excommunicate. In a wayward, lower class man, a right motive cannot be touched early in his church life, and he must be moved where best he can, if by any means he shall be saved.

Important points have been omitted under this inquiry of the right line of action, but the main concern is with the inquirer in his relation to instruction, admission into the church, development, discipline, benevolence, Christian organization and work. With the right line of action and the blessings of God there will arise, in the future, churches of great numbers of Christians, both men and women, born out of the filth and degradation of these lower classes, and taking their place with fellow Christians throughout the nations. For the coming of that time there must be wisest method, sacrifices of many lives and ceaseless toil.

## FIRST SPEECH.
### By the Rev. J. HEINRICHS, A. B. M., Vinukonda, Kistna.

The subject of the *Social Condition of the Lower Classes* has already been ably presented in the papers. It will be necessary, however, to make a few additional explanations, in *Mālas and Mādigas.* order to throw some light on the remarks which I wish to make. In the Telugu country, where our mission works, the non-caste people are called Mālas and Mādigas, and form about a fourth part of the population. Some are farmers, others farm-labourers or serfs; while others live by day labour or cooly work. There are also artisans a nong them, for many Mālas are engaged in weaving, and the so-called caste occupation of the *Their occupations.* Mādigas is leather-dressing and shoe-making. Some of these who have landed property are in comparatively comfortable circumstances. I baptized a Māla last year, who is said to possess Rs. 2,000 worth of farm land, cattle and houses. The farmers then rank first in independence, then come the

|  |  |
|---|---|
| Fifth Day. | artisans, next the day-labourers, and last the serfs, who, I think, constitute the larger bulk of the outcastes. |
| Debt. | Debt is common among all classes, but these last are almost sure to be in debt to the farmers for whom they work. This fact makes serfs of them, otherwise they would simply be labourers hired by the year. If one of these becomes a Christian he is likely to be asked to pay up his debts at once. If he can do so, he is free to seek some other work; if he is unable, the farmer can and does cause him great trouble, not infrequently selling his house by auction and leaving him and his family without shelter. The abject poverty of these people is so well known that I need not enlarge on this subject. |
| Debased condition. | In their heathen state these non-caste people live submerged in ignorance, superstition, filth and indifference as to their social improvement. They have not even the consciousness of being ignorant. Superstition is an outgrowth of their heathenism and idolatry. They take to dirt as naturally as we take to cleanliness, and since they know no better they are quite indifferent as to the consequences. It is only after Christianity has come to them that they begin to shake off the shackles with which they were bound for centuries and turn their faces toward higher ideals. Here, then, I think, we can properly discuss the next question: |

1.—*How far are missions called upon to ameliorate this condition?*

As a rule, the endeavours of missionaries to improve the condition of the heathen socially, however loudly that may call for the assistance of the philanthropist, will prove hopeless. All that a missionary can do is to prevail upon the Government to

|  |  |
|---|---|
| Aid of Government. | suppress slavery, the eating of carrion and similar moral evils from which these people are suffering and to aid them in getting possession of land and other means of an independent existence. Their customs and habits are so ancient and sacred to them that they will not abandon them simply because they are told to do so. Appeals to their reason or moral sense are fruitless, for in the majority of cases these people are unreasonable, and their moral sense needs first to be developed in order to be made productive of good. Neither has the missionary time to engage in secular matters, nor cash enough to supply the demands that would be made. |

Only he whom the Son of God makes free is free indeed. **FIFTH DAY.** After Christ has entered the heart of these people and they are made obedient to the Spirit, they will also have faith in the missionary's message and the superiority of his social, moral and religious ideas. They will, on accepting Christ as their Saviour from the sins and evils of this world as well as the everlasting misery of the next, not only learn the Ten Commandments by heart, but try to practise them in their daily lives. They will try to keep the Sabbath holy, endeavour to speak the truth, look upon adultery and bigamy as crimes, will cover their bodies, comb their hair, keep their houses clean and whitewashed, abstain from eating carrion, and do a great many other things which they formerly did not do; and that, not always from personal and religious conviction, but simply because the missionary's religion inculcates these principles and they have faith in him. Thus it will happen that in villages where heathens and Christians live side by side, the latter have on many occasions reaped the practical benefits of their new religion, while the former had to suffer the consequences of their old mode of life. In Ponnaluru, of the Nellore District, ninety Sudras were swept away by cholera last year, while all our Christians living close by escaped.

*Christ can make them free.*

*Cholera.*

If it be true what our religion teaches, that godliness is profitable unto all things having the promise of the life that now is and of that which is to come, there is no reason why missionaries should not try to ameliorate the state of these poor people socially as well as morally and spiritually. To instruct them in the divine arts of Christianity, such as cleanliness, the proper care of the sick, the training of children, the duty of diligence and thrift, &c., is certainly within the domain of our duty toward our fellowmen. This fact that the religion of Christ is practical in all its bearings is one of the striking object lessons which Christianity is constantly setting before the people of India. He would be a madman who deprecates this argument, and a poor missionary who does not avail himself of it. A tidy, clean Christian home, in which the whole family is seen to be better clothed, better fed, whose children are better taken care of and are being educated, to whom better ministry comes in sickness, with the care and attention of the missionary to look after their interests and help them

**Fifth Day.** forward in life, is an object lesson not lost upon their heathen neighbours.

**National customs.** The condition of the people will not be ameliorated by interfering with such national customs as are consistent with the spirit of Christianity. Such habits, however, as the incurring of large debts at marriages, funerals, for tombstones and jewellery should be discouraged. We all like to see the Christians get along well in this world. To help them to get their wrongs redressed and to aid them in acquiring land and the means of an independent livelihood are certainly within the sphere of the missionary's duties. *He should help the people only to help themselves.* A people thus developed will furnish splendid material to build up a self-supporting church in India—an ideal which we are all trying to realize.

**Golden opportunities.** II.—The next inquiry as to *the opportunities it affords for mission work*, can be answered by saying they are golden.

The common people heard the Saviour gladly 1,800 years ago and they do so still to-day. The working of the Gospel in the first centuries was from below upwards, from the slave to the emperor. And it seems to take the same course in India. Not that the richer and more influential caste people are not being reached, but the indications are that the Rajahs and Brahmans and Sudras, as classes, will not become Christian until the lower strata of society have embraced the Gospel.

**Their receptive condition.** The social and political oppression in which they have smarted for centuries has softened their hearts and made them receptive of the Gospel of freedom. Christianity may and does attract them by its material and social rather than by its spiritual and moral aspects at first, but is this to be deprecated on that account? What does it matter, after all, as long as they are attracted and won to Jesus Christ? In many an hour of distress and oft-repeated times of calamity they had been treated by their own people, as the priest and Levite treated the fallen and bleeding traveller; Christianity comes to them now as the good Samaritan. Can we wonder that their hearts are touched? They think that the missionary has influence with Government. In times of famine he was the dispenser of untold good to them. He has kept thousands from starvation, and is always ready to champion the cause of the poor and oppressed. This moral support goes a great way with the Hindus.

*Fifth Day.*

The fact, moreover, that these people have no caste to lose in becoming Christians, affords a golden opportunity for mission work. They will not be ostracized by the caste people if they join our faith any more than they are already, and while they have comparatively little to lose they have much to gain by their change of belief.

*No caste to lose.*

So well is this known that we are not infrequently addressed in the following manner:— "What advantage do I derive from your religion?" "Will you care for my stomach as well as for my soul?" Who will accuse these poorest of the poor for being somewhat concerned about the terrible realities of life? Some of the converts, such as the caste people, often lose their whole possessions and families in becoming Christians, and as for the Mádigas, from which class the majority of our Christians have come, they lose that part of their support which they derive indirectly from their religion.

It is not so important, therefore, to philosophize concerning the motives which bring these people into the fold of the Christian church, as to deal with the fact that they do come, and come in large numbers. We are quite satisfied if God uses what seem to us unworthy or mercenary motives to produce a spiritual result in the long run; and if, perchance, those who at first come for the loaves and fishes should also hunger after the Water and Bread of Life.

III.—*Mass movements towards Christianity more or less arising from it.*

We understand that this social condition favours the reception of Christianity by the depressed classes, and he is the most successful missionary in gathering in large numbers, who espouses the cause of these poor people the most. Those mission-stations where the people have been liberally helped in times of distress and famine have witnessed the largest accessions to their ranks. The mass movement which assumed such large proportions in our mission soon after the famine of 1877 and 1878 extended to what was then known as the Ongole field, embracing Ongole proper, as well as Cumbum, Vinukonda, Narsuraopetta and Bapatta which are now independent mission stations. The statistics as given in our last annual report give

*Statistics.*

21,329 as the number of Christians belonging to Ongole, 8,200 to Cumbum, 6,907 to Vinukonda, 6,202 to Narsuraopetta and 2,546 to Bapatta. All the rest of our stations have less than a thousand members. The largest increase in Ongole took place fourteen years ago, when from the 16th of June 1878 to the end of December of that year 9,606 persons were baptized. That movement has continued with more or less force to the present time and extended to those places which previously formed part of the Ongole field. Cumbum reported 3,239 as received by Baptism in 1891, Ongole 2,140, Vinukonda 867, Narsuraopetta 776, and Bapatta 218. All the rest of our stations had less.

*Fifth Day.*

In speaking of this movement as assuming such large proportions immediately after the last famine, a few facts need to be borne in mind so as not to attribute it wholly or even principally to the famine. (1) And first of all is the fact that the Gospel had been faithfully preached in all those places before mentioned for many years previous to the famine. Since 1866 the missionary with his assistants had visited every town and hamlet of the Ongole field with the preaching of the Word, and since 1870 there had been a wonderful succession of revivals which brought the people in by hundreds, if not by thousands. "It pleased God by the foolishness of preaching to save them that believe," and the famine was used as a corroborative means of bringing in the masses. (2) Dire calamities, such as plagues, fires, floods and famines play an important part in the economy of Providence and enter into the agencies God uses in converting men. The Apocalyptic rider on the white horse, who is represented as going forth with battle-bow and royal crown, "conquering and to conquer," is followed by other riders symbolizing war, famine, pestilence, and these are seen working together with the Gospel for the extension of the Kingdom of Jesus Christ in the earth. (3) In the Ramapatam field, which joins that of Ongole, there was no such general movement, yet over 600 were baptized in the latter half of 1878. In Nellore, where almost as much relief work was done, both in town and villages as was done at Ongole, excepting the contract for the construction of 3½ miles of the Buckingham Canal, the movement was scarcely felt. This is a significant fact if the movement be attributed to famine relief. Ramapatam, according to the last annual report, numbers only 604, and Nellore 646 church members.

*Previous preaching.*

*The Apocalypse.*

*No general rules.*

The movement, once begun, is likely to continue for the following reasons:— *(Fifth Day)*

*First,* a divine reason. He who has begun this good work is likely to continue it. Although I cannot entertain such an extreme view as a few of our missionaries who believe that every one of these thousands have been truly converted through the the agency of the Holy Spirit, I still believe that the Holy Spirit has been and is in the movement. I am unable to comprehend, however, how the Holy Spirit can work on the masses apart from the individual. He did not at Pentecost. The only conclusion, then, at which I can arrive is this: that whereas the Holy Spirit has moved a great many, he had nothing whatever to do with the moving of some. *(Permanence of the movements. Divine reasons.)*

*Second,* human reasons. An important motive which brings the people to us is not their own, but must be credited to the account of those who bring them in. They have been spoken to so long and invited so frequently that they do not see why they should not yield at last. Everybody knows that the Christian's is a good religion. Besides, many of their relations have joined already, or are joining, and among Hindus a movement of any kind carries great weight. They are not willing to lead, but are ready to follow. Indian movements of any importance, whether towards Christianity or in any other direction, are gregarious. It is mainly through family connections that truth wins its way among the Telugus. A person is soon followed by his relatives, and these in turn by their relations in distant villages, till whole communities become obedient to the faith. First, it may be a slow arithmetical progression, two, four, six, when suddenly it changes by leaps and bounds to something akin to a geometrical progression, twelve, twenty-four, forty-eight, &c. *(Human reasons.)*

IV.—*The dangers incident to such movements and the right line of action with regard to them.*

Masses are likely to come in for baptism who may be converted to Christianity and not to Christ; they may have "a mind to become Christians" without having been truly born again. Their Christianity thus becomes one which is acquired and not experienced. I dare not deny that the Holy Spirit is instrumental in inclining their minds toward Christianity, but I fear that in a great many cases he does not get an opportunity to go *(Dangers.)*

much deeper. Thus a nominal and acquired faith is apt to be accepted for one produced by the agency of the Spirit. A formula is easily learnt, and the answers to certain numbers of questions in a catechism are easily committed to memory; but does that constitute New Testament Christianity?

*Baptizing without teaching.*

There is the danger of acting out only the first part of the commission to preach the Gospel to the people and then baptize them, and of forgetting and neglecting the second part—to teach them to observe whatsoever He has commanded us. It is easy and delightful to baptize large numbers, but is harder to be conscientious in acting out the second part of the great commission as well.

*More than can be cared for.*

Another danger will arise if more are received than can be properly cared for. If not gathered into properly organized churches, where they can be spiritually trained and cared for, these masses will form so much dead-weight on our hands.

*A secularized church.*

Then, again, if the people come in from other than spiritual motives the church is in danger of being secularized. There is danger of heathenism living within the pale of the church. It is all right to excuse this state of affairs by saying there was a devil among the twelve disciples and a Simon Magus in the apostolic church, but we should remember at the same time that the first went and hanged himself and the latter was anathematized.

*The right line of action.*

I have hardly time to indicate the right line of action with regard to them. Let me briefly say: The mercenary motive should be discouraged from the beginning. No worldly prospects should be held out as inducements. But we should do our utmost to lift these people up to a higher plane of Christian man and womanhood.

Only persons who are genuinely converted, who are truly born again by the power of the Holy Spirit, who have an experienced, and not an acquired faith in Jesus Christ as the only Saviour from their sin, should be admitted into the church. This is what Baptists regard as a scriptural prerequisite to baptism. This spiritual element will furnish us a proper basis to work out the biblical idea of a Christian church.

And then they should be properly organized into churches, and not be left to idleness and decay in a large mother church. Let new colonies be formed as centres of Christian influence and power.

## SECOND SPEECH.

*Fifth Day.*

By the Rev. J. STONE, C.M.S., Bezwada, Kistna.

It has been my privilege to labour among these lower classes, more or less, for the last 17 years, in the Kistna and Godáveri Districts. It seems to me rather a pity that one of the writers of the papers, and the previous speaker with myself, are all from that part of the mission field, because naturally much of our experience will be the same, and we cannot, therefore, add as much in Conference as we would wish on this great subject. After considering the paper written by Dr. Scudder, and having read a good deal about the movement in Madras, called "The Pariah movement," and other parts, it seems to me that our people have, to some extent, a few privileges which those farther south in India have not. For instance, I remember no case in which a man of lower caste was called upon to step aside and lay down his burden to allow a man of higher caste to pass by; and I think, I may say, that in most of our villages the lower class people are free to come and go as they please, at the same time they are, in the fullest sense of the word, out-castes. They labour under many, many disadvantages, in every way. We find that the sites of their hamlets are very unsuitable and very unhealthy, and that the land is cultivated up to the very walls of the houses, with the result that the whole, during the rice cultivation season, is surrounded by water. I had occasion to go to several of these villages, very recently; and, when I attempted to go, I was told that it was impossible to walk, and impossible for anyone to take me. However, I managed, partly by walking, without boots or stockings, and partly, by being carried, to get to one of these villages. And what a sight met one's eyes! The whole surroundings were one mass of mud and pools of water. Can it be wondered at that we find these people dying off by hundreds, and by thousands, by cholera and other diseases? They have the worst of water, and under no pretence whatever are they allowed to draw water from the village wells: and they are so in the hands of their creditors, that they are liable to be sold out at any time. It is true, that the village schools profess to admit children of these classes, but only with the result that in a short time they have found it too warm for them and have had to leave. Again, we find that in many instances they are not allowed to enter the law courts, or magistrate's courts. I know this statement is at times denied, but I do not make it on hearsay. I speak what I have seen. I have seen over and over again Pariahs and Mâdigas standing outside the magistrate's court and giving their evidence through a window, and more than once, when I have remonstrated with the officials concerned, I have been told that the court was too small to allow them to come inside, when it was large enough to accommodate twice the number of Brahmans or Sudras. Then, again, as to their moral condition. It is most pitiable. As Dr. Scudder says in his paper: "There is scarcely a day in the year, when they are not guilty of breaking most of the Ten Commandments."

But now I wish to pass on to the more important question of how far missionaries are called upon to ameliorate this condition. I would say that a great deal of care and caution is necessary. We need to pray for the guidance of God's Holy Spirit that we may know what to do. We should take care not to present ourselves to these people in a false light, as relieving officers, but as those who are anxious to bring them to Christ. In most cases we should find it quite enough to try to help those who come to us. But the motto that I would adopt is, "Help those who help themselves." I feel, however, we cannot do anything for them without trying to evangelize them, so the first step should be to have real evangelistic service. I have had many, and we know that, especially with a violin and singing, we have no difficulty as a rule in gathering the majority of these people in a hamlet gathered together: and I have thus spent many happy times, often up to 11 o'clock at night, talking and preaching to these people. Our addresses to such should be simple, full of the Gospel, and suitable illustrations. Then again, I would say, we should do all we can to give these people a thoroughly good primary education. We should try to establish schools in every village for these lower classes. I would lay great stress upon night-schools. Many of the young men are willing, after a hard day's work, to go to the night-school, and study two hours or more to improve themselves. In many instances, where I have seen such schools established, they have been attended with the very best results. In one instance, some of the best

*Sidenotes:* Fifth Day. Want of privilege. Moral condition. How to assist them. Evangelize them. Educate them.

evangelists in a mission district were thus prepared and brought into mission work. We should endeavour to teach them all we can concerning their rights as citizens, but at the same time we should press upon them the importance of being loyal and obedient to all in authority.

In an industrial school I think we have a lever amongst the lower classes. Large numbers of children, especially boys, are being educated in our mission schools. Many of them become agents, but all cannot engage in mission work, nor all are fitted for this, although they are educated. If we had technical schools, in which to teach trades to those who did not join any mission, they would be the means of considerably elevating the lower classes. They would teach them to be industrious, and would lead them to independence. Our Christian lads who did not become agents might enter these technical schools, and instead of the various trades being confined, as they are now, to separate castes, we might have our Christian carpenters, and smiths, &c., scattered all over the country, each, we might hope, doing his best, by word and deed, to extend the Saviour's Kingdom in this land. When I first came to the country, it was just in the midst of the famine of 1877-78, and seeing distress all around me, I was most anxious to relieve all I could; but I stand here to-day to say, that from my experience, giving money, or lands, is a great mistake. I have seen the evil of it, and although I have never given away much either in the shape of money or land, yet in nearly every instance, when I did thus give help, the results were most unsatisfactory. If assistance be granted in this way, it must be done with the greatest care and wisdom.

And now passing to what are called the opportunities which this work affords. I say, they are great, they are immense. The lower classes of this country are beginning to realize that it is only through Christianity that they can rise. They feel that missionaries are their friends, and doubtless many enter the Christian Church from no higher motive than "to do better," as they often express it. But even in this way, by careful teaching and the Holy Spirit's help, many have come, and are still coming, to a saving knowledge of the truth, as it is in Jesus.

With regard to mass movements, I have not had much experience. After the famine of 1877-78, we had whole hamlets coming over and putting themselves under Christian

*Fifth Day.*

*Industrial schools.*

*The present opportunities.*

*Mass movements.*

instruction. They were carefully taught, some for one or two years, and a great many of them were then baptized, and have, with very few exceptions, remained faithful. I cannot help thinking that if these classes are assisted more on the lines I have briefly referred to, we shall even have larger accessions to Christianity in our own C. M. S. Mission.

But how are we to guard against the dangers? is a question before us and a most important one. The opportunities are great, but the dangers are great also. There is the danger of people mistaking what Christianity is, and so missing it; there is the danger of many joining the Christian Church from unworthy motives; there is the danger of being satisfied with a low standard of spiritual life, and no effort made to grow in grace and in the knowledge of our Lord Jesus Christ. The dangers, however, have been fully dealt with in the papers, and so I prefer to pass on to the right methods of guarding against such evils. I think we must lay down as a general line of action not to be in a hurry to give baptism to such as come in masses; there must be considerable periods of probation —until they know, and have experienced the truth, as it is in Jesus. There must be continual teaching, rebuking, and exhorting, before they are admitted to communion in the church. We must teach them that they have a cross to bear, a battle to fight, and that it is only through much tribulation they can enter into the Kingdom of God.

The meeting being now open for discussion,—

Rev. A. ANDREW, F. C. M., Chingleput, Madras, said:—I shall confine myself to the first point, "How far are missionaries called upon to ameliorate the condition of these people." I have read the papers written by Dr. Scudder and the others, and must state that with much that is contained in these papers I heartily agree. When I arrived in the mission field I began to study the condition of the people among whom I had come to labour. I soon discovered that there was a condition of things which we missionaries should not tolerate, and so set about doing what I could to ameliorate their condition. I think we missionaries ought to have the true Christ-like philanthropic spirit, and whether the people are Christians or not, we should do all we can for them. I saw that education was practically neglected among the Pariahs, and that, if anything were to be done at all, it would be through missionary agency. I thereupon wrote a letter to the Director of Public Instruction, bringing this to his notice, with the result that a special grant of 50 per cent. was given for each Pariah pupil who passed, in addition to the ordinary grant, and that a building grant of Rs. 25 was to be given in aid for schools erected for this class. This applied to the whole Presidency. Then in 1889 I began—and I believe I was the first to begin it—an investigation of what was called the "Pariah Question." I studied the question, and prepared a statement on it and sent it to the Government through the Collector of the Chingleput district; but nothing was done so far as I know. Then I went home on furlough, and I determined to do something while there. I went straight up to London, and called on Mr. Samuel Smith, and had a long talk with him on the subject. He thereafter introduced me to Sir John Gorst, Under-Secretary of State for India, with whom I had also a long conversation. He was deeply interested and said: "You are the first man who has come in this way and had a talk about the depressed classes in India." He told me he could not initiate anything himself, and could take no action unless it was referred to in Parliament. So I went to Mr. Smith, who laid the case before Parliament, and Sir John Gorst answered. As a result of this a dispatch was sent from the Secretary of State on this very question calling upon the Government of Madras to do whatever they could for the amelioration of this people. About simultaneously with my action at home, the Madras Missionary Conference sent a memorial on the same subject to the Madras Government. What has been the result of all this? A great deal. Some say that the Government of Madras has done nothing, but I am confident that it has done a great deal. It has given an order that certain lands, which have fallen into the hands of Government through the failure of the land-holders to pay the land tax, shall be put in a separate register, and that grants of this land may be given to respectable Pariahs who are cultivators. Of this land there are fifteen hundred acres available in the Chingleput district. And further, if any one will dispute the claim of any Pariah thus put in possession of this land, the Government says: "We will defend you in the Courts of Justice." Besides, village and house sites are to be granted wherever they are required, and education is to be on a generous scale. And lastly, any contract of slavery or of bond-service is null and void, and voidable at pleasure. The bond-servant or slave can run away and nothing can be done to him.

Mr. W. H. CAMPBELL, M.A., B.D., L. M. S., Cuddapah, said:—How far are missionaries called upon to ameliorate the condition of these people? They are for the most part miserably poor; they are unable to acquire land or to practice any handicraft which would enable them to rise into a position of independence; they are, as you have been told, in many cases, debarred from entering the courts of justice or walking along the public

*Fifth Day.*

The Pariah question.

Personal influence.

Government action.

Poverty.

**Fifth Day.**

**A new life.**

streets, and they are treated by their social superiors with a contempt and scorn which cannot fail to degrade and depress. The great and significant fact for us is that a new life has entered into this people. They are no longer content to remain ignorant and degraded; they believe that the time has come to improve their condition and assert their rights; they appeal to us in Christ's name for sympathy and help. Some brethren look on this movement with something akin to fear and suspicion, and dread any action which would tend to make the people discontented with their lot. I have no sympathy with such timid doubters. Our Lord Jesus Christ took up no such position. Where there is injustice and oppression His message is not a message of peace but of war; He came "not to send peace but a sword." As Christian men and women, above all, as Christian missionaries, we are bound to do all that lies in our power to help these people to throw off their bondage. The people will not rest content in their present state; of that you may be assured. In one part of the country at least they are discontented with their lot and resolved to better it. I do not believe that Government interference, or even missionary assistance, can solve this problem. "Who would be free themselves must strike the blow." The great work for us is to

**Prepare them.** prepare the people for the struggle which must inevitably arise, so that they may enter upon it with no low evil motives, but as Christian men whose only desire is to obtain what is just and right. We can do much to prepare them, and to help them to assert their rights. We can do this in many ways,— by helping

**Many ways of helping.** them to take up Government waste land, by teaching them useful arts and industries which will make them, to a great extent, independent of their richer neighbours, by giving them a good elementary education, which is one of the best means of preparing them to occupy a higher and more honourable position in the land. But all these are only subsidiary. The one and only power that can really elevate these poor ignorant people is the Gospel of Christ. If we lead them to the Saviour He will make them free.

The Rev. J. E. DAVIS, B.A., C. B. M., Coconada, Madras. said:—I have been very much interested in this subject. A great deal has been said about the lower classes and the diffi-

**Why Missionaries can reach them.** culties of elevating them. There is one thing that comes home to me more than all else, and it is this: that the Missionary Societies are the only ones who can reach and elevate the depressed classes in the true sense of the word. The work is too uninviting for others to enter the field. We have not far to look in the Missionary's *Guide Book* (the New Testament) before we find attention drawn to the depressed classes. When the disciples of John were sent to ask Jesus whether He was the true Messiah or should they look for another, we read that

"In that very hour He healed many of diseases, and said: 'Go tell John that the blind receive their sight, the lame walk, the lepers are cleansed,'" the depressed classes are being cared for. This will assure John that I am not of this world, for he knows that kings and princes are not attracted to these classes. Again, Luke iv. 18: "The Spirit of the Lord God is upon me." Why? How do I know that it is not some other spirit? "because He has annointed me to preach the Gospel to the poor" (the depressed classes). Let us away with human philosophy about this matter. The precept and example of our Master settles the whole question. We will prove ourselves followers of Jesus Christ in proportion as we sympathise with the depressed classes and seek to lift them up. The whole need not a physician, but they that are sick. We cannot expect to see many converts from among the Brahmans until the Pariahs are gathered into the fold of Christ. We must not try to reverse God's order: "The first *shall be* last and the last *shall be* first." I believe the people who are lowest down have God's great heart going out to them most, and while I rejoice that God in His wisdom and power is able to save the educated proud Brahman, I also rejoice that the ignorance and filth of the lowest down-trodden Pariah is not sufficient to keep him out of the Kingdom of God. The Lord knew that every man could not receive a college education, and He made the plan of salvation so simple that a wayfaring man, though a fool, need not err therein. I would not say anything against the educational missionary. Every missionary does some educational work, or else he does not fulfil the whole commission. What we need to do for the lower classes is, first to make them disciples and then gather them into little churches and shepherd them. We should also provide them with primary schools and make them as efficient as possible. We must first reach them through their hearts and then instruct them. They do not grow in a day. All growth is gradual, but life is instantaneous. Let us be sure we have the Christ-life and God will help us to develop it. It is quite possible to develop the carnal mind which is at enmity against God, and is not subject to the law of God, neither, indeed, can be. There are no mushrooms nor oaks in the Kingdom of God, but *new creatures in Christ Jesus.* There has been too much said about some kinds of work being done for the present and some for the future. I wish to expose that fallacy. Any work that is not done for the present will not be done for the future; and any real work done for the *present* cannot help being full of possibilities for the future. God will hold us responsible for giving the Gospel to this generation and not future generations. Therefore let us work for the present generation. Some feel discouraged about the lower classes and cry, 'caution! caution!' What we need

*Marginalia:* Fifth Day. Our Lord's example. Every Missionary an Educationalist. The present and the future.

*Fifth Day.*

is to be sure we are working along the line of God's eternal purposes, and then there will be no room for discouragement. We need our vision clarified that we, like the prophet Isaiah, may see the end from the beginning, and cry out He shall not fail nor be discouraged till He hath set judgment in the earth and the Isles shall wait for His law. In the day when Christ makes up his jewels there will be no difference whether men have come out of the colleges or from the scum of the earth, for the Lord Jesus will change them and stamp them all with His likeness. Let us give ourselves to this work with all the power of our being and God will lift them up.

*A poor sweeper-boy.*

The Rev. N. E. LUNDBORG, Secretary, S. E. L. M., Saugor, C. P., said:—I have heard so many good things said about this subject, that it may be counted unnecessary to say any more about it; but I beg to be allowed to say a few words *to plead for the depressed classes*: certainly they are depressed; they are hated; they are very much abominated by the higher classes. I have in my charge a mission school. I might well say that the lower classes are not so depressed, as a speaker just now described them, in the South of India; still you may judge yourself of how abominated they are by a story I am now going to tell you. The above-mentioned mission school was well furnished, not only with all necessary school materials, but also with a staff of five able teachers, *one* of them being a Christian, as I had no more suitable Christians to place there. My fellow missionary, the Rev. L. E. Karlsson, had once taken care of a promising sweeper-boy, who wanted to learn. He taught him himself to begin with; but afterwards he one day asked me if I would permit the boy to enter the mission school. "Well," I said, "he is most welcome, because the school is for all." The same day I asked the schoolmasters if they were willing to teach a sweeper-boy. They all joined in saying that they certainly were most willing to do so; but, they said, "All the boys will run away." "No matter," said I, "I only ask if *you* are willing to teach?" About this, there was a long discussion, the end of which was that they all agreed. On a said day the poor sweeper-boy entered the mission school, and as soon as he had entered, the whole school, 150 boys and five schoolmasters, absconded. By this they thought to do away with the school altogether; but, thanks to the Lord, it was soon re-opened; but *none* of the former schoolmasters received back again. By this it is easily seen how much the lower classes are despised here. I ought to mention that the above said act, namely, their running away, was brought about not by the boys, but by the very schoolmasters who had promised to teach the sweeper. They were all of higher castes. They took the boys and formed a new school; but as *none* would pay for it, they themselves absconded one after another. They prayed me to take them back, but in vain.

The Rev. H. U. WEITBRECHT, Ph. D., C.M.S., Batala, Panjab, said:—Our experience in the Panjab, as compared with what we have heard to-day from South India, shows that there are considerable local variations in the condition of the depressed classes. We cannot say, in the Panjab, that our Government is indifferent to their wants and hardships: on the contrary, it has an open eye for them, and it is ready to assist missionaries in efforts for the amelioration of their condition, especially by liberal grants for low caste schools. I have found, too, ready help from Muhammadans and Hindu school inspectors in promoting low caste education. Still their condition is bad enough. How can we improve it? I take it that, generally speaking, the missionary who work among these people, will have his hands full enough in caring for them spiritually (which I take to include proper education) without assuming the rôle of a social elevator. There is, however, one thing which has not been mentioned this morning on which I am inclined to lay stress, that is, the work to be done among these classes by the medical missionary. He may, and should do, a great deal to improve their condition in coming generations. Multitudes of them die off like flies, from preventible causes, and for one reason or another they are not much helped by Government medical relief. Again, as to the dangers which exist in guiding the movements among the low castes. They are many and great; and some speakers have laid stress on the need for caution, while others have advocated the need of moving forward with the stream. But why should we not combine courage and caution, energy and wariness? The Lord cure our one-sidedness. If there are dangers, why, then,

> Let courage rise with danger
> And strength to strength oppose,

for we have the strength of Christ on our side. Yet we recognise the dangers, and to obviate them I cannot do better than summarise the counsels embodied by Dr. Uhl in his paper:—(1) Teach carefully before baptism: (2) Discriminate carefully among inquirers; admit them as individuals, not as bodies: (3) If no teacher is available, postpone baptism: (4) From the first teach them to give, and see that they keep it up: (5) Use preparatory stage of initiation or catechumenate, before baptism: (6) Exercise effective discipline. These movements are a great opportunity; missionaries of every kind may help in using it. Our educated Indian brothers who favour the National Congress for the advancement of their country have a magnificent opportunity to help in the emancipation of 50,000,000 of their countrymen enslaved by oppression or barbarism. If the church of Christ fail to draw them in, they

*Fifth Day.*

Government co-operation.

Medical missions.

Courage and caution.

| | |
|---|---|
| Fifth Day. | will drift in other directions. Let us unite our best efforts to bring them in! |
| | The Rev. J. L. PHILLIPS, M.A., M.D., LL.B., S. S. U., |
| The blind. | Calcutta, said:—There seems to be a good opening here for saying a word in behalf of the blind, of whom it is said we have not less than two hundred and fifty thousand in India. Mr. Knowles, of the London Mission in South Travancore, was hoping to be with us and call our attention to this subject, but he has been prevented from coming, so at his request I will say, what I am sure cannot fail of interesting all of you, that a new and better way of teaching the blind to read is now before us, and it is rapidly commending itself to specialists in this line |
| The Braille system. | of work. I refer to the Braille system, now known and adopted in France, England, and the United States, and for obvious reasons a great improvement upon the old Moon system. Mr. Knowles gave a pretty full account of this new system in the last October number of the "India Sunday School" Journal, from which I am able to give you a few points. He terms it "a very simple and inexpensive method by which blind children can be taught to read and write, either in English or in any or all of the Indian languages." Mr. Knowles explained the method to me several months ago when I was at his station, and having seen it tried there I am quite prepared to believe all he says concerning it. He says:—"All that is wanted to begin with is a simple writing frame which can easily be made for two or three rupees, or it can be bought ready made from the British and Foreign Blind Association, 33 Cambridge Square, London, W. This and some stiff brown paper is all that is necessary, and after the blind child has been taught to read, he can easily be taught to write out books for his own use, |
| Method. | or for the use of others." In brief, I may say that this is a plan of reading by means of raised dots on stiff paper, felt by the tips of the fingers, and all letters are made by various combinations of these dots. Sixty-two combinations represent all the letters or sounds of our Indian languages. The blind learn |
| Music. | music, too, and concerts are given by them by means of this system. I may only add that the Rev. J. Knowles, Martandam, South Travancore, or N. L. Garthwaite, Esq., M. A., of Kolar, Madras, will be glad to give you further particulars, and to send you specimens of the Braille system as adapted to our |
| Save them from mendicancy. | vernaculars. Let us begin in good earnest teaching the blind children to read and write. It is for these blind boys and girls that I am chiefly interested. We must save them from a life of mendicancy, and let us hope that many of them now begging bread from door to door will become true shining Christians and teachers of others equally afflicted. Seven centuries before the Messiah came Isaiah wrote:—"*Then the eyes of the blind shall be opened*," and if you read the fourth and fifth verses of the |

eleventh chapter of Matthew's Gospel, you will see by whom that prophecy was fulfilled. In His name I plead for these blind little ones of our streets, for "to open the blind eyes" was a part of His mission, Whose servants we are.

FIFTH DAY.

The Rev. J. PARSON, W. M. S., Dilkusha, Lucknow, said:—I have had for some years a little experience in working among the lower classes. I have had the advantage of working in two distinct provinces, and have been able to compare the condition of the lower classes in one province with their condition in another. In Oudh, besides working among the higher castes, I have laboured among Chamars, Pasis and Sweepers. In the Central Provinces I have spent months among Gonds, Kols and Chamars. I found a great difference between the social and religious condition and accessibility of the lower classes of the Central Province and those of Oudh. After this I was prepared to find great dissimilarity in their condition in the various provinces of India. Last week in this city, in our own Conference, composed of men representing most of the provinces of India, we threshed out this subject. In the course of our discussion we began to understand, as many of us never understood before, the differences and divergences in the condition of the many tribes and castes of the various provinces. We gathered that the condition of the Pariahs in the Madras Presidency is without a parallel in any other parts of India. The Pariahs are a special class, and work for their elevation needs to be carried on on special lines. Work among them seems to bear much the same relation to ordinary mission work among the lower classes that work among the slums of East London, where religious and social forms of work need to go hand in hand, bears to ordinary evangelistic work among the masses in England. We shall make a mistake if we attempt to introduce what is suitable for one field of labour into another for which it is altogether unsuited. The lower classes in many parts of India do not require much material aid; they require the Gospel of Christ.

Oudh and C. P.

The Pariahs.

The Rev. C. B. WARD, M. E. C., Yellandu, said:—In the part of the country from which I come, I believe that these people are by no means so numerous as they are further south, and their disabilities are not so great perhaps. There is reason to think that they gain something from the Muhammadan country, and the Muhammadans rather like to take the starch out of the Brahmans. And yet there are a great many and they suffer many disabilities. One especially is financial oppression. In the matter of getting the benefits of what they grow, they suffer great disabilities. The tax imposed by the Government is not so great, but it must be collected by somebody, and that person must get his support, and so it becomes burdensome. Then they suffer from the police. These men get about half as much pay as they can live on and they must pick up the rest from the people. I have been somewhat beyond the limits of the Nizam's Dominions, and I have seen something that these people have to suffer. There is a street in Badra Chellam over which no low caste man once was allowed to walk, and it was not until some enterprising person entered the place recently and took his servants with him over this street that the Brahmans yielded the point. In some places where I have been the heart of these people was filled with hope. I have noticed that in the Nizam's Dominions there is a feeling that from some source or other, from some where, help will come. But I would like to call attention to another most needy accessible people, certainly of this class. I refer to the aboriginals. Sir William Hunter some months ago read a profoundly interesting paper before the Indian Section of the Society of Arts in London, of which the following is a part:—" After 4,000 years of occupancy, it has not yet by any means closed up its assimilation of aboriginal tribes." And, according to Sir William Hunter, there are still in India fifty millions of human beings lying outside or barely inside the pale of orthodox Hinduism and Islam. Here, he holds, is the line of least resistance, along which the church is called to regard it as her principal immediate duty to advance. He says: " I believe that within fifty years these fifty millions will be absorbed into one or other of the higher faiths, and that it rests in no small measure with Christian England, whether they are chiefly incorporated into the native religions or into Christianity." This shows, as Sir Wm. Hunter remarks, that Christianity in India has a vast area of extension opened before it, even if it should for an indefinite length of time lessen the numbers, or even stay the advance of Hinduism and Muhammadanism. One-fifth of the people of India is a prize worth trying for, even according to the canons of ordinary probability. I was 43 days in Bastar last year, and such open, accessible, poor, naked people I have never seen or heard of in India. Day after day they heard us with deepest interest. We found them everywhere in a state of expectancy. From some source they look for help. If Sir Wm. Hunter be right, as we believe he is, the Church of Christ should promptly, vigorously and worthily give these poor aboriginals attention.

The Rev. J. E. PADFIELD, B.D., C. M. S., Masulipatam, South India, said:—There are two or three points of practical importance that I should like to emphasize in regard to the whole subject of the lower classes. Some of these remarks may perhaps bear more particularly upon one or two phases of the question that have been discussed at other meetings, but as I had not then an opportunity of expressing my opinion, I do so on the present occasion. In the first place, I would say, that I think it would be doing very serious harm if it were to go forth, as in any way; the desire of this Conference to lower the standard for baptism. Much that has been said at various meetings would imply some such notion, and I am sorry to say that experience shows the great need of caution here. With some missionaries it seems to be the rule to baptize upon a confession of faith, and I fear this is too often done when such confessions are mere empty words. I could at any time baptize whole groups of Pariahs if I were content with such a standard, but I believe that there can be no true saving faith that is not founded upon knowledge, and, considering the dense ignorance of the classes in question, such knowledge can only be acquired after a period of patient teaching and learning. As regards the mission with which I am personally connected, I have noticed that in the case of relapses into hertheuism, the cause has very often been the too hasty reception into the church by baptism. Another point I would mention is that one of the chief things that keeps down the lower classes and prevents their rising from their abject condition is the terrible curse of *debt*; and this applies not only to the heathen, but also to the Christian portion of these people. Here, then, is a matter that I think we should take seriously in hand. It is time that something were done to stop this terrible evil that is working such harm even in the Christian church. One phase of the evil that I would more particularly emphasize, is that our Christian Agents are so much infected with it. I think it will be universally found that few Agents are free from debt; and that often to the people under their charge or to the heathen amongst whom they are placed to labour. If the Agents are so lax in this matter, what can be expected of their people? One point to which we might direct our attention is the foolish expenditure at marriages. Our people, in imitation of their heathen neighbours, expend money at marriages out of all proportion to their means, and, to do this, a young couple will contract a debt that is a weight about their necks for their whole lives. As long as this is so universally the case we never can expect to get a self-supporting church. Last year in a village, in the mission district under my charge, and where the congregation has been founded some 25 years, the Christians expended some hundreds of rupees in foolish waste at their weddings, whilst the utmost that could be extracted from them for the support of their church was about twenty-five rupees. Ought these things so to be? Surely, some united action might be taken to put a stop to this evil at least, or to confine it within more reasonable bounds! and this is a matter that might well be taken in hand by each and all of us here assembled. With regard to the question of extending higher education to the lower classes, especially our Chris-

**Fifth Day.**

**Pariahs.**

**Exaggeration of motives.**

tians, I think but little can be done by special legislation or by a forced action of any kind. This is a question that will solve itself, and that is solving itself in a natural manner; any forcing of matters will only do harm. Many years ago when I had charge of a High School we admitted several Christian youths of Pariah origin and my school was immediately emptied. A rival school was formed, and for nearly a year I had little but empty benches, but firmness prevailed in the end, and the battle was won once for all as far as that school was concerned. The present head of that school told me some time ago, when alluding to this matter, that it was no uncommon sight to see a Brahman school-boy walking through the compound with his arm round the neck of a Christian Pariah school-fellow. Christians of any other caste or station are free to enter any of the schools or colleges in our Telegu Mission and the lower classes are availing themselves of the privilege in gradually increasing numbers.

The Rev. W. B. SIMPSON, U. M. S., Tiruvallur, Chingleput District, Madras, said:—There is an idea spreading throughout our villages, of which Mr. Tremenheer's report, previously referred to, is an evidence that the missionary is the real friend of the poor people, and we ought to take advantage of it; for, if we do not, the opportunity will go. When the Pariah has become a recognised factor, other bids will be made for his friendship and support. Indeed, I have myself seen a professed ascetic, accompanied by men and women of high caste, entering into the houses of Pariahs and using all their influence and persuasion to prevent them from becoming Christians. Lately, moreover, an association of wealthy Pariahs in Madras, called the "Ancient Dravidian Association" has been formed, which, under the influence of other Hindus, has refused the right of entrance to Christian members. It is a great mistake to exaggerate the motives under which these people come to Christianity, and to describe them in the devout spiritual language which we use in speaking of home churches. At its best, it is but the response to kindness, a fairly clear sense of material progress and a divine sense of moral progress. The Pariah has little theology outside his stomach, and small blame to him for that, since he has to work incessantly to put anything into it at all. One does find in individual cases men who are independent, who are landed proprietors, and who are keenly alive to the advantages of education. A few, through intimate personal relations, may also come from higher motives, but in the vast majority of cases such classes come because their material progress lies in the path of Christianity. Nevertheless, frankly recognising this, it is quite possible to use it as a beginning to work up to results altogether higher and of a different kind. General mass movements bring us face to face with a very serious question—must missionary Societies take the place of the caste man? The Pariahs are not provident, and always restricted in their means. Whenever there is a wedding, funeral or any other domestic ceremony, the caste man steps in and lends him money. Sometimes he is friendly; sometimes he is oppressive; but the borrower is always left in his power. Now if we are prepared to decline mass movements and are content to baptize in very small numbers, we can refuse to meddle in any such transactions; but if there are signs that the masses are moving, and we do urgently need mass movements, we cannot evade the responsibility. It is easy to urge difficulties and objections, but the complete answer is that in many cases this only can create the possibility of freedom of action. Fifth Day.<br>Care needed.

It is not our business to foment disturbances between the caste and non-caste man, to tell the latter that Jack is as good as his master, and in future Jack can be a gentleman. By all means cultivate friendly relationships with the caste masters wherever it is possible. Disabuse their minds of the fear of a universal strike and spirit of insubordination; but there will remain many cases in which the only way to save the non-caste man is to fight the caste tyrant by taking from him the power of starving his slave into submission. Help must, therefore, be given with great caution; re-payment of loans should be rigidly insisted upon, if necessary, even in a court of law. But the main thing to be attended to is that evangelistic and teaching agencies must be kept in thorough and constant operation. If these people are constantly taught, not so much Christian formulas as Christian truth, other difficulties will right themselves. With one more suggestion I close, and that is, that in every station where there are considerable numbers of low-caste people, a primary boarding school should be established in which as many of the children as possible should be gathered. This I consider absolutely vital to anything like real Christian life in future generations. Boarding schools.

The Rev. J. A. Graham, M.A., E. C. S., Kalimpong, Darjeeling, told a story of a young Scotch minister who, fresh from college, permanently ruined his influence in his new parish by asking a farmer if he were "leading in" on a day when the "stooks" were dripping wet. The inference from the story was that missionaries should be like ministers at home, in intelligent touch with the social interests of his people. At Kalimpong the population could not be called the "Depressed Classes." They were chiefly fairly well-to-do ryots, but with no rich class among them. As in most other districts in India, Debt was a curse. The mission could not do anything to remedy this so long as its own agents were in debt, and the general testimony was that few missions in India were not hampered in this way. It was intolerable that good people in the low The Scotch Minister.<br><br><br><br><br><br>Debt.

**FIFTH DAY.**

countries should deny themselves to send money, not for the catechist's family, but for the pockets of the money-lender. At Kalimpong the whole of the agent's debts had been paid (not with mission money)—every month their salaries had been judiciously "cut"—and now the majority of them were free men. And a rule had been made *by themselves that, whoever after his debts has been paid, contracts debt should be immediately dismissed from the mission service.* The result repays a thousandfold the effort bestowed on the subject, and now the mission will be in a position to help its own converts and the whole population regarding debt. Mr. Graham also told of other efforts made to assist the whole farming class through the introduction of silk, agricultural exhibitions, medical work, &c., &c. The mission did all it could to help the Government to carry out schemes for the benefit of the district. In doing so, the missionaries got at the sympathies of the people in a way they could not otherwise do, and broke down that barrier of suspicious opposition which naturally meets those going to a new district to preach Christ. It is a mistake to confine our help to the mission converts. They get "coddled" and the heathen are not won.

*Industries.*

The Rev. J. McLaurin, D.D., A. B. M., Bangalore, said:— There are just two or three points of which I wish to speak. The first is with reference to what should be required of them before receiving them to baptism—or what with us amounts to the same thing—receiving them into fellowship in the churches. I believe some knowledge of the Lord Jesus Christ as fundamentally necessary. I do not say how much, but at least a consciousness of their own need and a knowledge of the Lord as a Divine Saviour. I do not think they need know much about the character or attributes of the triune God or of the details of the scheme of Redemption. The "teaching all things" comes afterwards. If a person gives me credible evidence that he is trusting in the Lord Jesus Christ, I am bound to baptize him or receive him; second, I do not believe the Lord ever did or ever will send more of these people than we can care for. And I protest with all my might against the thought of keeping these poor people out in the midst of the vile heathenism about them, simply because the churches are too lazy or too stingy to properly care for them. I believe the Lord has sent more into Ongole field than the American Baptist Churches have adequately cared for, and I believe that the apparent decline in a great many cases is due to that circumstance. Another point is this matter of probation. You will understand from what I have said that I do not much favour it—I have tried probation. I have found that if a man wishes to deceive me, he will very soon find out that he is on trial, and then he will behave himself just as long as I am

*Amount of knowledge.*

*Probation.*

prepared to keep him on probation. I believe it is our duty to take these men and women into our churches as soon as they have given us evidence of having passed from death unto life, and not before.

The Rev. L. L. UHL, PH. D., A. L. M., Guntur, Madras, writer of one of the papers, said in reply:—It has been declared here to-day of the depressed classes that, if they become Christians, the Brahmans and other classes will be left without support and will be compelled to come in also. I must dissent from this statement, as the Brahmans are not dependent on the Pariahs, but on the Sudras, so that, as far as support is concerned, the higher in conjunction with the middle classes, may not be in the least affected by the conversion of the lower. I must say here that, while working for the lower classes and certain of ultimate success among them, I shall never be satisfied with this work alone. We must press our work among the middle classes, and only when these are led to Christ will the Brahmans and higher classes be left dependent and compelled to seek the Christian faith. The question of the relative difficulty of educational and of district work has been raised. I have engaged in both spheres of labour, and out of courtesy to my brethren of the institutions of learning, I must say they have the greater difficulties in many respects. The educational work is more demanding on the physical energies and the emotional nature. The district work among the churches has its supreme difficulty in the ignorance of the people, in a worry from their many requests, and in an anxiety arising from constant planning to improve them. I recall especially the relief I once felt, after a year of busy tours on horseback among the churches when, on taking the train from our station to Madras and passing some villages, I could feel a release from the clamours and importunities of the people who could not then run after me and present their many wants. As to the nature of the work among this people, I think there is much mistaken notion. The speakers were correct who said, "it is slow," "it requires dogged persistence." Then the results are not what they appear to be on the surface. Brethren are led to have too high an opinion of these Christian people from what they see and hear of them without going into inquiries about their whole lives—this is my judgment. Some one has said, to-day, that the poor appreciate the Gospel as the rich do not. This is true in America or in England, where the poor understand the Gospel and discriminate what its fruit is, but the poor in this land see only the physical benefits, do not understand the Gospel, and cannot appreciate its mental, moral, and spiritual results. I would emphasize what one brother said about the control of these people coming over from the degraded classes—"Here thorough organization is needed."

FIFTH DAY.

Effect on the higher castes.

Education.

Organization.

FIFTH DAY.

What another speaker said is equally important—" There must be continuity in the work." Yes, indeed, there will be no fruit, no church, no future, without complete organization and sustained work among the lower classes gathered into our churches. There must be no failure here, and I often wish I had more skill in organizing. We have heard to-day the statement, " Hundreds or thousands of these people have been baptized ;" and I wish to make an observation about the different usages in the admission of these people into the church. There are two entirely different views and practices on the subject—one of speedy baptisms, the other of baptisms after long probation. These two principles enter as chief factors into all methods of, and into all results from, work among these people. With one division of missionaries baptism is considered as the entrance to Christian life and to the church ; with another division it is regarded as a means of grace and a sealing ordinance to be cautiously administered after long probation. The one baptizes an individual on his own confession ; the other only after the candidate has deserved the confidence of others. These two methods of work must be kept in mind, as we hear and read these reports of accessions by hundreds and thousands. I desire to add here, however, my sincere conviction that, in a greater or less degree, there is a fearful truth in one brother's statement about " the prostitution of baptism," and I believe that among these degraded classes the ordinance is mostly received without an appreciation of its holy nature, whether in the case of those more speedily, or in the case of those more tardily, baptized. Such is the profound ignorance of the degraded classes and the nature of their minds. I call attention to the unanimity of opinion as to the magnitude of the work among these people. Speakers have called this opportunity " immense," " golden," and I point out that not only is the subject of the Pariah a prominent topic now, but work among these degraded classes is attracting the attention of the whole church and of the world, and is rapidly becoming a preeminent feature of missionary effort. However, neither this nor any other one work should assume supreme importance, for missionary labour should be a balanced, thorough and all-round work. Nevertheless, the special work under discussion will reach still larger proportions, and will call for a still larger share of attention. Referring to the condition of these people, speakers have given us a very different account from the different quarters of India. It would be extremely interesting to make the subject a matter of thorough study and inquire into the causes of the different social conditions of one and the same class. On the whole, there is a consensus of opinion that the condition of these people is far worse in South than in North India. And now a few words as to the results of

*The prostitution of baptism.*

*South worse than North.*

Christian efforts among these classes. Brethren have said, "these people are cleaner," "they try not to lie," "they come for bread, but get the Bread of Life," "they do not commit adultery." Now I doubt these general statements. I have lived and worked long among these people, and I find a vast amount of lying, deception, adultery and uncleanness. They do not understand that salvation means deliverance from lying, quarrelling and licentiousness. Do they get the Bread of Life, though coming for bread only? I say yes, some get it, others will get it by and bye, but most of them will get it in their children in the generations to come. We as missionaries are imposed upon by these people, because of our hopes and expectations. Time fails me to speak of other matters.

One speaker wished to know how many of the 21,000 which Mr. Heinrichs reported as belonging to the Ongle field had gone back. In reply, Mr. Heinrichs said that, though they had kept a careful record of those who had been excluded, there were not known to him more than one hundred who had gone back last year.

*Fifth Day. Unsatisfactory result.*

## XIV.—MISSIONARY COMITY.

### AFTERNOON SESSION.
LARGE HALL—2 TO 4·30 P. M.

The Rev. G. W. OLVER, B.A., W.M.S., Secretary, London, *in the chair.*

A passage of Scripture was read by the Rev. J. P. Jones, and prayer was offered by the Rev. W. B. Simpson.

### FIRST PAPER.*

By the Rev. A. CLIFFORD, M. A., C. M. S., Calcutta.

INTRODUCTION.—Comity is rather an academic term. It, perhaps, may not be altogether superfluous in so mixed an assembly as this to remind ourselves that it is simply a translation of a Latin word which means friendliness, civility, courteousness.

When that has been said, it may be thought by some strange that it should be necessary to connect it with such an adjective as "Missionary." We are disposed to ask: Must there not be somewhat of redundancy here? May we not almost say that "Mission" and "Missionary" include in themselves the idea of *comity*, *i.e.*, what is courteous—friendly?

To that question we may certainly answer, Yes. The ideal mission cannot be other than a courteous body, the ideal missionary cannot be other than a friendly man. That is true. Sobered experience teaches us, however, that though it is disastrous to let our ideals slip, it is wise not to count too much

---

*The following paper was read before the Calcutta Missionary Conference in 1890. The writer has been asked to revise it with a view to its being used as one of the introductory papers at the Decennial Conference. On looking through it, however, he finds that it is so full of reference to the particular occasion which called it forth, *viz.*, the appearance of Bishop Thoburn's paper on the same subject in the *Harvest Field*, that it would be of little use to revise it, unless revision is to mean a complete re-writing of it. On the whole, therefore, he thinks it best that if it is to re-appear again, it should be in its original form. Dr. Thoburn, it is hoped, will forgive the repeated references to his name.—A. C.

upon men, and bodies of men, always behaving quite ideally. If we expect perfection, our credulity will sooner or later, probably, receive a rude shock, and our excessive optimism may be transformed into a still more exaggerated disgust. The fact is that *Missionary* is after all but a species of the genus *Man*. Even when we are dealing with good men, Christian men, we are still not allowed to forget the sage saying that "there is a good deal of human nature about man." The Old Adam is, we may well believe, crucified in the missionary, but he sometimes struggles not a little before he is made an end of. Nor does the wisdom of the new man become fully grown in him in a day. Our own experience must tell us *that*; and if we want to know why this Conference, which is, thank God, in itself a standing witness to the reality of Christian unity and brotherhood, should yet think it desirable to spend an hour or so in the discussion of the subject which is before us now, we may probably find a sufficient reply, if we go into the confession-box of our own heart, and each one of us ask himself whether the feelings which make for comity have always held complete sway there. There may be failing in the man, if there is failing in one thought of his heart. There may be failing in the body of men, if there is failing in one individual. While, therefore, we hold fast to the highest ideals of missionary character, and aim at the noblest standards, prudence bids us keep our eyes open, and though we may pray for human perfection, not to be too supermundane to recognise the expediency of some *ad interim* arrangement which assumes that it is coming rather than come.

FIFTH DAY.

The question before us now is: How can we best secure that missions and missionaries shall live and act up to their ideal of comity, and in their relations one to the other, be always just, courteous and friendly, and never grasping, inconsiderate and jealous.

How to act up to the ideal.

Now the difficulties which have from time to time arisen have, we cannot blind our eyes to the fact, been much aggravated by the great variety of organization which exists among Protestant Christians. If, instead of being split up into a dozen bodies, we could but do our work as one disciplined force, animated by one great plan, which had been matured in, and which might be modified by, mutual counsel, nine-tenths of the occasions for

**Fifth Day.**

clashing which now occur would probably be non-existent. However, I do not allude to our divisions in order to discuss them, but only to recognize them as unhappily part of an existing state of things which we may regret, and which we may seek to remedy, but which obviously cannot be immediately done away with, and, therefore, must be taken into account and made the best of.

The actual state of things is that this Indian Mission field is being worked by a considerable number of church bodies and societies, all of which have certain peculiarities of organization, or dogma, or custom, to which they attach importance, and which, however much they may desire to subordinate them to the great elementary principles of the Gospel which all hold in common, they still feel to be of sufficient moment to make it at least desirable that their converts should adopt them too. The problem is how, under these circumstances, to promote a working harmony among all these different sections of the missionary army.

**Alternate methods.**

II. ALTERNATIVE METHODS OF MISSION COMITY.—In a very able paper on the subject of Missionary Comity,* which was written for our Conference, and which one cannot but greatly regret was not read before it, Bishop Thoburn has expounded to the Christian public two alternative methods for the furtherance of missionary harmony. One represents what he calls the traditional doctrine, the other a doctrine which he would substitute for it. I need, I believe, make no apology for referring somewhat in detail to that paper now. It would, indeed, be hardly pardonable in me were I *not* to refer to it. Whether we agree with its conclusions or not, all will feel thankful that such a remarkably clear and vigorous statement of an important view of the case has been put forth. The traditional view, as Bishop Thoburn states it, is substantially as follows:—Let each non-Christian country be mapped out into separate divisions, each Mission Society confining its operations to one or more of them, and not going over the appointed boundary. Let there be also a code of intermissional rules forbidding all such actions as are unfraternal, and enjoining to courtesy and friendliness. I am prepared to accept this as a general statement of the traditional

---

\* See *Harvest Field* for February 1890.

doctrine, except that I am not aware that, in North India at any rate, any written code of intermissional rules exists. We may take it for granted, however, that there is an unwritten one.

The new doctrine which Bishop Thoburn would substitute for this is: Give up all artificial arrangements and boundaries and rules as rather worse than useless. Assume that missionaries will naturally live and work together in complete harmony. Let them court co-operation in work rather than distinctiveness of sphere. For correction of unfraternal conduct trust to the power of public opinion, with occasional reference, when necessary, to home authorities. For the rest, take for granted that each missionary will act as a Christian gentleman.

Bishop Thoburn's paper expounds at considerable length the two views here set forth, stating the objections he feels to the first, and the superiority he sees in the second. It will be well, perhaps, if I very briefly run through the charges which he brings against the traditional doctrine. They may be stated thus:—

1. Defined mission districts imply boundary lines. But boundary lines are very liable to become themselves causes of dispute, and so tend to promote difficulties instead of removing them.

2. The system of territorial districts is unfair to late comers, who may claim as much as early ones their right to work where they deem themselves most wanted.

3. The so-called "occupation" which Missionary Societies claim for certain districts is often a great unreality, and in few cases can it, in any intelligible sense, be held to mean that the whole population have the Gospel brought to them. The result is that many souls are practically deprived of the message of salvation.

4. Next, the system ignores four important things:—
(a) That there may be several distinct races and languages within one district, each of which might claim a mission of its own.
(b) That converts have themselves the right of choosing what Christian body they will attach themselves to. (c) That the normal state of things is for Christianity to spread from man to man and village to village, regardless of artificial boundary lines. (d) That Christian preachers are called by the Holy

*Fifth Day.*

*Bishop Thoburn's objections to old methods.*

<sup>FIFTH DAY.</sup> Ghost, and so cannot be subject to territorial distinction made by man.

5. Lastly, with regard to the code of intermissional rules which the traditional doctrine contemplates, a fatal objection may be urged, *viz.*, that, however excellent those rules may be, they must be practically useless, as no authority exists, or can exist, for enforcing them.

III. OBSERVATIONS ON THESE METHODS, THE OLD AND NEW. NOW, IN DEALING WITH THESE CRITICISMS, I venture to make the following observation :—

<sup>The abuse wrong, not the use.</sup> FIRST—The weight of *more than half of the objections seems to fall, not on the system criticised, but on the abuse of it*. For instance, surely the system contemplates that the districts chosen or assigned will be of a size proportional, and not disproportional, to the ability of the Society which undertakes to work them. It is an abuse of the system, if the districts are hopelessly and impracticably big.

<sup>A district, not a preserve.</sup> AGAIN, the system makes no pretence that I know of to absolute finality in the recognition of districts. It is an abuse of the system, if such absolute finality is claimed for it, as would preclude redistribution of territory or exclude new brethren who, going the proper way to seek it, desire a sphere of work. I should feel deeply and strongly, that a system which was justly chargeable with the crime of excluding the influence of Christ's Gospel from thousands, or even millions of souls in any particular region, on the ground that the region is regarded as the *preserve* of some Society, would stand at once self-condemned. No one with any love for souls, or loyalty to Christ's command, or indeed with any sort of missionary conscience, could defend it for a moment. But I cannot admit that the system in question is chargeable with anything of the sort; it is only the abuse and the perversion of it that is so chargeable.

<sup>Division an expediency.</sup> NEXT, I would remark that no one, I presume, supposes that the system which Bishop Thoburn criticises is anything more than an arrangement of expediency, recognized by foreign Missionary Societies for their work as *foreign* Missionary Societies. It is a *temporary expedient* for evangelizing purposes and for nurturing the infancy of congregations of converts. When the indigenous church in any particular district is strong enough to be self-governing, self-supporting and self-extending,

the foreign Society's work will be done. The foreign missionaries will pass to regions beyond, and their boundary system will naturally depart with them. But if this be so, I think it will be seen that the point of some of Bishop Thoburn's remaining objections is considerably blunted. For instance, it may perhaps be said with truth that the mission "district system" does practically ignore the freedom of a young community of converts to attach themselves to some body other than that which was the means of bringing them to a knowledge of Christ. I am prepared to admit Bishop Thoburn's allegation. But for my part, I question whether it is a good or a normal thing for a young Christian community to have such freedom, till it is in a position to support and govern itself. And when it is in a position to support and govern itself, neither the missionaries, nor any one else, are likely to trouble it with difficulties about the boundary question.

The objection that the district system interferes with the natural progress of the church from village to village, regardless of artificial limitations, seems answerable in the same way. *When the church becomes self-extending* the work of the foreign missionary will be done. He will thankfully vanish, and foreign arrangements about boundaries with him. Lastly, may we not say that the objection that the "district system" ignores the call of the Holy Spirit to preachers to go preaching wherever led, may be met on the same grounds? Again I say, when self-supporting preachers, or preachers maintained by self-supporting churches, go forth to preach the Gospel to their heathen neighbours, the foreign missionary and his boundaries will have had their day. He will say "Good-bye," and "God speed the better method." Meanwhile, however, I am apt to be a little sceptical about the *foreign-paid* preacher who tells you he has received a call to work in his neighbour's vineyard. I am not sure whether such a brother is not more closely following Divine leading and Apostolic example when he keeps within his own borders. I would ask him at any rate to *try the spirit* that inspires him; for it appears to some to prompt to confusion rather than peace.

I am disposed to think, then, that the array of objections to the old system which have been brought forward must be considerably reduced, and that those that remain are not of very overwhelming weight.

*— marginalia: Fifth Day. Apostolic example.*

FIFTH DAY.

The new proposal.

IV. IS THE NEW METHOD BETTER?—I now proceed to make some observations about the new method for the promotion of comity which it is proposed to substitute for the old one. It is, as I have already stated, this: Give up assigned mission districts and intermissional rules. Assume that missions will live in amity and co-operate for work. Trust public opinion to correct unbrotherly conduct. Believe that missionaries will respond to the exhortation to behave in all their inter-relations as Christian gentlemen.

Now no one can doubt that the new doctrine contains some very salutary advice. We shall all do well to take serious heed to it. It is a wholesome thing to be recalled to our ideal, as we are here recalled. For all this we may be grateful. When, however, we come to ask what helps to the preservation of comity, the doctrine gives us, in place of the old arrangements which are to be discarded, I am bound to say that I can find nothing at all—or nothing at all beyond kind exhortation and somewhat sanguine expectation.

No safeguards.

I remarked at the beginning of this paper that it is well to hold fast to the highest ideals, but it is also well to have something to fall back upon in case people fail to act quite ideally. It appears to me that the new doctrine, without sufficient cause, throws over some of the most important of our present safeguards, and only gives in their place something which we have already, and in any case, it gives us nothing substantial to fall back upon. For whether defined mission districts and intermissional rules exist or not, we in either case assume that, ordinarily speaking, missionaries, in so far as they are brought together, will live in amity and aim at co-operation. In either case, we say, let them behave as Christian gentlemen. In either case we are not without the restraining influence of public opinion and the possibility of an occasional sharp check from our home authorities.

V. THE OLD METHOD IS STILL NECESSARY.—We have then to ask ourselves whether we have now arrived at a stage at which it is wise to dispense with those safeguards for the preservation of comity which our predecessors adopted and handed down to us. For my own part, I do not think we have arrived at such a stage. It may be humiliating to have to say so, but that is the opinion I have come to, after over seventee years' experience of missionary life in India. I think we do need <sub>FIFTH DAY.</sub> safeguards beyond public opinion and check of home authorities, and I think we shall be unwise if we throw over the tradition we have received, because in some cases it has been abused, and the system it recommends not properly regulated.

And in saying this, I am not in the least insinuating, that I have ever found, or expect to find, my missionary brethren unkind, unfraternal, uncourteous or consciously inconsiderate. <sub>Missionaries</sub> All I imply is that I have found them *human*, and that I have <sub>human.</sub> known instances—not common ones, but occasional instances— in which lack of judgment and prejudice and (shall I say pardonable) partisanship would have led to unhappy and disastrous consequences, as I believe, were it not for these same wholesome restrictions which it is now proposed by some to abolish.

The fact is, I believe, that the very qualities which go to <sub>Reasons for</sub> make a man an excellent missionary sometimes also go to make <sub>the old methods.</sub> him a not perfectly desirable neighbour to his brother-missionary. Zeal, of course, need not be, and ought not to be, incompatible with that gentleness, that moderation, which St. Paul says, is to be known unto all men as our mark. Strong holding of our own convictions need not, and ought not, to make us illiberal as to the views of others. But as a matter of fact, the ardour which makes the effective evangelist often shows itself less pleasantly in another aspect as an indiscreet impetuousness; and the intensity of belief which makes the fervent and impressive preacher, under another form sometimes comes out as a rather bitter party spirit. I should be very sorry to accuse such brethren of not being Christian gentlemen. Their breaches of comity are the result of lack of judgment and lack of knowledge and absence of a wide experience of men and things, rather than any intentional failure of kindness and courtesy. And as I have said, the very qualities which sometimes tend to promote irritation and sense of injury in the minds of their Christian neighbours, are qualities which, in another direction, help to make them earnest and successful missionaries to the heathen. When some of the elders among us were boys, bullets, I believe, were usually made round. Modern science has somewhat progressed since then, and it is now found that the narrow-shaped bullets carry more impetus and travel farthest. Now I am not

**Fifth Day.** saying that the narrow missionaries are the most valuable. I am quite sure they are not. But they certainly carry impetus and often do work which perhaps is good work, even though they have travelled over a neighbour's frontier to do it. The brother who comes into your station and preaches in the bazaar and offers instant baptism to some ignorant low-caste men of more than questionable character, whom he leaves as an unwelcome legacy to your church, is not consciously failing in the conduct of a Christian gentleman; he is only an impetuous man who is blindly convinced of the infallibility of his own method. The brother who draws away your enquirer and administers baptism without your knowledge, is not intending to be discourteous or unfair; it is only that his devotion to his own denomination makes him feel it to be a conscientious duty to get as many adherents as he can. The brother who appears suddenly and tells you he hears you and your flock are very dead and he has come to revive you, has not the faintest notion that he is failing in urbanity and modesty. It is only that he is rather a crude Christian and has not perceived yet that his gifts as a preacher do not constitute a universal and unrestricted right to preach.

For such errors of judgment and mistakes of ignorance and crudity, we do occasionally want some sort of defence, and the district system and a code of intermissional rules, written or unwritten, supplies it, and for my part I should be sorry to see the safeguard abolished. It has been said, of course, that public opinion would act as a sufficient safeguard. Public opinion, however, generally means the newspapers, religious or secular. My experience of newspaper correspondence—even religious newspaper correspondence—about missionary grievances, leads me to the conclusion that the less we have of it the better. To go to the newspapers, even before believers, now-a-days is, in my opinion, as undesirable as it was to go to law before unbelievers in St. Paul's days. Rather than do that, I would say let us take wrong and suffer ourselves to be defrauded. Newspaper correspondence, as a remedy for the lack of missionary comity, is generally like putting a blister on the wound instead of an ointment. It promotes bitterness, it provokes hard word for hard word, and it calls a sneering audience round who delight to say, "See how these

*Newspaper controversy.*

Christians snub one another." Let us rather settle our differences, if we have any, quietly. The private opinion of a few wise and good men is really more weighty than the public opinion of an uninformed and unthinking multitude.

I believe then that, except in big towns, where it is impracticable, *missionary comity is distinctly promoted by a judicious application of the "district system."* I trust that system will not be hurriedly upset, or upset at all, without providing some far more effective substitute than has as yet been proposed.

It is an immense blessing to be able to work in quietness, in peace and in order. It is an immense blessing to be allowed to follow your own method of evangelization without the fear that some impetuous brother will come in unasked with an inconsistent and contradictory method. It is an immense blessing to be allowed to nourish up young converts without the disturbing influence of diverse doctrines assailing their ears on this side and on that. It is an immense blessing when a church is permitted to purify itself by admonition and discipline without the dread that some earnest, but not very scrupulous, neighbour will use the occasion for the aggrandisement of his own denomination and the enfeeblement of yours. These blessings are secured, to a great extent, by the district system. I am not prepared with light heart to throw them overboard.

VI. SUGGESTIONS AND CONCLUSION.—In conclusion, let me say this. A system may be good, but the method of working it may be defective. I am disposed to think our method of working the district system does need some regulating, and I should rejoice to see some definite attempt at regulation as a result of this discussion.

Bishop Thoburn complains, and I think with justice, that mission districts are often too large, and are sometimes claimed to be occupied by societies who do not work them thoroughly and cannot hope to work them thoroughly.

Here then is obviously a case for reform and regulation, though not, as I hold, for abolition. We may, perhaps, be told you cannot reform and you cannot regulate, because there is no authoritative body who can lay down laws for Missionary Societies, or enforce them if they were laid down. That is true. But it is, I venture to think, an over-statement. The missionary body indeed cannot institute a judicial department or a

**Fifth Day.**

*A committee of advice.*

criminal court for offenders, but it can appoint a representative committee of advice whose counsel would have immense weight in missionary circles, and whose arbitrations, though they could not be enforced, would generally be gladly invited and loyally accepted. Such a committee should never *initiate* advice, but it should give it candidly when asked. For instance, good men in Australia desire to send a mission to this country, and, after inquiry, come to the conclusion that a certain populous district in Bengal is very inadequately occupied and would present a suitable sphere for them. After communicating with the brethren immediately concerned, they might very properly refer the question of sub-division of the district to the committee of advice. I will venture to say that the counsel of that committee (which would be a strictly representative one) would be almost certain to be adopted, and probably with very happy results.

In the same way questions of special missions to particular places or languages within a district might be settled and wise lines suggested for securing proximity without interference.

I feel confident that there are men in this room now whose matured character, whose wise liberality, sober common sense, ripe experience, and acknowledged sense of justice, would qualify them to become weighty members of such a committee of advice; men who would see to the bottom of a matter and deal with things in a truly Christian and catholic spirit; who would know how to advise strongly without being dictatorial, and to arbitrate skilfully without being meddlesome.

I commend this suggestion to the consideration of this Conference as a conservative reform, and, while I am not so optimistic as to suppose that it would dispose of all difficulties, I believe that we should find in it a valuable help to the promotion of missionary comity.

## SECOND PAPER.*

By Bishop Thoburn, D.D., M. E. C., Calcutta.

The subject assigned to me on this occasion is not one which I should have selected if the choice had been left to myself. It is one which requires very delicate treatment, and yet one which cannot be discussed to any good purpose without a frank statement of views which are almost sharply opposite in character. It must be confessed that its discussion in public bodies like this Conference has not always been edifying, but at the same time the importance of the subject has not diminished, and it is felt by many that the present Conference cannot afford to ignore it. In order to prevent any possible cause of offence, however remote, I have carefully eliminated from this paper every trace of what might be called a personal element. None of the illustrations used refer to missionaries now in the field, or to events which will be recognised by the men of to-day. May I not venture to express the hope that all who take part in the discussion will do likewise, and not introduce any question which might possibly tend to substitute dispute for discussion, and thus defeat the purpose which we all have in view? *A delicate subject.*

That it is desirable to maintain friendly and fraternal relations among missionaries of all churches and societies, will be conceded by every one. That unfortunate differences sometimes arise in the mission field, will also have to be conceded, and if anything can be done to lessen these differences, and to promote fraternal good feeling, and as far as possible fraternal co-operation, by all means let it be tried. But we must not forget, what most persons who discuss this subject do seem to forget, that the questions involved are by no means new, and that a general line of policy has been followed in all the great mission fields of the world, without, however, securing the era of fraternal harmony which many think possible, if not absolutely necessary to success. At rare intervals a new proposal *Comity desirable.*

---

* I had intended to write a new paper for the Decennial Conference, but on the very day when I had hoped to prepare the first copy for the printer, a sudden and painful family bereavement broke up my plans, and I was constrained to substitute a paper published in the "Harvest Field" in Feb. 1890. A few paragraphs have been struck out, and a few added, but in the main the paper is the same as when first published.
J. M. T.

**Fifth Day.**

**The traditional doctrine.**

may have been made, but in the main the discussion is carried on along the same old lines, and repeated and conspicuous failures only seem to create a renewed cry for a policy which has been found weak from the beginning.

1. The traditional doctrine which, in outline at least, has been generally accepted on this subject, may be substantially stated as follows: Let each non-Christian country be divided into separate districts, and each society confine its operations to one or more of these, keeping rigidly within the geographical boundary line which encloses its fields. This, it is thought, will make collisions impossible, and at the same time secure a division of the great work to be done in such a way as to hasten its accomplishment. In the next place, let a code of intermissional rules be adopted, and made binding upon all missionaries, forbidding all such lines of action as are unfraternal, and enjoining all such duties as Christian love and courtesy demand. These two propositions cover, substantially, the whole ground, although in detail a few points might be added to them, but none that would affect the principle involved. Missionary authorities in Europe and America have generally approved both propositions, in theory at least, and both have usually passed unchallenged at the great Missionary Conferences held both at home and abroad. But in recent years the great mission fields of the world have been rapidly filling up, experience has been teaching many valuable lessons, missionaries have had opportunities for careful and wide observation, and the result is that not a few thoughtful workers in all lands begin to doubt the wisdom of the policy in which so many have put their trust.

The policy of assigning a separate field to each society is perfectly defensible if the object sought is solely that of making a proper division of labour, and at the same time occupying as much territory as possible. In the earlier stages of the work, and in countries of vast extent, like Central Africa at the present day, it is eminently wise for workers to agree upon such divisions where practicable, but the case is different when it is laid down as a fixed principle that missionaries must avoid one another in the interests of peace, and that these messengers of love must not aspire to a better standard of neighbourly living than was known in the dim twilight of the far-off era of Abraham and Lot. Many practical objections to such a policy have been brought to light in the progress of the work, some of which may be briefly stated:—

(1) These boundary lines are very apt to create the difficulty which they are intended to guard against. So, far from keeping the missionaries apart, and thus preventing causes of disagreement, the very line itself becomes a fruitful source of contention. At the last Missionary Conference in London one brother with admirable candour admitted that his mission had suffered more trouble from disputes about boundary lines than from any other question. A boundary line is often a very shifting quantity, and it is nearly impossible to prevent contentions when dealing with vast regions in which there is no actual occupancy, while there is nearly always a strange, and not very reasonable, eagerness to grasp as wide a territory as possible. It is by no means certain that the good effects which are often claimed for this policy are at all owing to it. The instances often cited are merely examples of the wisdom and good sense of the parties concerned. They would almost certainly have made the arrangements they did if no such rule had ever been enacted, whereas the advocates of the policy omit to notice that the contentions over which they mourn are too often caused, not by actual injury, but by a trespass upon an imaginary boundary line. For instance, if a brother in China hears that an agent of another society has settled a hundred miles north of him, he will naturally think nothing of it, except to thank God that another missionary has come to China. But if his society has drawn a line two or three hundred miles north, and told him that all the territory inclosed by that line is within his jurisdiction, he at once feels that he is an injured man, and protests against the advent of the man, for whose coming he would otherwise have felt thankful.

(2) These territorial allotments are unfair to those who come latest to the mission field. We must remember that Missionary Societies are constantly multiplying, that every few years a new society appears in such a field as India, and that its agents will naturally look around for the most suitable sphere of labour within their reach. It must puzzle them not a little to be told when they reach Bombay, that very little of India is open to them, that all the centres of influence have been

FIFTH DAY.

occupied and are practically closed against them, and that they must seek some field which thus far has been neglected by their more fortunate brethren who came earlier upon the scene. It will be said, no doubt, that they should nevertheless go to some remote district where no missionary is found, but those who proffer this advice would possibly be slow to accept it if they themselves were the parties concerned. A man has a right to work where he can do the most good, where he believes himself to be most needed, and there may be reasons, perfectly clear and satisfactory to him, why he should not go to a vacant place which is pointed out to him by others. The distribution of workers can never be successfully accomplished by mechanical processes. If, for instance, another Alexander Duff were to land in Calcutta, representing a new society, it would be absurd to insist that he must betake himself to some unoccupied district of some remote province, upon which no missionary or Missionary Society has any claim. A strict and rigid application of this policy would work, not only unfairly, but almost disastrously to any vigorous society which wished to enter the Indian field in strong force.

Extent of one's field.

(3) The custom has been for the agents of each society to decide for themselves the extent of the field which they are to occupy. Some of them have made their selection with wisdom, while others have chosen fields which they had no reasonable prospect of fully occupying for years, if not centuries, to come. Experience has proved that it is nearly impossible to persuade such men that they are grasping at more than they can possibly reach, and hence we have inequalities of the most singular kind among what are called the separate mission districts of India. In one small province we find seven societies represented, working at no great distance from one another, and I may add, without any serious collision with one another, while near at hand may be found a district, four or five times as large, feebly occupied by one society, and jealously guarded against what are called the encroachments of other missionaries. A very slight study of missionary maps will show how marked these inequalities are, and this evidence ought to convince any candid observer that the policy is a practical failure in its application to India.

(4) In its practical application this rule has tended to shut out the Gospel from vast regions where it would otherwise have penetrated. It will seem incredible to those in England and America, who so earnestly advocate this policy, and yet it is a simple fact with which many of us in India are painfully familiar, that good men often object most strenuously to the advent of missionaries of other societies into regions where they themselves are not able to give the Gospel to the people. One case, of many, will illustrate what I mean. A good man proposed to plant a missionary among a tribe of people who were utterly neglected, to whom no one had gone, and to whom no one was proposing to go, but was forbidden by some missionaries who lived at a great distance from the place in question, on the ground that their society had taken up the whole province in which the tribe was included. The enterprise was accordingly given up. The poor people are still living in their darkness, and the men who kept the Gospel from them will, in all probability, be in heaven many years, possibly generations, before any other messenger of the Gospel will attempt to reach those precious souls. Let no one say that this is an extreme instance. It is one of many, and beyond all doubt this rule is operating to keep the Gospel from millions of people to-day. In fact, it is so impracticable in a country like India, and in the nature of the case must work so directly against the free progress of the Gospel, that I do not hesitate to say that a rigid enforcement of the rule would put back the evangelization of India a thousand years.

*Fifth Day.*
*Has shut out the Gospel.*

(5) The word "occupy" is used in so flexible a way that it often misrepresents the facts. For instance, a good man, a very good man, once wrote to a brother missionary that he had occupied a district containing a million of people, and hoped the brother would not enter it. The occupation consisted in sending a native preacher to live in a small town, and preach in its bazaars and the surrounding villages. Had there been any plan for extension, or any resources to make extension possible, this might have been called an occupation in part, but many years have since passed without any vigorous attempt being made to occupy the field. A district is not occupied because a missionary station has been established within its borders. Missionaries who have lived in their station for years

*What it is to "occupy."*

FIFTH DAY.

An illustration.

have been startled to find people living within a few miles of their doors who had never heard the name of Jesus Christ. What, then, shall we say of the million, or perhaps two millions, who live in other parts of the so-called "occupied" district?

I am indebted to my friend Mr. Rouse for a definition of the word "occupy," which I think covers the case. A blockade of a coast is never respected so long as it remains a paper blockade. Unless war vessels are stationed along the coast, no one pays any attention to it. So with a proclamation of missionary occupation. The district must be actually occupied, not merely at one point, or even three or four points, but practically throughout. That is, every man in the district ought to be able to reach a Gospel messenger without walking more than ten miles. If there is a place twenty, thirty, or perhaps fifty or sixty miles from the mission station, which does not receive a visit from a Gospel messenger more than once a year, it ought to be considered open to any one who can actually give the Gospel to the people.

Charges of interference.

(6) This policy annoys and harasses men who love unity and concord, and seek peace and pursue it, and yet who are constantly put in the wrong by accusations of interference with the work of others. Any man with the mind and heart which a true preacher ought to have, cannot but feel grieved and pained when accused unjustly of the sin of hindering his Master's work by marring the labours of Christian brethren. Charges of this kind are made far too freely, and very often without a shadow of just cause. The policy in question never fails to afford a weak man some plausible foundation for an accusation against unoffending neighbours. The man who obstructs his brother's work is a great transgressor, but the man who unjustly accuses his brother is not a whit less guilty.

(7) This rule ignores the fact that within a given field there may be different races, or castes, or languages, and that one society may not be able, or may not choose, to do all the work to be done. For instance, Santhals and Bengali people may live side by side. One missionary may wish to work for the one people and another for the other. If the society in occupancy will do all the work, well and good; let no one interfere with its agents. But if a tribe, or a caste, or a

separate people of any kind, are wholly neglected, outside people should certainly be permitted to come to these neglected people with the Gospel. This is a practical question at the present time. Some are giving their exclusive attention to the aboriginal tribes, some are working among low caste people, while others avoid the lowest castes altogether, and in the nature of the case, vast multitudes of people in India must be overlooked, if this rule be rigidly enforced, or if it be applied, as many missionaries in the country interpret.

(8) The rule ignores the freedom of converts. As generally interpreted, it assumes that all natives who become Christians within a given area, shall be assigned to the missionary working within the area in question. It is taken for granted that the converts will do as they are told, but as a matter of fact they are by no means always willing to obey such directions. Any one who has observed the course of events in other countries, ought to be wiser than to expect that such a policy could be enforced in a country like India. In ninety-nine cases out of a hundred, sincere converts will wish to follow those who first bring them to Christ, and in ninety-nine cases out of a hundred they will do better under the care of these persons than under any others. It is said, I know, that Mr. Moody sends his converts to all the churches represented in his meetings, but Mr. Moody would not, and certainly could not, send his converts to churches out of sympathy with himself. He could not, for instance, send them to parties who would teach them, as their first lesson, that what Mr. Moody considered conversion was a delusion, and yet, if he were a missionary in India, and tried to apply his evangelistic policy, he might meet with this very difficulty. I must beg to protest that I am not drawing upon my imagination. I once knew a Scotch minister, anxious to avoid every appearance of what he incorrectly called sectarianism, to send the names of forty converts of a union meeting to a clergyman in India. Not the slightest notice was taken of the letter, and I believe that nearly every one of the forty was utterly neglected, and in due time drifted back into carelessness and indifference. A lesson which missionaries in all foreign countries are very slow to learn is, that the humblest converts have rights. It is for them to say what their ecclesiastical affiliations shall be, and if, for instance, they chance to live within the limits of a field in

*Fifth Day.*

*Freedom of converts.*

FIFTH DAY.

Interferes with progress.

which the missionaries tolerate caste, no low caste convert should be compelled to join such a mission. It was recently said in print, that at this present hour there is a whole village of inquirers in South India, willing and anxious to be baptized, but who are denied their right because they chance to live a very short distance beyond a boundary line which was laid down many years ago by parties long since dead. These poor people, for reasons which they have a perfect right to entertain, refused to go to the missionaries to whom they were sent, and hence are kept in nominal heathenism, contrary to the spirit of the New Testament, and contrary to the spirit of Christian justice.

(9) This policy interferes with the normal progress of the Gospel. We ought to look forward to the time when Christianity will free itself from the narrow limits of the mission house and mission agencies, and begin to advance over the country from heart to heart and from village to village, by a steady process of normal growth. Whenever it becomes a living, indigenous Christianity, it will advance in this way. In some places we see indications of such advance for which we ought to be devoutly thankful. I was told recently that the well-known movement among the Telugus in Southern India is steadily creeping northward. It is becoming more and more a normal outgrowth, and it will advance from heart to heart and from village to village on lines which no human wisdom can either mark out or obliterate. We may as well try to legislate against the advance of white ants as against the advance of a movement which is simply a normal outgrowth of vital Christianity. In western Rohilkund, on perhaps a smaller scale, a similar advance has been noted. The people have relatives or fellow caste-men, and becoming earnest Christians, they speak to these friends of Christ, who in turn becoming interested, wish to be Christians, and in this way Christianity has crossed the Ganges at many points and is moving westward. The missionary, or the native preacher, as the case may be, does not lead, but follows such a movement as this. He is told of inquirers in such and such a place, goes over to them, baptizes them and organizes them into a church. If India is ever to be a Christian empire, similar movements will be witnessed all over this vast country. But all such movements will ignore the artificial boundary lines which have been laid

down by men who could not anticipate the developments of the coming years. I have been much perplexed by some of these movements myself, but some years ago became convinced that the only way open to one who wished to follow where God led, was carefully and conscientiously and tenderly to nourish and cherish every such development of normal Christian growth. Missionaries everywhere should hail every such appearance with joy, and pray that what is the exception may quickly become universal.

(10) This policy ignores the special call which the Holy Spirit so often gives to the Christian preacher. Paul and Silas were Spirit-led, and they planted permanent churches where they preached. If India is ever brought to Christ, many successors to these men will yet appear. Could such men work, in India, as Paul worked? It is constantly said that Paul never built on other men's foundation, but this policy forbids a man to dig for his own foundation. If, when Paul reached Philippi, he had been met by a deputation of brethren, telling him that they had a monopoly of all the foundation-laying in Greece and Macedonia, and directing him to go elsewhere, he would have instantly replied, "Not for an hour!" It is not probable that India will ever see another Paul, but that she will see hundreds of men of like spirit is certain, and we should open a way for them rather than close it against them.

*Fifth Day.*

The "call" of the Holy Spirit.

II. Let us in the next place glance briefly at the proposed code of intermissional rules. Such a code, if agreed upon with practical unanimity by all the Societies interested, would no doubt be of value as a guide to young missionaries, and it would also greatly influence public opinion, which in the long run will be found the chief factor in settling points in controversy. But it is nearly certain that any attempt to give such rules the force of laws will end in failure, and probably aggravate the evils which they are intended to prevent. A somewhat elaborate code of this kind was actually adopted in the Punjab about a quarter of a century ago, but it proved a dead letter, or nearly so, from the first, and at present seems to be unknown. A code of laws cannot be effective without a judiciary to expound them, and an administrative department to enforce them. We have only to fancy a civil code in India, with every plaintiff and every defendant assuming the function of advocate, judge

Proposed rules.

**Fifth Day.**

and jury, in order to see how absurd it is to propose a code of laws which can neither be officially interpreted or enforced. This explains why it is that nearly all attempts in this direction seem to foment discord rather than allay it. How could it be otherwise when both plaintiff and defendant attempt to pass judgment on the case in dispute?

**Study of human nature**

A close and faithful study of human nature will greatly assist us in considering this question. Missionaries are very much like other people, and will continue to be like other people. When any two human beings differ warmly over any question, it is amazing how clearly each one can see his own side of it and how blind he is to the merits of the other side. As a matter of fact, has not the average missionary this infirmity in common with other men? And, if so, what possible use is there in laying down a law for him which he will be sure to interpret in the light of his own interests? For instance, a missionary is asked to intervene in a neighbour's quarrel, and allows his feelings to lead him into the dispute. He is reminded of a rule forbidding such meddling, but at once replies, "*This* is a case of gross injustice. I am merely helping the weak," etc. Or, a discarded helper comes to him for service. He accepts him, and, when reminded of the rule against such procedure, replies, "Yes, but *this case* does not come under that rule. *This* man is in the right," etc.

**A Committee of Reference.**

It has been suggested that a Committee of Reference might be appointed, and that all disputed questions might be referred to this body, but this would only be adding to the difficulties of the case. Could such a Committee enforce its decisions? And would all missionaries be willing to submit their cases to such a body? Would not a certain class of men always be ready to show special reasons why each one's own particular case should not be sent up to such a Committee? In important cases a reference to such a Committee might seem fitting enough, but it is extremely probable that many trifling differences would be magnified by such a reference, and in this way a dignified committee would be made to figure in a ridiculous light by being made the frequent recipient of undignified complaints.

**Change of policy.**

III.—If, then, we are to have no code of rules and no mission boundaries, can nothing at all be done to promote a proper

spirit of comity among missionaries? Beyond all doubt some- <small>FIFTH DAY.</small>
thing can be done, but not on the old lines.

First of all, there should be a radical change of policy. We should for ever discard the notion that missionaries cannot dwell together in love and harmony. Instead of saying, How good and how pleasant it is for brethren to dwell apart in *comity*, let us boldly and firmly maintain the ground that it is a good and pleasant thing for brethren to dwell and work together in *amity*. As a matter of fact, we all have reasons to know that brethren of different societies who live and work side by side have fewer differences than those who live far apart. We ought to be ashamed to proclaim to the world that we cannot work side by side. I saw Christians of two societies last year in a common assembly day after day, taking counsel together, and waiting on God together, and it was impossible to distinguish between them. How much better this than to keep them separated as if they belonged to separate castes! We need not plant our stations in the same towns for the mere sake of exhibiting our fraternal love, but let us no longer shun one another's presence, and thus almost ostentatiously proclaim to the world that we cannot live together.

(2) As far as possible, both missionaries and converts should co-operate in their common work, especially in meetings <small>Co-operation.</small> for the promotion of their spiritual life. Instead of having a Committee of Reference for the settlement of disputes, two or more societies might have a joint committee for the promotion of their mutual interests. In former years the London and the Methodist Episcopal Missionaries in Kumaon had such a committee, and the plan worked admirably. It is infinitely safer for us to attempt to legislate in the direction of practical amity, than to attempt deliberately to make provision for the demands of future discord.

(3) For the correction of unfraternal conduct, and of all conduct which may be hurtful to our common cause, we must depend chiefly on the power of public opinion, with now and then <small>Public opinion.</small> a reference to the home authorities. We may as well assume, once for all, that offences of some kind will come. It has been so since the beginning, and will no doubt continue so. Some of these will be trivial enough, but others will be grievous. In recent years, in India at least, every missionary is a public man.

**Fifth Day.**

*Character of the individual.*

*A Christian gentleman.*

Missionary opinion is a distinct and potent factor in the empire, and when a man is tempted to do a brother a wrong, or to do himself a wrong, nothing will restrain him so much as the recollection that what he does will be made public. Every missionary of moderate experience knows that there is an unwritten code by which the missionary public will judge every case which comes before it, and respect for this code will powerfully restrain those who might otherwise be inconsiderate. As a matter of fact, the force of this opinion has been distinctly recognized of late years, and in my opinion it has done much to promote good feeling among missionaries, and to prevent what under other circumstances might have been serious, or even disastrous, differences.

(4) But, after all, the question of peace and concord must depend very largely upon the character of individual missionaries. Not long since a missionary was giving me a history of a sad dispute in a local church, in the course of which he said, "If Mr. P. had not been a Christian gentleman, he could have carried off most of the people and have broken up the church. But he was a gentleman, and refused to interfere in any way, and in time the difficulty was settled." If we must have a code, let it contain but one rule, and let that rule be,—Every missionary shall be a Christian gentleman. A Christian gentleman will not offend in any of the following particulars:—(*a*) He will not meddle in a neighbour's dispute. If asked, he will act as a peace-maker, but in no other character. He will not even think of trying to profit by such a dispute by assuming charge of one of the parties to it. (*b*) He will not receive an excommunicated Christian, unless it be after very satisfactory repentance and reformation. (*c*) He will not enter a field where another missionary is successfully working and try either to appropriate his harvest or seize his opportunities. In other words, he will not in any way meddle with another's work. (*d*) He will not, however indirectly, entice another's helpers by offering them increased pay. If he does this under the pretence of obeying a religious conviction, especially on some non-essential point of doctrine, he is not quite a gentleman, and much less than a Christian. (*e*) *Per contra*, he will not attempt to bind his helpers down to a low salary for life, refusing to give them certificates of character if they wish to leave, and thu

virtually making them his bondmen. The Christian gentleman is bound to respect the rights of his Native brethren. (*f*) He will not accept as true every evil story brought to him about his brethren, nor will he lend a sympathetic ear to those who speak disparagingly of other missionaries. The missionary who is willing to listen to such talk will never fail to hear false or distorted stories about his brethren. (*g*) He will not engage in undignified disputes about trifling matters which are unworthy of his attention. (*h*) He will not make himself unhappy because others do not work according to his ideas or methods, remembering that each worker standeth or falleth to his own Master. (*i*) He will not assume rights or privileges, either of action or judgment, which he does not freely concede to every other worker in the field.

This list might be extended, but it is needless. It only remains to be said that after all precautions have been taken we may expect to find ample opportunities for the exercise of our Christian forbearance. We are not much better than our fathers, or much farther advanced than our brethren in Christian lands. We may expect to see thoughtless brethren transgress at times, and we may expect to see sensitive brethren bring unjust accusations against those who have done them no harm, but in either case it ought not to be a very serious matter for Christian men to bear and forbear, and go on with their work in quietness and love. Life is too short, and eternity too near, for Christian missionaries, of all living men, to waste their time and destroy their peace by disputes about matters which in nineteen cases out of twenty have no value whatever. *Need of forbearance.*

Christian workers in the home-lands have quietly settled down to their several tasks, with the accepted policy that they must live, and love, and labour, side by side, and surely we in India can do the same. It is the best policy, because it is the only possible policy. No other has ever proved successful, or ever can prove successful among men who enjoy the full measure of civil and religious freedom which is rapidly becoming the heritage of the whole wide world. Let us accept the comity which Christians in England and America accept, and therewith be content. *Home-lands.*

## FIRST SPEECH.

By the Rev. F. ASHCROFT, M.A., Raj. Pr. M., Ajmere.

**FIFTH DAY.**

There is no need to waste time in defining missionary comity. The two able papers in our hands make that unnecessary. Indeed, they go over the whole ground from the only two possible points of view so thoroughly that very little more can or need be said. The great object of comity among Missionary Societies is to make the work of all more efficient. We are still only beginning our work, and, whatever may be necessary in the future, we are still at the stage when the best work will be done by different societies working in different territories. Large territories, containing over a million inhabitants, might still be given to each society, and, when this is so, it seems a thousand pities that there should be overlapping, or friction. Our object is to carry the Gospel message as quickly as possible to all, and so each society should take up some definite district proportionate to its strength and try to evangelize it completely. To believe that work done by others is just as good as work done by ourselves is sometimes difficult, but we must remember that it is all work done for one Master. If, then, it is honest work, we ought to look upon it with satisfaction, even where the organization at work is different from our own. This requires a spirit of forbearance and sympathy, which it is surely not too much to expect to find in all Christian workers.

*Much land unoccupied.*

*Separate districts.*

There are several reasons which make work in separate districts advisable in the case of societies which yet regard each other with brotherly love and trust. One of these is that each has an ecclesiastical *organisation* peculiar to itself. Although we do not wish the Church of India to reflect all our Western differences, we who are workers cannot rid ourselves of them. Since, therefore, they exist, it seems better to work apart than together, so as not needlessly to perplex our converts. With this are subordinate differences of doctrine and practice that point in the same direction. The different great societies represent different churches, and the view they take of such questions is fundamentally opposed. Take for example the *rite of Baptism*. The Church of England believes it carries with it regenerating power. A missionary of that church will therefore naturally be careful to satisfy himself as to the reality of the belief of the convert asking it. The Presbyterian Church

*Baptism.*

holds that it is the seal of a relationship established between the individual soul and God. The Presbyterian Missionary will, therefore, demand evidence, that that relationship has been established. Other churches regard it as merely an initiatory rite of admission to the church, which again they look upon as a great training school for true conversion, and missionaries of such churches will naturally admit all who profess to believe in Christ, without enquiry into their motives or knowledge. Now, societies thus distinct in their view of this important question can only, by working in one another's district, perplex and bewilder converts, who cannot understand why one church should admit so readily and another with such difficulty. Only confusion can result from contradictory practice in the same district.

FIFTH DAY.

Then, again, the different societies take different views of *discipline*. One missionary is thinking of the church as a Spiritual Society, in which no unclean thing may dwell, and in his desire to preserve the purity of the Bride of Christ, he is severe in his treatment of offenders. Another, instead of looking at the question from the point of view of the church, is thinking of the individual who has offended a weak brother to be treated indulgently and readily received back upon a profession of repentance. There is truth in both views, but both should not be exemplified in one district. Offences severely punished by one society should not be condoned by another. It should not be possible to pass from the one to the other in order to escape the discipline of the more severe. It is almost impossible without definite rules of comity to prevent this coming and going, and the simplest rule would be that two societies so differing should not overlap.

Discipline.

Then there are different ideas about *the pay and standing of agents*. One society believes in educated agents, another in illiterate. One pays highly and the other gives a bare subsistence allowance. When the two are working in the same territory, among similar people, this gives rise to no end of trouble. The one society is constantly losing its best men to the other. Moreover, one society will only ordain men who have had a complete training and who are called to a church, but another will ordain partially educated men as local preachers. Hence inevitably, jealousies will arise among the agents that will do

**Fifth Day.**

**A Comity Committee.**

much to hinder the work. This passing of agents from one society to another, in many cases without enquiry, has been a scandal in the past, and will be so in the future, wherever two societies differing fundamentally on this question, work side by side.

Mr. Clifford's suggestion, therefore, seems a wise one, namely, to have a Missionary Comity Committee, consisting of representatives of all societies working in India. Of course, it would only have, could only have, advisory powers, but it would not be easy to disregard the advice of such a council, and the probability is that in most cases of friction its decision would be accepted by the parties concerned. The work of such a Committee would be as follows: First, to advise new societies anxious to begin work in India as to what districts to take up. This would be a great boon. No doubt as enthusiasm for mission work extends in Europe, America and Australia, new and powerful societies will wish to help in this great work. Let us have a representative council of existing missions able and ready to tell them of the real needs of the field and of the places where they can give most effectual help. Secondly, to advise existing societies as to the territories they claim. It is quite true that some of them have claimed vast districts as their own, quite out of all proportion to their strength, and that their work in great parts of such district has been only, and can be only, nominal. In view of fresh societies coming out to work this should be rectified, and this Advisory Committee, in the case of an application from a new society, might revise the territories of existing societies, and call upon them either at once to greatly increase their staff of workers or to give up a portion of their territory to others ready to enter. Each existing society, burdened with large districts, might be asked to indicate to the Committee the portions of their territory they have so far been unable to undertake. Thirdly, to arbitrate in cases of friction. These unfortunately do sometimes arise, and the fact that there is no final court of appeal prevents an early settlement. It is all very well to say the public prints will decide. We deprecate public discussions of such questions. A Representative Committee, commanding the respect and confidence of both parties, could much more wisely and effectually settle the question. It would not be necessary always for the whole Committee to act, but it could appoint arbitrators to act in all such cases. Fourthly, to arrange simple rules as to the transfer of agents from one society to another so as to prevent the present heartburning that undoubtedly exists.

*Fifth Day.*

In conclusion, let me illustrate what I have been saying by a practical case. The American Episcopal Methodists have recently entered Rajputana where we Presbyterians have been working for over thirty years. We have not been able to overtake the whole of that vast province, but in one part of it we are fairly strong, namely, in the Ajmere District. Will it be believed that the Methodists felt themselves compelled to begin work there. Of the sixteen Native States of Rajputana, there were five or six into which we have not been able to enter, with large cities, towns and villages waiting to be evangelized. Why did they not begin work in one of these? Why should it be necessary to settle down beside us? Perhaps it will be replied, Why should they not? Well, their methods are different from ours. We, Presbyterians, rightly or wrongly, believe a man should not be baptized until we think he understands what he is doing and is sincere in his action. Our Methodist brethren do not seem to think that necessary. They baptise in hope of future real conversions, as Dr. Johnstone, of Jubbalpore, indicated in his speech. So they have baptized in the villages, round about Ajmere, hundreds whom we would never dream of baptizing, and thus in the same district we have men in our mission baptized and called Christians who at the very most in the other would be only probationers. This must result in evil, and such a case would have been dealt with on its merits by a Missionary Comity Committee.

*M. E. C. encroachment.*

## SECOND SPEECH.

By the Rev. H. GULLIFORD, W. M. S., Bangalore.

He remarked that though the two papers advocated two different kinds of policy, yet in many points they were in substantial agreement. It would be well to emphasize those points. There were three cases where it was desirable to have some kind of regulations, because they would enable missionaries to work together more harmoniously.

**Fifth Day.**

**Missions side by side.**

I. The first case was where missions were working side by side in different areas. They have adopted the territorial system and are loyally working it. In the natural course of events the work should develop. It will spread right up to the boundary line, and if it spreads so far it will inevitably go beyond. Ought a mission to follow the work across the border? If the mission working on the other side of the boundary were willing to take up the work and carry it on, he would say that we ought not to follow it. If, however, the other mission were not able to take up the work, he would say it was the bounden duty of the mission to cross the boundary so that the work might not suffer. There need be no unpleasantness. The two missions could meet, consult together, and re-arrange the boundary between their respective fields of labour. In connection with this, it would be well to consider the question: "Ought we to follow our converts when they leave our districts and go where other missions are labouring?" As a rule, it is not advisable to do so. Letters of commendation should be

**Letters commendatory.**

given them, and they should be directed to join the mission working in the neighbourhood to which they have gone. If that mission should impose tests of membership, to which they had not been accustomed, or which was not clearly warranted from God's Word, then it would be necessary for the mission to exercise pastoral care over the converts. Such cases would, however, be rare; and the transference of converts from one church to another would show the real unity that exists amongst evangelical Christians. Reference was made in Bishop Thoburn's paper to work on particular lines, and he advocates the necessity of going wherever that particular work would lead. The speaker thought this would lead to much friction. If there was a work amongst the low caste, and it spread into the territory occupied by another mission, that mission ought to care for it. It would never do to have two missions in one place, the one having a church composed of caste people and the other one composed of non-caste people. A church should include all castes alike, or it fails to exhibit the true brotherhood of man in Christ. It might be possible to combine missions for a specific work, the one solitary example of which was the Christian College, Madras. If more were done on those lines greater harmony might be secured. The general principle at the basis of both papers was this: No interference with the work of another mission. For this purpose, except in large towns, the territorial system was the best. Those territories, however, should not be larger than a mission could occupy. The occupation should moreover be real. If a mission could not occupy the territory that it claimed, it ought not to adopt a "dog-in-the-manger" policy, and refuse to allow any other mission to enter.

*Fifth Day.*

II. The second case was where missions were working in the same place. Bishop Thoburn's suggestions for harmony in such cases were admirable. Christian courtesy would suggest the few simple rules necessary for harmonious and united work. One rule should certainly be that no mission should receive an agent or member from another church without reference to the missionary or pastor of that church. Nothing was really gained by taking members from other churches. The Kingdom of Christ was not advanced by work of this kind. If there were kindly reference, all cause for annoyance would disappear. Another rule should be that no agent or member of another mission under discipline should be received till he had made his peace with that mission. Much scandal had been caused by missions acting in this way. Men who had committed gross sins, have gone to other missions when they have been subjected to discipline, and have at once been put into positions of responsibility to the great injury of the work of God. A reference in all such cases is absolutely necessary. The man comes and tells a pitiful story, and makes himself out to be the worst-used man in the world. But, when the other side of the story is told, one's pity speedily vanishes. Our native brethren are often the cause of these transfers without reference. They should strive to maintain the purity of the church to which they belong. It has been said in one of the papers that the territorial system ignores the right of the convert to choose his own church. In most cases where a man wishes to change his church, he has no clear conception of the difference between the one he leaves and the one he wishes to join. There are generally social or personal reasons for the change; religious conviction has nothing to do with it. We should not emphasize our differences; we should not instruct our converts in the causes of these differences; we should rather so worship God that a Christian will feel at home in whatever place of worship he may be.

*Missions in the same place.*

FIFTH DAY.

The establishment of new Mission.

A Comity Committee.

III. The third case in which rules of missionary comity were needed was in the establishment of new missions. During the last decade no new mission of any great importance had begun work in India, except the Salvation Army, which was conspicuous by its absence from the Conference. If a new mission wishes to begin work in India it would naturally not desire to build upon another man's foundation. It might be necessary, perhaps, to have a base of operations in a town already occupied. But in order to know what territory was occupied, a good missionary map of India was needed—a map that would show all the stations occupied by all the missions at work in India. The speaker would like to publish such a map in connection with the *Harvest Field*, if support were given to the movement. Such a map would show large tracts of country unoccupied by any society where there would be ample scope for a new and vigorous mission. This would to some extent meet the need of new missions. It was, however, desirable to have some Council of Advice, such as Bishop Clifford had suggested. One Council for the whole of India would not do, for it would be practically impossible for such a Council in Calcutta to have the local knowledge necessary to arrange misunderstandings in the Panjab or Travancore. The speaker thought that the difficulty might be met by making the present local Missionary Conferences more effective and by organising new ones. Each local Conference should include a certain area, and the missionaries living at a distance might be regarded as country members. They might not be able to attend regularly; but in any special case they might be present. These local Conferences had in many cases found a way to remove friction between missions; and if the body were large enough it would command the respect of those who might appeal to it. At present it was exceedingly difficult to know what Missionary Conferences were held. He knew of Calcutta, Madras, Bombay, Bangalore, Lucknow, Allahabad, Benares, and Lahore. There might be more; there ought to be more. In the organisation of these local Missionary Conferences, and in the frank discussion of questions that arise between mission and mission in these Conferences, the speaker thought the solution of difficult problems of missionary comity would be found.

## THIRD SPEECH.

*Fifth Day.*

By the Rev. J. SHILLIDY, M.A., I. P. M., Surat.

In the papers of Mr. Clifford and Bishop Thoburn two theories in reference to this subject have been formulated. The first and oldest we may call the Territorial Theory; the newer, the Free-Hand Theory. In reference to these I may at the outset express my own opinion that if "Territorialism" keeps at times, as has been alleged by Bishop Thoburn, a million people from hearing the Gospel, keeps even a very much smaller number, then I trust this Conference will ring its death-knell; and, on the other hand, if the newer policy brings new men who, with a wave of the hand, set aside the workers of previously established missions, and pooh-poohing their slow and laborious methods and limited results, trespass on their incontestable field of labour, then I trust, too, that no uncertain sound will go forth from this Conference about the character of such work. I express the mind I hope of the great majority of the members of this Conference when I say, that in the Indian mission field we do not want dog-in-the-mangerism, and just as little do we want swash-bucklerism.

*Two theories*

I. *What is it that leads to breaches of comity?*

*Breach of comity.*

(1) One of the causes is the overlapping of mission fields, or the intrusion of new workers of other societies into fields already occupied. I will be reminded that so-called occupation is not always effective. Quite possibly it is not, and certainly it never is in the estimation of the intruders. I will make bold, however, to say that there are still in India many districts not only unoccupied, but unclaimed even by any Missionary Society; and, though I can't claim any special knowledge of the missionary geography of India, yet I could point to several such districts. Let those in search of new fields of labour go to the unoccupied ones. But from what I have seen of such cases, that is the very last thing the new-comers want to do. They in some cases deliberately raid the older mission fields: by bribes and promises and misrepresentations they seek to gain, not from the heathen, but from the older mission, adherents to their cause. Or, again, the new brother comes along where others have laboured for years, oftentimes in bitterness of spirit and deep searchings of heart over the little fruit they can show, and with his newer methods reaps

*By intruders.*

**Fifth Day.**

*S. A. encroachment.*

immediately an abundant harvest and counts his converts by hundreds. This is no fancy picture. Only a few years ago the S. A. erected a church building, which they called a "Barracks," in North Gujarat, and that church was erected where and for whom? In a Christian village, founded and established at very considerable expense by another mission, and not for the use of converts from heathenism, but for Christians perverted from the older mission. That Christian village was the only one of its kind among the three thousand towns and villages of that district, and the district immediately north of it, and though in hundreds of these the Gospel had never been preached, yet the new-comers passed by the 2,999 heathen villages and settled down in the one little Christian village. It is unnecessary to characterize such proceedings as these.

*By lack of concentration.*

(2) Another cause of difficulty is the exceedingly expansive tendency of some missions. They are not satisfied with one or even two fields of labour, but must occupy several provinces with an agent or two in each. These missions have yet to learn the important lesson of concentration, for unless their agents are geniuses, it is seldom indeed that a man can make up three or four different Indian languages, so as to work efficiently in all, and so support their fellow-labourers of the same mission elsewhere. The expansiveness shows itself, too, in other directions. We have heard of a young missionary of this class, leaving his own particular portion of the field and invading that of another mission, baptizing so-called converts almost at the door of another missionary, and then leaving them to their own sweet will without guide or teacher. This newer type of missionary knows nothing, as a rule, of the so-called converts or their motives, beyond that they have expressed a desire to become Christians. I think this Conference will agree that the less we have of such work the better.

*By difference of views.*

(3) But another cause, and when two missions come closely in contact in the same field, the chief cause of breaches of comity, is the difference of views regarding agents and methods of work.

*Standard of knowledge.*

(a) For example, some missions rightly or wrongly insist upon a very different standard of a preliminary education, both secular and theological, from their home representatives, and the same principle is carried out in the acquirements demanded from their respective agents in the mission field. This might not matter very much, did it not at times also happen that the defectively educated mission agent is in receipt of the highest salary, which very naturally produces dissatisfaction on the part of those in the neighbouring mission who are better educated and who know that they are.

(b) Then, again, there is a wide difference of opinion about the reception of converts into the church, which has become more and more accentuated in recent years. One man will baptize any individual, even if the man be profoundly ignorant of the fundamental principles and obligations of Christianity, if he only confesses Christ and expresses a wish for baptism. Another proceeds more leisurely, and insists upon an intelligent idea of what the convert is confessing, and some evidence of the genuineness of the faith he is professing. Where these diverse methods are in operation in the same town or district the result must almost inevitably be utter confusion.

*Firm Day.*

*Reception of converts.*

(c) Still further, there is a perennial source of heart-burning in the reception of each other's agents or adherents, and especially of those under discipline. When a convert's views of theology and church order are suddenly developed under the disciplinary process, then woe betide the theology he accepts or the church receiving him. We are told that converts should be at liberty to join other churches if they see fit. Who questions that, if the change be the result of prayerful enquiry and intelligent comprehension of the difference between two given sets of views; but to encourage change on any other conditions is simply to put a premium on perversion. There is nothing perhaps more painful than to see men whom you know from long and bitter experience to be liars and thieves and worse received into a neighbouring mission, and, notwithstanding warnings given, promoted to positions of influence, perhaps enrolled as preacher, of the Gospel. But why not receive them on their repentance? it is said. Why not, indeed; but let those who knew the character of their offence be judges of the quality and quantity of the repentance.

*Agents.*

II.—*Is there a remedy for our difficulties; and, if so, what?* Generally, I concur with what Mr. Clifford says in his paper. The best remedy, it seems to me, is what may be called a modified Territorialism carried out in a spirit of Christian forbearance and charity.

*Remedies.*

**Fifth Day.**

(1) Let each mission, old or new, concentrate its efforts on a field that it can efficiently work; and in any case where a mission has a large field that it can't so work, let it willingly and thankfully relinquish a portion of it to those who are prepared to help in it.

(2) Except in the eight or ten chief cities of India, there should not be more than one mission at work in any one place, and when two missions occupy the same field, distinct portions of it should be assigned to each.

(3) Then, again, when it is known beforehand that the lines of work of any two missions are widely different, let them for each other's peace and comfort keep as far apart as possible.

(4) Missions working in the same or adjoining fields should make an effort to secure the same standard of efficiency in their agents and the same rate of pay and allowances for them.

(5) Councils of conciliation might at times be tried, but I have not much faith in them because, if properly representative, which they should always be, there is just as much danger of the judges differing as there is of the parties who appear before them, and this would only make matters worse.

**St. Paul's example.**

The great missionary apostle prided himself on not building on another man's foundations, and he thought he had "the Spirit of God." Some nowadays seem to look out for foundations to build upon, and I have never heard of their doing so, except under the professed guidance of the Spirit. The Spirit that prompted Paul was apparently a very different one. Many of us will be satisfied to have a portion of that Spirit which rested on Paul, and to walk, however feebly, in his footsteps.

The meeting being now open for discussion,—

**Breaking golden rules.**

The Rev. N. E. LUNDBORG, Secretary, S. E. L. M., Saugor, C. P., said:—Although this is indeed a very important question, yet we feel sorry to learn that there are bodies or denominational institutions which seem certainly to be interested in it and to lay down rules how to deal with one another in this respect; but when it comes to pass that these theories are brought into practical use, they themselves are the first to trample the golden rules under their feet. During this five minutes I shall not have time to say very much of the common rules and regulations that ought to be observed by every society; but I will briefly tell you some of the facts which we have experienced in our Lutheran Mission in the Central Provinces. I will first tell you how we have obtained our mission stations. When the well-known missionary, the Rev. James Dawson, in Chindwara, died, and the Free Church of Scotland had no suitable person to send there, they invited us to take over that station; and they also offered us as a present their property, namely, the school building with some furniture, the papers of which are all with me certifying the truth thereof. And we never touched the mission work there before this was done. In regard to Saugor and Narsinghpore, our missionaries went out on a tour to search for a mission field in 1878. They went to consult with the much-esteemed C. M. S. Missionary, the Rev. — Champion, in Jubbulpore. Hearing that we wanted a mission field, he said, among other things, to our missionaries: "There is a station (Narsinghpore) which we used to visit from time to time by sending our catechist there; but if you would like to take up that station, we would be very glad to give it up for you;" and we said: "Very well." Further, he said: "There is also a large station (Saugor) which we have taken up, so far that we have a catechist stationed there; but if you would be pleased to have that station, we shall hand it over to you;" and we said: "Very well." And so he added lastly: "We have also a catechist there, a good old faithful man, if you like you shall have him also;" and we said: "Very well." That good and faithful man (Jan Ali) worked there with us more than two years, until his dear wife one evening—he having been to the bazaar for preaching—found him on his knees in prayer; but when she called him to come and dine, there was no reply; he had gone and joined those who kneel down before the throne of God. And so we have been toiling on, time and years have passed by. In Narsinghpore we have of late had good ingress; several have been baptized and the Word of God seemed to become a power among the people; there were a lot of people under instruction and there was a good prospect. One day, our missionary there, suddenly came to know that there had come another missionary in, and he had already baptized several persons there. After sometime he also paid our missionary a visit; and in his conversation he said, among other things: "I have come to do mission work in Narsinghpore, and I see that the Lord has blessed my work gloriously, so I intend to ask you if you will sell your bungalow!" I will finally also mention how that new missionary used to swell his number of converts. In conversation with the people, who had, as aforesaid, heard the Word of God for years, some perhaps for a shorter time, he used to say among other good things: "Do you believe in the Word of God?" Reply: "Most certainly I do." "But have you also taken the sign of such a belief?" "What sign?" "Well, bring me a vessel with water and I will show you." The water was brought and the show consisted in their baptism. "Now you are a Christian!"

*Fifth Day.*

*Instance of comity.*

*A second instance.*

*Narsinghpore.*

*An interloper.*

*His behaviour.*

**Fifth Day.**

Whereupon, I am told by trustworthy authors, there were people ready to bring that man in court for deception. I shall not express my opinion upon that sort of missionary comity, *sat sapienti*; but I beg to close with a few words of advice from one of the best of missionaries that the world ever have seen, namely, St. Paul the Apostle, who says: "*Not to boast in another man's line of things made ready to our hand,*" II. Cor. x. 16; and : "*Let no man suffer as a busybody in other man's matters,*" I. Peter iv. 15.

The Rev. L. L. Uhl, ph.d., A. L. M., Guntur, Madras, said :—I have written and spoken during the forenoon of this day on the extreme difficulties met with in work among the degraded classes. I am not alone in my estimate of the low grade of mental and Christian life among these people, for every one of the missionaries in our Lutheran Mission agree with me in this estimate in every respect. The case of our Christian people being as it is, there is imperative need of co-operation among the several Missionary Societies working in the same or neighbouring territory. In our Lutheran Mission, in the Telugu country, we have an illustration of all the possible conditions of missionary comity and amity. On one side of us, which I shall designate as our right, is an honoured society with which we are working in comity. On another side of us, which I shall call our left, and also among us, is a different society, one honoured also, with which we have not been able to co-labour either in comity or in amity. With the society on our right we have kept one boundary for fifty years, and only on inquiry and permission have the members or teachers of one mission been received by the other. These were fifty years of harmony: the two missions could unite together against deceivers and disciplined members, and could pursue their policy of work without interference or interruption. Sweet are the memories of those fifty years of comity, and that comity continues. With the society on our left we worked together in contiguous territory, but without comity. Members and teachers of all sorts were received by this mission from us, and that despite all our protestations. This continued for thirty-six years, when the same mission began work in our territory, where it has now been labouring for fourteen years without amity. The hindrances and evil to missionary work in those fourteen years are indescribable. In my own soul have I been filled with bitterness, because of the state of things ; nevertheless I have tried to put away all this bitterness and come up here to counsel peace. Yet what peace is it to be brotherly for two weeks and then be in conflict for nine years and fifty weeks! I say we have had fifty years of comity with the society on our right, and the work has been harmonious and blest ; we have had thirty-six years of contiguity of territory, but without comity, with the

*[margin: Comity on the right, not on the left.]*

society on our left, and then fourteen years of overlapping of territory and of work, but without amity, and the whole has been an unsettling of Christians, a strife and a pain. Comity is to be preferred, if it can be realized, for it is the ideal of co-operation in missionary work. If comity is impossible, we must by all means have amity. There are many members present here from the society I have designated as on our left, and I have a glad word to say to this body, viz.,—that there is prospect of amicable arrangements being made for jointly conducting our work in the same territory, members of both missions desire such arrangements, and I do hope that before the next Decennial Conference meets, we shall set an example of amity for all missions. Moreover, I do beg this Conference, I earnestly beg its members, to do something towards securing either comity or amity among the Mission Societies it represents, and so save the churches from confusion and strife, and bring about a better state of affairs in the congregations, especially among the untrained and undeveloped people.

Fifth Day.

The Rev. R. A. HUME, M.A., A. B. F. M., Ahmednagar, said:—My object in speaking is first to give a testimony, and second to give a message from the American Marathi Mission. In the Ahmednagar District our Mission and the S. P. G. Mission work side by side. We have a good many differences, and when we worked without a definite agreement regarding territory and the employment of agents, we had a good deal of unpleasantness. But now, for about fourteen years, we have a definite written agreement on these points. Though at times some questions have arisen, yet on the whole the agreement has been a mutual advantage, and non-Christians have seen much less of the evil of Christians contending among themselves. Secondly, at our last mission meeting the American Marathi Mission sent a message to this Conference, suggesting that it pass a resolution that no mission should employ a member of another mission without first asking of such mission what it had to say regarding the man. That is the way in which the Government ordinarily treats candidates, and if followed in a liberal spirit among missions, it would be in the main a mutual advantage to all parties.

The A. B. F. M. and S. P. G.

Employing another mission's agents.

The Rev. J. L. PHILLIPS, M.A., M.D., LL.B., S. S. U., Calcutta, said:—I could gladly keep my seat in this session of the Conference, had I not been entreated by brethren in many parts of India, who are not present, to speak for them on this subject. Too strong words cannot be spoken for thorough and sustained Christian fellowship among ourselves. We must preserve peace in our own ranks if we would hold high the standard of our adorable Lord in this land. I plead for what has been known for these centuries as the Golden Rule, or putting it negatively, if you please, let us beware of doing to any brother

The golden rule.

FIFTH DAY.

what we should not enjoy his doing to us. Particularly in this matter of native helpers, let there be a good understanding among us that no missionary accepts or employs a man disciplined or dismissed by another mission without his bringing satisfactory papers from his former field.

Letters of commendation.

Scandal and sorrow will be prevented by our adhering strictly to this rule, which you all know some Protestant missionaries are notoriously violating. Mr. Gulliford's suggestion about commending our members to the fellowship of other churches in places where they go, and find no church of their own order, is excellent and should be heeded in such a field as ours. This would save immense confusion in many cases, while it cannot but promote Christian fellowship.

But it is the effect from the heathen around us that I am concerned about. Our peace impresses them with the beauty and power of our holy faith, and our discord must turn away the hearts of some from the truth they fain would accept. Our blessed Saviour prayed for His disciples "That they all may be one, as Thou Father art in Me and I in Thee, that they also may be one in Us; *that the world may believe that Thou hast sent Me.*" Our spirit and conduct towards one another are telling upon the non-Christian multitude surging all around us, and you and I, and every missionary here and in all India, are making it either harder or easier for these Hindus and Muhammadans to believe in the Lord Jesus Christ. I now distinctly recall how

An act of amity.

years ago, in one of my earliest camping seasons in Bengal, the Christian courtesy of a beloved brother of the Church Missionary Society impressed the heathen of a large *sudder* station where we chanced to meet for the first time, and where his native assistants and mine came together on the Sabbath for worshipping one common Lord. With all my heart, I say, let us honour and help one another. Look not every man to his own things alone, but "let every one of us please his neighbour for his good to edification." So shall our courage and strength be multiplied for aggressive service.

Love and courtesy.

The Rev. T. S. JOHNSON, M.D., M. E. C., Jabalpur, C. P., said:—Christian love and courtesy, rather than districting the country, are the principles upon which to settle this question. Districts join each other, and a previous speaker made mention of continued friction with a mission in an adjoining district. A brother from Rajputana laments the coming of another mission into his district, and baptizing hundreds of people whom he says he "never would have baptized." But it is to be hoped that many of those ignorant, low-caste people will accept Christ and be saved, and their children become intelligent Christians, which certainly should be cause for rejoicing rather than otherwise. As to helpers, I have long ago decided to employ no man, not even from my own mission, without proper recommendations, and will even then be slow to do so, because such men as I want are too busy in the work to be seeking employment. An understanding about salary is one of the very needful things.

*Fifth Day.*

The Rev. J. P. JONES, M.A., A. B. F. M., Madura, said:—I also have a grievance in this matter, but will refrain from ventilating it, for I remember that a well-known writer insists that every one who has a grievance is liable to be a bore. I believe that both the papers presented to us have an element of truth in them. I am strongly in favour of territorial limits, but I am equally strongly opposed to the method of some missions and societies of retaining large tracts of country which they marked out for themselves a half century or more since, but which they have throughout these years only nominally occupied; indeed, have shamefully neglected. I maintain that it is the solemn duty of such missions to *shorten* their cords and invite other societies to occupy a part of their field. Let us see more generosity and justice in this line. Now, if a new society comes into this land it has to pass many bright and promising but pre-empted fields, even though they are practically untouched by Christian influence and are rarely the scene of any Christian activity, and go away into remote corners in search of an "unoccupied" field. I would that missions and societies could be made to feel that the only right they have to claim a field is that of full occupancy in the present or early future. Bearing this fully in mind the territorial limit has its decided advantages. Besides the negative benefits referred to by the other speakers, I believe that it has the positive merit of presenting before us so many separate and distinct methods of mission work, each one with its peculiar advantages and representing some points of excellence for our emulation. It is thus a stimulus, an inspiration, and almost a revelation to any one of us to take a tour of observation among our sister missions that are thus allowed to perfect their own peculiar ideas and methods of work. I heartily agree with the former speakers in reference to comity, so far as our treatment of each other's mission agents and Christians is concerned. We cannot be too careful in this matter, as nothing is more easy than to listen to one side of a story, and that usually the wrong one, and give employment to a man or receive so-called Christians without making the slightest inquiry with their past connections. Comity and amity here can only result in rich blessing to all parties concerned.

*A man with a grievance.*

*Benefits of comity.*

The Rev. W. HOOPER, D.D., C.M.S., Jabalpur, said:—It may be worth while to mention that at Allahabad we have never found it difficult to maintain the comity of which we have heard so much, but can scarcely hear too much. There, a division of the district, among the several missions engaged, is greatly facilitated by nature, as it is almost equally divided into the portion between the Ganges and the Jumna, the

*An instance of comity.*

**Fifth Day.**

**A comity committee.**

**Harmony most desirable.**

portion south of the Jumna, and that north of the Ganges. So the first was kept to by the Baptists, the second by the American Presbyterians, the third by the C. M. S. Now, indeed, the Baptists have retired from the district, so that the Presbyterians have the whole south of the Ganges, and the C. M. S. the whole north of it. This division of labour is, as I have said, particularly easy at Allahabad; but I am sure there can be no insuperable objections to it anywhere. We have practised the same comity in our mutual relations in work in the *city*, as in the district. We arrange the different preaching-places among ourselves, so that the same is occupied by different missions at different times; and when, some years ago, our work was threatened by the activity of the Arya Samaj, and police regulations had to be made to prevent collisions between them and Christians, the different missions acted *together* in the arrangements that were made. Some speakers have advocated the establishment of a general Missionary Comity Council for the whole of India, while others have maintained that its work would be better done by local Conferences among the different missions in any particular locality. It seems to me that both these are desirable, for neither can do the work of the other. By all means let the local inter-Mission Conferences, where established, endeavour to compose all difficulties which may arise between the missions; and, where not established, let them be so with all speed. But, for the double purpose of acting where *no* such Conferences exist, and of forming a sort of court of appeal when the local Conferences are unable to arrange matters satisfactorily to all parties, let us by all means have a central Committee or Council, whose decision no missionary or mission may disregard, without incurring the penalty of being made, so to speak, outlaws from the brotherhood of missionary comity.

The Rev. G. H. ROUSE, M.A., LL.B., B. M. S., Calcutta, said:—Territorial division is good to a certain extent, but it is not the chief thing. There may be united action in proximity and discordant action at a distance. The point to emphasize is that all missions should seek to work in harmony and not interfere with one another's work, by taking people and agents from other missions. Insist upon this, and we shall have the one essential thing, and it will matter little whether we are close by or distant from one another.

The Rev. A. CLIFFORD, M.A., C. M. S., Bishop-Designate of Lucknow, writer of one of the papers, said in reply:—I have little to add to my paper on the subject of comity. It was written two years ago for a special occasion, but I think my views have on the whole been confirmed since, and to-day's discussion has certainly tended to strengthen rather than weaken them. All that has been said to-day against, what I may call the "district system," has been said against the *abuses* of the system, and can hardly be held to hold good as arguments against the system itself. Every system is liable to abuse, and advocates of the "district system" would be the first to admit that where the system they uphold has been perverted and made the excuse for a "dog-in-the-manger" policy there is need to apply remedies. But we are not at all prepared to say that the remedy is the abolition of the system itself. Such a committee as I suggest at the close of my paper is, I believe, not an impossibility. It would have much influence in adjusting difficulties, and though its suggestions could not be enforced, there is a high probability that they would generally be adopted. Such an inter-Society Committee exists I believe in London, and is found useful there. I see no good reason why a similarly constituted one should not work here. Or, if preferred, there might be local inter-Society Committees for the various provinces of India. However, the moral sense of the Conference will condemn the forcible invasions, by one mission, of the sphere of another. Such high-handed methods of evangelization cannot possibly be right. They err against the first principles of Christian charity. There must at least be communication and consultation with the parties concerned before entering the district where they work. But, brethren, with our 284 millions of non-Christians, almost untouched with Christian influence at present, does it not seem preposterous that we should be talking about infringing on one another's work? Who can doubt but that there is room for all, if all do not insist upon rushing to the easiest or more promising fields? A little sacrifice and self-control and good feeling is what is wanted to put the matter right and keep it right.

Fifth Day.

Bishop THOBURN, D.D., M. E. C., Calcutta, writer of one of the papers, said in reply:—I have noted with much satisfaction that most of those who have spoken have taken my side of this question. It is very true some of them do not seem to be aware of the fact, but both in the spirit and in the letter of the discussion they have been with me in the expression of their views. A careful reading of my paper will show that I appreciate as highly as anyone the evils of dissension and the unspeakable blessings of love and unity. It is because I appreciate these blessings that I deprecate the traditional policy which most Missionary Societies have long since adopted, and advocate the introduction of something better. I shall omit all reference to the personal matters which have been thrust into the discussion by two or three of the brethren, save to say, that so far as Mr. Kerry's remarks are concerned, I wish to say here, publicly and frankly, as I have said in print before, that the S. P. G. Society has a just ground of complaint against the mission which I represent, but I knew nothing of the occurrence until two and-a-half years after it had transpired, and to this day the S. P. G.

The traditional policy.

FIFTH DAY.

Not a new theory.

Wide-spread organizations.

Society has made no representation of the case to me. For some reason, which I do not profess to understand, Mr. Kerry has espoused their cause with great zeal. I shall make no further reference to my old-time friend's attack upon us, but beg to call your attention to his omission to account for the presence of three societies in the little field to which he has called your attention. If this policy is as good as is here represented, how is it that it has so signally failed, not only in this case, but in so many others like it? All the speakers seem to think that they are advocating the introduction of something new, whereas they are really apologizing for something which has been on trial for a hundred years and has conspicuously failed. Mr. Kerry has unwittingly borne testimony to this fact. In a district close to Calcutta, under the very eyes of all the missionaries, three societies have come together in adjacent villages in spite of the rule, and the complaint is made that a fourth has also appeared upon the ground. If you will read my paper you will discover that my chief accusation against this policy is that it has been on trial for a hundred years and has failed. I say this again, not only with reference to the territorial question, but also the proposed rules of the committee of reference. This latter feature of the traditional policy has never been a success anywhere. It was tried in the Punjab about twenty-five years ago, and was so complete a failure that within five years very few missionaries in that region knew that it had ever existed. I once asked a brother up there how it was working, and he simply laughed and said that no one had paid the slightest attention to it from the first. You will notice that all the speakers who defended the traditional policy omitted to notice the fact that more than one organization has already spread all over India. The Anglican Church, for instance, meets you everywhere. The Roman Catholic Church, also, is planted in every part of the empire. The Baptists, English and American, have their stations dotted all over India. The mission which I represent has likewise spread far and wide. Some of you, on the other hand, belong to missions which have, and prefer to have, a limited district. Your policy may be the best one, but do not forget that others have adopted a different policy, and whether you like it or not they have been working out on lines which they could hardly avoid under their respective ecclesiastical systems. Surely, any one ought to see that it is simply a waste of time to talk to one of these organizations, which has already spread itself out throughout the empire, about gathering its forces together and retiring into a corner which may be set apart for it. But if we are to divide up as proposed, no division will be possible which is not a fair one, and which does not re-distribute the whole territory of India. But the very mention of such a proposal shows its practical absurdity. We must not part with reason in our desire to adopt good measures. I distinctly advocate a new policy, and yet a policy which is not new. It is that which we have all had from the beginning. No rule can permanently work successfully in India which is not adapted to Britain and America as well. In all Christian lands where free thought is tolerated and religious freedom enjoyed, Christian people learn to live and work together, respecting one another's rights, appreciating one another's labours, and succeeding in their respective tasks. It would bring utter confusion and endless discord, to say nothing of disgraceful quarrels, into any part of England or America, if an attempt were made to parcel out the country into districts to be occupied by single organizations, and then to lay down a code of rules and create a committee of reference either for the prevention or the settlement of disputes. The very proposal would be scouted, if made by the whole Christian world. Sooner or later we in India must awake to a realization of the fact that we are at least as good as our brethren in the home lands. We must exercise the charity which is exacted there, to say nothing of the common sense which is expected from Christians there. I think, too, that we all need to remember that no rule or policy can change character. We are all very much alike. Our infirmities are the infirmities of the race. We are so constructed, with our two eyes, two ears, and double brain, that each one of us has a double vision and a double sense of hearing. It has often seemed to me that human beings are peculiar in having their sense of vision and of hearing preternaturally acute when a wrong is suffered, and strangely paralyzed when a wrong is inflicted. We see the injury done to us most vividly, but are almost blind when a wrong chances to be inflicted by us. I fear that missionaries are exactly like other people in this respect, and we would do well to admit the fact at once, and not assume that in the nature of the case, after we have adopted our policies and rules, all of us will see exactly alike and everything move along with admirable smoothness. At the very best we must bear and forbear, and instead of providing a policy which shall put a premium upon public accusations and counter-accusations among brethren, let us adopt the policy of the New Testament. Let us remember that we are all brethren; let each one do his own work in his own way, and not get unhappy because a neighbour works upon a different basis, or perhaps is unbrotherly or possibly forgetful of our rights. If a man of this kind chances to come into our neighbourhood, all the rules and policies which could be adopted by all the societies and churches of the world would not change his character or make him a more desirable neighbour. I have reached my present views on this subject somewhat slowly, but chiefly by the light of my own experience. When I

*Fifth Day.*

One rule in India, Britain and America.

Effect of rule on character.

Experience.

**Fifth Day.**

came to India a third of a century ago as a mere youth, I was posted to Naini Tal. I did not dream that I could injure anybody in this wide world by doing a little work for the Master, but when I attempted to visit a sick soldier in the hospital I found that I was giving offence. When I went to hold a meeting among the soldiers I was regarded as an intruder. When I organized a Sunday-school, in a place where no Sunday-school had ever been held, I was positively compelled to close it ; and even when I attempted to bury the little corpse of a missionary's child by rites which the bereaved mother chose, I was obliged to have a little grave dug on the mountain side, and conduct the burial service there, so as not to trespass upon what was regarded as an ecclesiastical right. Do you wonder that at the very outset I became wearied beyond expression with this first exhibition of a spirit which is in essence not very different from that advocated to-day ? Then I had to look out for boundaries beyond my little station, and I became so wearied, if not disgusted, with the difficulties which beset me, that I rashly determined to preach no more in English, and held to my unwise resolution for a number of years. At a later day I felt impelled to work elsewhere under special circumstances, but at every step I have encountered the same extraordinary opposition. When I ventured to preach in Cawnpore I was requested to retire to the other side of the river. When I went to railway men who heard no one else, I was chided and requested not to interfere with another's labours, and thus it went on year after year, while I constantly felt oppressed by the fact that just at the point where it seemed to me most clear that God was calling me to a special work, opposition was sure to manifest itself. I could not but feel, and I cannot but feel to-day, that this traditional policy, however different its originators may have intended it to be, has an inevitable tendency to work in the way I have described. It hinders the Gospel, dear brethren, beyond any doubt. It interferes with Christian freedom of action, and creates ten times as much strife as under the best circumstances it can prevent. Look, for instance, at the present situation.

*Applications for workers.* At this very hour I have applications from fifteen thousand persons belonging to the depressed classes, who ask me to send them teachers or preachers to show them how to become Christians. I cannot disregard such an opening, and yet I cannot lift a hand to help any one of those fifteen thousand persons without transgressing this policy which so many of you are advocating to-day. You will tell me to make the work over to others, but there are no others to take it. There are missions planted in most of the districts where these people live, but some of the missionaries will not, and others cannot, do work of this kind. Some do not think that their work lies among the depressed classes; others say that they have too much already in hand and cannot add to their burdens. One dear Anglican brother told me that he and many of his brethren would be only too glad to join in the work, but that every one of them was carrying as heavy a load as he could endure. Others again have not the peculiar training, or skill, or knowledge, or whatever you may call it, which will enable them to do this kind of work. I make this remark with reference to some of our own missionaries as well as to others. Not every one *can* do this work. Now I can get men who can do it, and I can take it up at once. I ask you, and I put the question before the whole Christian world, ought I, dare I, to turn my back on these people and leave them to the uncertainties of the future, simply because some good men years ago laid down boundaries over which certain missionaries in coming years were not to pass? Time will shed much light on this whole question. I have often been regarded as an intruder, but some of the sweetest recollections of my missionary life are those connected with the change of views which missionary brethren have undergone on this subject. I have known men to contend earnestly for the old policy through a course of years, and in the end become fully convinced that the new policy is the better one, and to admit that they had stood in their own light in trying to prevent brethren from taking up a work which they did not fully comprehend. May I mention one instance: a brother missionary once called on me and remonstrated with me for beginning work too near to his own post. We reasoned together in the best spirit, but could not agree. He felt that I was about to injure him and his work, but before the end of the first year he cordially admitted that our presence near him had been a blessing and only a blessing to his people. He stated that, so far from hurting his work, he had received more new members into his church during that year than in all his previous ministry, and crowned his noble acknowledgment by sending a contribution in aid of our work. May this not happen in the case of some of the alleged injuries which you so painfully feel at the present day? will it not be possible that our dear brother from Rajputana, when we meet ten years hence, will look back upon the events of the decade and say that our entrance upon that field has turned out very different from his fears? If, for instance, he finds in his own mission five thousand converts from among the depressed classes, all of them soundly instructed up to the Presbyterian standard, and all of them living in peace with their Methodist neighbours, will he not then say that he miscalculated the results of what he now regards as an unwarranted intrusion upon his field? It used to be said of the Methodists in the early days of their history, that God had raised them up to be peculiarly the evangelists of the poor. Our noblest trophies have been won among the poor in other lands, and may it not be possible that

*Fifth Day.*

Possible results.

**Fifth Day.**

**Seek to do God's will.**

God is choosing even some of us here in India to be in some peculiar sense His messengers to these awakening millions among the depressed classes? If others are not listening to their cry, if others fail in some way to reach them and to lead them to Christ, and if we find the agents who can do it, and who will take up the work; in the name of our common Master, my dear brethren, let me ask if it may not be that we are right, and some of you wrong, in our views on this subject? May it not be possible that instead of injuring your work or trespassing upon your grounds that you are hindering us in a field which would be left untilled for half a century if we did not enter it?

Time has many lessons in store for us. We all have much to learn; we all make mistakes. But we need only to seek to do the will of our common Master, in order to avoid inflicting any actual injury upon another's work. God's work never operates against itself. It cannot do it, and cannot be made to do it. Let us be sure that we are each and all doing His work, and then we shall be found helping and not hindering our brethren, both near and far. May God bless you all.

# XV.—WORK AMONG ANGLO-INDIANS AND EURASIANS.

## AFTERNOON SESSION.

SMALL HALL, 2 to 4·30 P.M.

The Rev. T. J. SCOTT, D.D., M. E. C., Bareilly, N.-W. P., *in the chair*, who said :—We have before us a most important subject. It must not be thought that this is not a subject suited to a Missionary Conference. In the matter before us, we have a vital missionary question. Christian people, in thinking of mission work, often look away from home to some foreign field or people on whom they are willing to expend their money and sympathy, while they do not seem to see real missionary work near their own door. We must not overlook the great importance of giving the Gospel to all Anglo-Indians and Eurasians in the Indian empire. They are here to stay, and are certainly to be a powerful factor in the destinies of India. To the mass of the people they represent or misrepresent Christianity. Saved, they can powerfully influence the evangelization of India. They can bring to bear on the country something of the energy and dominant spirit that marks the European. The English language is becoming the dominant foreign language from Egypt all through to China and Japan. It is to be the common language of commerce and enterprise, of diplomacy and of general evangelism. How important, then, that the people in question at this meeting, and who speak this language, be fully influenced by the Gospel. We cannot afford to neglect this work whatever else we may do. It has been too much overlooked in the past in our zeal for other forms of work. We may rejoice that more attention is now paid to this matter.

*[Margin notes: FIFTH DAY. A Missionary subject. Here to stay. English.]*

## PAPER.

By the Rev. Herbert GOULDSMITH, M.A., C. M. S., Calcutta.

**Fifth Day.**

*Introduction.*

Work amongst Anglo-Indians and Eurasians is a subject which could be dealt with from many different points of view. In this paper I purpose only dealing with that part of the work which comes more directly under my notice. I will leave for others the discussion of work amongst the greater number of Anglo-Indians, namely, the Military, Indian Civilians, Planters, European merchants, &c., and confine my remarks to the domiciled Europeans and Eurasians residing in India. To simplify terms, I will use, throughout the paper, one expression to embrace both the domiciled Europeans and Eurasians, and call them Indo-Europeans.

*Use of the term Indo-Europeans.*

*The importance of the work.*

I.—*The importance* of the work amongst Indo-Europeans is sadly overlooked in the excessive zeal for direct mission work amongst the heathen. English-speaking people have souls to be saved as well as Hindus and Muhammadans; but because there is less romance about it, because the results are not so striking, and because the work is conducted in the English tongue, it is often looked upon as inferior and of little consequence. A quarter of a million of precious human beings, with immense powers for good, and at the same time terrible opportunities for evil, dare not be passed lightly by. The subject may be put forward, however, in another way, and that a more striking one, before a Missionary Conference. Work amongst Indo-Europeans is absolutely necessary from a missionary point of view.

*1. On its own account.*

*2. As a help to direct Mission work.*

*(a) By removing an immense obstacle.*

Sir Andrew Scoble, speaking at a meeting in London, said: "Let me tell you that, if, whilst sending missionaries to the heathen for the purpose of preaching the Gospel to them, you are neglecting the claims of the Europeans and Eurasians in that country, you create a class of missionaries who do infinitely more harm to God's Church than all the heathen together can do, because every European and every Eurasian who neglects his duty as a Christian becomes *a missionary of evil* to the people around him." The inconsistency of professing Christians must be the greatest obstacle to the spread of Christianity: yea, more than an obstacle, an absolute opposing force. Let this be overcome and removed, and how much more easily would missionary work flow on. Well may a strict Parsee, a pious Hindu, or a devout Muhammadan think himself a far superior being to the many around who, while professing the name of Christ, live in every way opposed to the principles of Christ's teaching.

The power of the life is far greater than the power of words, and, if only Indo-Europeans lived out the life of Christ before the heathen, the effect would be marvellous.

Why is it that now after 100 years of missionary work in India there is the constant cry, "Send us more helpers from over the seas," when at the very door of the mission field there is a recruiting ground capable of producing officers and men well suited for the work? The answer is simply this: The recruiting ground has been neglected. If only greater pastoral and educational care had been given, there would have come forth from all sides, ere this, earnest and willing volunteers for the work. From among the Indo-Europeans there are some now at work, and right royally too; and there is material for many more if only greater care and more money was given for their training and preparation.

May God stir the hearts of missionaries in the field and the hearts of lovers of missions at home to believe more in their fellow-countrymen in India, and to take such an interest in them that they will not rest till everything in human power has been done to raise and help a people that will warmly respond to all sympathy and love.

II. *The difficulties of the work* are often brought forward as a proof of the hopelessness of it; but surely no one believing that with God all things are possible could on that account turn aside from it and have nothing to do with it. The difficulties are great and very real, and should be well understood, that thus greater sympathy and help may be given for the work and the workers.

The variety of social grades amongst the Indo-Europeans and consequent lack of unity amongst them is one of the chief hindrances to any successful work on a large scale. The differences are not mere fanciful ones; there are wide divergences in every way, and to look upon Indo-Europeans as all of a class is to make a very gross mistake. Each class seems to need special

Fifth Day.

(*b*) By forming a powerful witness.

(*c*) By producing a recruiting ground for Mission workers.

3. Missionaries and Friends in England ought to take greater interest in it.

The difficulties of the work.

1. Social.

(*a*) Social grades.

**Fifth Day.** thought and special method for reaching it. The social differences often of people residing in one street is very striking, though none the less perplexing. This makes house to house visitation a great problem, and well-experienced visitors are necessary for this branch of pastoral work. There is good reason for the upper-class, well-educated Indo-Europeans feeling hurt when they are classed, as they often are, with the poor, uneducated, thriftless people who wear English clothes, and, at times, speak the English language.

(*b*) **Poverty.** The class just referred to, as differing so entirely from the upper and middle classes of the Indo-Europeans, is a large and very trying one. The terrible poverty which prevails amongst them seems to expel all thoughts of anything higher than mere existence. To get along, no matter how, with a certain amount of liberty, is the great life object. The valuable report of a Pauperism Committee for Calcutta has lately revealed a fearful state of things. 16·6 per cent. of the Indo-Europeans are receiving charitable relief, or, to put it in another form, 7·9 of the Europeans and 22·3 of the Eurasians are paupers. When these figures are compared with the amount of pauperism in England, it is concluded that in no county in England is there as large a proportion of the population in receipt of charitable relief as among the *Europeans* in Calcutta, or *one-third as much as among the Eurasians*. Poverty of this description can at once be seen as a great social and spiritual problem to deal with. It is very hard to arouse people to the need of preparing for the future, when the mind is taken up wholly and solely with the present. Government at present feels that nothing further can be done than is being done, but what the Government cannot do the Gospel can, for, when the Gospel once penetrates into the inner being of a man, how soon it raises the general character and enables the man to be independent of his fellow-men in his reliance upon God.

(*c*) **Houses.** Much social evil can be traced to the very insufficient house accommodation, and in this the poor especially suffer, though the middle classes also are effected by it. Home life, in its simplicity as known in England, is the one thing wanting in India. The privacy, the domestic barriers so precious to a home, are sadly absent, and terrible results follow from their loss. The sanitation, too, though clearly greatly improved from what it used to be, is far from perfect, and must be the cause of a good deal of the bodily and mental weakness so common among the poor.

But, while speaking of the social difficulties of the work, there must not be omitted the prejudice which exists against Indo-Europeans and the utter neglect of them as a consequence arising from it. It is indeed hard for a Community to be shunted on all hands: let Christians beware, and especially Christian workers, of ever throwing a reproach against them. And let one practical result of the discussion of this subject in the Conference be an increased sympathy for the Community on the part of missionaries and their fellow-workers.

There are moral difficulties, alas, as well as social, to contend with, such as are not so manifest in England. The standard of morals is fixed very low indeed. The Rev. S. A. Barnett, after a visit to the East, writing of his impressions of India, well hit the mark when he said something to this effect. Missionaries have been presenting the Gospel to the people before proclaiming the Law. The Law and the prophets must come before the Gospel of Love and Pardon. As a consequence of this, Sin, in its intensity, is seldom felt. Gross immorality is constantly spoken of as a thing of naught. Lying is very prevalent, and debt is only too common. The ground needs much ploughing, and constant hoeing is required.

In addition to this, there is a spirit of indifference and general carelessness, arising to a great extent from the relaxing climate. Who does not feel something of this spirit after toiling through the summer's heat and the autumn's rains? Reason for it there is undoubtedly, but the fact remains, and in it there is an immense obstacle to the reception of the Gospel. A constitution so weakened with indifference is easily effected with the disease of Hindu Fatalism.

Closely allied to this indifference is the want of perseverance so common among the younger members of the Community. It is complained of by employers of labour, as represented in the report of the Pauperism Committee above referred to, but it no less hampers the progress of spiritual work.

Here, then, are some of the social and moral difficulties. The difficulties call loudly for further help, and it is for Christian England to stir herself and, by taking greater interest in the Indo-Europeans, to remove the difficulties, and so, as shown in

*Marginal notes:* FIFTH DAY. *d* Lack of interest towards the Community. 2. Moral. (*a*) Low standard of morals. (*b*) Indifference and apathy. (*c*) Want of perseverance.

the earlier part of the paper, remove one great obstacle to direct missionary work.

III. From these remarks, concerning the difficulties of the work, it might be conjectured that there was no encouragement. This is not so; encouragement there is, and has been, but yet it has not been without a good deal of failure, and much yet remains to be done. Look first at the spiritual side of the work.

The services in the places of worship are, on the whole, very fairly attended, although attendance entails to many ghari-hire and often exposure to the heat or rains. These services must be a power, especially where godly, earnest men are placed over the flock, and in time they must tell on the moral and spiritual tone of the people. But beyond the regular attendants of the churches, there are, as always, large numbers who seldom enter a place of worship. How are these to be reached? The clergy and ministers are mostly so occupied single-handed with the duties of their churches and the business connected with them that they have no time for visiting those not members of the congregation.

Up to the present there have been only a few voluntary lay workers as far as I can ascertain; and here is a great weakness in the churches' power in India. What is needed are good preparation classes for young men and for young women to stimulate them to the importance of voluntary work for God, and at the same time to instruct them in the way of working. A more organized system of house to house visitation is immensely needed, great though the difficulties be. This, with the distribution of carefully selected tracts and the visiting of sick or wavering members of the churches, might well be entrusted more into the hands of lay helpers after due preparation. A Young Men's Mission Band, started some 15 months ago in connection with the C. M. S. Church in Calcutta, has proved the value of such workers. Three evangelistic meetings have been conducted every week by the members of this band. The 14 or so young men have themselves been helped by thus working for God, and who can doubt but that much good has followed the words spoken. Others probably are working on some such line, but there is room for much more to be done in this direction.

Temperance work amongst young and old is well received, and proves itself a useful ally to direct evangelistic work. Drunkenness is not a besetting sin amongst the Indo-Europeans, but still there is sufficient cause for the existence of total abstinence societies in connection with every church.

*Fifth Day.* (c) Temperance work.

Work amongst the children is the most hopeful of all. On it depends almost entirely the success of the future; unless early impressions are made, and much care bestowed to protect the young mind and heart pure from the surrounding corruptions, there can be but little hope for the coming generation. Children in India so quickly turn into the men and women of India; the early marriage system drives many, almost against their will, and before they know anything of the world, into the despair of want and responsibility. It is impossible to expend too much care on the children's spiritual training. Much is being done in the Sunday Schools, and there is good reason for encouragement.

(d) Children's work.

But this leads us to the educational aspect of work amongst Indo-Europeans, a part of the paper which calls for special attention at this Missionary Conference. What are Protestant Churches doing for the young Indo-Europeans? Look at the report once again of the Pauperism Committee; see the list of free scholars in the schools in Calcutta. Boarders in schools, either free or paid for from charitable funds, total 957; of these, 451 are in Roman Catholic Schools. This proportion is alarming, but is as nothing compared with the next table. Free day scholars in schools 780, and of these 663 are educated by Roman Catholics. Then from the latest report of the Inspector of European Schools in Calcutta and Bengal, it can be seen that the Roman Catholics are educating over two-thirds of the European and Eurasian children. Is it not time that Protestants should awake to their neglect and stop this rapid encroachment on the part of the Roman Catholics? Since the above tabulation of free scholars in Calcutta, a free day school has been started by the C. M. S. Church, the Old Church, and the need of it has been vindicated by 60 being enrolled the first month, and by there now being 110 on the rolls. This is encouraging, but there is opening for much more if only funds were forthcoming. In the higher education, again, the Roman Catholics take the lead—young men and girls are sent to their colleges and

2. Educational.

(a) Roman Catholic Education.

FIFTH DAY. convents because they give a better and cheaper education. It is not because Protestant parents prefer Roman Catholic instruction for their children, but because the Roman Catholics offer greater advantages at cheaper rates. True, indeed, is the old saying, "Give me a child till he is twelve, and you may do what you like with him afterwards." Here, then, is a crying need for the children of Protestants, more free education for the poor, and better higher education for those anxious to pass the much required University examinations.

(b) Need of technical education. Beyond this, the importance of a technical education for the poor should be much emphasized. The *Indian Churchman* thus wrote on this subject two months back: "Sir Andrew Scoble was in favour of affording greater facilities for University education. Mr. Orr, of Madras, thought that a technical education was the thing to be aimed at. We believe the latter is right. Everybody must expect to have to work either with his head or his hands. The native has, at any rate, in the subordinate departments of head work, thrust out the Indo-Europeans, not that he can do better work than the latter, but he does the same work for less money. On the other hand, he has a rooted objection to working with his hands, and this objection will not be overcome for many generations. Here, then, is a field open to the Indo-European, in which he will not find many rivals. He has, on the whole, a finer physique than the native; he takes more readily to manly exercises, and he has not, or, if he has, he has no business to have, any objection to manual labour." Could not something practical be done to further this technical education?

3. Social

Space will not allow more than a reference to encouragement and hints regarding the social aspect of the work. Enough to say, many harmful customs are being broken down, but that there still lies before us a battle against the early marriage system—

(a) Customs. against the extravagant customs at weddings, baptisms, and funerals, and against the ruinous habit of borrowing money and of constantly living in a condition of debt.

(b) Model houses. There is a stir in Calcutta amongst members of the Eurasian and Anglo-Indian Society in the direction of improving the dwellings of the very poor, commonly known as *kintols*, and it may well be hoped that schemes for model dwelling-places will soon be realities.

Truly, the work amongst Indo-Europeans is important; undoubtedly the difficulties are great, and the encouragements but small, yet nevertheless the spiritual future of the Indo-Europeans shall be a bright one if only Christian people will take up the work with a will, and be determined that in God's name it shall be a success.

"Not by might, nor by power, but by My Spirit, saith the Lord of Hosts."

---

## FIRST SPEECH.

By the Rev. D. Osborne, M. E. C., Mussoorie, N.-W. P.

*Fifth Day.*

*The importance of this community.*

The insertion of this topic in the programme of this Conference demonstrates its importance, and that from a missionary stand-point, whether viewed as direct missionary work, or as exercising influence of the most powerful kind upon missionary work, the subject is one whose importance cannot be overstated. That which was once a business mart has grown into an empire, and the company of traders has become a nation. This nation, both from its position and numbers, cannot be ignored. They are growing rapidly,—approaching half a million at least; and as the governing race, occupy a position of commanding and unique importance. No Christian worker can afford to overlook them. Their souls need to be saved. They are in peculiar peril. Their very supremacy and national advantage expose them to the subtlest danger. Men—young men—nurtured in the bosom of Christian associations at home, breathing the aroma of prayer and piety, thrust out here amid all the temptations of sensuous gratification and heathenish godliness. Surely, if ever men needed spiritual help, it is the British born and British descended in India.

*"Debtor to all."*

And none surely have a higher claim upon the sympathy and service of the Christian worker. The soldier protects him, the tradesman ministers to his wants, the engineer charts his way for him, the official preserves peace for the safe prosecution of his labours, the planter, the telegraph operator, the railway mechanic, the office clerk,—all help him forward and make his work easy and agreeable; surely he cannot but feel like Paul that he is "debtor" to them all, and, like him, resolve in

|             |                                                                 |
|-------------|-----------------------------------------------------------------|
| Fifth Day.  | acquittance of that debt—"So, as much as in me is, I am ready to preach the Gospel to you ...... also." |
|             | But if these facts be ignored, the unquestioned, powerful influence of such service upon missionary work in India entitles |
| Sir Andrew Scoble. | this subject to the weightiest consideration. Surely Sir Andrew Scoble did not overstate the case when he said:—"Let me tell you that, if, whilst sending missionaries to the heathen for the purpose of preaching the Gospel to them, you are neglecting the claims of the Europeans and Eurasians in that country, you create a class of missionaries who do infinitely more harm to God's Church than all the heathen together can do, because every European and every Eurasian who neglects his duty as a Chris- |
| A Sikh's view. | tian becomes a *missionary of evil* to the people around him." In Patiala, where our mission recently established a station, one of my best personal friends, yet most resolute opponent to my work, is the educated station-master, a cultured Sikh gentleman. I hardly visit that station, but he immediately provokes combat with the thread-bare, yet none the less galling sneer: "Look at these Christians of yours, these European gentlemen and ladies"—pointing to the swarms of racers, actors, dog-fanciers, &c., who visit that city—"Why don't you convert them, instead of coming to turn us away from our faith?" |
| A paradox.  | It is to me a paradox and a puzzle that whilst all missionaries and Christian workers agree in painting the godless Anglo-Indian and Eurasian in darkest colors, and in affirming that their evil example and questionable morality are a powerful obstacle, nay, an absolute opposing force to the spread of the Gospel; so many gather their garments around them and "pass by on the other side," maintaining that it is none of their business, *they* must preach to the heathen, and to the heathen only. Surely, even on the low ground of expediency, this is poor wisdom. It would be poor farming for a tiller of the soil to say: "My business is to plough, to harrow and to sow the seed; I have no concern with the noxious weed which cover the ground, and which, I know, must nullify my best efforts and choke the tender shoots when they appear." |
| The work to be done. | 1. Consider the work to be done. It is to get the nominal Christianity of India soundly converted to God, and not only so, but to so animate it with spiritual life, as that all its influ- ence and power may be actively exerted for God and |

for truth in India. The nominal Christianity consists of three strata,—the British born sojourner, the domiciled, well-to-do Anglo-Indian, and the poor, neglected Indo-European; and it would be hard to say which of these three classes, in a moral and spiritual view, is at the top, and which at the bottom. For, serious as the view of poverty, ignorance and social degradation may be in some aspects of the life of the poorer Indo-European, we deliberately believe that the neediest and most pitiable case, spiritually, is that of the upper-grade European in India. The "needy poor" must give way to the needier rich. An educated native gentleman, who travelled with me to Bombay, said: "The impression we entertain of Englishmen in high positions in India is, that nine out of ten possess no religion at all."

*Fifth Day.*

Here is the work to be done—to turn this nearly half-million souls to God, to transform them from "missionaries of evil" to missionaries of righteousness. Think of the thousands of society Europeans, polished and cultured, magnanimous and just, yet devoid of even outward regard for religion; of the great army of gallant men to whose loyalty and devotion we are indebted for the safety of this great empire, yet whose lives and practice contradict the plainest declarations of the Gospel; of the exiled planter, the wandering surveyor and engineer, the migratory railway mechanic, with scarcely the opportunity of hearing the truth: and of the indigent, ignorant, and degraded mass of poor Indo-Europeans, suffering all the pangs of poverty and social degradation, without ambition or aspiration, often without heart or hope for better things, sunk in pauperism and vice—look upon these, a veritable valley of bones—very dead and very dry—and you are constrained to ask as did Ezekiel: "Can these bones live?" And yet, remember, this work lies at the very threshold of missionary work in India. It is as the stone at the grave of the dead Lazarus of heathenism within. It must be removed before Lazarus can rise. Is it not extraordinary that many who talk with absolute indifference or despair of the spiritual and social elevation of the low Indo-European, affect to believe in the conversion of the heathen? No heart or hope for their own flesh and kin, professing the same Gospel, bearing the same name, hoping for the same heaven, and yet persuading themselves that they have mighty

*"Take ye away the stone."*

*Fifth Day*

zeal for the heathen! Is this possible? We have found, after careful observation, that those who talk most loudly of being called to the heathen only, who will pass by a wandering brother without a word of counsel, admonition or sympathy, make but poor missionaries to the heathen; whilst those whose hearts throb with love and pity alike to all, who, while steadily pursuing their own work, do not neglect an opportunity of serving an erring brother by the way, are the most successful after all in gathering sheaves for the Master.

*How to work successfully.*

2. Glance at the qualifications and conditions necessary for successful work. There is no patented secret of success in Christian work, and "work among Anglo-Indians and Eurasians" is no exception to the rule. The first necessity is unaffected love for these souls and earnest devotion to their welfare. We have, I am afraid, been commiserating the "poor Eurasian" too much. Our love has frozen into pity. We have been revolving his case and studying plans for his social and spiritual amelioration, until we have insensibly evidenced the gulf between him and ourselves by our very solicitude. We have been so occupied with his distress and degradation that we have pushed him further away from us, and have built a barrier without knowing it between the poor degraded thing and ourselves. And here I cannot help saying that I deprecate from my heart the necessity, if necessity there was, for coining, during the last twenty years or so, the unique and unscientific designation *Eurasian* to distinguish a certain section of Anglo-Indians. I

*Eurasian.*

characterize it as unique, since no other nationality in the world is named after its descent, but by its *habitat*; and I call it unscientific, since it is neither definite nor distinctive. A name is like a boundary fence, demarcating, distinguishing, defining, all round. It would be obviously unfair to fence off on one side, and to leave the other open for all kinds of marauders. The term Eurasian walls off a section of the Community from the pure European, but, on the other side, who can possibly restrict encroachment? The veriest scallawag who affects a coat and mounts a hat, may change his name from Ján Sing to Johnson, and announce himself a Eurasian! And this is actually done in thousands of cases, and the "poor Eurasian" is charged with the muck and the mire of this motley mob. Our friends have taken care to invent a name which *excludes* the possessor from themselves, but who cares what it *includes?* Notice the practical effect of this in the doleful report of the Calcutta Pauperism Committee which shews that 22·3 of the "Eurasians" are paupers and then gravely states that this is three times as bad as in the worst counties of England! Nor is it to be forgotten that the origin of this name is shrouded in an assumption of immorality as libellous as it is unwarranted. A Bishop of the Methodist Church confidentially informs his readers that "This mixed race, be it remembered, has not sprung from the marriage relation;" and after a few weeks of cursory skimming upon the face of Indian affairs, gravely observes: "This class of people, as a general rule, are most unfortunately situated." While an Anglican Bishop, in those barbarous days in which the whites and the darks were compelled to sit apart even in church, is said to have observed, with more emphasis than delicacy, "*You* are the sinners, and *these* are the fruit of your sin." I am not surprised that with such an assumption, a name was invented to fence off the unfortunate bearers of it from respectable society, but I am amazed that those for whom it was devised failed to detect the *bar sinister* upon its brow, and received the novel designation with complacency instead of indignantly repudiating it. FIFTH DAY.

Whatever view be entertained as to the merits of this controversy, it is certain that such a basis of thought is not calculated to produce that earnest and cordial love which is necessary to successful work among this people. It may bring about pity, solicitude, condescension, but these will not unlock the heart and give access to the soul. The love of Christ, beaming from the eye, tingling in the hand-shake, thrilling the voice, leaping from the heart and grappling with the best sympathies of the one whom we wish to serve—abolishing distance, removing barriers, bridging chasms, is the one, only and all-sufficient factor which can take the heart captive for God. Love necessary.

With this there must be a faithful presentation of Christ as a living Saviour—as able to save unto the uttermost. Not a homeopathic dose of the Gospel,—a mere trituration—with the saccharine of mere profession or ceremony; but such a presentation of Christ as will break down the mountains and fill up the valleys, as will unhorse the consciously superior from Truth necessary.

**Fifth Day.**

their pride, and lift up the degraded and fallen and poor and out-cast to the high plane of Christian manhood. This class of persons will not come to us, we must go to them. In Allahabad, where I laboured for ten years, it was my practice to devote one day in each week to the special work of visiting *serais*, lodging houses and the abodes of the poorest in the back alleys of the native city, bearing relief in shoes and clothing, and preaching the Gospel of Christ to the poor, the fallen and the ignorant. The recompense continues to come to this day in transformed lives, reconstructed homes, youth rescued from vice, ignorance and poverty, now earning an honest and sufficient livelihood, adorning the profession of godliness by consistent Christian character.

**Education.**

Nor can I dismiss this cursory view of the conditions of success without at least alluding to the necessity of educating the young of this Community in the principles of true, vital religion. It has been shewn that the Romish Church is educating more than two-thirds of the children and youth of our growing Anglo-Indian community, and even in the remaining less than one-third, there is a very small fraction under the active influence of evangelical truth. Is this not deplorable? Have the Evangelical Churches in India then surrendered the future generation to the opponents of truth, or do they fondly hope that sowing briars they shall gather figs by-and-bye? It is true that the Romish Church, in its educated priests and accomplished nuns, who give their service to education without personal advantage, have facilities for this work of an extraordinary kind; but does not this very fact accentuate a deficiency of the most serious kind in the spirituality and vitality of our religious work? Is there not found in our churches devotion and consecration equal to this emergency? Would to God that a recognition of the supreme importance of preempting the youth and childhood of our Community for truth and pure religion, might be so impressed upon our hearts and conscience as to become a controlling force, constraining us to wise and concerted action.

**The outlook.**

3. Glance at the outlook of this important work. Much has been done and is being done, and we have reason to thank God and take courage. Truth and righteousness are dominant, and public sentiment is on the side of morality and religion.

Churches and societies have been established, and many of them have become centres of light and blessing. Revivals of true religion have taken place at many points, and a witnessing band of Christians have been raised up. No one has done more for India in this particular service than William Taylor, now Missionary Bishop in Africa. His work is not to be measured by the number of nominal Christians converted to God, or by the churches where his enthusiastic faith enkindled a glow of soul-saving zeal; its influence has touched with light and warmth and blessing every church and mission in India, and its inspiration is felt in every religious movement. All this is encouraging; still there is hard work to be done. It is to be feared that evangelical religion is not keeping pace with the growth of the Community. The great need of the day is a revival flame among the nominal Christians in India. Many of our churches are inactive and without fruit. There are communities to whom no preacher has gone. It is impossible that fitting spiritual ministration can be afforded by means of the regular ministry to all the numerously scattered groups of professing Christians in India; but may it not be hoped that living witnesses from among the laity might be raised up in increasing numbers to testify of the truth to their fellow-countrymen? *Fifth Day.*

And this naturally leads to the observation that here is a recruiting ground for our ministry and missionary work which has scarcely been improved as it deserved. That some have been raised up and are preaching the Gospel ably and successfully is sufficient demonstration that the field is fruitful; that so few have been brought to the front proves that but poor diligence has been employed to develop the resources to hand. If but one devoted and capable preacher of the Word had been raised up in India, a leader of God's host, it would for ever have silenced the doubt as to the successful issue of this problem, and would have inspired the most earnest and hopeful endeavour to find others. But has this been the case? The theory is held universally that the country is to be evangelized by means, chiefly, of its own sons; and yet the practice directly contradicts the theory. It is frequently regretted, and amazement is expressed, that so few of our promising Anglo-Indian youths offer themselves for the ministry; but it is a *Recruiting ground for the ministry.*

**Fifth Day.** fact that in certain sections and under certain conditions there has been an encouraging advance in getting promising recruits. It is a notable fact that in the wake of William Taylor's work, a goodly array of recruits—some of them relinquishing positions of honour and high emoluments—joined the army of workers. How was this? Would not the same result follow similar conditions elsewhere? Given a genuine spiritual revival, and as surely as the divine fire touches the hearts of the people, the seal of a divine commission will rest upon the brow of some. But more than this is needed. "The spirit and the bride say come." Have we been quick to recognize the divine seal, and faithful to accept such in the name of the Lord? Have we been diligent in seeking, joyful in finding, patient in training, hopeful in receiving them? Is it not true, in some quarters at least, that honest aspiration has been discouraged and hope disappointed by the difficulties put in the way of Christian service? As one personally acquainted with many aspects of this hopeful field, I must do the many devoted, true-hearted volunteers for this service from India, of both sexes, the justice to affirm that they are not seekers of honour or emoluments in asking for equal rights with the foreign missionary, but they feel that in such a service no distinction of colour or nationality are admissible. With these foreign brethren, they are willing to accept a crust with joyful gratitude, and have done so again and again; but they cannot persuade themselves that any differentiation, save that of capability and experience, ought to rule in this matter. Let these things be borne in mind, and the door of welcome swung more widely open, and I feel convinced that this field will yield a host of harvesters with sickles glittering for the sheaves. With heartfelt gratitude I notice striking advance even in this matter in the religious sentiment of India; with profound thankfulness I behold many, of both sexes, raised up in this country, taking the first rank in this blessed service; and I cherish the hope that hundreds, nay thousands, of consecrated and capable workers shall go forth from the recruiting ground into the ripening fields of this great land.

## SECOND SPEECH.

*Fifth Day.*

By the Rev. Isaac F. Row, Secretary of the Anglo-Indian Evangelization Society, Poona.

In my judgment there is no subject on the programme of the Decennial Conference more important than the one we are to consider this afternoon. Mr. Gouldsmith in his paper has dealt more especially with this work in the larger stations, leaving it, as he says, to others to deal with the spiritual needs of the large number of "Anglo-Indians" scattered throughout the length and breadth of this great empire, and having their abode in small stations and out-of-the-way places, where they are more or less cut off from the regular means of grace. For several years past, as an Agent of the A. I. E. Society, my own work has been in this direction, and it has led me to travel very much, so that I have had unusual opportunities of becoming acquainted with the great spiritual destitution that prevails amongst these widely scattered ones, brought up in the Christian faith, but now as "sheep without a shepherd." I have in the course of my travels, again and again, met with individuals, who have told me that I was the only minister of the Gospel who had ever visited them in their lonely stations. When in Assam some years ago, I spent a month in a large tea district where there were quite a number of English and Scotch families, and I learned that they had only been visited *twice in twelve years* by a clergyman, and even then these visits had only been made through the request of some of the married planters who had children whom they wished to have baptized. During all these years these people had been without any religious serivce whatever, so that their spiritual condition was indeed a sad one. I spent a month in that district, and was most kindly treated, and had the privilege of preaching the Gospel there several times. After leaving that station I spent a week at a large jute centre where I found a good many persons (mostly Scotch) who had not had a religious service for three years—the last service prior to my visit having been held there by an evangelist of our society. When I went to Assam I was asked to give three months to evangelistic service in that field, but I found such terrible spiritual destitution there, and met with so much encouragement in my work, that I remained more than six months, and the following year went

*"Scattered sheep."*

*In Assam.*

*No religious service.*

*Fifth Day.*

*Planters, miners, &c.*

again for several months. Besides this experience amongst the planters of that great Province, I have also done a good deal of evangelistic work amongst the tea and coffee planters of the Neilgherries and Coorg, the gold miners in Mysore and the Wynaad, and along several of the lines of railway. The latter affords great opportunities for earnest Christian effort, and I feel that we owe a great debt of spiritual service to the hard-worked, and in too many instances, underpaid railway employees, many of whom have but little opportunity for Sabbath rest and church privileges.

Mr. Gouldsmith has rightly urged in his paper the importance of this work among Anglo-Indians—1st, on its own account, and 2ndly, *because of its practical bearing on the great missionary work*. With reference to this latter point, it is utterly impossible to urge too strongly the need of more attention being given to this branch of Christian service in India.

*Its bearing on missionary work.*

I am sure that all those who are engaged in direct mission work amongst the native people of this country, will agree with me when I say that after sixteen years' experience and wide observation, I am of opinion that what the Rev. Dr. Baldwin recently said of China, at a missionary meeting at Mr. Moody's place at Northfield, America, is equally true of India. Dr. Baldwin was for many years a missionary in China, and is now one of the missionary secretaries of the Methodist Episcopal Church, and at the meeting referred to, he spoke impressively of the great difficulties, and also of the triumphs of missionary work in China. The greatest of all the formidable obstacles to the progress of Christianity in that land he affirmed to be, not in the people, not in the customs, not in their idolatry, because these can be overcome, but in the ungodly lives of men from Christian Europe and America.

*Dr. Baldwin's opinion.*

*L. M. S. Report.*

In a report of one of the missionaries of the London Missionary Society in India, published not long ago, the following appears:—" Rani Khet, being a military hill sanitarium, the European community is composed principally of soldiers, *a class whose influence so materially affects our work among the natives*, that we feel our efforts for their moral and spiritual welfare must be unremitting and vigorous."

In a recent number of the *Indian Witness* of Calcutta, there is the following passage by the Editor, an old and experienced missionary:—"It is now twenty-five years since, the first time, we were interrupted, while preaching on the streets to Hindus and Muhammadans, by the arrival of a couple of European soldiers the worse for liquor. It was for us a most startling and humiliating experience. We dropped our eyes in shame; our arguments for Christianity based on the perfect morality of its Founder were swept away by the conspicuous immorality of men who, among Hindus and Muhammadans, were known and designated as Christians. Years before this incident, in the confidential talk a missionary often enjoys with his non-Christian pupils, we had heard of this and that officer of the Government who, in some way or other, had shown disregard of either the doctrines or morals of Christianity, and had failed as representatives of a distinctively Christian civilization. And widening the circle of observation, we have from time to time learned the sad truth that not only in the different branches of Government service, but also among the representatives of the Christian faith generally, there is too often an undeniable failure to apprehend the responsibility of their lives as nominal Christians in a non-Christian land." *[margin: First Day. A sad incident.]*

Such testimonies, as to the urgent need, and the great importance of this "work amongst Anglo-Indians," *even from a purely missionary stand-point*, might be multiplied indefinitely, and we may well hope that as a result of our consideration of this subject to-day, there may be a revived and ever-deepening interest in this branch of Christian service, and that the churches at home may be led to realise, as never before, that those who are engaged in it, are in a very real sense *missionaries*, and bearing a very important part in the great work of trying to win India for Christ. For the purpose of reaching the isolated and scattered "Anglo-Indians" of whom I have spoken, and amongst whom I have been for so many years labouring, it seems to me that an *Unsectarian Itinerant Ministry*, such as that of the "Anglo-Indian Evangelization Society," is eminently adapted. *[margin: Appeal for interest. An unsectarian ministry.]*

At present we have but very few labourers for this great work, but I trust the great Lord of the harvest will lay it upon the hearts of His people to pray that we will thrust out more labourers into this harvest field, and that the time may soon come when this deep need shall be so met that even in all this vast *[margin: More labourers required.]*

*Fifth Day.*

*Scripture precedent.*

empire there shall be none of "our kith and kin," isolated and neglected as to justify them in casting at the Church of Christ the reproach, 'no man careth for my soul.' In the great commission to go into all the world and preach the Gospel to every creature, there is the special obligation to go first to 'the lost sheep of the house of "Israel," and in the parable of the lost sheep what a lesson there is for us in the example of the good shepherd who left the ninety and nine to go off into the mountains and seek the one sheep that had gone astray, and finding it, having more joy over that one, than over the ninety and nine.

I myself could tell of many delightful experiences of this kind, when the Spirit of God has led me into some very out-of-the-way spot to try and teach a poor isolated and lonely soul brought up in the Christian faith, but now cut off from all religious privileges, and surrounded by the deadening and blighting influences of heathenism. It has often been painful to me to be compelled, for want of time, to decline pressing invitations to pay prolonged visits to such persons.

From a *missionary point of view*, how important is the salvation of these individuals, when we remember that in almost every instance they stand as the only representatives of the Christian faith before hundreds and thousands of the native people of the land.

What a power for good or for evil thus centres in and around these single individuals called Christians, and as such read and known of all about them. How glorious the result if they be walking worthy of that sacred Name. As the outcome of the Rev. C. Grubb's recent mission amongst the planters of Ceylon, there is now, I am informed, a good deal of interesting and successful mission work carried on by converted planters amongst the coolies employed on their estates, and we may be sure that whenever an "Anglo-Indian" becomes a true Christian, he is made alive to his responsibility with reference to the salvation of the people about him, and he manifests a practical interest in the great work of Christianizing this land. If there were time I could give interesting illustrations of this in my own experience, but others are to speak after me, and I will therefore now conclude by earnestly hoping with Mr. Gouldsmith that "missionaries in the field, and lovers of missions at home, may be led henceforth to take such an interest

*The Rev. C. Grubb's mission.*

in their fellow-countrymen in India, that they will not rest till everything in human power is done to save them."

*Fifth Day.*

The meeting being now open for discussion,—

The Rev. C. A. E. Diez, Basel Mission, Kasaragod, South Canara, said:—Although a foreigner I can give proof that I have a right to speak on this subject. It was God's good way to send me to the late Rev. Samuel Hebich. This man with a Pauline spirit preached to everybody. He devoted himself also to regular English preaching. I have witnessed how European officers and ladies were truly converted by his powerful preaching at Cannanore and other places. These conversions are the strongest possible proof of the renewing power of the Gospel which God grants to the heathen of this country. Why should we omit to strengthen the fort from which we sally forth to take the enemy's fortress? Besides the Pauline practice, ties of blood also give me a right to speak. I had an English wife, and English blood runs in my children's veins, and this increases my interest. Now, what I am most anxious to say on the subject, I may be permitted to read from my paper on "Romanism," pp. 24-25. *We owe attention to Europeans and Eurasians.* Although we are a missionary body sent for the conversion of the heathen, we are surely no priests and levites who intend passing by our own kith and kin in danger as to body, soul and spirit!—Let us *befriend* our own unfortunate countrymen and countrywomen in this country who, as often without, as through their own fault, are exposed to many sufferings, and are often in danger of becoming renegades, through offers made unto them.—*Dissuade* evangelical parents from sending their children to Roman Catholic institutions, where they are in danger of imbibing another spirit and forfeiting their happiness. There are mothers who require to be reminded of their high calling to educate their children for God. A little smattering in French, music, drawing, &c., acquired in convents, is too high a price to pay for spiritual shipwreck. Let us *take to heart* that many European and Eurasian parents, owing to different circumstances, among which the low exchange is one, are forced to keep their children in India and to send them to Roman Catholic institutions in order to get them educated. We do not disparage what is being done, but we are certain far more ought to be done to meet the want. There is enough of evangelical money, self-sacrifice and energy to build and keep up boarding houses for such boys and girls in high and healthy localities where they might be educated at cost price. A sound of alarm to the evangelical churches all over the world is certainly not out of place.

*St. Paul an example.*

*Our duty.*

*To befriend our fellow-countrymen.*

*R. C. schools.*

*Protestant schools necessary.*

FIFTH DAY.

More willing now to work.

Mrs. SORABJI, I. F. N. S., Victoria High School, Poona, said:—I come forward to speak on this subject, not as a European or Eurasian, but as a *Christian*. I have had much to do with Eurasians, during the forty years that I have been working in the mission field, and I have known many who have shone for Jesus all their lives. In years gone by, I must admit, they did not readily or willingly engage in missionary work, nor encourage their children to do so; but of late years, the feeling has wonderfully changed. Given Christian influence and training, they make as earnest and devoted workers as any other class. I know a dear Eurasian missionary lady in this very city (Bombay) who for many years has been devoting her life to this work, in whole-hearted consecrated service, and God is using and blessing her more and more. And I know there are others scattered throughout this land. I could tell of some dear boys and girls—once my pupils—who have now gone forth into the world; and are not only living honourable and useful lives, but are doing their best to further Christ's Kingdom.

The lack of Evangelical schools.

The Rev. H. C. STUNTZ, M. E. C., Naini Tal, N. W. P., said:—I would emphasize the remarks of Mr. Diez about the lack of Evangelical Schools for European and Anglo-Indian children. I am amazed that no English or Scotch Society has taken up this as a part of its regular work. So far it has been left almost wholly to American missions to provide these classes with schools in which children are taught the way of salvation by simple faith in Christ. Rome is awake whoever else sleeps. Look at her magnificent real estate and territorial equipment for this task! She has scores of lakhs invested in India, and indents indefinitely upon Europe for priests and nuns to maintain schools for the classes who must set the pace for the native church in India for another century. I am amazed at the almost criminal apathy of Protestants in this matter. It is high time that we awake out of sleep. We have overlooked the source of supply for mission-helpers and missionaries. God has placed such a source at our doors. Missionaries have too long permitted themselves to be swayed by the opinion of godless Anglo-Indians as to the possibilities of the Eurasian and domiciled Anglo-Indians. This source can be tapped best by schools in which the youth are captured for Christ and imbued with the missionary spirit. God has permitted me to see some of this class led to Christ, and from among them some are now effective helpers in the Gospel, while working at their own professions, and others are intending to enter the work as missionaries. I would not minify other agencies. I call attention to the schools.

The possibilities of Eurasians.

The Rev. S. W. ORGANE, Secretary, Auxiliary Bible Society, Madras, said:—During my residence of twenty-six years in India I have worked a good deal among Eurasians, and I can

speak highly of their Christian life and conduct as a Commu- *Fifth Day.*
nity. Some of the brightest Christians I have known have
been in their ranks. I can also bear favourable testimony to *Many are bright Christians.*
their liberality as may be seen by the long list of their contri-
butions to the society I represent. In my opinion Europeans
ought to take a deep interest in those who are, to a large extent,
of their kith and kin, and approach them in a kindly spirit.
In particular I bespeak a warm interest in those of them whose
work compels them to live in out-of-the-way places, and in the
families scattered over our lines of railway, shut off as they *Many are quite neglected.*
are from regular ministerial oversight. Some of these seem
almost to lose sight of the Sunday, and often when travelling
I have known many to make use of any means and to bring
forward all kinds of excuses for non-attendance at services
which I have held among them. I regret the unwillingness
of some Eurasian congregations in the South to receive as a
minister one of their own class and also the readiness with
which many Protestant parents send their children to Convent
Schools.

The Rev. David REID, M.A., B.D., Minister of Wellesley *The Anglo-Indian.*
Square Free Church, Calcutta, said:—So far as a pastor of
a congregation of Anglo-Indians and Eurasians is able to do
anything towards heightening the moral and spiritual tone of
this Community and building up among them a strong and true
and attractive type of Christian life, he is telling directly and
most helpfully upon missionary work. A good deal is heard *"Wicked lives" an over-statement.*
about the wicked lives of Englishmen and Scotchmen in India,
and no doubt there is, alas! considerable foundation for the
report. Still the matter is probably overstated rather than
understated. At home, a man whose heart is bent on sin is
often kept in the way of outward decency and of attendance *Environment.*
upon religious ordinances by parental and social and traditional
influences. In India, these external restraints are to a great
extent removed; the man has little motive for appearing better
than he really is; he lets us see the worst of him. There is
an honesty and openness and absence of hypocrisy about much
Anglo-Indian worldliness and unrighteousness.

Unbelief is often fostered by travel and life in heathen lands, *Reasons for unbelief.*
and unbelief, more or less pronounced, is widely prevalent
among Anglo-Indians, and has to be reckoned with and wisely
met. In many cases a young man drifts or is led into sinful
and irreligious ways unwittingly and unwillingly; and even *A wise suggestion.*
the worst man has generally some soft place in his heart at
which he can be approached—some blessed memory of a father
or mother or godly home. When a young man is coming out
to India his friends ought to write and announce his arrival to
some one of us missionaries or ministers, near whom he will be;
and we ought to welcome him and try to engage his interest,

FIFTH DAY.

A "lay" Missionary's testimony.

The position of Eurasian workers.

Government makes no distinction.

and, where possible, his practical help in our work. If Anglo-Indians have often been to blame in standing aloof from missionary work, missionaries have sometimes been to blame in standing aloof from Anglo-Indians.

Mrs. F. L. McAFEE, Lady Superintendent, Government Training College for Mistresses, Ahmedabad, Guzerat, said:— I feel some diffidence in speaking on this platform, as I cannot, in the generally accepted sense of the term, claim to be a missionary. Yet in the Training College under my charge I have four Anglo-Indians, and no less than twenty-three native Christian young women and girls studying in the classes with my Hindu students. I think, therefore, I may almost claim to belong to that large but somewhat despised body—the " lay missionaries." And as such, perhaps, I may be permitted to say a few words.

A great deal has been said at some of these meetings about Eurasians and domiciled Anglo-Indians—chiefly I may say of a depreciatory character. At the meeting held in the large hall to discuss the problem of " work among women," some of the European and American lady missionaries publicly expressed their surprise that their " Indian sisters," the domiciled Anglo-Indians and Eurasians, volunteered in such small numbers for mission work. It was, therefore, generally agreed that the various mission societies should be urged to send more agents from Europe and from America to labour among this class, so that the latter, when converted, might devote themselves to the work of the Lord. In reply to this, I would say there are hundreds among the domiciled Anglo-Indians and Eurasians here who are not only converted men and women, but who would gladly come forward for mission work were they only treated properly by the missionaries! But it is a lamentable fact that many mission agents, while seeking to break down caste among the heathen, yet have caste amongst themselves. To many interested in missions, it seems a sad thing that zenana missionaries sent out by Christian societies to teach high caste Hindu women that God hath 'made of one blood' all the nations of the earth, should yet often treat with marked contempt such of their fellow-workers as happen to have a few drops of Hindu blood flowing in their veins. I think it only right, however, to add that I, too, have not always been free from this un-Christ-like prejudice, but I think I can say that for many years past God has been gradually thinking this out of my heart. As regards the respective status of the workers, I would submit that there should be no covenanted and uncovenanted service in the Christian Church. Even in the Government service to which I belong (and which I was sorry at one of these meetings to hear termed immoral), when a man or woman is appointed to a post, he or she rises by order of seniority in that post irrespective of the place of his or her birth or education. Amongst the ladies of the Government Education Department no distinction is made between those of us who were born and educated in Europe and those who were born and educated in Asia. The assistants receive their promotion according to seniority, and when the senior posts fall vacant become Superintendents, irrespective of the place of their birth and training. But in the mission it is, I regret to say, not so. A lady appointed in this country for educational work takes a subordinate position and remains in that subordinate position for ever. I will give one illustration which, though seemingly trivial, means a great deal more than would appear on the surface. It is a common custom among zenana missionaries to speak of the young lady educationalists appointed in this country as "the girls," while those appointed direct from home are always styled "the ladies." It is true that from a Christian stand-point the term lady need not be considered so desirable, especially when (so far as I remember) it is used but once or twice in Scripture, and then in condemnation, as "Thou saidst I shall be a lady for ever." Still if this term be so rigorously maintained in missions for educated workers appointed from the other side of the water, why not for those appointed on this side? I would ask in conclusion whether it is not sufficient to take the life out of any people—to render them indifferent in fact to all mission work—when they *know* that, however capable the men and women of their Community may prove themselves to be, however trustworthy and reliable, yet that the mere fact of their having received their training in India, or worse, of having received their appointments here, dooms them to be servants, for ever and ever.

*Fifth Day.*

"Ladies" or "girls."

The Rev. J. E. Newsom, A.M., B.D., M. E. C., Cawnpore, said:—It is a wrong policy to work for others and neglect Eurasians. Neglect of people in India in whose veins flows English blood will prove disastrous. Their's is destined to be a position of influence for good or for evil. They are largely the moral, social and political intermediate power between the masses and the rulers of this country. To neglect them is to neglect the medium through which much of the philanthropy must pass down to the idolatrous millions. It is to forget the counteracting, destructive influences they will have upon all good done to the natives alone. Let us do all we can for the native, but do a great deal more than is being done for the Eurasian. While it would be a vast improvement to do even as much for them as is being done for the natives, yet they demand comparatively much more. They especially need schools adapted to their poverty. But few can send their children to the hills for education, and from the lack of cheap Protestant schools in the plains, many children out of Methodist, Baptist, Presbyterian,

The position of Eurasians.

More schools needed.

| | |
|---|---|
| Fifth Day. | Church of England and other homes are being sent to Roman Catholic schools because of their cheapness. The church of Rome evidently counts it her wisest policy to provide such schools for these children regardless of cost. Shall we be less wise than they? Shall Protestant philanthropy awaken to its privileges only after it is too late? Children never return from these schools to their churches and homes the same as they were |
| More should be done for them. | before. I have worked among English speaking people for two years, and the necessity of a decided advance on all lines of Anglo-Indian and Eurasian interests, especially among the poorer classes, has steadily grown upon me. With their exceeding poverty and spiritual dearth; with liberal Government assistance just beyond their reach; with missionary interests largely passing by them; with the native from below and the foreign European from above increasing their difficulties, my heart has begun to bleed for them. May God in his Providence raise up men of large means and of liberal hands to establish orphanages, endow schools, and found other charitable institutions for these much neglected people. |
| The fate of orphan children. | Miss A. M. ANDREWS, S. F. E., Ludhiana, Punjab, said she wished to lay before the audience a terrible need that had lately come under her own notice, viz., the fate of little European children in out-of-the-way places, should they be left orphans. Not long since one such, a little girl 17 months old, came into her hands and through the goodness of God she had been able to find her a comfortable home. Her history in brief was that at 6 weeks' old she was left entirely an orphan in a place where there was no other European.* Her mother died at her birth, her father, a few weeks later, of cholera. A good woman who heard of the facts sent to find the infant that she might adopt it as her own; *knowing as she did that in such places infants thus left were taken and brought up by native cooks and barbers.* What their future is to be can easily be conceived. When found, this child had been kept by the cook for four days. When she was nine months old, the little one was a second time left fatherless; for eight months the widow struggled on, but at last unable longer to provide for the child, she had to seek for her some other home. Would Christian friends take into their earnest consideration the awful fate awaiting such orphans as these, who are left *alone* in the midst of a heathen population, and see if some regular system of search and rescue cannot be organised by which they may be saved and placed in Christian families or institutions. |
| Anglo-Indians are neglected. | The Rev. J. L. PHILLIPS, M.A., M.D., LL.B., Sunday School Union, Calcutta, said:—I left the other sectional meeting and came in here because the subject is one that interests me much. First, as to Anglo-Indians. I believe we are not doing enough for them. In some stations we are skipping over |

our countrymen entirely, and I believe wickedly, in our eagerness to reach the heathen. Our Sunday School Mission is finding work for some of these Anglo-Indians, and I am delighted to tell you that within twenty months several tea and coffee planters in India and Ceylon have opened schools for the children of the coolies of their estates. I believe we missionaries have been to blame in some places for standing so aloof from this class, and for not interesting these countrymen of ours in our daily work. I have found that it pays to do so in more ways than one, and some of them have helped me right royally in school, medical, and other lines of effort for the heathen. Some of these Europeans in India are godless and grossly immoral, and these need us still more. I find nothing in my Lord's Great Commission that warrants me in passing by a profligate Englishman or a drunken Scotchman for the sake of reaching Hindus or Muhammadans: and His significant "every creature" embraces all sinners. And as to Eurasians, I wish to testify, here and now, that in my thirty thousand miles of journeying throughout India and Ceylon during the past two years, I have found no more devoted toilers in my own department than some men and women of this class. Indeed, you know that our Sunday schools would be terribly crippled in many places, all over this land, were the East Indian or Eurasian helpers to be withdrawn. In some schools they are doing all the work, and doing it well. These workers deserve more encouragement, and this should not be given grudgingly either. They should be trained for still better service in the Church of Christ. I believe I am right in saying that those missions are doing most for this class and for the heathen, too, that are devoting most attention to employing and qualifying Eurasian agents for the varied lines of missionary service. There is a bright future before Eurasian Christians of integrity and industry in India. Let us honour them, trust them, promote them, and share with them the toils, and the trials, and the triumphs, too, of this great work of publishing the glorious Gospel to these millions of idolators and Muhammadans. And the best plan I know of for dealing with both these classes before us at this session is that laid down by the great apostle in the twelfth chapter of the Epistle to the Romans and the tenth verse.

*Fifth Day.*

*Their help in S. S. work.*

*Helping them is true mission work.*

## XVI.—CHRISTIAN LITERATURE.

(a) Vernacular, (b) English, (c) The Scriptures, (d) Colportage.

---

### SIXTH DAY.

Wednesday, 4th January 1893.

---

### MORNING SESSION.

Large Hall, 10 a.m. to 1 p.m.

---

Eugene Stock, Esq., Editorial Secretary, C. M. S., London, *in the chair.*

The Rev. J. Bruce read a passage of Scripture, and the Rev. Dr. Boggs offered prayer.

### FIRST PAPER—Vernacular Literature.

By the Rev. H. Haigh, W. M. S., Mysore City.

Fifth Day.

It cannot be needful in a Conference like this to emphasise the importance of literature as a missionary agency. Our activity in vernacular education is wholly mistaken, unless we are ready for corresponding activity in literature, for books are the true corollary of schools. Although modern schools have obtained their popularity largely through the energy of the missionaries, they will hereafter retain and extend it independently of their aid. Nothing is plainer than that, as the days go by, our proportionate influence in the education of India will grow smaller, while our opportunity and responsibility in the sphere of literature will be enormously enlarged. Under these circumstances our discussion to-day ought to be anything but academic. Are we producing vernacular literature of the right kind and quality? Are the arrangements of the societies such as to enable us reasonably to do this? Are we securing that what is produced gets into the hands of the people and is read

I fear that none of these questions can be answered satisfactorily. Missionaries as a rule are so placed that they have no leisure to write books; the literary instinct, where it existed, dies of inevitable repression, and the literary habit fails. What books do issue are produced under the strong pressure of some momentary necessity. They are born in a day and—live for a day. They come at the urgent desire of a committee, rather than from an inward impulse that will not be denied expression. The result is plain. Our literature lacks breadth, strength and form. It is hardly of the type which must ultimately lead India safely through the dangers of its great transition. It is important, then, that in this Conference, we should consider carefully wherein lies our failure or defect, and boldly define to ourselves what we ought to do. *Sixth Day.*

I.—There are some things which it is needful to say in regard to the general character of missionary vernacular literature.

i. I venture to suggest, first, that it should be much more closely related to the thought and life of this country than it has hitherto been. Think of the great majority of the books prepared for our Native Christians: in form and spirit, in everything but words, they are simply English literature done more or less idiomatically into the vernacular, and always with much loss of meaning and suggestiveness. So it has come to pass that the Christians of India are receiving an essentially English training, and they are thereby, infallibly and inevitably, being made strangers and foreigners to their Hindu brethren. There are no points of approach between the two. The language of the one has no grip on the other, recalls no memories, suggests no common starting place, but suggests rather a great gulf fixed, so that those who would pass over cannot. By providing books for our Christians so completely unrelated in thought and so largely unlike in style to the literature on which India has been feeding for centuries we are fast creating a new caste in India—a caste which, however rapidly it may grow within, must steadily decrease in power without. *Adaptation necessary.*

Speaking broadly, the missionary literature of India has been translation. This may have been inevitable, and is not a matter to be complained of; but the question is: Has not translation been fundamentally misunderstood? The standard of trans- *Standard of translation.*

**Sixth Day.**

—lation which has been prescribed for the Bible has been allowed to assert itself all too imperiously in the rest of our books. The Bible work of the past claims from all of us the most reverent acknowledgment; it has been done, generally, with a conscientiousness which it would be impertinent to praise. But, candidly, is the reproduction of the original text, idiom for idiom and almost word for word, even to the particles, true translation? After all, the book remains essentially a foreign book. Those who labour at it as students will extract much good from it, but for common Christians it is a stumbling-block, and to non-Christians it simply makes no appeal. The letter is successfully retained, but the spirit is not all there. It is like fire photographed instead of fire transferred; the warmth and cheer are gone out of it. The true idea of translation is not the substitution of a set of words in one language for a similar set of words in another. It is rather the effective conveyance to readers of the exact idea, without addition or subtraction or change of emphasis, that was conveyed to those into whose hands the original was put. Carried out to its legitimate issues this definition would permit the utmost freedom in regard to words and idioms, and might even compel sometimes a change of figures used. It would imply an amount of labour in comparison with which the usual method of translation is almost child's play. And it would especially necessitate this: *that the hands of the translator should be continually on that literature which most widely influences the people and out of which their thought and language have been formed.* But though the trouble implied is beyond expression, the result of translation on such a principle would be to make the people feel that the Bible is one of their own books—powerful, attractive, one that cannot be ignored.

**The Bible.**

It is probably undesirable that we should spend time in this Conference in debating the different methods of Bible translation which have just been indicated, though the subject is one which before long will require to be most carefully reconsidered. What it *is* important for us to dwell upon is this: that the method adopted in Bible translation has been far too closely followed in all our other work, and has vitiated it incalculably. Whatever we may say of the letter of the Scriptures there is no reason why, *e. g.*, the letter of commentaries should be reproduced; nay, no reason why whole sections of the English Sixth Day Prayer Book should be laboriously transverbated when its petitions and aspirations can be rendered in characteristic Indian phrase and measure. To continue to supply books prepared on the old plan will be to continue fatally to denationalise our Christians—far more fatally than by taking off their tuft of hair, or changing their food or costume. The principle I contend for, then, is this: *that the books which we publish should be carefully related to Hindu thought, expressed in its terms, done in its style, adopting where it can its positions, and leading on, still in Hindu fashion and in its terminology, from points of agreement to essential points of difference.* In this way we may, perhaps, be able to furnish an effectual exhibition of legitimately "Hinduised Christianity."

*The Prayer Book.*

*Hinduised Christianity.*

(a) In view of this principle I would suggest that no greater service to the Christian Churches in India, or to non-Christians, can be rendered than that some man should, for each language, reproduce the Gospels and Epistles in free paraphrase. Making it his one aim to leave on the mind of Indian readers the exact impression which the original was likely to leave on *its* readers, let him feel himself wholly unfettered by any tradition as to the way in which his aim ought to be accomplished. Let him expand into a sentence allusions which instantly appealed to the original reader, but which are difficult now; or, better still, if he can find it, let him substitute an Indian allusion which will answer precisely the same end. Let characteristic Hebrew and Greek expressions be displaced by characteristic Indian expressions. Let difficult foreign figures yield to simple and indigenous illustrations. And let the style throughout be full, flowing, resonant, such as the ears of these people love — anything provided only that the book is made to live and the impression left is accurate. No harder task can be set a man, but it would be worth a life-time of labour to succeed in it.

*Paraphrase.*

(b) There is another application of this principle which is just now becoming urgent. Large numbers of low caste and non-caste village people are joining the church, and accessions from these classes are sure to become still more rapid and numerous. The language of these people is almost always a rude but vigorous *patois*. They speak in short, sharp phrases, largely in the concrete, and abound in exclamation and interro-

*Patois.*

**Sixth Day.**

gation. Anything outside their *patois* is practically unintelligible. Certainly the Bible is a closed book to them in its official translation. Not only are the terms used utterly beyond them, but the length and complexity of most of the sentences makes the book a despair to them. But a paraphrase exactly after the manner of their speech is quite possible. It might be sufficient to prepare the Gospels and one or two selected Epistles: these would serve as an introduction to the Bible in its authorised version. The majority of the people whom I have in view cannot read; but they could understand this when read, and would be allured by hearing what was plain into trying to learn to read it for themselves. A Bible in *patois* is, in view of the course the churches are taking, one of the most important tasks to which we can set ourselves. I know no other way so good for bringing the root ideas of the New Testament into controlling contact with the minds of these people.

**Naturalize Commentaries.**

(c) The principle for the recognition of which I am pleading will bear application in every part of our literature. What could be more fatuous than to take an English Commentary and translate it after the ordinary fashion into a vernacular? Certainly the truths we have to expound are one, whether for English or Indian readers, but the point of view, the emphasis, illustration and application must be as different as India is from England. In preparing our commentaries should we not be wise to begin by providing a new text? The Bibles of India have not yet, generally speaking, appeared in their final, or even in very long-enduring versions, and variations in the new text

**Suggestions.**

would provoke interest and suggest thought. Supposing, when this was ready, we judiciously circulated interleaved copies: catechists might be asked, during a given period, to make a note of proverbs, illustrations, quotations, or common expressions which have any bearing whatever on the text before them; three or four reliable and sympathetic non-Christian scholars, representing different sections of the community and different ranges of literature, might be asked to note special classical books or passages from them touching on the subject-matter of the text, whether in confirmation, contradiction or illustration. Supposing after this that the author set himself to work from the materials thus gathered into the best results of European exposition, would he not be enabled, as in no other way, to relate his whole book to the country for which it is intended? A commentary prepared in this way, though the labour of it would be formidable, would do that work which is needed above all—naturalise the Bible for India, making it a new power in the hands of our Indian fellow-workers, and a new attraction for those among whom they work.

Thus far I have chiefly referred to the literature of education; but the literature of stimulus, of comfort, and of leisure requires exactly the same treatment. Let us, in particular, be careful that our books for Native Christians shall not isolate them from their fellows. Such books must freely assimilate to themselves all that is worthily characteristic of the great literature of this land, and add to it the elements which Christianity can alone supply. We shall then no longer be chargeable with creating a Christian foreign caste, of an inferior European type, but we shall nourish those who will become at once distinctly Indian and yet indubitably Christian.

ii. Our literature should begin to take on such a character as will compel the serious attention of the really educated vernacular Hindus. Between Hinduism as such and Christianity there has never yet been a fair fight. On our side there has been a good deal of skirmishing by means of tracts and brief handbills; but we have not yet by our literature seriously disturbed those who ought to be the real expounders and defenders of the Hindu faiths. The books that would assault the citadel, and make the enemy bring into play its heaviest arms have still to be written. Such opposition as we have had has furnished itself for the contest with weapons drawn from the armoury of Europe. Those weapons will be ineffective though harassing, but when they have failed Hinduism will not have been conquered. It will then begin to look into its own armoury and another phase of the war, more momentous, more interesting and much more desperate will begin. It is our true policy to precipitate that phase of the contest. We must by some means rouse those who are at the back of the people, and who have hitherto regarded our efforts disdainfully and at a distance. When once we touch them, and drive into them the apprehension that the existence of their systems is seriously imperilled, we shall find ourselves in the very Balaclava of our

*Sixth Day.*

*Fair fight desirable.*

SIXTH DAY.

war: so furious will be their defence, so exciting and decisive our victory. The hastening of this collision will, in the main, have to be the work of literature. We cannot get at those who will be the most powerful and obstinate defenders of Hinduism by means of preaching; they will not come to hear us. English education will lessen the number of their followers and diminish the sympathy of some who still remain with them; but beyond that it will not affect them. Books, however, can reach them, and, in so far as they are strong and true, will compel their attention and extort a reply. How poor we are in literature of this type is patent to everybody. It could not be otherwise. Busy men make time for an occasional tract, but in presence of the duties which crowd upon them and will not be denied attention they fear even to contemplate a larger and more exacting enterprise. Is it not possible, however, for missionaries to make a beginning in the direction I have indicated, by taking some of the most popular and influential Hindu books, and sending them forth with Christian annotations? The *Bhagavad Gita* may stand as a type of the book I mean; in Kanarese we have *Gnanasindhu* and *Anubhavamrita* and every language will have similar books. Some of them, doubtless, contain things that are objectionable or fantastic or utterly useless; but they are books which the people like, and to touch them would be instantly and infallibly to touch the people's interest, and it might also, not unprofitably, draw forth their hostility. Such annotations as I have in view would point out fallacies, suggest deficiencies and set forth succinctly the answering or correcting truths of Christianity. Apart altogether from the benefit which such books would bring to our Native Christians by indicating, as nothing else could, the comparative strength and illumination of Christianity, they would do much to fix the anxious attention of the most influential vernacular-speaking Indians on our methods and sentiments.

iii. But while we boldly attempt to reach the most difficult classes we must also produce literature that closely affects the every-day life of the common people. Newspapers are becoming common in all the vernaculars, but they are generally of such a type that it would be no difficult matter for a Christian newspaper to take the lead among them. The art of newspaper-editing is one that vernacular literary men have not yet very fully

*Present literature insufficient.*

*Annotate Hindu books.*

*Christian newspapers.*

mastered. They will master it by-and-bye, but in the meantime we have a great opportunity. It must be, always, a *bonâ fide* newspaper that we issue. It must deal frankly with the dominant interests of the hour, burking nothing, but always, from the stand-point of the Sermon-on-the-Mount, touching them decisively, independently and interestingly. Such a paper will find a place for ruling market prices and for the weekly calendar; it will deal in the most practical way with health and sanitation, with agriculture and the diseases of cattle; it will ventilate social questions, and in political matters, it will take the part of the well-informed and honest friend of the people. Nor will a paper of this kind seriously lessen its chances of popularity if every issue is made distinctly evangelistic— carrying a straight and vigorous call to religious concern, and pointing definitely to Christ as the true satisfaction of man's needs. The value of such a paper is obvious. It links Christianity to the common life of the people. It makes Christian men important factors in moulding non-Christian public opinion. It familiarises the people with aspects of things which will be presented to them by nobody else. In Native States particularly it enables us effectively to claim due consideration for Christians in local legislation. But beyond all this it affords our preachers an easy introduction to the people, and, if properly managed, will go to scores of villages yet unvisited, thereby preparing the way for them. It may be necessary to sell such a paper at slightly lower rates than those which at present commonly obtain. But with careful management it will be possible to do this without involving the societies in any serious expense. In the Mysore country a weekly newspaper of this kind has steadily held its place for more than five years past.

*Sixth Day.*

II.—But if our literature is to be of the character, and to do the work which I have indicated, it will have to be produced under conditions other than those which obtain at present. As a rule, no man is responsible for books, but every man is responsible for so much else that the writing of books is all but an impossibility. Perhaps the most practical remedy is this— that where a society finds itself possessed of a man (or men) who have special literary taste and power and an adequate grasp of the vernacular, it should recognise his gifts, and relieve him as far as may be of duties which can easily be done by

*New conditions necessary.*

**Sixth Day.**

**Literary missionaries.**

**Obstacles to literary work.**

**Set apart men.**

others, so that he may have a certain portion of his time absolutely secured for following this great vocation. The proportion of men possessing these aptitudes will never be embarrassingly great, and it might properly be demanded that a man should have made distinct proof of his calling before his brethren recommend that partial relief which he needs to enable him to do all that is in him. I suggest partial relief rather than the complete setting apart of men, as the least that societies ought to do in acknowledgment of their duty to literature. I suggest it also in the interest of literary missionaries themselves—for if their productions are to be fresh and strong, they must be born of living and intimate contact with the people. It would be a calamity to release men from preaching and debating and judicious visiting in order that they might sit in their studies and write books. But they might, usefully, be relieved of the care of schools, of heavy financial work, of building and of incessant itinerancy. There are many men who can do that admirably: let them; and let those on whom is bestowed the rarer literary gift have opportunity granted to exercise it. At present the accumulation of routine duties bids fair to prevent all really important work in literature. Accounts *must* be kept, journeys *must* be made, schools *must* be examined, and meantime the man with a book pressing on his brain can do nothing at it steadily, nothing when the pressure is greatest, but goes on worried, wearied, the victim of a great purpose which cannot fulfil itself. This, if not the picture of a common, is at any rate the picture of an actual experience, and where such cases exist societies are not getting the most out of their representatives. Is it not desirable that the brethren connected with our larger missions in India should ask themselves, in their annual committees or synods, whether they have not one or two whose partial designation to literature would bring permanent and invaluable repayment to their work? It cannot be, that, if unanimous and urgent representations in regard to this matter were made to the Home Committees, they would persistently refuse the extra help which such a designation would imply.

But more than this is needed. It has at various times been suggested that each large society should set apart one man for literature. The suggestion does not wholly commend itself to

me, unless it is desired to multiply denominational books. A
better arrangement would be that missions should combine
within each language-area for the appointment of one man (or
two, if the reading population is very large), whose whole time
shall be given to promoting the literature of his vernacular.
He should be a man of literary bent and training, possessing
the instincts of a journalist, and yet having a real appreciation
of, and some capacity for, producing the more permanent kinds
of literature; one who could direct others as well as write
himself, and who would make it his buisness to draw out
the best writers in his area. In many places there is already an
appointment answering to this—that of editorial secretary to
local Tract Societies. But that appointment is generally an
honorary one, and given to a man who has already quite enough
to do in the sphere in which his own society has placed him.
The position ought to be a great one, and its possibilities can
never be adequately worked out until a man is free to devote
himself entirely to it. As to the support of such men: the
societies of each area should contribute proportionately, and
make up exactly what he would receive from his own society.
This principle of combination has already succeeded in education, notably in the Madras Christian College, and it would
be both a fitting and economical thing that Missionary Boards
should try to apply it in promoting Christian literature. The
cost would not fall very heavily on any one of them. But
there would be other expenses, for such a Literary Agent
would need a staff and would have to travel. These ought to
be provided for by some one great central organisation existing
specifically for the preparation and distribution of Christian
literature throughout India. Such an organisation would give
unity to this great work, would represent it to the Christian
Churches of England, America and Australia, would raise funds
for it, and would make grants-in-aid to the various areas, to be
supplemented by local contributions and spent under the
direction of a local Committee acting with the Literary Agent.
This, in brief outline, is the scheme that commends itself to
me. Fully to arrange it will require time and much communication with England and America. But it seems to me
feasible, and the existence of ONE recognised Christian Literature Society for India would be an enormous gain. Pending

*A Sixth Day.*

*Local R. T. S. Secretaries*

*One C. L. S. for India.*

**Sixth Day.**

**A Literature Department necessary.**

some such arrangement, however, would it not be possible for the missions of each area to induce their societies to jointly guarantee the support of a man, to select him and set him to work, for the present, as editorial secretary to the local Tract Society and editor of a vernacular Christian newspaper?

This much is certain: that whatever plan we ultimately agree upon, we must urge unceasingly that our Home Committees should substantially recognise literature as one of the most important departments of their work in this country. India has already been the home of one great literature, and Christianity, before it has done its duty, will have to make it the home of another—stronger, purer, more practical—a literature that shall set forth a truer theosophy, teach human duty more humanly, and in its gathering glory throw a fresh halo around Him "of whom the Prophets spake," and who has been everywhere, even if unrecognised, the Inspiration and Goal of all true religious writing. No society has adequately responded to its sublime opportunity until it has begun to give practical encouragement to the fulfilment of this great purpose. Let us lay it upon the home churches with an importunity which they cannot withstand. And then, on our side, let us link our wide-embracing message to all that is best in India, and thus find a legitimately effective setting for the figure of the Oriental CHRIST.

## SECOND PAPER.
## ENGLISH LITERATURE.

By J. MURDOCH, Esq., LL.D., C. L. S., Madras.

**English.**

At every Decennial Missionary Conference, Christian literature has formed one of the subjects; but on this occasion Christian literature, in *English*, has a separate paper. The spread of English education and the influence of its recipients justify the division.

*Importance of English.*—English is still more valuable at present in India than Greek was in the times of the apostles. It affords the means of reaching educated men all over the country. It contains also the greatest treasures of knowledge ever accumulated. "Whoever knows that language," says

Macaulay, "has access to all the vast intellectual wealth which Sixth Day. all the wisest nations of the earth have created and hoarded in the course of ninety generations."

*Spread in India.*—Statistics are not available as to the number who can read and write English; but on the 31st March, 1891, out of 3,682,707 under instruction in India, it was studied by 353,515*—nearly ten per cent.

Statistics.

The following publications were registered within British India during 1890-91 † :—

|  | English. | Total. |
|---|---|---|
| Bengal ... ... ... ... | 177 | 1,739 |
| Assam ... ... ... ... | ... | 22 |
| N.-W. Provinces and Oudh ... | 86 | 1,107 |
| Punjab ... ... ... ... | 46 | 1,577 |
| Burma ... ... ... ... | 3 | 149 |
| Central Provinces ... .. | 1 | 13 |
| Berar ... ... ... ... | ... | 13 |
| Bombay ... ... ... | 84 | 2,044 |
| Madras ... ... ... ... | 219 | 1,022 |
|  | 616 | 7,686 |

The total number is considerably less than the previous year, because mere reprints do not now require to be registered. It will be seen that Madras and Bengal head the list with regard to English publications.

*Home Literature.*—This is imported in increasing quantities. So far as Indian readers are concerned, it consists chiefly of text-books and novels. The former are required for the numerous University and Government Examinations; the latter, for the comparatively small number who read for pleasure. The English classics have a fair sale, probably because they are supposed to be good aids in acquiring a knowledge of the language. Formerly Reynolds was considered the "Prince of novelists." His writings had nearly as large a circulation as those of all other works of fiction taken together; but their sale has fallen off considerably. One firm claims to have made a specialty for their Indian Railway Bookstalls of translations from French novels. Those of Zola have been forbidden to be sold, but they are said to be procurable in other quarters.

Text-books and novels.

---

\* *27th Statement of East India Progress*, p. 200.   † *Ibid.*, pp. 206-209.

**Sixth Day.** Books describing the dark shades of European life are popular with some.

**Free-thought Depôts.** A few years ago, a vigorous effort was made to circulate infidel literature. Madras had two "Free-thought Depôts." There seems less of it now; but, under an innocent title, a pernicious book, advocating free thought and free love, is kept on sale in all the great cities. Though publications of the Ingersol type may not be so widely diffused as before, it is to be feared that this does not apply to the works of writers like Herbert Spencer and others. The idea is very general among educated Hindus that Christianity has been given up by enlightened men in Europe.

As the standard of English education rises in India, home publications will be more and more appreciated. At present most Indian readers have too imperfect a knowledge of the language to understand complex sentences and foreign allusions; while many home tales are quite uninteresting to them. Still, already the cheap reprints of Cassell and other publishers meet with a fair sale.

Attention is invited to the numerous English publications of the Religious Tract Society which, both in get up and in subject matter, take a high position. They are obtainable at the different Tract Depositories at rates generally ten per cent. below those of other publishers.

**What has been done.** The principal classes of English Christian literature published in India will be briefly noticed.

(1) RELIGIOUS LITERATURE,* BENGAL.—The first publication in English relating to Christianity seems to have been *The Precepts of Jesus*, selected from the Gospels with an intro-

---

\* Valuable service has been rendered by the American Methodist Episcopal Mission, the German Missions, and some others in providing Christian literature; but the work has been mainly supported by the grants of the Religious Tracts Society, which, during the last decade, amounted to £ 36,412-9-10. The issues of the Indian Tract Societies are given below as far as available. The progress is encouraging.

|  | 1872-81. | 1882-91. |
|---|---|---|
| Calcutta Tract Society | 1,576,251 | 7,732,265 |
| North India do. | 660,994 | 2,727,550 |
| Punjab Religious Book Society | 339,517 | 2,215,397 |
| Gujarat Tract Society | 177,032 | 623,076 |
| Bombay do. | 1,120,404 | 1,987,810 |
| Madras do. | 6,591,891 | 12,132,652 |
| Bangalore do. | 1,580,861 | 1,915,200 |
| South Travancore do. | …… | 1,545,400 |

duction by Rammohun Roy, published in 1820. It led to a long controversy with the Serampore missionaries. The original pamphlet contained only 74 pages; the "Appeals" in its defence extended to 430 pages. Among the more important works which followed may be mentioned, *Vedantism, Brahmism, and Christianity*, by Dr. Mullens; *Dialogues on Hindu Philosophy*, by Rev. Dr. K. M. Banerjea; the trenchant exposures of *Brahmoism* by the Rev. Dr. Dyson; *Fulfilled Prophecy* and *What Think ye of Christ?* by the Rev. J. Vaughan.

Sixth Day.

The Calcutta Tract Society, during the secretaryship of the Rev. Dr. K. S. Macdonald, has circulated a large number of English tracts. Including those from home, the gratuitous issues in 1890-91 amounted to 213,516, out of a total of 964,271.

*North India and the Punjab.*—The strength of the Allahabad and Lahore Societies has been given to the vernaculars; but a few useful publications have been issued in English, as the Lectures by the Rev. Nehemiah Goreh, &c. Dr. H. Martyn Clark has dealt vigorously with the Arya Samaj. Sir William Muir's *Testimony of the Coran* is very valuable. The numerous interesting little books by A. L. O. E., though printed in South India, were written in the Punjab.

*Bombay.*—Various tracts by the Rev. G. Bowen, and a valuable series of *Papers for Thoughtful Readers* have been issued; but the most important publication of the Bombay Tract Society has been the Rev. Dr. Murray Mitchell's *Letters to Indian Youth on the Evidences of Christianity*. Ten editions of it have been printed, and an eleventh is now in preparation.

*Bangalore.*—Numerous small Scriptural tracts were written by the late Rev. B. Rice, and some publications for educated Hindus, by the Rev. T. E. Slater, have been issued.

*Madras.*—The Madras Tract Society, though established in 1818, printed very little in English till 1872. A series of *Short Papers for Educated Hindus* was then commenced, which has been kept up, with more or less regularity, ever since. The editions have gradually risen from 5,000 to 20,000. Supplies are sent post free all over India. Three Companion Volumes, to accompany the Scriptures distributed by the Bible Society among students passing University examinations, have been published. The English circulation of the Madras Tract Society in 1891 amounted to 319,324, out of a total of 1,706,726.

SIXTH DAY.

Of late years the Christian Vernacular Education Society, now the Christian Literature Society, has devoted special attention to English publications for educated Hindus. They include a series of Scriptural instruction for the young, and examinations of the various forms of Hinduism; but most advocate social and moral reform, or may be classed under the head of General Literature with a Christian tone.

(2) *Periodicals.*—Including newspapers, publications of this class are very important as they constitute nearly the entire reading of many educated Hindus. They have also the advantage that any impression produced can be followed up.

Thacker's *Indian Directory* gives a "Newspaper and Periodical Directory;" but so many changes take place that accuracy is almost impossible. The Directory for 1890 includes 619 entries, of which 352 are wholly or partly in English. Of newspapers issued by non-Christian Indians in English, Bengal has the largest number, including two dailies and several weeklies. Bombay has one daily and one weekly entirely in English, but several Anglo-vernacular weeklies. Madras has one daily and two weeklies.

There are several Periodicals, weekly, monthly, and quarterly, issued by Missionaries and Indian Christians. They are useful in their place; but, as space is limited, those intended primarily for non-Christian readers will alone be mentioned.

"The Epiphany."

*The Epiphany.*—This has been published weekly for the last ten years by the Calcutta Oxford Mission. It contains four foolscap folio pages, and is sold at ¼ anna. The circulation is about 200 in India and 80 at home. It is purely religious. The circulation is mainly among Christians, but the writers are frequently Hindus. "Its main aim is to argue out publicly and before the world any objections which may be brought against Christianity, so that every sincere inquirer will have his difficulties honestly and fairly met." It may be read with advantage by missionaries who wish to become acquainted with the current of Hindu religious thought.

"Young Folks."

*India's Young Folks.*—This may be mentioned, though it is intended more for Sunday School scholars than for non-Christians. It is a monthly illustrated magazine, containing twelve quarto pages, published fortnightly at Lucknow by the American Methodist Episcopal Mission. A single copy is Re. 1

a year; with postage Re. 1½. Explanations are given of Sunday School lessons, and the contents are fitted to interest and instruct the readers. The circulation is about 1,200. The receipts equal about half the expense.

*The Madras Christian College Magazine.*—This monthly, issued by the College, is now in its tenth volume, and contains 64 pages royal octavo. "It seeks to awaken or keep awake an interest in higher things and in every social, moral, and literary question affecting India present and future." The annual subscription is Rs. 5; to students, Rs. 3½. The circulation is from 500 to 600.

*Progress.*—This monthly illustrated paper, published by the Madras Tract Society, is now in its thirteenth year. It contains twelve royal quarto pages. The aim is to diffuse Christian truth; but, to secure subscribers, the contents are varied, including descriptions of places, biographical and historical sketches, news—literary, scientific, and general, &c. One page is devoted to Indian students. The subscription is only eight annas a year, exclusive of postage. Three copies may be sent by post for half an anna. The monthly circulation in 1891 was 2,650. The Religious Tract Society supplies the paper at half price. With this help *Progress* is about self-supporting.

It would seem that no purely religious paper, intended for non-Christians, can be made at present to meet its own cost. *The True Light*, a fortnightly paper containing eight royal quarto pages, was commenced at Lahore in 1890. The subscription was Re. 1½ a year, postage included. Though started under favourable circumstances and well conducted, the issue of September 1st, 1891, stated that the paper was published at a loss. "We should be willing to lower the terms of subscription, if we could make sure of say 500 subscribers. At present we have not half that number." The appeal for additional subscribers was made in vain, and in January, 1892, the paper was discontinued.

*Non-payment of Subscriptions.*—One great difficulty connected with periodicals in India is to get subscriptions paid. It was said of an "Anna Magazine," once published in Calcutta, that half the subscribers never paid, and the other half very unwillingly. Subscriptions to *Progress* must be paid in advance. A reminder is sent when a subscription is due; but if not remitted, the paper is discontinued. There are losses in this way, but with Indian subscribers it probably works best on the whole.

*Past and Present.*

(3) *School Books.*—The early Educational Missionaries attached great importance to School Books. Dr. Duff says in his *Missionary Addresses :* "'Give me,' says one, 'the songs of a country, and I will let any one else make the laws of it.' 'Give me,' says another, 'the school books of a country, and I will let any one else make both its songs and its laws!'"

In 1839, Dr. Duff, Mr. Lacroix, and other missionaries established the Calcutta Christian School Book Society. There were numerous good school books published at home, but they wished others more decidedly Christian, and "suited to the exigencies of the country." The Christian Vernacular Educational Society,\* so far as its publication department is concerned, was established for the same object. While its school books have been largely used by some missions, it is not the case with others. The use of Home "Readers" in India was thus condemned by the Education Commission :

"Adapted or unadapted, the books that are most suitable, because conveying the most familiar ideas, to English children, are most unsuitable to natives of India. Though often compelled to read about such things, the Indian learner knows nothing of hedge-rows, birds-nesting, hay-making, being naughty, and standing in a corner." p. 346.

The Rev. Dr. K. S. Macdonald, in a paper read before the Calcutta Missionary Conference in 1889, described the present favourite "Readers" of this class in some Bengal missions "to be as thoroughly swept of all Christian thought as the School Book Society's expurgated texts." Government Readers, prepared on the principle of "religious neutrality," are also largely used in some mission schools.

It is a truism that means should be adapted to the end on view. Neither Home or Government Readers are fitted to promote what ought to be the grand aim of mission schools—the evangelization of the pupils. A return to the principle of the

---

\* The total issues of the Society, in English and the Vernacular, of all classes of publications, during the last two decades, have been 5,091,176 and 7,303,745 respectively. English and diglots formed about one-fourth of the whole. The work has been very largely self-supporting. Until recently, the home funds went almost exclusively to education.

early missionaries is strongly recommended by missionary committees at home. [Sixth Day.]

Besides school and college text books, properly so called, very much has been done of late years in the preparation of keys and catechisms to cram for examinations. The Bengal Publication Report says that "Even B. A. students depend on keys, and do not take the trouble to consult books of reference." The University authorities are endeavouring to take means to abate this evil. [Keys, &c.]

4. *General Literature.*—In this direction little has yet been done in India. The limited funds of Christian societies have been more than required for publications of a directly religious character. Useful Knowledge Societies have been established, but they do not excite sufficient enthusiasm to work them with any degree of vigour. [Limited Funds.]

The Christian Literature Society has lately begun to aid in supplying the want. The aim is to provide cheap books on subjects interesting to Indian readers, written in language sufficiently simple to be understood by those whose knowledge of English is not very extensive. Descriptions of countries, biographies, historical tales, natural history, fables, anecdotes, &c., have been issued, both separately and bound together in volumes for school libraries. Catalogues can be obtained on application.

For the above class of literature, the main dependence must be upon home publications. [Production.]

*Difficulties.*—The writer of this paper has been one of the Secretaries of Publishing Societies for more than forty years. His greatest difficulty has been to get MSS. for publication. The almost invariable answer to an application for them has been, "I pray thee have me excused. I have no time." The work has been left to a comparative handful of writers or it would have almost ceased.

The two, now living, who have done most in this direction are A. L. O. E. and the writer. The pen must shortly drop from both their hands: an earnest appeal is addressed both to zenana ladies and to missionaries to take up the work. [A. L. O. E.]

**Sixth Day.**

In 1890 the Calcutta, Madras, and Bombay Missionary Conferences passed the following Resolution:

"That in view of the spread of education in India and the growing need of the Indian churches, it is highly desirable that Missionary Societies should recognise Christian literature as a department of evangelistic effort, and that select men, who have shown the requisite ability and inclination, should be set apart for it; being supported, as before, by their respective societies and reporting to them; but working in connection with Christian Publishing Societies."

**Help solicited.** When, however, Missionary Societies are asked to set apart suitable men, either European or Indian, as recommended above, the reply is that they cannot be spared from other work; and so the claims of the Press are neglected as before.

There are upwards of eighty foreign missionaries engaged in colleges. One would naturally look chiefly to them for the supply of *English* Christian literature. As a rule, classes do not meet on Saturday and there are long vacations. Any, so disposed, could find time, now and then, to write a short paper, suitable for a fly-leaf, and one lecture a year, which might be published after delivery. It may be objected that examination papers absorb all the leisure time. If necessary, less should be done in that direction for the sake of evangelistic work.

But literary help should not be confined to educational missionaries. All others who come in contact with educated Hindus might co-operate. The most efficient help will eventually come from Indian Christians. One or two have already done excellent service, like the late Babu Ram Chandra Bose. They should address appeals to their countrymen, somewhat like the Greek and Latin apologies of the second and third centuries.

The current of Indian religious thought should be watched in the papers which are the popular guides. It is an excellent plan to cut out the most important articles and paste them in a blank book. The writer has adopted this course for thirty years, and now has about twenty-five folio volumes of classified extracts. Much good may sometimes be done by letters to the Native papers.

Besides purely original works, home publications may be adapted to India. *Phulmani and Karuna*, by the late Mrs.

Mullens, one of the most useful books ever printed in this country, is based on *The Last Day of the Week*. SIXTH DAY.

*Interchange of Publications.*—This should be done to a greater extent than at present. The Catalogue of the Calcutta Tract Society does not contain the title of a single English publication of the Bombay Tract Society, and *vice versâ*. The two societies might as well have been located in different planets. Every publication should be utilised as far as possible. Interchange.

*Circulation.*—Under this head, space permits only a few remarks directing attention to one important channel for the circulation of English Christian Literature, *viz.*, *Colleges* and *High Schools*. Circulation

The sale might be entrusted to a teacher. From the liberal discount, the cost of carriage would be met, and commission at the rate of two annas in the rupee might be allowed.

The sales will depend very much upon the interest taken in them by the professors and teachers. Lists of new publications should be entered on the Notice Boards, and if attention be directed to them, they would find purchasers.

It is to be hoped that the Bombay Decennial Conference will give an impulse to Christian Literature, commensurate with the progress of education and the increasing intelligence of the people.

---

In connection with Dr. Murdoch's paper the following letter from the Christian Literature Society to the Conference is given:—

"The Committee of the Christian Literature Society for India begs respectfully to submit to the Conference some considerations on the vital question of the Production and Circulation of Christian literature in India.

The Committee feels that the time has arrived for a new departure in this important work, in view of the great and far-reaching results of education, and of the vast numbers who have now passed through the Government, and missionary schools and colleges, for whom no suitable provision has been made to satisfy the new intellectual appetite which has been created, and the deeper wants of the spiritual nature which have been awakened, and to so large an extent unhinged.

If we add to the number of readers returned at the last Census, the proportion attending schools and colleges who were able to read, but were not included in the Returns, and those who have since passed from them into society, there cannot be fewer than fifteen millions in India who have been taught to read by the modern system of tuition, so different from the old routine. Of these, probably not fewer than a million and a half have been taught to wield that powerful instrument of thought—the English language—

in itself a most precious gift, but liable to be used to the injury of the recipient and to the society of which he is a member. The Native Christian community, also, now numbering, with those of Burma and Ceylon, more than three-quarters of a million of Protestant professors, claim special care for their growth in knowledge, that they may, by their intelligence and strength of character, adorn the "Doctrine of God our Saviour," and become a power for Christ among their countrymen.

That it is full time for devising some system of co-operation between societies in India and England, which shall secure a great extension of the circulation of Christian literature, is evident, not only from the great increase of this number of readers, but from the increasing difficulty felt by Book Societies of India in raising money; and a similar difficulty experienced by undenominational societies of a like kind in England. Fresh interest must be awakened on the subject in both countries so as to increase the resources for this great work. It is not a matter of *choice*, BUT OF NECESSITY. The old way of working has been useful in the past, and has done much good; but it has not kept and cannot keep pace with the needs of India, and every year it is becoming more and more difficult. The crisis in India is desperate. It is not a question about sending out a few thousands, or even millions, of tracts and little books. The question is, *Can we meet the mental and spiritual needs of the educated masses of India?* Can we meet the inquiries raised by a too exclusively intellectual education? Can we satisfy the craving for literature, and deliver the youth of India from feeding their appetites on mere secular books, or from the temptation to read infidel or impure and polluting works? If we cannot meet needs like these we fail in our object, and are unfaithful to the trust committed to us in this critical period, when India is awakening to a changed and eventful future—a future of Christianity and moral and social progress, or a future of infidelity, discontent, and corruption.

THREE PARTIES are interested in this work of the Production and Circulation of Christian literature, especially in India:

1st and chiefly, Missionary Societies at home and their agents in heathen lands. These may be regarded as one. Their work, and aims, and interdependence are such as to make them inseparable, and these societies and their agents are more than any others interested in the Production and Circulation of Christian literature. They cannot carry on the work without literature in its different branches, and before Tract and Book Societies were originated in the mission-field and at home, *the entire work of producing and circulating literature was carried on by each mission for itself, at great cost and inevitable waste.* This fact is now too much lost sight of by both Missionary Societies and missionaries in India when this subject is under consideration.

2nd. The second parties interested are the *local Tract and Book Societies in the mission-field,* formed by the union of missionaries of different denominations and the Christian members of the foreign community in these lands, so as to economize the time, labour, and money of the different societies and their agents, and to avoid the ruinous waste inseparable from individual efforts in such work as the writing and printing of books.

3rd. The Tract and Book Societies *in this country*, including, as the most important of all, the Bible Society, to which we shall not refer further than to emphasize the inquiry in their paper to the Conference, on the important principles of co-operation in the circulation of Bibles by the same agents employed in the circulation of books and tracts. These home societies have come to the aid of missions and their missionaries by co-operation with the local Tract and Book Societies abroad. The latter are indispensable for selecting and publishing the best original and translated works suited to the wants of the people in their varied spheres of operation; but they are weak and comparatively powerless for want of the funds which societies in this country can provide.

The great problem to be solved is, How to get these three parties to co-operate in carrying on the great work in which all are interested, so as to give to each a definite object, and get from all the largest amount of work, and to give the greatest stimulus to increase liberality on the part of the supporters of our Tract and Book Societies (in which we include C.L.S.) at home and abroad?

*Co-operation in the production and circulation of Christian literature.*— The Committee does not feel competent to lay down, or even suggest, rules for co-operation in this important work, but would respectfully submit for the consideration of the Conference the following facts and principles on which practical rules may be formed.

Taking into account the three parties interested in the production and circulation of Christian literature as above described, we would observe:

1st. That the production of literature naturally divides itself into two distinct and independent operations. (*a*) The *production of manuscripts*, either original or translated. This clearly falls to the hands of missionaries and other native or foreign agents, paid or voluntary, connected with the Missionary Societies in this country (with the exception of such English works as may be suited for circulation in India). They alone know the language and can enter into the ideas and feelings of the people among whom they labour, or of whom they are brethren. The societies at home should regard this as an important part of the work of their agents of all kinds in the mission-field. They should take note both of what their agents do, or neglect to do, in this department of work, in which all who have the talent for it ought to engage less or more. They ought also to strengthen the hands of missionaries so as to leave time for such work, and in some cases relieve any engaged in an arduous and necessary literary engagement from some other portion of his labours. Weak missions of a purely sporadic character, in the long run weaken the society employing them, and retard the establishment of the Kingdom of God in heathen lands. (*b*) The other division of the production of literature is the most costly one of *printing* in its different departments. This, which at first fell on each Missionary Society, now falls to the

the Book and Tract Societies of India and England; and as it demands more than the monetary resources of all these societies, it is a question worth considering, whether or not a division of labour and expense cannot be devised for giving the societies in India and England a more definite object, by which a larger measure of interest and liberality in the supporters of these societies could be called forth. The present system obviously fails to elicit contributions to Book and Tract Societies in India, and those in England have a hard struggle to increase or even maintain their income. If these societies in India continue so largely dependent on *subsidies* from those in England, that source of revenue will be dried up, leaving them more helpless than ever.

2nd. The *circulation* of literature also naturally devolves on Missionary Societies and their agents in India, while we would not by any means throw upon them any heavy burden of monetary responsibility. They alone can select and stimulate and superintend native colporteurs, and they can influence their converts to do a great deal of voluntary work in this way. It seems to have been a doubtful advantage for Book and Bible Societies, either in India or in England, to undertake this work. Missions and missionaries from the first felt this to be their duty, while naturally enough they were glad to devolve it on those who wished to share in the work. The Book and Tract Societies of India have abandoned this direct employment of colporteurs, and societies in England now feel the moral responsibility for their employment as intolerable as the monetary burden.

3rd. The Tract and Book Societies of India have an all-important work to do in the selection of suitable manuscripts for publication, and bearing a share of the cost, either as at present by printing a certain number of manuscripts, or by some other way, in which by a more obvious division of labour, free from the appearance of overlapping, they may more fully develope liberality both in India and in this country.

4th. Book and Tract Societies in England, including the Christian Literature Society, in common with those in India, should make it their great aim to produce books and tracts for circulation by missions in India at such a price as will allow of their being sold at a profit, which will largely cover the expenses of the colporteurs and other modes of distribution, and by a judicious co-operation with the Bible Society the cost of colportages would be so reduced as to make their employment no material burden to Missionary Societies, while their more efficient management by their natural guardians—the missionaries—would bring a far richer blessing on the work of Bible, book, and tract circulation.

That the Conference may be guided by wisdom from above in the consideration of this important subject, and that a rich blessing may descend on its great assemblies, is the earnest prayer of your Brethren, the Committee of the Christian Literature Society for India.

Signed, by authority, JAS. JOHNSTON, *Secretary*.

SIXTH DAY.

## THIRD PAPER—THE SCRIPTURES.

By the Rev. S. W. Organe, B. F. B. S., Madras.

The need of every land is a faithful and intelligible translation of the Scriptures, and on the Christian Church devolves the duty and privilege of supplying the want. The circulation of the book in printed form and the proclamation of its wondrous truths by the living preacher are inseparably united, and, in the main, are interdependent. The Bible often travels without the preacher, but, as a rule, I believe, God intends that the two shall go together, each contributing towards the enlightenment, conversion and sanctification of human hearts and lives. No missionary can succeed without the sacred volume, and his aid in its translation and dissemination is an imperative necessity. That the Bible should be freely offered to all men is a position that, happily, in these days, is beyond the region of controversy, and this involves the whole question of translating, printing and circulating the Scriptures. It is an accepted principle that distribution should, as a rule, be by sale. *The Bible.*

We look back with admiration at the work accomplished. To-day the Bible, in whole or in part, speaks 350 tongues—a noble monument to the genius and skill of consecrated effort—while it is estimated that well nigh 200,000,000 copies have been scattered among the nations. But lest we be tempted to rest satisfied with the achievement of by-gone days, let us be deeply impressed by the fact that, in these closing years of the 19th century, the proportion of the human family yet untouched by the Living Word exceeds the number of those who possess it. *350 languages.*

The subject of this paper is wide and comprehensive, but its limits do not admit of more than an indication of leading plans and methods of work and of the briefest reference by way of historical statement. As all my Indian life has been spent in the Southern Presidency, I can only write from local experience, and I am far from presuming to say that fixed rules can be laid down for, or any one system be made applicable to, every part of this great country. In certain broad features the lines will no doubt be similar, but in others there will be considerable divergence. We have much to learn from each *Local experience.*

**Sixth Day.**

**B. F. B. S. work in India.**

other, and a free interchange of opinion and a comparison of methods will be greatly to the advantage of all.

Apart from the Baptist versions, the British and Foreign Bible Society now issues the Scriptures, in whole or in part, in 43 of the Indian languages and dialects, 10 of these being in the South. It also publishes 3 versions in Ceylon, and 5, confined to portions, I believe, in Burma. Each language has its complete Bible, most of the major dialects have the New Testament, and many of the minor ones a Gospel or other Portion. The total annual circulation exceeds half a million copies.

**Madras Auxiliary.**

The Madras Auxiliary was founded in 1820. The following figures exhibit its operations in 1891:—Local income Rs. 24,705-1-2; Circulation 177,417 copies (free grants 2,853, the rest by sale); Printing operations 222,400 copies; Branch depôts 60; Colporteurs 63. In addition to circulation within the presidency we periodically supply, through the local Auxiliaries, the Tamil and Telugu Scriptures to Burma, Ceylon, the Mauritius, South Africa and the Straits Settlements. Besides our own operations, the Kanarese Bible, the Tamil Bible and the Telugu New Testament are separately issued by the Bangalore Auxiliary, the Leipsic Lutheran Mission and the American Baptist Mission, respectively. The total united circulation is about 200,000 copies a year.

**Translation.**

I. *Translation.*—In a brief general paper, the chief aim of which is to deal with methods of circulating the Scriptures, expansion under this head would be out of place. The discussion of so vast and far-reaching a subject calls at once for a special and lengthy treatment. My few remarks therefore will be in the way of suggestion and enquiry. It is, however, a subject of great importance, and one which will press more and more to the front till every Indian language has its standard version.

**The vernacular Bible.**

The preparation of a version that will stand as a literary model and as a repertory of Christian terminology is a gigantic undertaking, demanding an accurate and extensive knowledge of the original languages and of the tongue into which the Scripture is to be translated. The time is gone by for translating from a translation. From beginning to end a translator should have vividly present in his mind the great object of his work, *viz.*, the communication of eternal truth and the moral and spiritual elevation of a nation. He should also ever remember the various and dissimilar classes by whom the book will be read. The standard of translation should be faithfulness to the original with idiomatic rendering; on the one hand, it should not descend to the vulgar form of the colloquial; nor, on the other hand, aim at the poetic style which is unknown to the common people. The version needs to be in dignified vernacular, sufficiently pure in style to be acceptable to the most elegantly speaking among the higher and cultivated classes, yet simple, perspicuous and intelligible to the masses. At the same time it should be borne in mind that the work is a translation, not an exposition; not a paraphrase giving a human view of the Bible, but the living, speaking Word. It is well to follow the middle course between the two extremes of an over scrupulous literality and a merely paraphrastic style. The qualifications for the task will be found not in a single scholar but in a company of scholars.

A few practical points may be noted here.

(1) Strict fidelity to the original, compatible with approved, idiomatic usage, should be the capital rule of every translator of the Bible.

(2) Where there is no difference in the meaning, it is advisable to have one uniform word or phrase for each original word or phrase, and not to translate by different words.

(3) There are difficulties in the way, but it will be well if the Indian translators can agree as to the use, in cognate languages, of uniform terms for the most important words, such as God, Lord, Spirit, Creator, Sacrifice, Salvation, Heaven, &c.

(4) Frequent changes in a version lead to confusion, and on this and other grounds are undesirable.

(5) Caution is necessary in the translation and publication of Portions in a dialect, as with the advance of education, many of these dialects will cease to be spoken.

(6) Now that the results of scholarly research are embodied in the texts on which the English revised Bible is based, has not the time arrived for a general comparison with these texts of those Indian versions which do not require elaborate revision?

(7) On the score of economy, and by way of removing the stumbling-block caused by the circulation of rival versions, it is

*Margin notes:* Sixth Day. Suggestions. Uniform words. Frequent changes undesirable. Comparison with revised version. One version in each language.

of the first importance that every effort be made to secure the issue of only one version in each language. The case may be different in other parts of the empire, but in the South the variations in any one of the languages are no longer felt to be of such a nature as to warrant the perpetuation of more than one version in that language. With many others I long for the discovery of such a basis of agreement as to the rendering of βαπτιζω, the Greek prepositions in connection with it, and the *Great Commission,* as shall unite Baptist and Pœdo-Baptist in the one common work.

(8) In the South light is needed as to the desirability or otherwise of issuing versions in the Roman character. Where native opinion on the question has been sought it has generally been adverse.

(9) My experience of the circulation of the Urdu and the Dakhani versions leads me heartily to approve of the effort now being made to provide one Hindustani Bible for all India.

(10) I do not agree with some who seem to think that the time has come for placing wholly in native hands the preparation of new versions and the revision of existing ones; but I am strongly of opinion that they should be more largely represented in the work. Many of them have, in recent years, considerably advanced in Biblical scholarship, and their judgment is indispensable in regard to idiom.

(11) Translators deserve more sympathy and help in their work than they have usually received in the critical examination of their tentative texts and in suggestions of various kinds from missionaries and native pastors.

(12) The harmonious working of Revision Committees is not without its difficulties. When isolated from their brethren many excellent men arrive at the conclusion that they are right on a disputed question and others are wrong. Discussion by correspondence not infrequently confirms the belief or prejudice. Personal conference and united fervent prayer are the best means of effecting agreement.

*II.*—CIRCULATION—*Production.*—Natives now look more critically than formerly both at the contents of a book and at its general appearance. Hence it becomes necessary on this, as on other grounds, to send forth the Scriptures printed with good ink, in clear, readable types, on paper of fair quality and in strong and attractive styles of binding. The sale of Portions <small>Sixth Day.</small> has been considerably enhanced by the use of covers of striking colours with a neat border.

A few suggestions may be offered here:—

(1) The Bible should be issued in at least two types. A <small>Suggestions.</small> large type edition is indispensable for pulpit and family use. The old quarto has mostly given place to the super royal 8vo. size. Many of the readers are advanced in life, and the reading is done generally at night and by dim oil lamps.

(2) The cry for a small volume is general. By the use of <small>Type.</small> thin paper we have produced a popular edition in Tamil $6\frac{3}{4} \times 4\frac{3}{4} \times 1\frac{3}{8}$ inches. We have also successfully introduced the crown 8vo. size. If a medium size is called for, the demy 8vo. meets the case. The New Testament for separate sale admits of greater variety of paper and type.

(3) The issue of Portions in the smallest type has not answered. The most popular size for the larger books is the super royal 32mo., and for the smaller the demy 32mo.

(4) The great usefulness of references and marginal readings <small>References.</small> is admitted. As soon as the text is fixed there should be at least one reference edition of the Bible.

(5) I strongly recommend the introduction into one edition <small>Maps.</small> of each vernacular version of the six maps of the British and Foreign Bible Society with the names transliterated. Our Native Christians say that these maps are most helpful to them.

(6) With the rapidly increasing demand for the Scriptures <small>Cost.</small> the double question of cost and selling prices will come to the front. At present our cheapest vernacular Bible is sold at 12 and the New Testament at 4 annas a copy. We have long desired to provide one edition of each for 8 and 2 annas respectively, and have hesitated only from want of the necessary funds. One means of effecting a general saving is the printing of large editions. Another is the saving of two-thirds of the cost of composition by the striking off of Portion editions, by the process of re-making up, from the matter of the Bible and New Testament editions.

(2) *Free Grants.*—Free distribution is now less common and is carried out with greater discrimination than in the early years of the Indian Auxiliaries. Then the Christian community was small, education was backward, and the know-

ledge of the best methods of Christian work was in its infancy. Experience has since proved the truth of the principle that books like other things are valued in proportion to their cost. The Bible should be placed in the hands of the people in the way best calculated to secure that it be intelligently read and profoundly reverenced. The principle of circulation by sale is perfectly sound, but there should be enough of elasticity in its application to admit of free grants in special cases. In the case of individual applicants—not very numerous—two essentials are necessary,—a sincere desire to read and understand the book, and inability to pay for it. In the majority of such cases the sincerity of the applicant is best tested by offering a copy at a reduced rate. To charitable institutions there is scope for free gifts on a larger scale. Orphanages and poor schools, hospitals and dispensaries are the recipients of the society's gifts. On the formation of jail libraries, we placed the Bible in them in every language spoken by the prisoners. To each of the principal railway stations we have supplied an English and a vernacular Bible, and to every travellers' bungalow an English Bible. Some of the police stations have also received grants. Believing in the wisdom of bringing the truth to bear on the higher and the educated classes, we distribute English Bibles, Testaments or Portions annually to the successful candidates at the University examinations, and we are presenting a Bible in superior binding to each of the Rajahs and leading Zemindars. In every instance the grants are made by the Madras Committee, and after minute enquiry. It is stipulated that the books form part of the property of the institution, for which the person in charge is responsible. In the case of students it is recommended that in the larger centres, the volumes be presented publicly by one of the resident missionaries, and be accompanied by a lecture or an address. The presentations to native princes are made in person by missionaries who have thus excellent opportunities for proclaiming the Gospel in the palace.

(3) *Depôts.*—The large area embraced by an Indian Auxiliary can only be effectually covered by keeping a stock at each local centre to serve as a source of supply to surrounding districts. The depôt meets the want, and is an economical arrangement. In places where the population is small, it may

be located in a mission building. In large towns a room may be rented or built in some suitable spot, the cost of up-keep to devolve, in whole or in part, on the Bible Society. Outside, affix a well-painted sign board with the words *Bible Depôt* or *Bible and Book Depôt*, in English and in the vernacular. Embellish the inside walls with a few Scripture texts and pictures, and altogether make the room as attractive as possible. Where the reading population is large it is desirable to incorporate with the Scriptures the publications of the Religious Tract, the Christian Literature and other similar Societies. The sale of one class of books re-acts favourably on that of the others, and by the union, the cost of management is divided. A Reading-room is a valuable addition. Besides supplying the visitors with wholesome literature, many of them are led to search the Scriptures. The room may also serve for addresses and lectures.

<small>SIXTH DAY.</small>

The success of the depôt system depends in part upon the intelligence and devotion of the Native Christian in charge, and also upon the interest taken in it by the missionary supervisor. The advantages are many. The depôt supplies all classes in the town and neighbourhood. It leaves the colporteurs more free to do their legitimate work of travelling to out-lying villages. It also calls forth local liberality by showing that the society has a real existence.

<small>Their success.</small>

Of the 60 branch depôts in connection with the Madras Auxiliary in 1891, 23 received money grants amounting in all to Rs. 1,914. With one exception the individual grant lies between Rs. 12 and Rs. 120 per annum. Rs. 60 a year is the more usual amount. The salary of the depôt-keeper varies from a small sum to Rs. 10 a month, according as he gives to the work a part or the whole of his time. The sales at these depôts last year consisted of 32,171 copies, and the proceeds amounted to Rs. 4,410. The subscriptions from the districts where the depôts are located were Rs. 8,566-2-9.

<small>Madras Auxiliary.</small>

(4) *Colportage.*—The systems of colportage adopted by the various Auxiliary Bible Societies in India are on somewhat similar lines. The agency has taken a leading part in spreading the Scriptures, especially in country places. Sometimes it has accompanied the missionary, sometimes followed, but more frequently it has preceded him. In many districts, the first

<small>Colportage.</small>

SIXTH DAY. ingathering of converts to the Christian Church has been due to it, and it shares the honour of many a subsequent harvest with the Missionary Society. Altogether, it has been a wonderful pioneer in the removal of the spiritual darkness which for ages has covered the land.

The first colporteur for the city of Madras was appointed in 1848. Our present organization dates from 1857. Through its instrumentality, 1,559,323 copies of Bibles, Testaments and Portions have been circulated, and have realized Rs. 82,868-15-1.

The old system has been attacked in recent years, in some instances with not overmuch discrimination or fairness. Confessedly it is not, and so far as I am aware, has never been held up as an ideal system. The work if well done involves separation from home and friends—distasteful to the average Hindu—hard travel, exposure, and, in some cases, danger. On this account, and notwithstanding its comparatively liberal scale of pay, it has, as a rule, failed to attract men of a higher standard of Christian life and devotion than the majority of subordinate mission agents.

On several grounds, the time has come for modifying the present system, and if the Missionary Societies are prepared to give the necessary help, this system should ultimately give way to more economical methods. In this respect it is possible to do to-day what could not have been safely attempted a quarter of a century ago. Some of our missionaries believe in the old system if worked by capable men, and others are not yet prepared to try new methods. Consideration must be had for the men who have grown grey in the service of the society. Changes involving ultimate abolition, will need to be carried out wisely and gradually. It is altogether too big a question to be settled by a stroke of the pen.

Methods. The method of procedure that commends itself to my judgment is to the following effect:—

(1) That except in special cases no fresh agents be appointed. Where immediate abolition is not advisable, fill up vacancies as far as possible by transfer.

(2) Locate no colporteur in a station furnished with a depôt.

(3) Confine the sales of colporteurs to non-Christians, except where small bands of Christians have no other means of access to the sacred volume.

(4) Pay the men less salary and allow a larger commission. I suggest, as a rule, a sum not exceeding Rs. 6 per mensem to commence with and Rs. 12 as the maximum, with a commission of 50 per cent. on Portions and 25 on Bibles and Testaments.

(5) Give no commission on sales to Christians, to colleges and schools, and on expensively bound Bibles.

(6) By way of increasing efficiency, itinerant missionaries should be encouraged, as far as possible, to take colporteurs with them on their tours, and, where practicable, to include them in their instruction classes. Supply them with simple commentaries, magazines, &c. Periodical examinations for the agents, such as have been carried out by the North Indian Auxiliary, including prizes for the three or four best men, are desirable.

(7) By way of a test let the men in the course of their journeys be instructed to write to the supervisor from the chief centres.

(8) I see objections to selling on Sundays.

(9) The qualifications of an agent should include a general knowledge of the Scriptures, ability to explain in a simple way the fundamental truths of Christianity and to answer common objections against it.

III.—*The work of the future.*—The wave of missionary feeling that is passing over the churches in Western lands is already bearing fruit in India in an addition to the staff of labourers, in the more vigorous working of old fields and the occupation of new ones. The Native Church is growing in numbers and there is a marked increase in the general reading population. One result of this advance will be an enhanced demand for the Bible and greater facilities for its dissemination. By each of these considerations the Bible Society is directly and powerfully affected.

The promotion of the translation, revision, printing and binding of the Scriptures is her legitimate work, and she will, no doubt, be equal to the demands that are made upon her in these directions. But with the prospect before her of a heavy outlay for additional versions, for revision, and for production on a larger scale, at prices much below the cost, is it unreasonable to ask that the churches represented in the Indian missions either assume the responsibility of distribution or that they provide the expenditure it involves? This is a question

**Sixth Day.** that calls for the careful, generous consideration and resolution of the Decennial Conference. It may not be possible to decide outright the details of any proposal, but a general principle may be laid down for subsequent development.

I venture to offer a few general suggestions on the question of the dissemination of the Word of God:—

**Agencies inadequate.** 1. It is freely admitted that the present agencies all combined are inadequate to the needs of India. If the Bible is to be taken to every village and hamlet in a reasonable time, we must devise new methods and put forth far greater effort than in the past. Any scheme or any number of schemes that may be proposed will have to be conditioned by the resources available as to labourers and funds.

2. A word in regard to those fields which are unoccupied or but partially occupied by Missionary Societies. In this Presidency the mapping out of district for permanent and systematic **Tours.** Bible work has usually been preceded by a Bible tour, and based upon the experience gained in the course of it. These journeys have been undertaken at our expense, by vernacular-speaking missionaries, assisted by catechists or colporteurs, and have ordinarily lasted from a month to six weeks each.

**Room for improvement.** 3. The present methods are capable of improvement and extension. In connection with each Auxiliary Society a Branch might be established in every well-populated centre, with a good working depôt, and agencies for taking the Scriptures from house to house and for the collection of funds, all to be under the direction of a local Committee in communication with the Committee of the Auxiliary. As long as the present system of colportage lasts it is worth while to work it efficiently. I would confine it chiefly to country places. The town circulation may fairly be left to missionaries, Bible women, mission agents and voluntary workers.

**Help needed.** 4. But additional help is wanted and we are limited in expenditure. The plan most ready to hand, it seems to me, is distribution by subordinate mission agents. As far as I am able to interpret their views, the majority of our missionaries are in favour of such a plan, but a minority fear that this dual arrangement will have the effect of diverting the men from preaching and of turning them into mere book hawkers. This fear need not exist if it be clearly laid down

that sales are to be effected not at fixed times and in fixed **Sixth Day.**
places, but generally in the course of the preaching tour. In
many parts the plan has been tried and has succeeded. A
catechist is fully equipped for his work only when he can
follow up his message by the fuller statement of it in printed
form.

5. Many of the mission agents may be willing to undertake Labour of love.
this additional work as a *labour of love,* but the majority will
expect remuneration for it. As a class they are certainly not
overpaid, and I would therefore offer them some inducement,
not in the shape of salary, but that of commission on sales.
The scale of allowance need not be absolutely uniform, but
generally the experiment may be tried of 25 per cent. commission on Bibles and Testaments and of 50 per cent. on
Portions. The demand will be chiefly for Portions, and a
packet of these is light in weight and small in compass.

6. Village school-masters might be vendors of the Scriptures. School-masters.
Students in training institutions and boys in boarding schools
may, with advantage to themselves and their future work, make
house-to-house visitations in the place where they reside and
in the neighbouring villages. I advocate the erection of a
Bible stand at weekly markets, fairs and festivals. The
principal railway stations offer a splendid field for labour, of
which we have largely availed ourselves. Let soldiers and
sailors not be lost sight of. Members of congregations, both
European and native, can do much in the way of voluntary
Bible circulation, and their duty and responsibility in this
direction may well be pressed on them. Other methods might
be stated, but it is sufficient to have indicated the chief of them.

A few other points may be mentioned :—(1) The extension Minor points.
of railways has an important bearing on Bible circulation, as
indeed, on the planting and working of missions. (2) There
should be free communication between Bible Society Committees
and missionaries with the double object of obtaining advice
and avoiding friction. (3) It is most advisable to advertise
the publications of the Bible Society in railway guides and in
the leading newspapers and magazines. (4) Deputation tours
on behalf of the society are invaluable in the way of instructing
audiences, establishing local organizations, and, generally, in
consolidating and extending the work. (5) When mistakes

Sixth Day.
Opinion asked.

are discovered in versions in circulation particulars should be communicated to the Secretary of an Auxiliary. (6) Opinion is wanted on (*a*) the selling prices of the Scriptures, and on (*b*) mixed systems of colportage. (7) Is it advisable for the Bible Society to issue Scripture selections, such as "The Sermon on the Mount?"

In closing I would re-affirm the leading practical points on which the opinion of the Conference is specially desired:—

(*a*) The best and cheapest methods of circulating the Scriptures.
(*b*) Whether the circulation should devolve mainly on the Missionary Societies.
(*c*) If the circulation is to remain chiefly with the Bible Society, what proportion of the expenditure the Missionary Societies might be expected to meet.

S. W. ORGANE,
*Madras Auxiliary Bible Society.*

December, 1892.

---

In connection with Mr. Organe's paper, the following letter from the British and Foreign Bible Society to the Conference is given:—

"THE EFFECTIVE CIRCULATION OF THE HOLY SCRIPTURES AS A BRANCH OF MISSIONARY ORGANISATION.

The Committee of the British and Foreign Bible Society in London beg to call the attention of the missionaries assembled in Bombay for the Decennial Conference to a topic of considerable and increasing importance. Its treatment in this paper can only be of a general character. If the proposal comes to be put widely into practice, adaptations in detail to special localities would need discussion and settlement in correspondence with individuals.

By *effective* circulation is meant such as results from a genuine desire to possess the Scriptures for the purpose of *reading* them. Something more than mere curiosity is desired. A real thirst for the Divine Book usually arises only from close or repeated *personal* discussion respecting its object and character. Proper cases for the free gift of a Portion, or Testament, or Bible may follow such pesonal dealing. But in the Committee's opinion and experience, mere general gratuitous distribution, if taken as the rule, produces little good, and involves a wasteful, or even harmful, expenditure of funds which at best do not suffice for the evangelisation of the world. In proof that some real desire to search the Scriptures has been created, the rule should be to claim some payment, however small, before the book is given.

In endeavouring to promote effective and fruitful circulation of the Scriptures, the British and Foreign Bible Society has borne heavy expenditure for colportage in missions. Financially it would have been much cheaper to give away the books for nothing. The numerical circulation might in that way have been larger for the same money. But most missionaries think with the Committee that more real good is done by sales. It is time, however, to consider whether sales cannot be effected at less proportionate cost, and with even more real efficiency than heretofore in districts where missions are in full operation. Where there is a mission staff, including native agents, and a body of native Christians, could the machinery for Bible circulation form with advantage a regular part of the Missionary Society's organization? The Committee of the British and Foreign Bible Society would submit this subject to the consideration of the brethren from the great missionary centres in India, and ask for all the information and advice upon it which they can supply.

The Committee do not at present express any opinion on the question in either direction. They wait for more complete materials upon which to form their decision and take action or not. They have no wish to abandon any work which is properly the duty of the Bible Society, or to shirk expense which fairly belongs to it. But the Society's funds have of late proved inadequate for meeting all the increasing demands made upon it. Any expenditure which can be reduced without loss of efficiency should be saved, that funds may be released for expansion elsewhere. If greater missionary success would be attained by a change of method, it would be matter for serious consideration whether the change should not be attempted. There are missionaries who think that the circulation of the Scriptures should always be accompanied by more complete evangelistic teaching by living agents than the constitution of the British and Foreign Bible Society makes allowable for its colporteurs. But if this plan is desirable, it would become possible, if the Bible-sellers were *employés* of a Missionary Society, and the application of the Bible Society's funds to defray the cost of the circulation were only in proportion to its books sold. This could be effected by a fixed discount, or even with an added subsidy, if circumstances required it, given at the time the books were purchased from the Society's depôts. Cash payments at the time of purchase would save the missionaries from any further trouble in settling accounts with the Bible Society and in furnishing it with returns of sales.

In stating these points, the Committee are not advocating the suggested system, but only noting considerations which have been advanced for it. When they put a question here or there in this paper, it is only to elicit information or opinions in reply. They are often pressed to make the Society's rules more elastic, and to permit the colporteurs in some countries to carry more than the Scriptures for sale. The Society's first law, and its comprehensive constituency, are a bar to such a change. But it is only fair to point out that if the work were done by volunteers from the native Christians, or by the *employés* of a Missionary Society, and the charge on the Bible Society's funds were regulated by the sales effected of its books, missionary superintendents would get the wider instrumentality they seek, and the cost of a salesman for general Christian literature would be reduced. One man would travel in place of two, and the expense would be met from two sources. The Bible Society would still bear its share in the labour and cost of providing the books of Holy Scripture. It would still have to care single-handed for pioneer circulation, and that in countries where missions are scarce or feeble.

These topics were to some extent discussed at a Conference held at the Bible House on July 23rd, 1891. Delegates connected with twelve Missionary Societies were present, but several did not consider themselves authorised to vote on a resolution which was proposed, and which was carried by a large majority of those who did vote. Its form was as follows:—" Resolved that this Conference desires to record its conviction that greater economy and increased efficiency in circulating the Scriptures might be secured, if the various Foreign Missionary Societies would, wherever possible, themselves undertake this work,—the expense of carrying it on being still, where needful, largely defrayed by the different Bible Societies."

If it should appear to the Decennial Conference that arrangements on the above lines in suitable areas would extend the diffusion of Holy Scripture more economically and effectively than at present, and would enable the missionaries to feel a greater *missionary* interest in the work and to supervise it better than now, resolutions to that effect would, of course, greatly facilitate the bringing of the subject before Missionary Committees at home with success, should the Bible Society decide to pursue that course.

THE BIBLE HOUSE, LONDON."

*November,* 1892.

# FOURTH PAPER—CHRISTIAN LITERATURE. SIXTH DAY.

By the Rev. G. P. TAYLOR, M. A., B. D., I. P. M., Ahmedabad.

In responding to the request to prepare for submission to this Conference a paper on Christian Literature, it has seemed to me that I shall best serve the purpose of our meeting by briefly indicating the main lines on which the Irish Presbyterian Mission in Gujarat carries on a fairly successful work in connexion with its Tract and Book Society. *The Gujarat Tract Society.*

I. In the earlier stages of the mission, some forty or fifty years ago, while as yet the Christian community was small, and the agencies requiring superintendence but few, the pioneer missionaries were able to devote a considerable portion of their time to the writing of tracts and Christian booklets. In later years, however, the work of the mission stations, especially at those occupied by senior missionaries, has so largely developed that it is no longer possible to give the same time and attention as formerly to the production of Christian literature. As a consequence, though occasionally new books are issuing from the mission press, the majority of the recent publications have been reprints of older works. Indications indeed are not wanting that, in the future, the writing of new tracts in the vernacular will devolve not so much upon the European missionary as upon educated native converts. For instance, of the three new publications issued in 1891 by the Gujarat Tract Society while one, "The Harmony of the Gospels," was prepared by Rev. Mr. Scott of Rajkot, the other two, "The Heart Book" and "Stories from Early Christian History," were translations into Gujarati by our first native pastor and his eldest son. As pointing to a like conclusion is the fact that in the more recent numbers of our mission monthly magazine, "the Dawn of Truth," fully five pages out of every eight have been contributed by the native members of the Church. *I. Production. Reprints. Converts increasingly helpful.*

The reprinting of tracts issued first many years ago lies in some cases open to a serious objection. Those early publications were, owing to the necessities of the times, of a character largely *Evangelistic rather than controversial tracts.*

**Sixth Day.**

destructive and controversial; but now the state of matters is greatly changed. A generation has grown up different from their fathers. Western science, Western education, Western modes of thought have moulded anew the minds of many, and under the overruling hand of God the object which the first missionaries perforce set themselves to accomplish, the weaning of worshippers from superstitious and debasing practices, has been in a measure effected by agencies divine indeed yet not distinctively religious. It now becomes us to recognise the altered circumstances of the times, and in our tracts and books present a constructive plea for the Gospel, emphasizing not so much the strange contradictions of Hinduism as the sweet reasonableness of Christianity.

*English tracts.*

Another feature of the times calls for especial notice. The wide and rapid spread of English education, not in the cities alone, but even in the smaller towns of Gujarat, has produced a demand, formerly unknown, for short and simple tracts in English. To supply this demand our missionaries have indented on the Tract Depôt at Madras, our deep obligations to which we gratefully acknowledge. The English publications for Indian readers, edited by Dr. John Murdoch, have proved of the greatest service, and the admirable papers on Social and Religious Reform, the Short Biographies, the Manuals for Students and Teachers, and the recently issued Papers for thoughtful Hindus, are coming more and more into request. It is imposible to tell the good that may be done by these excellent publications, so well adapted to the present period of India's unrest.

*Vernacular tracts.*

Further, we cannot overlook the needs of the growing Christian community. As the bounds of the Church extend and her numbers increase, it becomes an imperative duty to provide wholesome intellectual food for our flock. The works issuing from the secular press are as a rule far from elevating in their tendency, and if the members of our Christian Church, especially those living at a distance from any mission-station, are to be supplied at all with good moral reading it can only be through the more effective working of our Tract and Book Societies.

Another with us comparatively new demand in the matter of Christian literature has arisen in connection with the training of a native pastorate. A pressing need is felt for text-books suitable for adoption in a Divinity School, books thus of a more advanced scholarship than those employed in the ordinary mission schools. This want, however, we merely mention here, inasmuch as the more appropriate time for its discussion would be when the subject of "the Native Church, the Training and Position of its Ministry" comes up for consideration. SIXTH DAY.<br>Text-books.

Our tracts are all printed in the Mission Press at Surat, which was the first of the printing-presses in Gujarat. The workmen employed are, with one or two exceptions, Native Christians. We have found that tracts generally command a better sale when bound in brightly-tinted covers. Indeed, in the majority of cases the villagers are induced in the first instance to make their purchases, not so much because of the contents of the tracts, as on account of their neat and attractive appearance. Whatever the contents be, they recognise that in return for their money they have in their hands a pleasing and pretty booklet. A short striking title to a tract goes a long way towards assuring its popularity, while pictures also help the sales, and the larger the pictures the better. In this connection mention should be made of the beautifully illustrated tracts generously supplied by the children's special service mission. The full-page (quarto) engravings are executed in England, while all the letter-press is printed after arrival in this country, with the result that these tracts are, as to workmanship, far superior to anything issued from the native presses. A dozen or twenty, neatly bound in cloth, make a handsome volume which serves admirably as a pictorial prize-book for schools. The Surat Mission Press.<br><br>Bright covers.<br><br><br><br><br>Striking titles.<br>The children's special service mission tracts.

II. The financing of a tract society is a matter of very considerable difficulty, but certain principles may be laid down as being generally applicable. The wholesale price of the publications, say the nominal price less 25 per cent. discount, should be determined by the cost of production, being fixed only slightly above that figure. Vernacular tracts must be priced very low, otherwise they become simply a drug in the market. In our own society of 141 different publications no less than 104 sell at, or under, one anna each, 22 of these being priced at only one pie each. For English tracts, on the other hand, a higher sum can be charged, but even of these only few should cost more than four annas each. In order to obtain satisfactory II. Finance.<br><br><br><br>Selling price.<br><br><br><br><br><br>A fixed price.

SIXTH DAY.

sales it is absolutely necessary that in all retail dealings the colporteur should keep strictly to the full published price. If under the hope of immediate gain he ventures upon selling his books at a reduced rate, it is well nigh impossible for himself or for others who a few months later come after him in the same field to effect any sales at the original prices. Substantial discount once having been allowed, the honest man who charges sixteen annas in the rupee will find no customers. Underselling is perhaps the surest way of ultimately stopping all sales, and not unfrequently it has been found that a serious falling off in the sales at any station was traceable to just this cause.

On the much vexed question as to the method of payment of colporteurs, or of others engaged in the circulation of books and tracts, there exists a very wide difference of opinion and practice. The scheme which is now adopted at all the stations of our mission, and which after having tried several other expedients we have found most effectual in increasing the yearly sales, is as follows. The tracts issuing from the Mission Press are sold at about cost price (three-fourths of the full price) to the missionaries resident at the different mission-stations, the carriage from Surat being charged to the purchaser. Our evangelists while on tour may take a supply of these tracts with them on condition of their selling them at the full price, of which three-fourths must be returned to the missionary, while the remaining fourth is the commission allowed them for their trouble. Thus the missionary receives back the entire sum he had paid, and the cost of circulating tracts in this way by the agency of evangelists is merely the amount required for carriage. On the other hand, our colporteurs, who receive no fixed salary, yet maintain themselves solely by the sale of tracts and books, may purchase them at one-fourth of the full price. These men also agree to sell always at the full printed price, of which thus three-fourths fall to themselves and one-fourth to the mission. The latter, accordingly, on the sales thus effected, loses two-fourths of the full price, and hence the cost of circulating tracts by the agency of colporteurs amounts to half the total value of the sales *plus* railway charges. For example, tracts, the cost of production of which is about Rs. 75, have a selling price of Rs. 100. These are

Evangelists receive 25 per cent. of retail price.

Colporteurs.

supplied wholesale to the missionary for Rs. 75. An *evangelist* will sell them retail in the towns and villages he visits for Rs. 100, paying of this sum Rs. 75 to the missionary, and keeping Rs. 25 as his commission: so that, exclusive of cost of carriage, the expense of circulation is *nil*. A *colporteur*, however, also selling them retail for Rs. 100, pays for them only Rs. 25, that is to say, Rs. 50 less than the cost of production: hence in this case, exclusive of railway carriage, the cost of circulating Rs. 100 worth of tracts amounts to Rs. 50. We have found that the men engaged solely in this work cannot obtain a livelihood on less favourable terms.

The paying a fixed monthly salary with a comparatively small commission on sales is, in our opinion, a great mistake, the colporteurs having then no special incentive to push their sales vigorously. An admirable society which has long done good work in the Bombay Presidency would, we believe, have stood in a better financial position to-day had it been possible for it to adopt some other method than that of engaging its colporteurs on a fixed salary. In the report for 1890 we find the total proceeds of sales amounted to some Rs. 850, while, irrespective of commission and travelling allowances, the salaries of its colporteurs reached Rs. 1,850, or more than four times the amount (Rs. 425) that would have been due on the lines of our work in Gujarat. As one result of the strict economy that has marked the management of our Tract and Book Society, it has been from the outset an organization independent of the home church. The Religious Tract Society of London supplies, free of charge, all the paper required for the printing of our tracts, and the small deficit after crediting the receipts from sales is contributed by friends in this country. These private subscriptions amount to about Rs. 500 a year.

The free distribution of tracts may have been necessary when Christianity was regarded as a new and strange religion, and when its claims to general recognition were disallowed; but those days are already past, and the need for gratuitous circulation no longer exists to the same extent. Also tracts received for the asking are, as a rule, not so much appreciated as those for which a price has been paid. However, in some of the more out-lying stations private members of our Christian community have with our hearty encouragement visited the dharm-

*Sixth Day.*

Monthly salaries a mistake.

Free distribution of tracts.

SIXTH DAY.

shalas or other public resorts, and presented tracts to all who were able to read.

Locality.

III. As to locality we have often found that good sales can be effected on virgin soil distant far from any mission-station.

New Districts.

A few years ago one of our Christians undertook at his own instance a tract-selling expedition into Cutch and North Kathiawar, where in little more than two months he disposed of nearly 7,000 tracts and booklets of the aggregate value of Rs. 120. Hindu fairs, or *melas*, also provide a favourable opportunity for sales. Last year at the Vautha *mela* the agents sold in addition to a great many tracts and books their entire stock of 128 gospels. "If they had taken more they could have sold more." In cities where our tracts have circulated for many years past the demand is not so brisk as in the rural districts, though even in cities considerable sales can be effected by means of courteous canvassing. In recent times we have been able to dispose of a very considerable number of tracts at railway stations. Through the kindness of the Traffic Manager of the B. B. & C. I. Railway free platform passes have been granted to some of our colporteurs, who now meet most of the trains at the large stations of Surat, Broach, Baroda, Anand, and Ahmedabad. The enormous increase in passenger traffic makes this department of tract circulation singularly encouraging, and by this agency seeds of truth are being scattered far and wide over vast stretches of country.

Fairs.

Railway stations.

Results.

IV. The results effected so silently by tracts cannot easily be tabulated or even estimated, but the history of our mission bears strong evidence to the great good that they have done.

1. Founding of the mission in Gujarat.

When, more than fifty years ago, the veteran missionaries of the London Mission were sadly and anxiously questioning whether they should not abandon this mission-field, lo! two Hindus appeared at the gates of Surat, inquiring for the missionary's house. They had come from a village a hundred miles to the north, and as the warrant for their coming shewed the tracts they had been reading, which invited all who might wish to learn further about Christ to visit the missionaries in person. These two men stated that in their district many were reading Christian books, that there was a large sphere of labour open among the villagers, and that they themselves would gladly receive baptism. Such was the origin of the first mission on the banks of the River Mahi, the parent of the present mission with its two thousand converts. Of the two native pastors, associate-members of the Presbytery of Kathiawar and Gujarat, one, a Bhrahman of Rajkot, ascribes his first religious convictions to the reading of a Church History which he had received as a prize in a mission-school. The late lamented Rev. Hormazdji Pestonji, who worked for years in connection with our mission, traced his first knowledge of the truth to a copy of one of the Gospels and a couple of tracts placed in his hands at Daman by a missionary on tour towards Gujarat. Within the last three years three Brahman youths, each of fair education, have, through the reading of tracts, sought and found admission within the church, of whom one is now engaged in the sister mission at Baroda, another in Ahmedabad, and the third is under training at Anand. Several indeed of our best converts were first led to serious inquiry by means of the printed Word, but to relate the cases in detail would necessitate transgressing the limits assigned to this paper. This much, however, we can confidently affirm that the history of the past teaches us a lesson 'large writ' that God has set his seal of approval on the noble work of disseminating Christian literature, and that He has granted an abundant blessing to accompany this special branch of Christian effort.

*Sixth Day.*
*2. Rev. Nathu Hari.*
*3. Rev. Hormazdji Pestonji.*
*4. Three young Brahmans.*

V. *Suggestion.*—Having regard to the increasingly felt need of new tracts and books in the vernacular to meet the modern phases of Hinduism and its changed attitude regarding Christianity, would it not be well if this Decennial Conference were to impress on the home churches the desirability of relieving from all other duties a senior missionary in each mission where a different language is spoken in order that he may have leisure to prepare such tracts and books for early publication?

*Suggestion.*

---

## FIRST SPEECH—COLPORTAGE.

### By the Rev. A. W. Prautch, M. E. C., Thana, Bombay.

I desire in opening to state that I will confine my remarks to colportage; other speakers who are better able will deal with the production of literature and the translation of the Scriptures.

*Colportage.*

SIXTH DAY.

*Salaries more than sales.*

*Old plan unsatisfactory.*

Let me first draw your attention to the paper from the Bible Society in that part beginning :—"In endeavouring to promote," &c. (*see above*), and to that from the Christian Literature Society where it deals with "circulation" (*see above*). I want to clearly state that in my opinion the time has come when the present system of Bible Society Colportage must be stopped, because it is inefficient, extravagant and expensive. I feel that the Bible Societies ought to confine themselves to producing the Scriptures and organize colportage only where there are no missions. Surely every missionary ought to value the circulation of the Scriptures, and devise some way of putting them in the hands of the readers on his district. I am further convinced that the sales of colporteurs are out of proportion to their salaries. To read at random from a Bible Society Report, the proceeds for the year, for one colporteur were Rs. 37, while the salary and allowances were Rs. 178, making a cost of Rs. 5 to sell Re. 1 of Scriptures. The total proceeds for all the colporteurs for the year were Rs 709; total expenditure was Rs. 2,233.

My contention is that either the readers were so few or the demand so small, that it did not profitably employ the colporteurs' time, and the same results would have been attained in sales by having it understood that the man is to preach, visit from house to house, talk to people about Jesus Christ, and sell them a Bible if possible. This is suggested by the Bible Society. You see the Bible Society could better afford to give the Bibles gratis to the missionaries, and even a subsidy on the sales, rather than maintain the present colportage method.

It is not a fact that if professional colportage were stopped, the *circulation* of the Scriptures would stop. To quote from a Bible Society Report: the sales from the depôt for the year were 54,218 Scriptures, which brought a return to the Bible Society; while colportage for the same period circulated only 16,679 Scriptures and cost Rs. 2,233, less the colportage proceeds Rs. 709. The cost of colportage could better have been spent on paying the cost of carriage on Scriptures bought by outstation customers, or as a discount or bonus on actual sales among the non-Christians, and by thus giving a discount to missionaries, they would be able to appoint their own book-sellers and pay them according to their individual needs. The colportage rules are very strict; not allowing a colporteur to spend part of his time at anything else, nor to sell other books than Scriptures, where the readers are few. The colporteur soon supplies the demand, and his services as a colporteur are no longer needed; but if he were a mission agent, paid by the mission, he could be put at the work he was best adapted for or combine several works.

It is a fact that colportage is looked upon as an inferior work, fit only for those who are unable to do anything better; and often it is made a sort of pensioner's place for some one the mission thinks it ought to provide for. One Bible Society Secretary told me that missionaries gave him the halt, lame, and blind as colporteurs, simply to have them provided for, thus turning colportage into an alms-house; so now he pays the railway fare of new candidates simply to see their physical condition.

I met another missionary who, when asked how his colporteur was getting along, said: "He is not doing much as a bookseller, but he is bringing up a family of seven children who will be church members." So the present Bible Society system is a success in one direction at least.

In the "*Harvest Field*" of November 1890, I pointed out some of the defects of the present colportage system. I find them still in existence, so I cannot do better than to again call attention to the facts. The colporteur's record does not bear looking at. In Bombay the sales seldom exceed Rs. 5 worth of books a month; the average is Rs. 4. This is how the account stands: Sales Rs. 5. While the salary of the colporteur is Rs. 12, and he receives 25 per cent. on the sales. A man, who seldom moves out of his own house, or takes any trouble to sell the books, can thus ensure an income of Rs. 13 per month. This is a sore temptation to a good man and a clear case for a bad man. The figures may vary slightly in other societies, but the plan is the same. At this rate the colporteurs will, in a few years, be able to lend the societies money to publish with!

"I do not object to the expenditure of money. I should like to see more spent, but differently. I know several missionaries who would go into colportage *at once* if the societies would allow 50 per cent. discount on their publications and pay freight. These terms would enable them to use local men for this work, whom they know thoroughly, and whose present work

*[margin: Sixth Day. An alms-house. Spend money differently.]*

**Sixth Day.**

might permit them to combine with it effectively that of colportage also. If the whole discount were not utilised in this way, it would enable the missionary to use his discrimination in the *free* distribution of Scriptures among the really needy."

My object is not to devise a plan to economize money at the expense of thoroughness or effectiveness, but I feel strongly on the question of retaining the present colportage system. It may have answered the purpose fifty years ago when missions were just beginning, but surely now with the number of converts and workers a change for the better might be made. The same money that is now *thrown away* on a few colporteurs might be used to better advantage in publishing and giving the Scriptures almost free to responsible people who will guarantee their circulation.

**The North India Bible Society.**

The North India Bible Society have this plan in splendid operation. The conditions are as follows:—

Discount allowed on all Vernacular Scriptures: price under Re. 1—75 p.c.

| ,, | ,, | ,, | ,, | over | ,, | 50 p.c. |
| ,, | ,, | ,, | English | under | ,, | 50 p.c. |
| ,, | ,, | ,, | ,, | over | ,, | 25 p.c. |

Roman-Urdu Bibles, at catalogue price, having already been reduced ... ... ... ... ... 80 p.c.

(1) The above must be sold at catalogue prices.
(2) They must be sold by those not receiving support from any Bible Society.
(3) The above discounts are not allowed for schools and prizes.

I approve of the above most heartily, as it meets every need and can be adapted to any mission field.

Too much emphasis cannot be laid upon the importance of circulating tracts and Scriptures. Many souls have been led to Jesus by these silent messengers of salvation. The truth is that most of the circulation of literature is done by a few missionaries, the others could do more if they tried. In this respect the Basel Mission leads all others. Every missionary and mission agent is a bookseller; every mission station has its bookshop; they thoroughly believe in colportage and *do it*. This to my mind is the ideal to work up to.

**The Basel Mission.**

Colportage is a trying work, as the colporteur meets with rebuffs, insults and contempt; he therefore needs the support of the missionary. He can best be helped by making him a regular member of the mission staff, and the missionary can make the post honourable by personally engaging in it. It is quite clear that if a missionary does not prize this mission agency enough to give it a place alongside his teachers, he does not deserve to have Bible Society money spent upon him. I continue to urge that the money spent now ought to be spent differently—really spend it where it would be utilised.

## SECOND SPEECH—COLPORTAGE.

By the Rev. J. AUSTIN THOMSON, Secretary, North India Bible Society, Allahabad.

The subject on which I have been asked to speak is the same as that on which the Rev. Mr. Prautch has just spoken, *viz.*, colportage. I agree with what he has said on some points, but I disagree with him on a great many others. My apology for speaking on this subject is that I have been engaged in this work of colportage for the last fifteen years, and I have had experience of it in England, in Japan, in Corea, and now in this country; and I have studied the work under varied conditions.

It is found necessary to support a large number of Christian men, both in Great Britain and in the United States, for the sole purpose of selling the Scriptures and religious literature, and I maintain that if this is necessary in so-called Christian countries, it is much more necessary in heathen lands. In this I disagree with the previous speaker, who has given it as his opinion that the present system of colportage is no longer suitable for India.

There is a great work to be done in circulating Christian literature in remote districts, where missionaries and evangelists seldom or never go, and this can only be done by men whose sole work it is, and who are paid a fixed salary for doing it. We have many instances of great good resulting from the sale of Scriptures and tracts in places where the Gospel had never been preached and where the name of Christ would never have

SIXTH DAY.

*Work extremely difficult.*

*Melas.*

been known, but for the humble colporteur carrying his pack of books far into the jungle and into the mountain recesses of Nepal and Thibet. For this reason I would plead for the continuance of the present system of having men employed for the sole purpose of selling the Scriptures and other Christian books.

It is true that the results obtained are not what they might be, but instead of condemning the whole system for that reason, I would rather ask your consideration of the causes of the poor results as compared with the expense incurred, and ask if something could not be done to remedy that which has been complained of, viz., the excessive cost as compared with the work effected. In the first place, I would call your attention to the extremely difficult nature of the work. It is one thing for a European missionary to sell books in a *mela*, and quite another thing for a native colporteur to tramp through villages, in which perhaps not more than one or two persons can read, offering his books for sale, and I submit that no comparison can be instituted between the two kinds of work. I have done both myself, and I give as my experience the opinion that while the former may be much more successful so far as sales are concerned, the latter is much more successful so far as results are concerned; and, after all, our work is not merely to see how many books can be disseminated for a given sum, but rather to effect as much good as possible by their circulation, and it is a fact that much of the Christian literature sold at *melas* is destroyed immediately afterwards, and indeed much of it is bought in order that it may be destroyed. This is not the case with books sold to the people at their own doors. They read them and value them, because they have paid for them. Again, the work of a colporteur is very hard. They have to leave their homes, sometimes for long periods at a time. They have to carry heavy burdens in all kinds of weather. They are often treated with great contempt when the nature of their business is known. Sometimes they are buffeted by the people to whom they offer their books, and often find it difficult to obtain food and shelter simply because they are Christians. Work like this requires men of stamina, as well as that they should engage in it for the love of it. I would like to ask the missionaries who are assembled here what kind of men have been given to the Bible Societies in time past to engage in this work?

*Sixth Day.*

I can only speak from a very short experience of the work in India, but my opinion is that the very worst type of native converts have been given to us for this important and difficult work; men who were in no way qualified for it, and who were useless for any other kind of work, but for whom the missionaries thought that something should be done: this is the kind of men who have been doing the work, and now we are reproached because the results are not in keeping with the cost. Shortly after I came to this country, I began to gather the colporteurs in the service of the North India Bible Society together once a year, for prayer and for examination in Scripture knowledge, for the men who sell the books are often asked to read portions and to explain them, and it is important that they should have a fair knowledge of Christian doctrine. I remember the first meeting of the kind we had, and the shock my feelings sustained when first I saw the men gathered together. A more motley group I never beheld in my life before. There were the old and deaf and maimed and partly blind. This was the class of men who had been recommended by the missionaries. But I am glad to say that a much better class of men is now being given to us, as was shewn by the fact that at the last examination held, four out of six prizes, which were offered for those who passed the best examination, were taken by men only recently employed. And more than this,—the average sales per mau is steadily increasing, and I trust that the objections which have been presented to you this morning to our present system of work will not long hold good. Give us better men, and we will do better work.

*Better men required.*

I believe that the time is not far off when the missions will realize in a greater measure than they do now the importance of this work of colportage, and that a colporteur will be an indispensable adjunct to every mission station. I believe that men ought to be trained for the work, and, speaking from a long experience, I can testify that there is nothing that will bring a man out as an efficient Christian worker, quicker or better, than two or three years experience in colportage. During the ten years I wrought in Japan, quite a large number of the colporteurs who worked under me became catechists and evangelists,

*A colporteur in every station.*

and some were ordained and entered the regular ministry. It pays therefore to train men for the work.

*The cost no criterion.*

Under the circumstances which I have mentioned, it seems idle to me to count up the cost of circulating each copy of the Scriptures as has been done this morning in your hearing. If the missions were to do the same thing with their converts, I wonder what would the average cost per head be? I fear it would run up into a good round sum.

Now, having stated some of the reasons why our system of colportage has not been so successful as we would like to see it, and having asked the missions to give us better men for the work in future, the next thing I would ask is that the missions provide the salaries of the colporteurs, or at least that the work of selling Christian literature be taken up more directly by the missions than has been done in time past. The Bible Society at home is beginning to think that the missions ought to do more in this line than they have done, and to relieve it of a share of the great expense attending the circulation of the Scriptures. And there is a good reason for this. As many of you are aware, the work in India is conducted on very different lines from what it is elsewhere. In Japan, for example, we had a rule never to sell Scriptures under their cost price; and as for some of the publications of the Tract Society, they were sold at a fair profit, excluding tracts, which were sometimes sold below cost, and occasionally given gratis. I remember having a serious difference of opinion with my revered friend Dr. Murdoch when he visited Japan about twelve years ago. As agent of the London Tract Society I had just published a book, and Dr. Murdoch thought the price fixed was too high, and that the book would not sell, but it sold, and the price of the next edition was raised to nearly double the cost, and yet it sold. But in India such a thing would be impossible on account of the poverty of the great mass of the people. As a matter of fact, the greater proportion of our books, both of the Bible and Tract Societies, are sold at prices ranging from a half to a fifth of their cost. When to this is added the great expense attending their circulation, as has been pointed out to you by Mr. Prautch, it will be seen that the burden that is laid upon the Bible Society is a very heavy one, and it is only to be expected that they should ask that the missions

*Missions to provide salaries.*

relieve them of a share of that burden. It is not proposed to give up the present system of paid colportage, but it is suggested that in the large cities, and in places where there are numerous Christians, that all Bible-selling should be done free of cost, so far as salaries are concerned, to the Bible Society. And this could easily be done. The Bible Society would be willing to allow commission to those engaging in the work so as to cover the expense and occasional loss connected with book-selling, or to help to pay the salaries of the catechists or evangelists who did the Bible-selling and who were thus taking the place of the colporteurs. In addition to the saving thus effected there would be other important advantages gained. Many of the missionaries, already overburdened with work, complain of the labour involved in keeping the accounts of the colporteurs with the Bible Society and the furnishing of reports of their work. By the method suggested the work of keeping accounts would be reduced to a minimum and no reports would be required. Again, the colporteur being entirely in the service of the mission would be more thoroughly superintended in his work than at present, and more interest would be taken in the results attending his work.

Another plan that has been tried with considerable success in the North-West is that of subsidizing colporteurs, the Bible Society paying one-half of the salary and allowing a commission to the man. Many of the missionaries urge that the colporteurs should be allowed to sell other literature as well as the Scriptures. If the Bible Society pays for the whole of a man's time, it expects to get what it pays for, but if only half his salary is drawn from the society, the man is at liberty to sell other books, so long as his sales of the Scriptures warrant the subsidy being continued. This plan, also, secures the better superintendence of his work by the missionary under whom he works.

*Plan of subsidizing.*

I will conclude by reminding you how closely the work of the Bible Society and the Missionary Society are related. The work of the missionary without the printed Word would be greatly crippled, almost paralysed. What helps the work of the former helps the work of the latter. I commend to your best consideration this work of colportage.

## THIRD SPEECH—COLPORTAGE.

By the Rev. H. U. WEITBRECHT, PH. D., C. M. S., Batala, Punjab.

*Literature for all classes.*

There is, doubtless, a disadvantage in having the subject in which one is personally interested, treated at the fag end of the Conference, but there is also this advantage in it, that after considering the methods and wants of each branch of missionary work, we are reminded how each leads up to this. Do we speak of work among the masses? The cry is for catechisms and plain books to meet the needs of the simple-minded villagers. Do we discuss the wants of the native church and its ministers? They ask us for commentaries to study, books of devotion to feed the spiritual life. In the session on the training of the young, how often was the call reiterated for Sunday School literature, stories and the like! The mention of the Roman Catholic controversy reminded us that we are ill-furnished with vernacular manuals on that subject. The needs of the educated classes bring to the front the claims of English missionary literature as a distinct branch of the work. For women special literature is needed. Our schools, to be effective, must be thoroughly supplied with high-class Christian school-books. And so throughout.

*Increase of readers.*

There was a remarkable unanimity in the session on education as to the need of prosecuting that branch of missionary work with vigour and thoroughness. But what is the moral or religious use of manufacturing readers, aye, and implanting a thirst for truth in their minds, if we fail to give them the reading that will satisfy these cravings? The mass of readers in this country is increasing year by year. In 1882 there were some 2,000,000 pupils in Indian schools; they now number 3,700,000. But what is the literature offered to this wider circle? Much of it is morally pernicious; more is ephemeral, and if we take the vernacular press of the country as its chief mental food, it will scracely be counted a harsh judgment to say that it leaves much to be desired, and is scarcely fitted to educate men even to a fair secular standard of judgment. Surely more support should be given to agencies like that of the late Christian Vernacular Education Society, now the

Christian Literature Society, which strives to minister to these needs.

We must not, however, ignore the work that is being done. To take only the provinces from which I come, we have for the Punjab a branch of the British and Foreign Bible Society and a Religious Book Society, which is, in effect, an auxiliary of the London Religious Tract Society. These two are under combined management, and they circulated in 1891, 47,000 Bibles, New Testaments and portions, 52,000 books, and 231,000 tracts in the various languages of the Punjab and the neighbouring tracts. Yet what are they among a population of, say, 30,000,000? Still these books are not without their effect. Not long ago *The Tribune*, a leading Lahore native journal, contained a paragraph commenting on what the writer called the spread of Christianity in the Manjha (the tract south of Amritsar) which is noted as the chief home of the Sikhs. He had often, he wrote, seen old Sikh women spelling out the New Testament in the Gurmukhi characters, and he doubted not that they knew far more of it than of their own Scriptures. Again, some time ago the Rev. Dr. Imadud Din, C. M. S., Amritsar (a Muhammadan convert, who has received the degree of D. D. from the Archbishop of Canterbury in recognition of his writings in defence of the Christian faith), was visited by the Wakil or minister of the Mihtar of Chitral, a Muhammadan State beyond the frontier. The Wakil said— "My master bids me say that he has heard of your writings against the faith. You are a *kafir* worthy of death, and were you in Chitral, he would depute no one else to do the deed, but would slay you with his own hands." Dr. Imadud Din replied: "Tell your master that were he able to slay me, God would raise up twenty more and better Imadud Dins from my spilt blood." Our Christian books thus go beyond the frontier to regions which the missionary as yet cannot reach. And, strange to say, controversial and other Christian books may be found in the catalogues of the Muhammadan book-sellers in Amritsar.

The great fault in our present methods of producing and using Christian literature, is the lack of thoroughness and system. As has been pointed out, our colporteurs are not unfrequently the poorest of our agents; and it is a fact as

*Sixth Day*

The Punjab.

The Rev. Imadud Din.

A strange visitor.

Improvement necessary.

**Sixth Day.**

lamentable as undeniable that the promotion of Christian literature is left to the spare time of such missionaries as happen to take an interest in it. If we wish that anything practical should issue from this session of our Conference, we must face these facts and set ourselves to remedy them.

First, then, let me remind you that an Indian Christian literature has its sources of support mainly in the two great societies already mentioned along with kindred societies in America. Now as regards the B. and F. Bible Society and the Religious Tract Society it is, alas! a fact that their income is stationary, while the needs of their foreign work are progressive. With all our heart we thank these great societies for the munificent support which they have given and continue to give us, and we appeal to the Christian public in home lands not to allow their resources to be straitened. But if we would extend our work as we should, we must make some effort toward self-support; and this we can best do by taking on our own shoulders to some extent the financial burden of the circulation of Christian books. We need to decrease the number of our colporteurs by weeding out of their ranks those who are unfit for the work, thus relieving the societies of their pay. On the other hand, we ought to train those whom we keep to efficiency in their work, no less carefully than we do our catechists or readers. Again we should see to it that our preachers (and we ourselves) do more to promote the sale of books than in time past. Also each mission school should be a book-selling agency and have its reading room. A liberal commission to school teachers may do much to make them book-sellers.

*Sell in schools.*

*"Readers" for schools.*

This leads me to another point. There are, to my knowledge, a good many mission schools in which Christian Readers are not used. This ought not to be so. It may be that some of our readers, good when they were first compiled, have fallen behind the times. If so let them be revised, and let our educational brethren lend a hand in producing suitable readers, up to the most recent requirements. They will find the publishing societies more than ready to print them, and thus remove a disfigurement and a stumbling-block to our work.

*Men set apart for literary work.*

Once more, how is the work of colportage, of literary production and distribution to be directed? This cannot be properly done till we have missionaries specially set apart for

the work. It cannot be really carried out by a man who  <small>Sixth Day.</small>
already has a mission on his hands. The papers submitted to
this Conference, especially the interesting one by Mr. Haigh, of
Mysore, bristle with excellent suggestions. But who is to see
that they are carried out? We ask our societies to give a
man for each language area, to devote himself to the direction
of this work. And this, along with many another need, can
never be fully supplied till we recognise the need, in missionary
work as a whole, of a system of reserves. No sooner is a  <small>Emergency</small>
special work started than it is liable to collapse for inefficiency,  <small>men.</small>
because it has to supply a vacancy caused by sickness or depar-
ture in some other branch, for there is no reserve to draw upon
to fill up the blank. What would be thought of the general who
elected to fight a battle with his forces scattered over a wide
line with no reserves to fill up gaps caused by the enemy's
attack? Yet this is the way in which most of our missionary
work is carried on. We appeal to the Home Societies so to
concentrate, strengthen and dispose the forces, God has given
and shall give us to provide workers in the cause of literature,
and roll away the reproach which is now too well merited, that
" the hungry sheep look up and are not fed."

---

## FOURTH SPEECH.

By the Rev. W. F. Johnson, D. D., M. E. C., Allahabad. (Read by the Rev. D. Phillips.)

The object of this paper is to discuss two questions: What
are the obstacles which hinder the wider spread of Vernacular
Christian Literature in this country? and, What can be done
to remove those obstacles?

When any one is sick, three things are to be done as soon as  <small>The disease.</small>
possible :—(1) Recognize the fact that disease is present.
(2) Get a physician to diagnose the case, and tell what is wrong.
(3) Apply appropriate remedies. In the case before us we all
admit there is something wrong: our Christian books and
tracts are not pushed into circulation as they ought to be.
The sooner, therefore, we inquire what the obstacles are, the
sooner they are likely to be removed. Some of them seem to
the writer the following: It is understood, of course, that each

**Sixth Day.**

of us speaks from his own quite limited experience, and from the standpoint of his own limited field. What is here written has reference to the region which looks to Allahabad for its supply, and chiefly to the work which has the Hindi language for its vehicle. It is, after all, not such a very circumscribed field, if there be, as has been claimed, 50 millions of people, who use the Hindi as their vernacular; still it is by no means India.

**Poverty.**

The *first* hindrance in our way is the poverty of the masses. Reading matter is to most people a luxury, and with these toiling masses the margin for luxuries is very small indeed. If a man has only from Rs. 2 to 4 per month to support a family on, the purchase of even a pice book will be an event, and the purchase of a rupee book something not to be dreamt of. Notice in our catalogues how small the sale of anna tracts is as compared with the pice ones, in spite of the greater value and attractiveness of the former. The people simply cannot afford the larger expense. We ought, in view of this fact, to try experiments in the way of cheaper get up in our publications. In some characters much space is wasted by using type larger than is needed. The Hindi is a great offender in this respect, but we are at the mercy of the type-founders, for, thus far, their type when very small has not been very easy to read. Cheaper paper also might be used. Hindu publishers should teach us a lesson in this regard, for they use scarcely anything but straw-coloured, or the very cheapest of white paper.

**Religious tracts unwelcome.**

The *second* hindrance is that our publications are chiefly religious, and as such have to encounter the natural aversion of the human heart to the truth. If our tracts were filled with the highly-spiced, evil-provoking material, which fills so many native books, we should hardly need colportage. Such books would almost sell without a seller. As the native proverb has it—"the liquor-seller can sit still in his shop, but the milk-seller must cry his milk from door to door." Now we cannot meet tastes of that sort, but something can be done to meet the objection, which looks upon our publications as dry and insipid. There is no question, but that many of our tracts have erred in that regard. They have been too didactic. If even new Christians are, as the Apostle tells us, unfit to digest strong meat, and require a milk diet, how much more those who are not even converts? Even the stronger digestion of the West, does not **SIXTH DAY** much relish dry dogmatism as food, how much more unpalatable will it be to the Oriental? But much may be done by the use of apt illustrations, well-known quotations from their own classics, witty fables, ingenious parables, allegory and the like, to render our writings attractive to those who would not otherwise care for them. In the proverbs of this and other lands there is a well-stored mine, that might be worked, for purposes of illustration, far more than it has yet been. The training of many of us has led us to be shy of fiction as a handmaid to Truth. But, surely, the literature of the day makes it very plain, that it is simply a question whether this most patent agency for influencing opinion shall be used for Christianity, or only against it. The people of India know little as yet of the fascination of this style of writing, but it will be a lesson easily learned, and not soon unlearned. It is much to be desired that those who have gifts of the imagination should use them in this direction. Why cannot more of our missionary ladies enter where A. L. O. E. and Miss Droese have shewn the way?

A *third* hindrance to the sale of our literature is that few see it. At all events it is not urged upon their notice. We little think how much of our own buying is brought about simply by our attention being called to things. Five minutes before the boxwalla appears, we would declare that we wanted nothing; but he makes a fair living out of people who live within twenty minutes' drive of a much better assortment than he can shew, simply because his things are spread on our verandah, and the shopman's are not. In short, by pressing things on our attention, he first creates the want, which he then proceeds to supply. This principle is the warrant for our colportage system. But unfortunately that system has proved extremely costly and wasteful. Can it not be improved upon? Instead of salary, can we not pay for each Tract sold, so that, as in ordinary avocations, a man's profits will depend on his industry? The objection will at once be raised, that in most parts of the country, a man could not sell enough to make a living, unless you gave him nearly all he received for sales; and if you did that, you would tempt him to burn large quantites of tracts, so as to draw their price. Probably the best scheme would be to employ, not colporteurs but others, who should have some other employment and do

*Not urged on people's attention.*

*Colportage*

this work in odds and ends of time. Catechists, Bible-women, teachers and school-boys might earn a welcome addition to their salaries or support, without interfering with their regular duties. Indeed, there is a plan already followed by some workers, by which anybody, Christian or non-Christian, might be utilized. That plan is, in brief, to allow one-half the price as a reward to the seller. A rupees worth of tracts are furnished to the seller for eight annas. He sells at catalogue price, and pockets eight annas as his commission. How is this loss of 50 per cent. to be met? The Bible Society would probably bear that loss, so far as its own publications are concerned. The Tract and Christian Literature Societies might not care to give so heavy a commission. But even if they only gave one-third, the worker could still by this scheme get Rs. 10 worth of tracts circulated, at an expense to himself of only one rupee eleven annas, and the cost of the freight. Any mission could well afford to give a small yearly grant to press so valuable and inexpensive an agency. One great advantage of such a scheme as this is, that it avoids the multiplication of accounts and labour of oversight, to both of which overtasked missionaries have a great aversion. Another is, that it enlists in our service one of the most powerful of human motives, self-interest, good pay for good work.

A *fourth* hindrance is by some held to be, that many of our publications are too polemic. Some hold that we should urge the simple Gospel, and make no attack on Hinduism or Muhammadanism. Such a rule loses sight of the very patent fact, that the missionary's first, chiefest, hardest duty in this country is to combat that attitude of contented indifference in which the masses live. Most of them have no conception that they have any need which you can supply, or that you have ought to offer them which is superior to that which they already have. Until that supercilious attitude can be overcome, it would seem as if the offer of salvation could have little meaning. Why should a man look to you for salvation, when he is conscious of nothing to be saved from, when in fact, he holds himself to be in a vastly better religious state than you are? By all means, go on making the Gospel offer, for there may be here and there a heart prepared to receive it. But the fact, that when seed is sown on unploughed, unprepared soil, here and there a grain will take root and grow, affords no argument against breaking up the soil with plough and harrow.

<small>Sixth Day.</small>

Of course, everything, in polemic discussion, depends on the loving and faithful spirit in which it is carried on. Bitterness and injustice are fatal here to any hope of good result. But attacks on false religions, if properly made, may even be popular. In fact, for years, among the best selling Hindi tracts have been the well-known "Párikshá" series, in which certain things, which needed to be said, have been said with much plainness of speech. We do not then regard this as an obstacle of any weight. Christianity must be polemic, because it is exclusive.

<small>A kind spirit.</small>

There is a *fifth* hindrance to the increase of our sales which seems to the writer a serious one, and that is lack of variety. How long, for example, would it take an active-minded Hindu to read the whole round of books and tracts yet published in Hindi? How often do men come to us to know what new publications are available, and how disappointed they are when we can tell them of nothing new. Our catalogues may shew lists that seem fairly long, but we must remember that these have been growing slowly through forty years or more, so that to many their contents are very stale. Of the men and women who use Hindi in their work, perhaps not one in ten ever prepares a book or tract for publication, or if they do so at all, prepare but one or two in a lifetime. Probably one reason for this is, that the examining committees of societies are too critical. So many manuscripts are rejected, on one plea and other, that not only the writers are frightened away, but their friends as well. Some of those who have written much could tell harrowing tales of their sufferings through perils of publishing committees. One wonders what chance some of the minor prophets, for example, would have had for reaching the public, if they had been dependent on our modern machinery. In the opinion of the writer so much critical strictness is a great misfortune in several ways. It not only keeps back many who would have done useful work, but it has had this bad effect, that the work we have is the product of few hands, and has been drawn upon one procrustean bed, till there is very little variety in it. Remembering that "many men have many minds," and that time is a wonderful sifter of printed matter, we would like to see our societies

<small>Lack of variety.</small>

Sixth Day.

Lack of funds.

Pictures.

Magic lanterns.

much more free in publishing what is offered and let the fittest survive.

And this brings us to another reason why our shelves shew so little variety, and that is lack of funds with which to print manuscripts. If your committees can only find money to print two or three new tracts a year, it is no wonder that they are very critical and very anxious to get the best worth for their money. Look how many missionaries depend for their tracts on the N. I. Tract Society, and yet if that society can collect subscriptions in any given year equal to the salary of one average missionary, it counts itself fortunate. That is not business. It is child's play. It would take five times the present available amount of funds to put that society on the right footing. I suppose that is measurably true of all the other societies. But if more people were putting their hands to this work, their interest would be enlisted and that of their friends. Now and then a well-intentioned failure would waste a little money but the general result would be increased efficiency.

There is a *sixth* hindrance, which will not be regarded as such by many, and that is the lack of pictures in our books and tracts. Here and there a worker had had an occasional unfortunate experience when using illustrations among Muhammadans, and as a result is shy of pictures altogether. But certainly to discard them is to reject what is always and everywhere an arm of strength. Pictures have two very great advantages. They do not need translation, they are the same in all languages. Again, what speaks to the eye makes a more vivid and lasting impression than that which addresses the ear. Who, in our day, would try to educate children without illustrated school books? Now, the principle here is the same, for the minds of the masses about us, so far as religious truth is concerned, are infantile and need similar methods. Those who use the magic lantern in their village preaching are not likely to entertain such ideas. They find how vastly the picture aids, not only to attract the crowd, but to make plain the message. Of course discretion must be used as to how, when and where to use illustrations, but their use instead of being discouraged should be greatly increased.

Doubtless, there is nothing new in the above suggestions, but they are points which seem to the writer very needful to keep constantly before us, with a view to force our publication work *Sixth Day.* up to a more satisfactory plane. If we are slow and lazy and negligent in sowing wheat, we may be sure that the adversary will be prompt enough in sowing tares. We have our opportunity. Let us improve it.

The meeting being now open for discussion,

The Rev. J. L. PHILLIPS, M.A., M.D., LL.B., S. S. U., Calcutta, said:—I wish to emphasize what has been said about Bible distribution. It is one of the cardinal features of our *Bible distribution.* Protestant churches that the Word of God is honoured and exalted above creeds and confessions. Now we must put *the Book* as well as the man in every part of our broad field. The man can never get on without *the Book.* We must have men wholly devoted to this great work. Madras has a man for its Bible Society, and I hope Calcutta will have one soon. We speak of it as the "benighted Presidency," but I assure you it has more Bibles in it to the square mile than any other part of the Indian Empire. There was never such enlightened curiosity concerning the Bible, never such eagerness for possessing it and perusing it as now in this country, and these facts add to our responsibility. We must take hold of this work ourselves and push it on and not stand by and look on, and let the Bible Society do it. Every missionary should be an active agent of the Bible Society. I was delighted to find so many of Mr. Organe's depôts in South India. Why not have a Bible Depôt in every missionary station? Let us try resolutely for this. My bungalow in Bengal had one, and I enjoyed the work much. Then again we should push the manufacture and sale of general *General* Christian literature in English and in the vernaculars. *literature.*

The missionary himself should be the colporteur *par excellence*, and dignify his office by faithful effort and so set an example to his native helpers. There are earnest men in all parts of India who always carry books with them. Our present Sunday School Secretary for Bengal accompanied me on a tour into Orissa as far as the shrine of Jagannath at Puri, and I found him selling Christian books all along our route. I liked what my good brother Dr. Weitbrecht said about training men for this work of selling our Christian literature. Well, one of the best way I know of for training helpers is by your own example. *Personal* Say to them: "Come on," and lead the way, and shew them how *example.* the work is done. Missionary example is wonderfully infectious sometimes. My book-boxes on tour were my best pulpit among Hindus and others. I can't forget how glad I used to be, when a *mufassal* missionary, seeing the boys following my cart begging for books, and sometimes crying, because the last book was gone, or they had no pice for buying one. It was the first

Napoleon who said, I think, that the Press was "the fifth great monarchy in Europe." It is far more to-day than then, and what it is to be under God, for the weal of men, depends not a little on what we missionaries do with it in these pagan lands, where the Gospel has liberated the intellect, and men are crying out for literature. The bad, the very worst, from the purlieus of Fleet Street and Paris, is coming into India like a flood of filth, and our young folk are buying it. Let us adopt the motto of the British Sunday School Union, and "*overcome evil with good.*" Let us multiply book-stalls on the streets. A countrywoman of mine, and a near neighbour in Calcutta, has lately opened a beautiful book-shop beside her front gate on the great highway. Let us "sow beside all waters." Our holy religion has created this growing appetite; now let us do all we can to satisfy it. In the near future as our work advances millions more of young readers will be eager for books. Let us insist upon purity and supply them abundantly. In short, *let us push things now.*

The Rev. J. CHAMBERLAIN, D. D., A. A. M., Madanapalle, Madras, said:—I come from a mission that believes that it is our bounden duty to do our share in providing a Christian literature in the languages of those we have rescued from heathenism. You have mentioned, Sir, that my mission had set me apart for such work. After thirty years of evangelistic work among the people coupled with medical work, and during twenty of those years giving a good deal of time to the translation of the Bible from the Hebrew into Telugu and its revision, our mission, three years ago, directed me to give my chief time and effort for the years to come to the preparation of a Christian literature in the language of the eighteen millions of Telugu people. One of my colleagues, the next senior to myself in the mission, has gone home on sick leave, and our mission has sent a unanimous resolution to our Board at Home, asking them to send him back devoted to the preparation of a Christian literature in Tamil as I am in Telugu, for we use both languages in our mission. It has been well said in the excellent papers, and by some of the speakers that what the growing Christian church of India imperceptibly needs now is not translations, however excellent, of Occidental works, but works on the same lines it may be, but brought out in an Oriental way, adapted to the genius and mode of thought of the people. The people of the East are so differently constituted and the traditions behind them are so different that often the literal translation of an English work will fall flat upon them or fail utterly to be comprehended. Let me illustrate:— Thirty-two years ago I was seeking to find some useable hymns, suited to English metres, for the use of our little Telugu congregation. An older missionary sent me a small book of hymns so prepared, with the caution, however, that the hymns were so literally translated as scarcely to be intelligible to the Telugu people. It was the work of a pious civilian, with perhaps more piety than facility of expression in Telugu. To test the matter of the intelligibility of these hymns I placed the Telugu translation of that beautiful hymns "Rock of Ages cleft for me" in the hands of my Telugu and Sanskrit Pandit and asked him to take it home with him and the next day give me in simple prose (Telugu) the meaning of the hymn. The next morning he came looking puzzled and ill at ease, saying that he had not been able to make a satisfactory rendering. On being pressed to give me what he understood it to mean, he said: "Well, Sir, I have noticed that every religion has its mysteries, and uses words in mystic senses. Not having been initiated into the Christian religion I do not know the mystic meanings of certain words. So you must pardon me, for all I can make of it is this: 'O very old stone, split in two on my behalf. Let me get under one corner of you'"! —No, let us have no literal nor slavish translations of even the best of works. If we are to give to the native church the treasures of our English hymnology, one should take a hymn and become thoroughly imbued with its sentiment, and then, casting the words and lines and verses of the English to the winds, bring out in pure Telugu or other vernacular the chief ideas of the hymn dressed in Oriental idiom and phraseology, and so of any work. We may translate ideas, but not sentences. And on many subjects works need to be prepared afresh from an Oriental standpoint for Oriental readers. To illustrate:— I am by direction of our mission, engaged in bringing out a large, thoroughly illustrated Bible Dictionary for the Telugu people. It is not to be a translation. For twenty years I have been preparing for the work. For that purpose I spent four months in Bible Lands, from Goshen by way of Mount Sinai and the Wilderness of the Wandering, all up through the Holy Land, and on to Antioch, Tarsus, Patmos, Smyrna, and Ephesus, seeking to become thoroughly imbued with the country, its history and its spirit. And now taking Smith's Bible Dictionary and Kitto and Rand and Schaff and *The Land and the Book*, and all other available books I read upon each subject, compare my own impressions and the following day dictate in the Telugu to my amanuensis what I think a Telugu man would want to know of the subject in hand. The Bible was an Oriental Book. What needs the most explanation to Occidental Christians often requires the least for Orientals; and, on the other hand, what centuries of Christian training and culture has made clear as day to Occidentals of the present century may require much elucidation for those just emerging from Hindu superstitions. It will take me years to complete the task, but I believe

*Sidenotes:* Sixth Day. "Rock of Ages" translated. Slavish translation useless. A Telugu Bible Dictionary.

**Sixth Day.** that such a work should be prepared for each of the people of India. The first volume I may perhaps be able to issue in a year. I have already in my house a new set of electrotype illustrations, costing Rs. 3,336, and the entire cost of the work, before it is completed, including my salary for the proportion of time I spend upon it, will be not less than Rs. 15,000. Thus our mission is trying to fulfil its duty to the growing native church, and I mention it as an incentive to other missions to do the same, or better, to surpass us. Let us all vow that the church of India shall have a Christian library of new vigorous Oriental works that shall help them to grow "unto the measure of the stature of the fullness of Christ."

The Rev. J. A. MACDONALD, C. L. S., Calcutta, said:—I would appeal to the members of this Conference to assist the Christian Literature Society in its efforts to provide school-**School books.** books suitable for missionary use. It is well known that in some of the vernaculars, after a century of missionary work, we have not yet obtained the kind of text-books which we desire. Many earnest workers have long groaned under the compulsion put upon them to use readers which are pervaded by heathenish sentiment, or, to say the least, are absolutely colourless in regard to religious influence. Our society is now preparing in Edinburgh a new series of English readers which will, in all respects, be brought up to the needs of time. And we are also preparing new readers in Bengali, Panjabi, and other languages of India. We beg of you to see that these books are, wherever possible, introduced into mission schools. Our society, which, under Dr. Murdoch's lead, had done so much in the past, is now aiming to extend its influence, but this can only be accomplished by the co-operation of missionaries themselves. Even when good school-books exist, we are met by obstacles to their introduction. In some parts of the country Government Inspectors, contrary to the provisions of the Government itself, use illegitimate influence to force upon the schools books in which they have a personal interest. To so great an extent is this carried that post-cards have actually been sent to the head masters of mission schools which insinuate that there is a risk in using the Grammar from Madras issued by Dr. Murdoch; and that the risk is a real one, all who are acquainted with the way in which the Inspectors may shape the examinations will easily understand. We desire emphatically to state that there is no real objection which can be urged against our books. But the Hindus and Muhammadans are in many instances actively opposing Christian books, and it is therefore necessary for missionaries to secure proper representation on the Text-Book Committees, and to unite in obtaining liberty everywhere to use the books which they judge most suitable, always supposing that these books satisfy the prescribed Government standards. We are also very anxious to get our works in general literature circulated amongst the people. During the last year we published over a quarter of million copies in Bengali alone, but the difficulty is to distribute the books; for there can be no doubt that the present method of colportage is very unsatisfactory. The discussion of this morning shews that we are all being led in one direction, and that is to make every mission agent a distributor of evangelical literature. Let the missionaries and their helpers distribute and sell our literature in their own districts, and in the process the men who develop a talent for the work may be employed in out of the way places as colporteurs. Too great importance cannot be attached to the distribution of Bibles and Christian books. A few weeks ago I had the happiness of baptising seven men; and I found that in nearly every case they had been led to confess Christ by the reading of the Bible, which they had obtained years ago from missionaries in various parts of the country.

*Sixth Day.*

*General literature.*

The Rev. G. H. ROUSE, M.A., LL.B., B. M. S., Calcutta, said:—This subject is of very great interest to me. I should like first of all to emphasize what has been said on the matter of translation. I have brought out some books of translations, and yet I do not think I have ever really translated one. I usually find that I have to make a different thing of it. The principle that I aim at always is to get the ideas into my mind, and then bring them out in such a way as the people will really understand. I think we should urge this upon our native translators also. I have seen cases where I could not tell what the Bengali meant until I looked at the English. There is another important matter, especially in regard to native helpers, and that is to insist upon a simple style. I think the tendency to use high language is being somewhat corrected by the newspapers. The newspapers have got something to say, and they naturally express it in a simple way. Let us insist upon it that translators and writers must use simple language—good language, but simple. Another thing that is very important, is the preparation of literature for women and girls. In this our lady friends can help us very much. If any line of thought takes well with the women, put it down and give it to the Tract Society. In Bengal and in some other parts of India we have some very short simple tracts for women. Another important point is the selling of books. I long to see the time when more Christian books will be sold by the native book-sellers. There is no prejudice against it as long as they can make money by it. What we have to aim at is to produce books at such a rate that we can actually sell them at cost and then get the native book-sellers to sell them at a profit. When we once reach this point there will be no limit to the number that we may produce and sell.

*Principles of translation.*

*Simple style.*

*Books for females.*

**Sixth Day.**

*Efficient colporteurs in the south.*

*Harder to sell than to prepare.*

The Rev. J. E. PADFIELD, D.D., C. M. S., Masulipatam, said:—I wish to speak on two or three points of practical importance in connection with the subject of Christian literature in the vernacular; but before doing so I feel it would be wrong not to refer to a remark made by a former speaker. It has been asserted by a gentleman, connected, I believe, with the Bible Society, that missionaries do not adequately assist the Bible Society in the matter of providing proper men as colporteurs. It was said and repeated, as a humourous remark, that the colporteurs he had had to deal with were the most miserable body of men to look at that he had ever seen—"the lame, halt, the blind," &c., &c. Now, whatever may be the state of things in the north, I would most distinctly say that it would be a libel to apply such a statement to the south, as far at least as my experience goes. We give good men for this work as we are as fully alive to its importance as the Bible Society itself, and we are not so shortsighted as to place useless men to carry on such an important branch of missionary effort. In speaking of Christian literature in the vernacular, I do not refer to mere tracts or small books of a like nature, but books of a literary character to instruct and build up the native church. Though no time has been specially given me for the task, I have, for a long number of years, done my very utmost to help to create such a literature as I allude to. I mean such works as commentaries on the Bible, books of Christian Evidences and on Church History and the like; but I confess that I have found it a much harder task to sell such books when prepared than the work of production itself, hard work as that may be. The fact is, I have not found that missionaries are sufficiently alive to the importance of this matter and they do not seem to make the special efforts one would expect towards diffusing good sound literature, even when it is prepared to their hand. I am bound to say that there are many exceptions to this rule, and I think I may also say the number of such exceptions is increasing; still the fact remains the same, that it is a difficulty to effect adequate sales, and thus there is sometimes a failure to persuade our great publishing societies to bring out works when prepared. We must remember that such books are sold at the lowest possible price, often at less than actual cost for printing and paper; hence if sales are slow or small the producer and publishers are discouraged. Some of my brother missionaries have said to me that there is no demand amongst their people or agents for such things. Very likely so, I reply, but we have to create a taste for such things if we do not want to see in the future an ignorant, unstable native church. We cannot afford to neglect this most important matter, or the church will have to suffer for it. I would venture to suggest the more general adoption of selling books and taking the payment in instalments—spreading it over a longer or shorter period according to the means of the purchaser. I have adopted this system myself, and have so sold many hundreds of copies of works, very many of a rupee and upwards each, and I have never lost money by it. Many of our people would like to buy a book but they may not be able to pay the money out in a lump sum. I have referred more fully to this matter in an article in the *Harvest Field* to which I would refer any one who may be interested in the subject. *(The Harvest Field, July 1891.)* Another point to which I would direct attention, and also one I particularized in the article alluded to, is the need of some periodical catalogue of Christian vernacular books already in existence. There may be books in existence which are not generally known and thus their distribution is restricted. As a matter of fact I know this to be the case. There is also the danger of toil and energy being wasted in producing books, similar ones to which may be already available. Some periodical catalogue of such books might be issued by a society or joint societies—say one for North India and one for the South—and this paper might be made attractive and useful by articles and contributions bearing on the subject of Vernacular Christian literature and Christian literature generally.

*Sixth Day.*

*Payment by instalments.*

*Catalogues needed.*

The Rev. M. Mody, Independent Worker, Bombay, said:—I do not think it always advisable to *sell* Bibles, as I know personally that there are many thousands who cannot buy at any price. You are aware of Mrs. Robertson's Society for the free distribution of the Scriptures, and nobody can deny the excellent work it has done for many years. Then, again, how much has been done by the free distribution of New Testaments in Hebrew among the Jews through the Rev. Mr. Wilkinson, of Mildmay, who was presented with thousands of pounds to distribute them freely. I am very much interested in both the Bible and Tract Societies, as through the reading of small tracts, I was led to embrace Christianity eventually. I think as our Tract Society is a Protestant and Evangelical Society, all the printed matters sold by it should be on the same principle. No one work bearing on or advocating High Church or Ritualistic views should have any place on its shelves. Romanizing books, like Hymns Ancient and Modern," ought not to be sold by our Tract Society. Besides, the members of the committee should be pronounced evangelical and Protestant. Those of them who cannot consciously sympathise with it on such grounds entirely ought never to be members of its committee under any circumstances. The Ritualists, &c., have their depôts in Bombay, and they can do as they like there, but, pray, let us have our society carried on entirely on the Protestant and evangelical principle. One word more and I have done. There is a great need of a daily Christian

*Free distribution.*

paper. We ought to have one of our own. Is it possible to have one? I know money for it is a great consideration, but God can supply the need if any one would undertake this work.

The Rev. T. J. SCOTT, D.D., M. E. C., Bareilly, N. W. P., said:—Some variation is now needed in the form of controversial literature. The ground in old forms of discussion against idolatry, caste, pantheism, &c., has been well covered. In the reforms of the country, such as Aryanism or in the atheistical tendency of the educated, we find a class of opponents needing a different kind of treatment. The style of some missionary controversial tracts is to be regretted. I have access to many native papers, and when I have come across something in them very harsh and bitter against a Christian tract, I have turned to it and found in it a style that had provoked the bitterness. Indians are the most courteous people in the world, and if treated courteously in discussion they will not revile. We should be guarded in the manner of our writing. We are much in need of Sunday School literature. The Methodist Publishing House at Lucknow is seeking to meet this want. This Press is seeking to build up a large endowment, so that it can turn out at available rates all that is needed in some of the Indian languages. It is hoped that sometimes this Press may be able to employ photo-lithographers and photo-engravers for making pictures especially suited to Indian Sunday Schools. Too much cannot be said of the importance of Bible distribution. Missionaries should give personal attention to this matter and not leave it too much in the hands of colporteurs. They should make Bible distribution in some way a part of their own mission work. The entrance of God's Word giveth life. We cannot estimate the impression the Bible has already made on awakening India. The observer can find it infused into the thought and woven into the modern literature of the country in a wonderful way. Surprising instances can be given of how many read the Bible. Many oppose the Bible, and it has been torn to shreds and scattered in the streets, and yet in the same town it has turned out that many read the Bible quietly in their homes and are more influenced by it than by their own religious books. This fact was testified too by a non-Christian friend who warmly averred that the Bible was the guide of his daily life, and that he had many friends who could say the same thing. Let us put the Bible into the schools and homes and hearts of the people in every possible way.

The Rev. H. J. BRUCE, B.A., A. B. F. M., Satara, said:—I wish to say a great many things in these five minutes; and in the first place I wish to say that I approve of what has been said in regard to the sale of books and tracts of any considerable size. It has been our rule not to give away any book that has a price put upon it, except in very special cases. But I wish to bring before this Conference an urgent plea for the greatly enlarged circulation of small two and four-page gratuitous tracts and leaflets. It has seemed to me that there is a great army of readers in all our cities and large towns, whom we do not reach by our ordinary methods. The Government schools are turning out such readers by the ten thousand. You know that they will not come to our street-preaching. You know that they will very seldom *buy* our Christian books. How then are we going to reach them with the Gospel message? It occurred to me that these little printed messengers might be sent in among those thousands, and for many years I have been engaged, as other work would permit, in preparing and sending forth these little two-page leaflets. It has been our aim to put into each one enough of the Gospel, so that a man may be saved by it, if he only will, through the aid of the Holy Ghost. In my experience these leaflets are gladly received, and we know that many, who would not come to our street-preaching, have received them, and read them, and that they carefully keep them among their treasures. We have known of some who have pasted them up upon the walls of their houses where they may be read many times, and where visitors may read them as well. And who can estimate the influence of these silent messengers when they are read by a man in the quiet of his own home, where there is no one to point the finger of scorn at him? In the city of Satara I have often employed a man to go from house to house distributing these leaflets to every reader, and it has resulted in a greatly increased knowledge of the life of our Lord Jesus Christ. What would you think of a general who should encamp his army before a city and content himself with capturing the few stragglers who came within his lines? Would he not rather pour the hot shot into the citadel itself and thus soon reduce it to subjection? And, in like manner, shall we not send these messengers of God's love to the thousands whom we are not reaching by our ordinary methods, that they, too, may become acquainted with the invitations of the Gospel? We are sending these leaflets abroad, by the thousand, to all parts of the Marathi country, and there are many to testify that they are doing good. All my native agents at Satara and at the out-stations are supplied with them for distribution to readers only. And at our place, where the Railway station is near by, our agents are instructed to visit the trains daily and distribute them to the passengers. These passengers are sitting in the train with nothing to do, from one to six or even twelve hours, and how gladly they take the tracts and read them. And I have myself heard, perhaps the only reader in a compartment, reading his tract aloud to the other passengers. We do not know where these leaflets go, but we do know that the truth is

| | |
|---|---|
| Sixth Day. | being widely scattered, and many people are becoming acquainted with the Gospel. |
| A Tract Society in Travancore. | The Rev. J. DUTHIE, L.M.S., Nagercoil, Travancore, said:— In the Travancore Mission of the L. M. S. there has been a Tract Society in full operation for more than forty years, during which time it has published upwards of five million pages. The Religious Tract Society of London has been most kind in giving grants of paper, and has also sent £20 annually for a good number of years. The remarkable thing about the society, however, is that it has been to a very large extent supported by the contributions of our Native Christians themselves. The Press at Nagercoil is doing a great work in the vernacular. As many as six Magazines are issued every month, a monthly hand-bill for free distribution, and two Quarterlies. Every effort is being made in the Travancore Mission to spread the blessings of education amongst the Native Christians. I would like to mention a fact of much interest. A lady in England, who, for many years, has taken a warm interest in the mission, sent £20 last year to Mrs. Duthie for Bibles. The plan that has been adopted is to sell the Scriptures to poor Christians only, at *half* price, and by that £20 about *one thousand* copies of the Bible and Bible Portions have been circulated amongst the congregations. |
| Colporteurs necessary. | The Rev. W. J. RICHARDS, C. M. S., Alleppy, Travancore, said:—We must not do away with the colporteurs, for they are preachers of the Gospel as well as book-hawkers. In Travancore and Cochin States they are welcomed as the men of the Bible by nearly half a million of Bible-reading Christians, who |
| The Syrian Church. | are lost to your statistics. At least 400,000 of the Syrian Christians of St. Thomas' are Protestants, in that they reject the supremacy of the Pope of Rome and read the Scriptures in the vernacular *with the approval of their Bishops* (or Metrans) *and clergy.* It is a great error in our missionary statistics allowing these to be included among enemies of the Bible, and I commend the correction to the industrious compiler of the missionary census. The above correction applies to the Jacobite or so-called *Unreformed* Syrians, as well as to the "Reformers." It is a good suggestion to sell Scriptures through the boys in our high schools. By means of Christian lads in this way I sold in one year, and received the money for, seventy rupees worth of |
| Bible sales. | vernacular Scriptures disposed of in the holidays. It requires trouble, perhaps, but is worth doing. Let me hand on to the missionaries in this Conference the wisdom I have had from others. Have a book-shop, *away from the mission-house if your quarters are not close to the high castes and bazaars.* No matter how small it is at first. Do not wait for a *site* or a nice house, but make a beginning and you will find it grow into a thing to thank God for. Last year I sold in our book-shop |

ninety rupees worth of Scriptures. You know how much that means, and of this sixty rupees worth was bought by Roman Catholics who are 'moving' in our parts. <small>SIXTH DAY.</small>

The Rev. H. HAIGH, W. M. S., Mysore City, writer of one of the papers, said in reply:—Mr. Bruce has been pleading for the free and extensive distribution of handbills. I practised that for a long time, but I found it was almost fatal to the sale of tracts and Scripture portions. During the last two years I have adopted a different method. Carrying with me both books and handbills, I hold up the former and say: "These books are thoroughly good and they are very cheap. Still, cheap as they are, I will give a present of a handbill to every one who buys a book." The bait almost always takes. I have sold large numbers of tracts in that way, which I could not have disposed of, if handbills had been available for entirely free distribution. There is one department of literature that has received but little attention this morning, and I should like to ask the Conference to consider it: it is the missionary newspaper. For some years past I have had charge of a Kanarese paper, called the *Vrittanta Patrike*. Every Thursday morning we send forth from our little press an issue varying from 1,500 to 2,000. It is a *bonâ fide* newspaper that we publish and every copy is sold. We discuss all the leading topics of the day in as frank and fresh a way as we know how and always from the distinctively Christian standpoint. People quite understand that now, and buy their paper, knowing what they will find. In every issue we try to carry to the people an urgent call to religious concern, and that part of the paper is as much appreciated as any. We do not mince matters; while speaking always with the greatest possible kindness and respect, we speak always with unhesitating candour. Now this paper is doing for us much pioneer work. We have only a limited number of evangelists, and they by no means cover the area within which we are working. But the newspaper goes to scores of villages which the preacher cannot at present visit, and is doing its work in a way that makes us devoutly thankful. Some time ago I went to a village where no missionary had ever been before. After some inquiry I found the head man of the place and sat down to have a chat with him. He was a fine old man, not educated, but otherwise well fitted to be a leader among his fellows. I asked him if any one in the village could read. "Only one man," was his reply; "I have engaged a Brahman to teach the boys of the village." This led me to remark on the advantages of education, if, for nothing else, yet at least for making them acquainted with all that goes on in the world. "Oh, we get to know that. On market days we hear a good deal from different people, and besides that there is another way." "What is that?" I inquired. "Why, sir, 

<small>How to sell.</small>

<small>Newspapers.</small>

<small>An illustration.</small>

736 CHRISTIAN LITERATURE.

**Sixth Day.**

every Friday evening, about this time, a newspaper comes to our village. It is called the *Vrittanta Patrike*, and I have myself paid the subscription for it." "But what good is such a paper to you?" I asked. "Why," said he, "when it comes I take it to the schoolmaster and a boy goes round to tell the neighbours. After a while they all come together and sit down under that great tree, as many as thirty or forty." "Then," said I, "do you have it all read through that night?" "No," he answered; "there is a great deal in the paper, and besides we have great talks about everything it tells us. We generally meet five or six times before finishing one paper, and then we are ready for the next!" The man had no idea who I was, and I encouraged him to talk freely. "What sort of things are there in this *Vrittanta Patrike*?" I inquired. "All sorts of things, sir. There is an almanac every week, and we always see what are the market prices in Mysore and Bangalore. Then it explains all that the Sirkar is doing, and sometimes tells the Sirkar that it is making mistakes." "Is that all?" I gently persisted. "No, it says a great many things about our customs. It is always telling us that idolatry is false and we have great talks about that; and every week there is something about a Great Guru, called Jesus Christ. The paper says that He is everybody's Guru. We have read a great deal about Him. He did a lot of wonderful things and He was very kind to those who were in trouble." Then growing confident, he continued: "Do you know anything about this Jesus Swami, sir?" The way was opened for my message, and I was able to deliver it to people who had been well prepared for it by previous reading and discussions. This is just one illustration of the work that may be done by a Christian vernacular newspaper. If properly conducted, it will find its way into scores of homes where a tract would never find entrance. And people are always willing to pay for a good newspaper.

**Forty years work.**

J. Murdoch, Esq., LL.D., C. L. S., Madras, said:—For more than forty years the compilation and circulation of Christian literature has been my main work. Long before the next Decennial Conference is held, the pen must drop from my hand. I would most earnestly appeal to my brethren to take up the work which I must so soon relinquish. During all these years help has been obtained only from a few. While some have had good reasons for declining, there is great truth in the proverb, "Where there's a will there's a way." A change of occupation relieves the mind as well as entire rest. During the rains and the hottest part of the year when out-door work is impossible, something might be done in the way proposed. The remark about myself applies to my beloved fellow-labourer,

**A. L. O. E.**

A. L. O. E. The most remarkable feature of modern missions is the rapid extension of women's work for women. It is lamentable, however, how little has been done by missionaries' wives and zenana ladies, with a few noble exceptions, to provide Christian literature for their Indian sisters. The Madras Tract Society has about 540 Tamil publications on its catalogue, but I think only four of them are by ladies. More has been done in some other provinces. In Western India Mrs. Bissell and Mrs. Edward Hume have done good service, still much more should be done everywhere. I would especially suggest a series of letters to Indian women, treating of their home life, social reform, the doctrines and duties of Christianity. Only ladies have the means of entering into the thoughts and feelings of the women, so as best to know how to present Christian truth and how to reach their hearts. Some may say, "we have no talent for writing;" such may do excellent service by promoting the circulation of Christian literature. It is disheartening to find, after tracts and books have been prepared, that they lie as lumber on the shelves. While some missionaries are zealous in this work, many take little interest in it. An American missionary, in South India, circulated annually about 20,000 Scriptures, books and tracts. He went on furlough, but under his successor the issues dwindled to a trifle. Christian literature is both useful in itself and auxiliary to every other department of missionary labour. In view of the growing number of readers, it should receive more attention. It is so far encouraging that there has been progress. I am not acquainted with the number of publications issued by missions during the last two decades; but those of the Indian Tract Societies have increased from 13 millions to 30 millions—an increase of 130 per cent. Let one hundred millions be the minimum number reported at the next Decennial Conference, and may many of you be spared to take part in it, while some may look down from above.

*Letters to women.*

*Increase of publications.*

The Rev. S. W. ORGANE, Secretary, Auxiliary Bible Society, Madras, writer of one of the papers, said in reply:—I am glad of the opportunity of saying a few words at the close of the Conference as a resolution of the British and Foreign Bible Society in regard to the dissemination of the Scriptures in this empire will be submitted for your acceptance this afternoon. I may remark that the suggestions on this subject in my paper are based on a long and pretty wide experience. Although we are far from having reached the ideal I can speak with some degree of pride and with much thankfulness of the success of Bible work in South India, where we have attained a circulation of a third of that in the whole country. I also rejoice in the fact that in 1891 our free contributions reached a total of Rs. 12,500, the greater part of which came from the poorer classes, and in which native Christian gifts have a prominent place. With the exception of the Nizam's dominions, in

*B. F. B. S. work in South India.*

**Sixth Day.**

**Sixty depôts.**

large portions of which you may travel without seeing a Bible, and the Ganjam district, our Presidency is now fairly covered with agencies. We have over sixty branch depôts, and from other smaller centres the Scriptures are spread over the surrounding country. The sales at railway stations, freely allowed by the agents of the companies, are considerable. I acknowledge that the agitation of Mr. Prautch has done good, and welcome him into our ranks. But long before this agitation began, as supplementary to the regular system of colportage, we were working on similar lines to his and with even greater economy. To judge of the results of his work his salary and travelling expenses should, in all fairness, be included.

**Financial position.**

I wish particularly to speak regarding the society's financial position. We are approaching an annual circulation in this country of 600,000 copies of the Scriptures, and looking at the rapid extension of mission operations, we may fairly contemplate the time when the circulation will reach a million copies a year. The present annual expenditure on colportage alone exceeds Rs. 50,000. I estimate that in the near future the expenditure on translation and revision will be considerably enhanced. Now it seems to me that if the society, besides meeting the heavy cost of translation and revision, is to print the Scriptures in ever increasing numbers and to continue to sell them so much below the cost, it is impossible that its limited resources can bear the additional cost of dissemination. The responsibility and practical direction of that part of our great work ought, I think, for the most part to devolve on the missionary societies, and if they give us the relief we seek the result will, I believe, be eminently satisfactory. If in general terms you approve—as I trust you will—of the proposal in the society's resolution, a scheme for practical working might be drawn up in the course of the year. And, further, as the Bible Society is far from being the wealthy corporation it is popularly said to be, I also bespeak your generous help in the way of effort to enhance its income.

**Increased circulations.**

The Rev. G. P. Taylor, M.A., B.D., I. P. M., Ahmedabad, writer of one of the papers, said in reply:—It would be well that this Conference should bear in mind that Christian tracts now find a circulation over increasingly large areas. During the last decade, while twelve per cent. represents the growth of the population of India, the number of readers has increased by fully thirty-six per cent. It thus becomes highly desirable that tracts and books containing Christian teaching should be supplied in numbers commensurate with the wide extension of the reading area. It was with much pleasure that I heard Dr. Phillips emphasize the point that wherever the man went the book must go. One practical reason why the book may well accompany the man is that owing to the generous action of the Religious Tract Society of London the production of Christian books in this country can be effected at a very small cost. By the free grant of all the paper for books brought out in accordance with its regulations that munificent society has placed Indian missions under a deep obligation, an obligation which to-day we gratefully acknowledge. A second very obvious reason why our preaching should be followed up by the written Word lies in the fact that while preaching an unguarded utterance may at times escape our lips or some word be spoken we would fain take back. When surrounded by a crowd of hearers the missionary occasionally finds himself the victim of a pusillade of questions, sorely testing both patience and temper. At such a time a single angry flash of the eye or contemptuous curl of the lip may undo much of the good he had hoped to effect. The printed tract, on the other hand, as the product of calm and careful reasoning, expressed in words deliberately chosen, may well be expected to present the truth in a more accurate and more winsome manner than is possible under the strain of heated discussion. Prior to the preparation of the papers presented to-day it was found impossible for the writers to meet and agree upon any mutually concerted method of treatment. As a consequence the subject assigned us has been viewed from four entirely independent standpoints, and under these circumstances it is a significant fact that no less than three of the four writers have emphatically indicated the urgent need that in each language-area men duly qualified should be relieved so far as possible from other work in order to their being expressly set apart for the production of Christian literature. On this point, I am convinced, there exists amongst us all a complete consensus of opinion. Of the speakers this morning Dr. Weitbrecht has referred very prominently to this need, while Dr. Chamberlain has informed us that what should be done *has been done* in the Arcot Mission, where one of the missionaries has already been designated for literary work. The need, however, is distinctly accentuated after the touching statement made on this platform by our revered and beloved father, Dr. Murdoch. For very many years he has devoted himself unsparingly to creating and fostering a Christian literature for India, but to-day we have heard from his lips, and heard with sorrow, that the pen must soon drop from his hand. It thus becomes at the present time an especial duty of the churches to see to it that the work so well begun should continue in the future, and that other workmen should rise to fill the posts of the honoured veterans who perforce must leave the field. Another, and strong, motive for the effective distribution of Christian literature is supplied in the present transition stage of India. A process of fusion is going on everywhere around us, and powerful solvents are acting on Hindu habits of thought and

*Sixth Day.*
Obligation to the R. T. S.

Set apart men for literary work.

Transition stage.

SIXTH DAY. life. This process we are utterly unable to prevent, even should we wish to do so. For my own part I would not have it otherwise. I believe in a God Who reigneth, and my heart-conviction is that all this national seething ferment is the working of the Spirit of the living God. Solution of the old fixed beliefs will certainly be followed, sooner or later, by re-crystallization, and the imperative duty that devolves on us as God's servants is to determine the form the near crystals shall assume. Master-founders tell us that in the casting of the huge bells for our ancient cathedrals a silver chalice would be melted down and poured on the mass of liquid brass, so might they hope the resulting tone would be rich and clear and full. Western civilization and Western culture are already fusing the grosser forms of Hinduism, but it is ours as missionaries of the Cross to pour in the pure silver, ay the gold, of Christian education and Christian literature, that at the last notes sweet and clear ring forth. Only so shall Young India, the India that is soon to be, issue from the crucible, beautiful with the beauty of Christ.

# XVII.—CLOSING MEETING AND BUSINESS ARRANGEMENTS.

## AFTERNOON SESSION.

### LARGE HALL, 3-30 to 5 P. M.

Bishop THOBURN, D. D., M. E. C., Calcutta, *in the chair.*

After singing a hymn, the Rev. J. Duthie read Psalm lxxii., and the Rev. Dr. Weitbrecht offered prayer.

SIXTH DAY.

This closing Meeting was occupied almost entirely in the discussion of various business details. Had there been sufficient time, it was intended to ask two or three of the oldest missionaries present to give a brief address. This was not possible. The few remarks made by the Chairman and the resolutions passed are given below:—

Bishop Thoburn said :—

In taking the chair this afternoon, I may be expected to make a few remarks upon the proceedings of the past eventful week, but the programme placed in my hand reminds me that I have very little time at my disposal. I must, however, congratulate you, and at the same time acknowledge God's gracious help, on the success which thus far has attended our Conference. In the first place, we have reason to be thankful that so many missionaries have been brought together from all parts of this great empire. In point of numbers the Conference has been more than a success. Those of us who were present in Allahabad in 1872 remember how thankful we all were for the attendance on that occasion. In 1882, we were not only still more thankful, but indeed quite amazed, to find more than four times as many present as had met at Allahabad; but here in Bombay we are almost, if not quite, stronger by two hundred delegates than we were in Calcutta ten years ago. In fact, our success in point of numbers has been a serious embarrassment to us on the present occasion.

A successful Conference.

From the numbers present.

**Sixth Day.**

**From mutual instruction.**

It is too soon to estimate the amount of good which has been accomplished during the past week in connection with this Conference. Indeed, the good accomplished by such convocations of Christian workers is seldom of a tangible kind, and can never be tabulated in those forms which, in these days of endless statistics, are so imperatively demanded. Many, if not indeed all, of us have learned new lessons of various kinds. We have gathered most profitable instruction from the experience of brethren and sisters engaged in similar work, but under somewhat dissimilar circumstances; and every missionary who has been here will return home wiser and better equipped for future service. We have undoubtedly received a new inspiration for the great work which is before us, as missionaries united in a common cause and engaged in a common task. God has so created us that we lean upon one another as if by a common instinct. The lonely worker may be a noble and valiant man, but unless he is one of those rare characters like Elijah of old, it will be impossible for him to put forth his best strength while toiling all alone in his remote field. It is very different, however, when such workers come together. They strengthen one another, and it is God's plan that they should thus strengthen one another. We should never despise or neglect meetings of this kind. We should employ every means and method which God blesses for our mutual edification and help; and beyond all doubt this is one of them.

**From increased brotherly love.**

One good result which undoubtedly will follow the meetings of this Conference will be the increase of brotherly love, which is invaluable to us when engaged in work of this kind. It is very true that not much has been said upon this subject, and no effort has been made with the specific object in view of increasing our Christian affection for one another. I do not mention this as an omission, for I should have been sorry to see such a specific object put forward in connection with the Conference. It is better to take it for granted, not only on this question but on similar questions, that as a matter of course all Christians, everywhere and on all suitable occasions, nourish and cherish that Christian love for one another which is a primary condition of Christian life and growth. I remember how marked this development of Christian love became, both at Allahabad and at Calcutta, as the sessions of those Conferences advanced from day to day, and I am sure that on the present occasion this growth has been no less marked. Many of you never before saw any considerable number of missionaries together, and never heard an experience brought from a mission that differed from your own. As we have looked one another in the face, and listened to one another's discourses, as we have joined in singing and prayer, and as we have mingled in social intercourse, we have been unconsciously drawing nearer and nearer together, and thereby making it possible for God to work more wondrously among us and through us on others. It is an essential condition of success in Christian work that the workers be not only of one mind, but still more of one heart; and in my humble opinion the greatest work that has been wrought in Bombay during these seven days has been that of uniting more perfectly and practically the hearts of all these Christian workers. India will be the better for it during the next decade. If we have not been perfectly agreed upon all the topics brought forward, we must all gratefully admit that there has been very much less disagreement than was at first anticipated. At least three of the questions submitted for discussion had been regarded as burning questions, each of which would probably give rise to a heated and possibly bitter discussion, but on each occasion we were most happily disappointed in this respect. That all have not been satisfied should not be a cause of any wonder, but we may well wonder that the dissatisfaction has not been greater. On some questions many of us differ widely and perhaps positively, but we should feel grateful to God that we are able to differ in love. I am sure, too, I may add that we differ much less than we did when we met.

And now, my dear brethren and sisters (and I am glad to be able to add the word 'sisters,' for it seems to me that at least half of the assembly before me is composed of Christian ladies engaged in missionary work), I need not add anything further. We part this afternoon to return to our homes and to our fields of labour for another ten years of toil. We shall not all meet again in 1902, but I trust many of us will still be found in India at the end of the next decade. Let us expect God to do great things for us: let us accept His gracious promises and go forth in perfect confidence that He will be with us, and cause

*Sixth Day.*

*India will be the better for it.*

*Our love greater than our differences.*

*Our trust is in God.*

**Sixth Day.** His work to prosper in our hands. Beyond all possible doubt, God has great things in store for us in this empire of India. Let us prove faithful to our opportunities and to our responsibilities, and if we do not meet again in 1902 in some city of India, we shall all rejoice, some on earth and the rest in heaven, over the great prosperity which God will vouchsafe to the toilers in His Vineyard in this great empire, where satan has for so long held his seat.

The following resolutions were then passed by the Conference:—

1. *Resolved:*—At the last session of the Decennial Conference held in Bombay, 1892-93, the members desire to place on record their heartfelt thankfulness to God for the stimulus they have received to continue, with renewed consecration, in the great work of evangelizing India; and for the good-feeling, unanimity of sentiment and Christian love that have characterized the whole of its proceedings."

2. *Resolved:*—That the following letter be printed and circulated:—

TO THE SECRETARIES OF MISSIONARY SOCIETIES IN EUROPE, AMERICA, AUSTRALASIA AND ASIA.

*Bombay, January 5th,* 1893.

The members of the Decennial Missionary Conference of India, assembled in Bombay, overwhelmed by the vastness of the work contrasted with the utterly inadequate supply of workers, earnestly appeal to the Church of Christ in Europe, America, Australasia, and Asia.

We re-echo to you the cry of the unsatisfied heart of India. With it we pass on the Master's Word for the perishing multitude, "*Give ye them to eat.*" An opportunity and a responsibility never known before confront us.

The work among *the educated and English-speaking classes* has reached a crisis. The faithful labours of godly men in the class room need to be followed up by men of consecrated culture, free to devote their whole time to aggressive work among India's thinking men. Who will come and help to bring young India to the feet of Christ?

*Medical missionaries* of both sexes are urgently required. We hold up before medical students and young doctors the splendid opportunity here offered of reaching the souls of men through their bodies.

The *women of India* must be evangelized by women. Ten times the present number of such workers could not overtake the task. Missionary ladies now working are so taxed by the care of converts and enquirers already gained that often no strength is left for entering thousands of unentered but open doors. Can our sisters in Protestant Christendom permit this to continue?

SIXTH DAY.

India has fifty millions of *Muhammadans*—a larger number than are found in the Turkish Empire, and far more free to embrace Christianity. Who will come to work for them?

Scores of missionaries should be set apart to promote the production of *Christian literature* in the languages of the people.

*Sunday schools*, into which hundreds of thousands of India's children can readily be brought and moulded for Christ, furnish one of India's greatest opportunities for yet more workers.

*Industrial schools* are urgently needed to help in developing a robust character in Christian youths and to open new avenues for honest work for them. These call for capable Christian workers of special qualifications.

The population of India is largely rural. In hundreds and thousands of villages there is a distinct mass movement toward Christianity. There are millions who would speedily become Christians if messengers of Christ could reach them, take them by the hand and, not only baptize, but lead them into all Christian living. Most of these people belong to the *depressed classes*. They are none the less heirs to our common salvation, and, whatever admixture of less spiritual motives may exist, God Himself is stirring their hearts and training their thoughts toward the things which belong to His Kingdom.

In the name of Christ and of these unevangelized masses for whom He died, we appeal to you to send more labourers at once. May every Church hear the voice of the Spirit saying, "Separate me Barnabas and Saul for the work whereunto I have called them!" In every Church may there be a Barnabas and Saul ready to obey the Spirit's promptings!

Face to face with two hundred and eighty-four millions in this land, for whom in this generation you as well as we are responsible, we ask, Will you not speedily double the present number of labourers?

Will you not also lend your choicest pastors to labour for a term of years among the millions who can be reached through the English tongue?

Is this too great a demand to make upon the resources of those saved by omnipotent love? At the beginning of another century of missions in India let us all "Expect great things from God—attempt great things for God."

SIXTH DAY.

For the reflex blessings to yourselves, as well as for India's sake, we beseech you to "hear what the Spirit saith unto the churches." The manifestation of Christ is greatest to those who keep His commandments, and this is His commandment—"GO YE INTO ALL THE WORLD AND PREACH THE GOSPEL TO EVERY CREATURE."

A. MANWARING,
J. L. PHILLIPS, M.D.,
*Secretaries, Decennial Conference.*

3. *Resolved:*—This Conference recommends the various missionary societies neither to employ agents nor members from other missions without proper reference to those from whom they came, nor to receive members under discipline without similar consultation.

4. *Resolved:*—That this Decennial Conference adopts the following resolution, already passed by the Missionary Conferences of Calcutta, Madras and Bombay—"That, in view of the spread of education in India and the growing need of the Indian churches, it is highly desirable that missionary societies should recognize Christian literature as an increasingly important department of evangelistic effort, and that select men, who have shewn the requisite ability and inclination, should be set apart for it; being supported as before by their respective societies and reporting to them, but working in connection with Christian Publishing Societies."

5. *Resolved:*—That this Conference desires to record its conviction that greater economy and increased efficiency in circulating the Scriptures might be secured, if the various foreign missionary societies would, wherever possible, themselves undertake this work,—the expense of carrying it on being still, where needful, largely defrayed by the different Bible Societies."

6. *Resolved:*—That this Conference hereby expresses its hearty appreciation of the efficient services rendered by the members of the business committee, especially Messrs. Manwaring and Phillips, and thanks them sincerely for their painstaking and laborious attention to their duties.

7. *Resolved:*—That the sincere thanks of this Conference be extended to the several Railway and Steamship Companies which have granted concessions to its members in travelling, both for concessions made and for the assistance cheerfully rendered by all their employés.

That the special thanks of the Conference be tendered to its esteemed friend and brother, Henry Conder, Esq., for his kind and unremitting efforts to provide for the comfort of the members in every possible way.

8. *Resolved:*—That the Conference tenders its warmest thanks to the Principal and staff of the Wilson College for the use

of their splendid building and grounds, and for their constant efforts to promote the success of the Conference.

SIXTH DAY.

9. *Resolved*:—That the members of this Conference tender their sincere and heartfelt thanks to H. E. the Governor of Bombay and Lady Harris, for the kind courtesies extended to them; also to the many friends in Bombay whose hospitality they have enjoyed, in whose sanctuaries their hearts have been refreshed, and whose many acts of kindness and courtesy have contributed to the pleasure they have derived from a brief stay in this beautiful city—the gem among all the cities of the Eastern World.

10. *Resolved:*—That a Standing Committee of thirteen members of the Conference, chosen so as to represent as fairly as possible all the leading missionary societies in the Empire, be appointed with power to represent the Conference in the interim of its regular sessions, to arrange for its regular meetings and to fill vacancies.

That the Standing Committee shall choose the place of meeting of the next Decennial Conference, but shall appoint a sub-committee of seven persons, four of whom shall be members of the Standing Committee, and three representatives of the Christian missionary bodies of the city in which the Conference is to meet. This Committee of seven shall have full power to arrange the programme, and make all other arrangements for the decennial meeting.

The following thirteen members to form the Standing Committee:—

Mr. W. H. CAMPBELL, L. M. S., *Madras.*
Rev. J. C. R. EWING, A. P. M., *Panjab.*
Rev. H. GULLIFORD, W. M. S., *Madras.*
Rev. J. P. JONES, A. B. F. M., *Madras.*
Mrs. LONGHURST, E. C. S., *Madras.*
Rev. D. MACKICHAN, F. C. M., *Bombay.*
Dr. J. L. PHILLIPS, I. S. S. U., *Bengal.*
Rev. E. SELL, C. M. S., *Madras.*
Mr. J. G. SHOME, *Bengal.*
Rev. E. S. SUMMERS, B. M. S., *Bengal.*
Bishop THOBURN, M. E. M., *Bengal.*
Rev. H. U. WEITBRECHT, C. M. S., *Panjab.*
Rev. L. B. WOLF, A. L. M., *Madras.*

The Chairman mentioned that letters had been received from the Bishop of Bombay, the Hon. Mr. Birdwood (Member of Council), W. Lee-Warner, Esq. (Secretary to Government in the Political Department), the Rev. Robert Clark, C. M. S., Amritsar, who was too ill to attend, and from their old friend the Rev. Dr. Murray-Mitchell, part of whose letter was read.

After the singing of the Doxology, the Chairman pronounced the Benediction, and the Conference was brought to a close.

## XVIII.—PUBLIC TEMPERANCE MEETING.

### HELD AT THE FRAMJEE COWASJEE HALL, ON

*Friday Evening, Dec. 30th, at 5-30 p. m.*

SECOND DAY.

The Rev. J. C. R. EWING, D.D., A. P. M., Lahore, who occupied the chair, remarked that the gathering of such a meeting in connection with the Decennial Conference was in itself significant of the interest taken by missionaries in the highest welfare of the people among whom they labour. The time has come when no Christian missionary can afford to occupy a neutral attitude on this question. A right position here is of the highest importance in its bearing upon our work amongst non-Christians, as well as upon the character of the Christian Church in India. The inculcation of total abstinence from all intoxicants is, I venture to believe, our duty, and such teaching can only have its greatest power when enforced by example.

The missionary's attitude.

The Rev. J. H. BATESON, General Secretary, Army Temperance Association, said:—

I propose this evening to devote the time which has been placed at my disposal to an account of the temperance work which is being carried on among the British soldiers in India. There are many societies at work, but all are overshadowed by one, which has the patronage of the authorities, the Army Temperance Association, which continues the good work commenced by the Rev. J. Gelson Gregson in 1862. At the present time the membership is 17,000, all total abstainers, but this does not represent our real numbers, as the troopships have already taken home many of our oldest members, and our returns do not include the drafts, whose names are kept a month on trial before being returned. There is every likelihood that in March we shall have 20,000 members. There are now 170 branches in India, including almost every corps, cavalry, artillery and infantry, and including men of all army "religions"—Church of England, Presbyterian, Wesleyan and Roman Catholic. Though

The army in India.

at any given time there may be 17,000 abstainers in the army in India, I do not wish to give the idea that all of these are staunch abstainers. On the contrary, about 9,000 may be accounted staunch abstainers and the remaining 8,000 belong to what we call "the floating population," men who take the pledge, and keep it for a time, but then for various reasons, a birthday, some annoyance, the renewal of some old acquaintance, St. Andrew's day or Christmas day, they leave the association. There is no need for such men to break their word as they have promised to abstain only so long as they *retain their pledge-card*. The results of the work of the association are highly satisfactory as regards the conduct, health and general physique of the members. At a meeting held a few nights ago Colonel Peyton, commanding the Durham Light Infantry, attributed the diminution in crime in the battalion under his command to the work of the association. For the year 1891-92 statistics shew that the percentage of trials by courts-martial in India were, among abstainers ·12 and among non-abstainers ·4. As regards health, a commanding officer supplied me with the following statistics when I visited his regiment a short time ago. The percentage of admission into hospital in the battalion under his command were among abstainers 2·6 and among non-abstainers 10·6. That our members do not suffer physically by their voluntary abstinence received a remarkable illustration at the Simla Football Tournament in 1891 and 1892. On each occasion the King's Own Scottish Borderers sent to Simla a Temperance Team to meet the finest regimental football teams in India, and on each occasion they carried off the challenge teams against all-comers. When total abstinence has this effect upon men under their command, as regard conduct, health and physique, it is hardly to be wondered that commanding officers not only give us their patronage but their active support. These facts disprove the now historical statement of Dr. Mortimer Granville, the champion of moderate drinking, that the principles of total abstinence have injured men mentally, morally and physically. The fact is that the A. T. A. gives to the world a great object lesson in temperance. Our members are exposed to the extreme cold of Sikkim and the Himalayas, to the heat of the plains in summer, to long marches and hard service, to all the temptations of large garrison towns, to the errors of a soldier's life, and yet

*Marginalia:* Second Day. Floating members. Courts-martials. An object lesson.

SECOND DAY.   with advantage to themselves as regards immunity from disease, and to the army, as regards freedom from crime, they are true to their pledge.

Difficulties.   There are undoubtedly great difficulties that have to be faced. One is with regard to the pledge, how to retain our members. A mere pledge is not sufficient, and we seek by all lawful means to encourage men to maintain a strict fidelity to it. Another difficulty is that so many are inclined to make a religion of their temperance, apparently thinking that when they have signed the pledge they have done all that God or man can expect of them. We even seek to set before them the fact that the pledge is only a means to an end, the devotion of their hearts and lives to the service of the Lord Jesus Christ. Many are the

Good testimonies.   testimonies I have received which shew that this end has been accomplished. Some time ago a soldier said to me : " I'm thankful I ever took the pledge, it was my first step towards Christ," and more recently I received a letter from another soldier in which he gave me the chief features of a military career which had been wrecked through indulgence, inasmuch as he had been reduced to the ranks through drunkenness and had been pronounced incorrigible, but at one of my meetings he took the pledge, had since given his heart to Christ, and has, to some extent, redeemed his character. Our desire and prayer is that such results should follow our work generally, and not as sometimes appears to be the case, in isolated instances.

Three-fold aim.   In common with other temperance organisations our aim is three-fold : we seek to prevent those who come under our influence falling into habits of intemperance, to rescue those who have formed such habits, and to help the reformed, many of whom are morally weak through indulgence, to preserve a consistent fidelity to their pledge. As regards preventive work, our first aim is to get the children of married soldiers into our Juvenile Branch. This is a new feature of our work, but already it gives promise of success. Then there are the drafts which every trooping season come out from England in large numbers, to take the places of the dead and invalided, and the many who under the short service system are transferred to their Reserves. Many of these drafts have the opportunity of taking our pledge afforded them before they leave England, then when the troopships are ploughing their way through the deep, the naval chaplains hold Temperance Meetings and take pledges, and before they ultimately reach their corps, where they are entertained by their Regimental Temperance Society, each man, individually, is asked at Deolali and Karachi to take the pledge. This work is done by volunteers, whose efforts have been attended with much success. They have shewn a devotion to the interests of their comrades which is most commendable. Of many a man it may be truly said:—

I live for those who love me,
  For those who know me true,
  For the heaven that smiles above me,
    And awaits my coming too.
For the cause that lacks assistance
  For the wrong that needs resistance,
  For the future in the distance
    And the good that I may do.

*Second Day.*

The fringes of another sphere of work have been touched. Fortunately, there is no drunkenness in the native army. God grant that there may never be. If it be true that drunkenness is spreading among the natives, the fear is that it may shew itself in the native army. Lest such should be the case a determined effort to enrol the native army would be justified, and would erect a barrier against the spread of intemperance in this section of the community. In the course of my present winter tour I addressed a meeting, at Baroda, of officers, non-commissioned officers and men of the Baroda State Army, many of whom took the pledge. Their Excellencies the Dewan and Commander-in-Chief were present. I was forcibly struck with the value of woman's influence in temperance work by an incident which His Excellency the Dewan gave as illustrating the interest which H. H. the Gaekwar takes in the temperance movement in his dominions. A number of the inhabitants of a certain village petitioned the Government to shut up a drink shop. On receipt of the petition a official was deputed to visit the village and ascertain the opinions of all the villagers. It was found that whilst the majority were in favour of closing the shop, a minority wished to keep it open. The wives of the men in the majority then approached the wives of the others and pointed out the evils which they suffered through their husbands drinking. They in turn approached their husbands, pointing out to them that the liquor-shop was a source of temptation to which they

*No drunkenness in native army.*

*Women's influence.*

**Second Day.** frequently yielded, and the consequence was that the minority were converted to the views of the majority. An unanimous petition resulted in the liquor shop being closed, though with considerable monetary loss to the Government. Our hopes for the future are based on this preventive work. If we can get the child of this generation we have the man of the next, if we can get the young soldier of to-day we have the old soldier of to-morrow, and if we can get the native soldier now there never will be the necessity for rescue work in the native army.

**Rescue work.** Rescue work next demands our attention. There are in the army a large number of men who have got into habits of intemperance. Their pay all goes to the canteen, and they are constantly in trouble through their drunkenness. This is particularly the case among the older soldiers. Whilst in the army, beyond certain punishments, they do not experience the full results of their intemperance; they are sure of their pay, their food, clothes and shelter. When they leave the army their case will be different, and unless they reform they will inevitably go to the wall, and drift into the hopelessly helplessly destitute population. Our duty with regard to such is manifest, we must

> Rescue the perishing,
> Care for the dying,
> Snatch them in pity from sin and the grave;
> Weep o'er the erring one,
> Lift up the fallen,
> Tell them of Jesus the mighty to save.

**Active members.** Every member has it impressed upon his mind that he must use his influence to save his comrades. He must go after them, and, if repelled, go again. These characters are the ones who are found within the wall of our military prisons, and each man is asked, the day before his release, to sign our pledge. If he does so, his name is forwarded, by the chaplain, to his corps, and on arrival there his temperance comrades extend to him a welcome and receive him into their midst. This work, which is the equivalent of the Prison Gate Brigades at home, has been the means of rescuing many a poor fellow. The hand he needed to raise him, was extended to him and he took it. In one of his policies Whittier describes two armies marching on the opposite banks of a stream. One

> "Marches to the drum beat roll,
> "The wide mouthed clarion's bay,
> "And bears upon a crimson scroll
> "Our glory is to slay."

> "Moves in silence by the stream
> "With sad yet watchful eyes;
> "Along its front no sabres shine,
> "No blood red pinnions wave,
> "Its banners bear one single line—
> "Our duty is to save."

Our duty, aye! and our glory too, is to save. The weak, the morally enslaved, the helpless, these should be the objects of our earnest labour, our care, our prayer, that we may save them from the degradation of drunkenness and lead them to the feet of Him Who is able to save to the uttermost.

Lastly, our aim is to help every member to keep his pledge. In the early days of my life in India I was in Mandalay with the Upper Burmah Field Force, and it was my habit at the close of each service to give the temperance pledge to all who might desire it. When I found the same men coming again and again to take the pledge, I asked the reason, and they said that they had no place to go to in the evening, except the canteen; so, how could they be expected to keep it? Upon this I went to Sir George White, then Commanding the Field Force, and with his help I was able to secure a temperance room in the palace, with the result that men, having a comfortable place of resort, games and papers, generally kept their pledge. This is the principle on which we work in India now. There are some who have nothing good to say for the Indian Government. So far as our work is concerned we obtain all the help we require— rooms, furniture, transport on the line of march, and a refreshment bar, from the profit of which we are able to purchase any comforts that may be required. It was said of a former drunkard in his hearing that he was in the gutter and a certain friend helped him out and put him on his feet. "Aye," he said, "and I should be in the gutter still if, when he put me on my feet, he had not stood against me and helped me to stand." We should ever seek to be strength to the weak, help to the helpless, above all commanding the weak and helpless to seek the help of Him through Whom we can do all things.

Depending for help upon the Holy Spirit we believe this temperance work to be of God. His blessing we seek and to

*Marginalia: Second Day. The Canteen. "In the gutter." The work is of God.*

**Second Day.** Him we ascribe the glory. A certain regiment, having received new colours, sang—

" 'Mid sword and steel, 'mid weal and woe,
" Unwavering and in faith
" Where'er these sacred banners go,
" We'll follow to the death."

With our banners above us, consecrated by love and prayer, we can truly say,

Where our Captain leads us
We may safely go;
Where our Chief precedes us
We may face the foe;
His right arm is o'er us,
He our guide will be:
Christ has gone before us,
Christians, follow ye!"

Miss Jessie ACKERMANN, Travelling Evangelist of the World's Women's Christian Temperance Union, said that the previous speaker had told them about a great organisation of men, but she wanted to speak on behalf of a great organisation of women, the largest organisation of women in the world, having half-a-million members in forty-seven lands. Its motto was a grand one—"For God and home and humanity." This Union had sent her to India to survey the land, and to prepare the way for other workers. She had a deepening conviction that the hour had arrived when every Christian man and woman should take a definite stand on the drink question. In pressing this home she was often confronted with the query, "Don't you think that alcohol is a good creature of God?" Alcohol is a good creature of God in the same sense that the devil is a good creature of God! The Lord made him a pure spirit, but he made himself into a devil by disobedience. Pure and healthful fruits were among God's best gifts to men, but men make them into the poison called alcohol, and then speak of that as a good creature of God, laying all the meannesses of man at the door of God! Then again she often met with good Christian people who smoke cigars and drink whiskey, and they told her that they did it with a good conscience. She could never learn, however, that they had any definite transaction with the Lord about it. If there were any of this class present, then she would affectionately say to them, "Just take that whiskey and those cigars

*Half-a-million women.*

*Alcohol.*

on your knees before the Lord, spend only one hour there, and if you can then continue their use with a clear conscience, I will say no more." "It is God that justifieth." No one would have any further right to say a word. Nevertheless she believed that if every drinking and smoking Christian would follow this plan every church would become a grand temperance society in itself. When the church opens to admit the whiskey bottle it opens its doors to the greatest evils that afflict mankind. There is only one course to be taken by those who are aroused on this question, and that is, to appeal to the Christian church to clear itself of all complicity with this curse. The church is to a great extent asleep and must be awakened to a sense of its duty.

*A Gospel movement.*

In conclusion, Miss Ackermann spoke of the way in which she, who was free from home ties, felt impelled to go forth into the world to oppose this evil which was making such havoc with the homes and happiness of other women, ruining their husbands and their sons. She felt very thankful that she was able to say that this great movement of women is a Gospel Temperance movement, it has the Lord Himself, and the strength of Jesus Christ at the back of it, with all the combined moral forces of the universe.

*Work among Natives.*

The Rev. Arthur PARKER, L. M. S., Benares, said :—The two speakers who have preceded me have given you accounts of work among English soldiers and work done by Christian women. It is my pleasing duty to relate what we have been trying to do in Benares in the way of work among natives of this country. Our society, oddly enough, owes its existence to an American lady, Mrs. Leavitt who, at the time I first came to Benares in the beginning of 1883, was visiting that ancient city in the interests of the same great organisation which Miss Ackermann represents to-day. As a result of her efforts our Benares Total Abstinence Society was founded, the members of which, with only one or two exceptions, were all Hindus and Muhammadans. It was not, however, till a year after that date that any unusual work was accomplished. Early in 1889 I received a visit from a man who had revolutionized the work of our society, and who has set an example to all Indian temperance reformers. The Mahant Kesho Ram Roy had for some years in his quiet way been a temperance

*An earnest worker.*

*Second Day.*

**Second Day.**

**A long meeting.**

worker but had accomplished little. In December 1888 he accidentally attended a meeting at which the redoubtable Thomas Evans of Mussoorie was delivering an address in Hindustani. One idea of the speaker seized the Mahant's mind, and that was embodied in the phrase: "Agar koi admi sharab piwe to uska hooka pani band ho jae." The meaning of that phrase I need not explain to my Indian hearers, but to others it may suffice to say that the meaning is simply this: "If a man *will* drink, then put him out of your caste." In simple English "Boycot him." It was on this idea the Mahant seized. It seemed to him that the sober well-educated members of the various castes of Benares had a right to protect themselves and their children against the contaminating influence of the drunkards of their community. There was one obstacle, however, to his putting this idea into practice. Hence his visit to me. He wished, he said, to have the presence of at least one Englishman and of as many educated Indians as possible at his meeting in order to assure his hearers *that the English Government was not forcing drink on the Indian people*. It was news to him, and he believed it would be news to many thousands in Benares, to know that the Government did not desire its subjects to spend their money in drink. "Will you," said he, "help me by being present to assure these people that in striving to be sober they will not be considered guilty of sedition." I need not say how readily I consented. The first meeting I presided over—a caste-meeting of the Ahirs or cow-keepers—was a great success. It commenced at nine p. m. and lasted till three or four o'clock the next morning. The stalwarts of the caste insisted upon a decision, and when the meeting broke up the result was that this large and influential caste, numbering 20,000 in all, was pledged to total abstinence. Other meetings soon followed, and the moral effect of that first victory was felt in them all. Now for four years that good work has been going on. We reckon now 60,000 persons in the lower castes in Benares pledged to either partial or total abstinence. The effect of our work has been felt by the drink-sellers, and has made itself manifest in the excise reports. The drink-sellers in Benares appealed to the authorities to stop the work of the Mahant, and were not a little surprised to find their appeals refused. The revenue for excise on native liquor has gone down steadily ever since 1887. In the Government report for 1887-88 the amount paid in still-head duty in native liquor in the Benares District was Rs. 1,49,741 and in the last report, that for 1890-91, the same item shews Rs. 86,790. The Mahant is still at work. He is now an agent of the Anglo-Indian Temperance Society and a most indefatigable worker. He has given up his whole life to this work, and although he has been threatened, his house robbed, and attempts even made to bribe him, he remains firm, faithful and indefatigable. I have been moved to relate this partly in order to stir up your minds, and especially the minds of my Indian, hearers to similar efforts in other parts of India, and partly because it illustrates very well one or two interesting aspects of temperance work in India. Let me then make an urgent appeal to missionaries on behalf of the temperance cause.

SECOND DAY.

First let me appeal to you as *Englishmen*. A little has been said of the great things the Government has done, and is doing, to promote temperance among the English soldiers in India. Would to God the Government had as great care for its Indian subjects! There is room, nay, there is need, for Englishmen in India to make it clear that the English Government is at least not on the side of drunkenness. I have told you why the Mahant wished for my presence at his meetings. Let me now relate an incident which will bring this need even more forcibly before you. In the rainy season of 1889, the Mahant and I visited a little village just outside Benares. We had been led to visit the place by an appeal made to the Mahant by the women of the village. When we reached the ferry which had to be crossed to get to the village, a company of the work-women of the place who were crossing at the same time poured their piteous tale into our ears.

Appeal to Englishmen.

There was a Government drink shop in the village. Their husbands who were fishermen were infatuated with the drink. Early in the morning these men bearing their burden of fish went into Benares, and having sold their stock returned and spent all their earnings in the drink shop. They themselves, poor creatures, in order to get food for themselves and their children, usually carried into the city the produce of their gardens or a few cakes of cowdung for fuel, and often it happened that, as they returned carrying a few hard earned

SECOND DAY.

A meeting near Benares.

pice, their drunken mates issued from the shop and robbed them of all they had. In the most pitiful manner, with their hands on our feet, they besought us to help them, "for," said they, "we are all being ruined." Entering the village the first building we saw was the miserable hovel where drink was sold. In the village was neither school nor dispensary nor even a good road. The only representation of our Government was the drink shop and an old lazy watchman. The latter when interrogated declared that the drink shop was a Government institution as much as he was. I need not tell you with what pleasure we devoted ourselves to the task of disabusing the minds of these simple folk of this foul calumny. As we left the village accompanied by a crowd of the delighted inhabitants, the drink-seller emerged from his den and cursed us as we went. The last words of his which reached our ears were these: "Where will the Government get its three lakhs of rupees from, if such people as you are allowed to go about in this way?" I am an Englishman and rejoice in the name, but that day I came near being ashamed of it. I claim for myself and for those that work as I do that we are the true friends of the Indian Government and of England, when we try to disabuse the minds of the people of India of the wicked lies which designing men for their own profit have told and are telling. For the last four years we in Benares have been trying to lift the fair name of the English Government out of the mire and filth into which it has been dragged of late. Cannot you do the same? I do not think that in Benares the people are more ignorant than elsewhere. But there a Government license is held to mean, and by some is proclaimed to mean, a Government *order* not only to sell drink, but *to drink.* I have found it so, and I feel sure if you care to inquire, you will also find it so.

As lovers of humanity.

Then I appeal to you as lovers of humanity and as missionaries of the Gospel of purity and freedom. In entering on this work I have been delighted to find how it has brought me into sympathetic touch with many right-minded, educated natives. In Benares the leaders of the local Arya Samaj have been some of our most loyal and hearty co-workers. Orthodox and heteredox Hindus and learned Moulvies have all been brought together and the common bond of brotherhood has been discovered and tightened. In conversation with such men I have had my attention directed more than once to the grave danger to the educated youth of this country arising from the drinking habits of *temperate* Englishmen. Heads of schools and colleges, and professors and teachers in such institutions have been mentioned to me as exerting, often unconsciously, a most pernicious influence in this respect. Education, we rejoice to see, is loosening the bonds of ignorance and superstition which have so long bound the Indian mind. But with this general loosening there should not surely be any falling away from native habit, any throwing off of restraints which operate to keep men in paths of honour and goodness. In the case of the drinking habit I am sure that even the slightest swerving from the path of total abstinence is misinterpreted and magnified by those who seek for some encouragement in vice, and not students alone but our servants are influenced by our example. I know that in my own case my servants have long marked and noted my example. Among them are some who are heads of the little communities to which they belong, and from them I have heard many a story of struggle on behalf of the cause of sobriety. Encouraged not by our words alone, but by our practice and example, they have fought many a good fight in the *panchayat* of their castes. To a missionary nothing could be more terrible than the thought that one of these weak brethren, who serve us with such faithfulness, has been caused to stumble or been made weak by the needless indulgence of a good master or mistress. For, not to men alone but to English ladies do we appeal that in their households as well as in their lives it may be clearly seen that they have no part or lot in this accursed thing. My friends, it is a light thing with you. I am persuaded it is a light thing, but to the servant behind your chair and the student who sits before you in class, it may be—this simple glass of wine—the beginning of the bitterness of death. Let me appeal then in the name of our common humanity and in the name of our Blessed Master on behalf, first of the ignorant poor who are being deluded by those whose interest is vested in the sale of liquor, and again on behalf of those who, as students and servants, come daily under the influence of our example. Let us so act that not one of these trusting in our light shall ever wake to the discovery that the light in us was darkness.

*Marginalia:* Second Day. Students. Servants.

## XIX.—PUBLIC MISSIONARY MEETING,

*Saturday, December 31st.*

LARGE HALL—at 5·30 P. M.

**THIRD DAY.**

**Bishop of Lucknow.**

The Rev. T. R. WADE, D.D., C. M. S., Amritsar, who occupied the chair, said :—At the commencement of this meeting I would say, and I think all will agree with me, that I am extremely sorry that the Rev. A. Clifford, Bishop-designate of Lucknow, is not here to take the chair at this meeting, announced in the printed programme, but as the ship in which he comes has not arrived in time, he and we are helpless, and in the emergency, at the request of the Committee, I have consented to take his place.

As your Chairman, then, I shall claim the privilege of saying a few words, and I do this the more readily as I see there is no missionary from the Panjab down on the list of those who are to address you this evening. I desire to direct your attention to three thoughts, THANKFULNESS, HUMILIATION, ENCOURAGEMENT ; *thankfulness* for the past, *humiliation* for the past and present, and *encouragement* for the future.

**Thankfulness.**

I. *Thankfulness.*—There are many subjects calling for our deepest thankfulness when we look back upon the past.

**Increase in the Panjab.**

As a missionary from the Panjab I might mention the great increase in the number of Christians that has taken place there in the nine years, 1881-1890, as mentioned in the "Statistical Tables of Protestant Missions" published this year. The rate of increase in the Panjab during these 9 years is given as 335 per cent. higher than that of any other Province in India. I could speak of the great work going on in the Central Panjab amongst the depressed classes, some thousands of whom have already been baptized, and the movement towards Christianity is growing and spreading, and at least one whole village has become Christian.

**The Frontier.**

As a missionary of the Church Missionary Society I could speak of a C. M. S. Frontier chain of Mission Stations from Simla in the north to Kotghar, Srinagar, Pehsawar, Bannu,

Dera Ismael Khan, Tank, Dera Ghazi Khan, and Quetta down through Sindh to Karachi, with important mission work being carried on in each one; sometimes prominence being given to medical work, as in Kashmir and Quetta, or to education, as in Dera Ismael Khan, or to hospitality as in the Hujra at Peshawar, and the missionaries, with the Scriptures in their hands translated into Kashmiri, Pushtu, and Persian are waiting to move forward to the regions beyond as soon as the closed doors are opened. I could also mention the names of individual converts, personal friends, with interesting histories and devoted and useful lives, such as the Rev. Imad-ud-Din, D.D., so well known for his learning and work for Muhammadans; the Rev. Kharak Singh with his knowledge of Sanskrit and work amongst the Hindus; and Dr. Barkhurdar Khan in medical charge of the Native State of Chumba, and his work amongst the lepers. As a member of this Conference, after all I have seen and read and heard of the great and increasing work being carried on by so many devoted workers, in so many places, amongst so many races and classes, in so many ways, and yet with such a manifest blessing resting upon the whole that by far the most and greatest difficulties arise from the very abundance of the blessings bestowed —there has not been room enough to receive them—but if not prepared to receive them I am sure we should all the more be ready to thank God for giving them.

And when, as a member of that Kingdom which Christ came to set up in this world, I extend my view and look out upon the world and see how Christianity is spreading in China and Japan, and North and South America, and penetrating into the very heart of Africa, whose soil now in our time and generation has been sprinkled and consecrated with the blood of Europeans and natives, true martyrs of Christ Whom they loved more than life itself; when I realize at all the extent of this Kingdom, its rapid growth and increasing strength—for if the cords of the Church of Christ are longer, as without all contradiction they are, I for one believe also that the stakes are stronger than ever;—when I see the doors of the world open as never before, means for travelling and printing unprecedented, the reins of the Government of the world, might I not say, and the strings of its wealth, in Christian hands; and when I see too that more of the followers of Christ feel their responsibility to

*Sidenotes:* Third Day. Imad-ud-Din. Growth of the Kingdom.

**Third Day.**

**Humiliation.**

**Encouragement.**

make known His Gospel in all the world according to His last command; a greater and more intelligent and practical interest taken in missions, and more prayers offered for them than before, I feel that our first thought on such an occasion as this should be one of thankfulness.

2. But if this should be our first I am equally sure our second should be one of *Humiliation*. There is abundant cause for the deepest humiliation. When at this time, the evening of the last day of the year, we examine ourselves and compare what we are with what we might have been, what we have done and what we might have done, then look at the standard of Christian life and the work of Christians, and compare these with what God asks us to be and offers us strength to be and to do. As for work the Church of God could and should take possession of the world for Christ. And yet in this one land of India in which we live and labour, which God in love and mercy took and handed over to the Government of a Christian people brought from the other end of the world, after all these years of power and opportunity not one in one hundred of the inhabitants is a Christian. And when in this last Decennial Conference of the present century we look out upon a world which God still loves, and for which the Son of God became flesh and died, with His unrepealed command still sounding in our ears, "Go teach all nations," and consider that some two-thirds of this world remain unevangelized after nearly 1,900 years, though God has always been faithful to His promises and much more ready and willing to hear prayer and bestow blessings than His people were to ask and receive, surely there is cause for us to humble ourselves before Him down unto the very dust.

3. But my last thought is one of *Encouragement*, and I say without hesitation, and I think you will all agree with me, that there were never more reasons for missionaries to be encouraged than there are now. Of course there are difficulties many and great, nor would I under-rate or understate them. Of all persons, missionaries, and of all missionaries the seniors who have spent decades of years in mission work, should know these difficulties best; but pile them up one on the other till they are like the Himalayas of this land, and in Christ's Name I would say, "Who art thou, O great mountain? before Zerubbabel thou shall become

a plain"; and this not by man's might or power but only by God's Spirit. Can there be a surer sign of a coming shower than when the drops begin to fall? And are there not many witnesses here now who can testify to the droppings falling from above in many places of this great land? and every drop is not only blessing in itself but also a sign and pledge of more to follow. Yes, "God shall bless us." "There shall be showers of blessings."

<small>THIRD DAY.</small>

The Christian student standing upon his watch tower can see visions plain, and signs and prophecies being fulfilled before him—great doors opening of their own accord before those who "go forth to preach the Gospel as a witness to all nations," the fig tree and all the trees shooting forth in the increasing light and warmth of an approaching summer, and he knows that as surely as day succeeds night and summer winter, so the rays of the rising Sun of Righteousness are already dispelling the gloom of the night of darkness, and the hope of His near coming brings forth for service best energies of the heart filled and consumed with His love. And thus we thank our God for all He has done for us and by us in the past, we humble ourselves and lie low and empty before Him at the present to be filled with His Spirit and clothed with His power, and trusting in Him we go forth with the greatest encouragement to carry on His work, for we remember that when the Son of God Himself gave the command, "Go teach all nations," He not only said that all power was given unto Him in heaven and in earth, but added the gracious promise, "Lo, I am with you always."

<small>The return of Christ.</small>

Kali Charan BANURJI, Esq., B. A., B. L., of Calcutta, said, in substance, that he regarded the missionary enterprise as an object-lesson on the evidences of Christianity. If, at any time, we ventured to point out any defects in its conduct, it was because he wished that its effectiveness as an object-lesson should be complete. He then related how, in the gracious providence of God, he had been brought within the sphere of its operations. Although as an infant, he used to visit a mission school, an astrologer's warnings led to his removal from all possible missionary influence, until years after, the repetition, by a fellow-lodger, of the lessons received on the "Sermon on the Mount" in a mission school Bible class, awakened in him a strong desire to join a mission school himself. He prevailed on this fellow-lodger of his to persuade his guardians to fall in

<small>Personal testimony.</small>

THIRD DAY.

with his desire, and he found himself a student in the Free Church Institution. When eventually he was led to the Saviour, he owed his conversion, under God, to close personal intercourse with one of his professors, a medical missionary, now in glory. The missionary had endeared himself to the whole family, and was always welcome to visit him, and pray with him, and for him, by his bedside, when suffering from illness. No more demonstrative evidence could be given of the desire of the missionaries to accept the people of this country on a footing of equality with themselves, than the fact that they brought the Bible to them, and offered to share with them the greatest gift of God. He believed that the success of the missionary enterprise depended, in a large measure, upon the attitude of the missionaries towards the people. That attitude should be characterised by love and sympathy, and by a readiness to receive them on terms of perfect equality, of which the gift of the Bible was the earnes.

*The missionary attitude.*

The Rev. J. E. SCOTT, PH.D., M. E. C., Muttra, N.-W. P., said:—

In the remarks I am about to make I do not wish to be understood as opposed to or to minify or disparage *any* form of mission work, for I believe in anything and everything that will help to bring about the conversion of this great empire. Education, higher, middle and primary; Medical, Industrial and Normal work, all have their place, and are useful in the accomplishment of this great purpose. But at this time I desire to enter a plea for one form of work, a work in which I have spent more than nineteen years of my life, namely, that of *direct effort to save and elevate the depressed classes.* And in considering this work for the masses there are three thoughts which I desire to keep uppermost. First, the advantages of and reasons for this work; second, the necessity for organization and system in its prosecution; and third, results which have been achieved.

*The depressed classes.*

*Advantages.*

I. And first as to the advantages. (*a*) When we are working among the depressed classes we are working for the majority. They throng about us on every hand. These are the people who fill the villages, who till the soil, who live from hand to mouth and often with little in the hand. We meet them *everywhere*, and to avoid them or to neglect their crying want would be wrong. (*b*) Working among these teeming millions of the poor is both natural and Scriptural. It is natural, for in building any structure one must begin at the bottom. No house can be built from the top. Nor could water be boiled by an application of heat from above. The normal method of all development is from the bottom upwards. It is Scriptural, for the glory of the Gospel of Him, Who was Himself a member of the great family of the depressed, is, that *"the poor have the Gospel preached to them."* It was to these that Our Lord and His Apostles devoted their lives. "Not many mighty and not many noble" were called in Paul's time. And the poor, the lame, the halt and the blind are in all ages the special subjects of the compassion and mercy of God, so that when we are doing this work we are following in the footsteps of the Master and emulating the example of the Fathers. (*c*) And these people are accessible. The high caste and rich are not. They hold aloof from the Gospel or actively oppose it. But the masses about us are glad to hear what we have to say. *"The common people heard Him gladly,"* and many of them in this land hear us gladly as we go to them kindly and humbly with the true word of life. The pure Gospel of peace and love and truth will always get a hearing among the common people. (*d*) They are not only accessible but they are *teachable*. *We can get at them* and they *want to learn*. They perish "for lack of knowledge." They "hunger and thirst after righteousness." They look up to the missionary as to one who can deliver them, and they are ever willing to follow his leading. Whatever faults the masses of this country may have, it cannot be said of them that they are not *docile*. Blessed be the missionary who, in the midst of such a multitude, is *"apt to teach."* (*e*) These poor, depressed people are also capable of the *highest development*. Mission work has been carried on long enough in India among this class of people to show that even from the lowest classes men can be marvellously trained and educated and developed. I have myself seen men, who were in youth sweeping the streets, now teaching the upper classes in the high school! The second master of one of the high schools of North India was a sweeper. Some of our best educated and most influential catechists and preachers are from among the substratum of society—from the depressed classes. The Gospel of Jesus Christ not only purifies the

*Margin notes:* THIRD DAY. A Scriptural work. They are accessible. They are teachable. Capable of development.

THIRD DAY.

Does not hinder high caste work.

heart but it wakes up and stimulates the mind in a wonderful manner. (*f*) And does working among the depressed classes—among sweepers and leather workers—hinder the work among the upper classes? It rather helps it. It is the Gospel of success which so warms the heart that even the high caste man comes to recognize the Fatherhood of God and the brotherhood of man. I think there have been more converts from among the upper classes where real Gospel work has been vigorously pushed among *all* classes—among the lower classes—than where the work has been coldly and exclusively confined to the upper classes—to the Brahmans and Thakurs of society.

Organization.

11. But in order to be successful in this, or in *any* mission work, there must be proper organization system in its prosecution. Look how Hinduism is organized against us. Look at caste and the richly endowed institutions of India. Muhammadanism presents a united front—cold, calculating, confident—against us. Can we afford to do *our* work in a careless, slipshod, desultory manner? *Let us organize.* We should lay out our work. *Plan* the work and *work* the plan.

M. E. C. system.

There should be system for reaching *the lost man.* In the church with which I am connected the work is divided into five conferences, over all of which there is a general superintendent. Each conference is divided into districts, supervised by a presiding elder. Districts are divided into circuits, composed of a number of towns and villages where reside a number of Christians or enquirers. Each circuit has its preacher in charge, and under him may be sub-circuits with preachers, teachers, pastor-teachers, Bible-readers, colporteurs, &c., &c. Each circuit has its conference for the examination of character and renewal of licenses held quarterly. And in each district is held a district conference for the supervision and investigation of the work within the towns of the district; and annually all the districts come together in annual conference, when the presiding elders and heads of circuits are examined and reappointed. Camp meetings, for purely evangelistic work, Worker's Conventions for practical, normal and literary work, and other meetings are held periodically. During this cold

Camp meetings.

season *six Camp meetings* have been held in North India, attended by not fewer than five thousand (5,000) Christians, scores and hundreds of whom from the lower classes were wonderfully blessed. I have, for the use of such meetings in my districts, a large tent which will seat a *thousand people*, and we have had it filled with earnest men, women and children seeking a blessing from God. Thus by laying out and faithfully and systematically presenting this work, great and most substantial and permanent results are gained.

III. That leads me in conclusion to speak of results, nearly all our success in India has been among the humble poor. The majority of our converts in all missions is from among the great majority. *These numerous, accessible, teachable, and trainable* classes are yielding fruit. They will come over to us by the thousands and hundreds of thousands. *We should be prepared for that.* In one mission alone in North India they are joining the Christian ranks at the rate of 2,000 *per month !* In my own district 200 a month are being baptized. There are places in other parts of India where *whole villages* are ready. Providence seems to point to this work as the present work of the church. *We are beginning a new era.* The embarrassment of lack of workers and lack of money will vanish if we follow the lead of the Divine Spirit in this work. When the multitudes come, good workers from among them—men like Amos from " among the herdsmen of Tekoa," and John, who fed on " locusts and wild honey "—will stand forth, and the masses, though poor, will be able to feed them and support them in the work. Let us, then, *work for* the *masses.* They are all about us. They call to us. Let us with humble hearts go *up* to our work, for it is God's work and *is* succeeding—*must succeed*—and when these, the *depressed masses,* are raised up into Christian life and liberty, then *the classes* will be left *below* them and must hasten to join them, or be left at a disadvantage in the great evolution of life. " Blessed are the meek, for they shall inherit the earth." " Blessed are the poor in spirit, for theirs is the kingdom of heaven."

The Rev. J. WILKIE, M.A., C. P. M., Indore, said:—

One striking feature of all the addresses we have listened to in the Conference has been the very cheering confident tone, especially marked when the oldest and most experienced missionaries were the speakers. There will not be any radical changes in methods, in all probability; but we certainly shall

**Third Day.**

Encouragement.

A nation awakening.

return to our respective fields stimulated and encouraged, as we realize what great things the Lord hath done for us throughout this land. And we may well be encouraged when we consider the task undertaken by the Christian church and the wonderful success in the past hundred years. We have undertaken nothing less than the upheaval and overthrow of one of the most ancient and most firmly rooted of the world's religious systems, with which has been interwoven, till it has become a part of itself, the whole social and moral life of the people—a people that in number are nearly one-fourth of the whole population of the globe With what contempt did Brahmanism regard the feeble efforts of the first missionaries, who without political influence or support, few in number and poor in this world's goods, first attempted to conquer this land for Christ! Had not the Brahmans in the past been able either to beat back or to absorb the religious movements that had attempted a landing upon their shores? Were Carey but to appear in our midst at this time, how his heart would fill with sincere thanksgiving? On all sides we see a nation, that for ages has been asleep, awakening to a sense of its possibilities and powers, shaking itself free from customs and superstitions, hoary with age and eagerly seizing on what to it seems better. Caste is not by any means dead, but has it not lost the respect of the great mass of the thinking people? Hinduism and Aryanism, Muhammadanism and Brahmoism are not dead: but does not the use of our methods shew the failure of theirs, and the adoption of so many of our Christian truths, as props to uphold their own, shew how weak it is even in their estimation? *Young Bombay or young Bengal* are no longer terms of reproach but rather are regarded as compliments. India is in a transition stage and hence exposed to peculiar dangers ; and so, whilst there never were so many opportunities and signs of the Master's favour, there also never were such serious threatening dangers that should call for redoubled efforts on the part of the Church of Jesus Christ. We as Christians are responsible for driving them from their old moorings and hence should equally seek to bring them into the only safe harbour, and especially so, as we see the battle raging around the great central truth of our Christian system, *i. e.*, the atoning Sacrifice of our Lord Jesus Christ. Many profess to admire His life and character, and not a few profess to imitate Him; but the Cross is, as of old, foolishness and a stumbling-block to not a few.

 To thoroughly understand what has been done we require to look back but a few years and compare it with the present. To turn to the field I specially know. Ten years ago at Indore the Agent to the Governor-General had refused to allow us to start a school in the British Residency limits, had refused to allow us to buy a property that was offered for sale, would not allow us any ground on which to build, told us we had no rights there and in other ways made it very difficult to carry on any Christian work. In June 1883 the late Maharajah of Indore issued, his so-called "*ultimatum*," in which he refused to allow us to carry on Christian work of any kind, in or out of our house, within his territory. It was given out, and by not a few believed, that no Christian work could be carried on in any Native State, but by the sufferance of its ruler. In September 1883 we touched bottom just before I set out, and met with the brethren of the different Conferences. Gratefully do I remember the helping hand of Dr. Ewing, at Allahabad, and Dr. McDonald, Bishop Thoburn and Mr. Kerry of Calcutta, at a time when the spirit had almost lost hope in the weary contest that had so long tried faith and patience. I must also refer to the kind assistance of Dewan Bahadur Ragunath Rao and Rao Bahadur K. C. Bedarkar, a former and the present Minister of Indore; and especially must I thank His Highness the present Ruler of that State for his continued kindness to us as a mission since.

 In 1883 we could get no land for any purpose; we have lately received not less than eleven acres from the present Maharajah. Then we were not allowed to start a school even in the British Residency, now we have our High School and College in the Residency, together with Vernacular and Middle School in the Residency, city and surrounding territory. Then we could preach nowhere, without the danger of serious interference, now we can preach anywhere; and within the last two years, in addition to kind words regarding the work we are trying to do, His Highness Maharajah Holkar has given over two thousand rupees to the mission. But we are especially cheered by the wide open door that everywhere meets us. Had we but the men and means the work might be indefinitely extended.

*Third Day.*

Trials in Indore.

THIRD DAY.

Bright prospects.

In India the day seems to be rapidly coming when our difficulty will be, not to get a few to come out and confess Christ, but to properly receive and train those who in crowds will then come flocking into the Christian church. We are not ready for that day yet, and our great aim at present should be the training of those who may be able for this great work.

The work is not ours, and we can only hope for success as we allow our Captain to work in and through us. One thought has been brought home to some of us at least—that all the methods are needed, and further, that we are not going to gain our end by spending our strength in opposing the methods of those who do not work as we do.

The work is Christ's, and so too are the results. Let us expect large things, and in the strength which He can give seek for them to His glory, and we shall, ere another ten years pass by, find our grandest hopes far exceeded, and in the end we shall all, as we have so often sung together here, " Come home rejoicing, bringing in the precious sheaves."

## XX.—PUBLIC MORALS IN INDIA.

MONDAY, JANUARY 2ND, 1893.

LARGE HALL, AT 5-30 P. M.

(*Meeting for men only.*)

Dr. J. H. CONDON of Mussoorie, *in the Chair*.

Prayer was offered by the Rev. C. Harding, after which the Chairman said,—

That the subject of the evening divided itself, in his mind, into three principal parts: (1) the opium traffic in relation to public morals; (2) the liquor traffic and public morality; and (3) regulated vice and public morals. He suggested that that meeting of the Conference should pass a resolution upon each. In regard to the first, a letter had just arrived from the Chinese Christian churches of Hong-Kong for the purpose of being read to the Conference. He would read the letter:— *FOURTH DAY. Three subjects.*

"*To the Ministers, Elders and Brethren of the Churches in India.*

DEAR BRETHREN,—Opium coming to us from the West is destroying with increasing rapidity the people of our country, and it is to be feared that, if it is not speedily suppressed, it will spread itself over the whole world. Happily, there are men in England who through love of Christ have come to love others also, and who, being themselves saved, have come to wish to save others. They have established in London a Society for the Suppression of the Opium Traffic, thus uniting their strength to remove from the world this great evil, this obstacle to the spreading of the Gospel of Jesus, and, though no very tangible result has as yet followed their earnest labours during a period of nineteen years, yet they are, as it were, in the building of a high tower, making rapid progress. Opium is one of the greatest evils in the world, and only the greatest benevolence and perseverance, together with the blessing of God, will succeed in removing it. *Letter from China.*

We have heard that representatives have been sent from India to England to set forth the evils of the use of opium, and to urge the men of England to suppress it, and, though meanwhile unable to do likewise, the churches of Hong-Kong are of one heart with you in your efforts for this good cause. We

**Fourth Day.** pray that God will graciously help the speakers, that they may speak with power, and that He may comfort those who are engaged in the work, as He once comforted Simeon, when He promised that he should see with his own eyes the Lord's Christ before he should taste of death."

Dr. Condon said he did not see how it was possible to refuse to act upon this appeal from Christian brethren in China. Christians in India, China and Great Britain must stand together in the name of the Lord against the iniquitous traffic in opium.

The Rev. M. B. FULLER, M.A., International Missionary Alliance, Akola, Berar, said:—The letter to which we have just listened appeals to us as men, as Christians, and as missionaries. It is the cry of humanity from China, and appeals to our human sympathies. It is the cry of Christian churches, and appeals to us as fellow-disciples of Christ, and as workers for Him. When the anti-slavery struggle was going on in America, after a discussion in the House of Representatives, the Abolitionists were voted down. Charles Sumner rose and said: "Gentlemen, we have been out-voted, but remember that *this question will never be settled till it be settled aright.*" So of this opium question.

*Cry from China.*

Shall we simply look to see this battle fought out by others, or shall we not rather do all that we can to help in it?

I have been asked why I refuse a Government grant for our Industrial Training School. A dying Scotchman called his sons around him, and told them what he had to leave them, and how they should divide it amongst themselves. He then said: "My sons, it is not much that I have accumulated for you, but remember this, there is not a dirty shilling among it." There are too many "dirty shillings" in the revenue of Government for me to receive such money for God's work. I would not receive a donation for our work from a liquor or an opium-seller; and as long as Government continues to be the sole manufacturer and wholesale dealer in opium, I will not receive its money for our work.

*Refusal of grant-in-aid.*

It is said that Government must have the revenue. When I visit the opium hells, the schools where men are graduated into perdition, I say to myself, "If Government must destroy men, soul and body, for revenue, then *I will lessen the need a little by refusing the grant for our school."* I therefore take pleasure in moving the following resolution:—

FOURTH DAY.

"Having listened with much interest to a letter upon the Anglo-Asiatic opium traffic from our Chinese Christian brethren at Hong-Kong, addressed to the ministers, elders, and brethren of the churches in India, and written expressly to be read at this Conference, we express our sincere desire that this unrighteous traffic may be immediately abolished, so far as the production and sale of the drug for other than medicinal purposes is concerned. In view of the fact that opium has no legitimate use except as medicine, we regard its manufacture for common consumption for sensual gratification as an unworthy occupation for the British Indian Government to engage in, and one that is adapted to confuse and corrupt the public conscience as to right and wrong. As representatives of Christ among the perishing millions of Asia, we can have no fellowship with the unfruitful works of darkness, but must, on the contrary, reprove them. We unite with our Christian brethren in other lands in appealing to the people of God in Great Britain to persevere in the conflict against the opium iniquity, with faith for speedy triumph through the mighty power of our Divine Leader and Head."

Proposal.

Rev. R. M. BAUBOO, of the Free Church of Scotland Mission at Madras, seconded the resolution.

A member of the Business Committee of the Conference here rose, and said that that Committee had decided that no resolutions should be submitted to the Conference.

Business rule.

Mr. Alfred S. DYER, Editor of the *Bombay Guardian*, said that his name appeared on the programme to speak at this meeting. When the Provisional Committee of the Conference asked him to speak, no intimation was given to him that resolutions were to be excluded. He knew nothing concerning that till he arrived at the meeting that night. If he had been informed that he was desired to speak without bringing his subject to a practical issue by a resolution, he would not have consented to be there. He disputed the right of a committee to bind a Conference in that way without consulting it. He hoped that meeting would not be thus bound, but would proceed with the resolution.

The Chairman ruled that the resolution would not be proceeded with in face of the opposition.

Mr. Alfred S. DYER rose and said he had that morning received a letter from Mrs. Josephine E. Butler with reference to that

FOURTH DAY. Conference. Mrs. Butler had been for more than twenty years the leader of the Social Purity movement in Great Britain. He would read an extract from her letter:—

Letter from Mrs. Butler.

"I have heard that there is to be a great Missionary Conference at Bombay early in January, and that you will be permitted to introduce the subject of morality in India. My heart beats high with hope, for it seems to me this will be the first note of the call to a real renewed battle in India on the subject of repeal and of moral purging, which cannot but end in victory in God's own time. It is heavy on my heart continually that our Indian army and other officials have so despised the voice of the British people and Parliament as to continue under a slightly altered form the abominable system. I know well what horrors, what crimes, what crying iniquities and cruelties this means to the poor native women and to our own soldiers. I feel in my soul what must be the anger of God and the pity of Christ about it all. I could wish I was young and strong once more to put my head, however feebly, to the work, but if I am old and worn in body, I am stronger in faith now; for in so much I have '*seen*' the salvation of God,' it would be a shame if I had not faith; and I write you this line to say that I shall be on my knees in prayer for you and your friends on January 2nd and following days."

Mr. Dyer said that Mrs. Butler's letter indicated the expectations with which a large number of Christians in Great Britain were looking toward this Conference. They were expecting the Conference to take action regarding moral questions in India. He had, therefore, come to that meeting prepared to move the following resolution:—

Suggested resolution.

"This Conference expresses its abhorrence of regulated vice in any form; it hopes that the Imperial Government will insist upon obedience by British officials in India to its instructions based upon the resolution of Parliament, of June 5th, 1888; that thus the practical official sanction of the sin of impurity may no longer exist in this country, to the corruption of morals, and hindrance of the progress of the Gospel, especially in the districts immediately affected. This Conference further affirms that it is the duty of the Government to, as far as possible, remove temptation from the path of British soldiers in India and to create conditions conducive to morality and therefore to health."

Mr. Dyer said that if permission was refused him to move that resolution, he could not degrade himself by speaking under the fettering conditions which the Business Committee had imposed.

*Fourth Day.*

Mr. Henry VARLEY, Evangelist, who then spoke, touched upon the relation of purity to health. He said the average of human life was thirty-four years. With Jews, however, for special reasons, the average was forty-six, and with members of the Society of Friends it was fifty-eight years. This illustrated the connection between a high moral standard and longevity. Mr. Varley then passed on to allude to the immoral and unscientific system of regulated vice which, he shewed from the experience of France, fosters the disease it is designed to check. It would be the same in India.

*Purity.*

Mr. Varley said the subject of the opium traffic could not be excluded from the question of public morals. It affected the morals of other places beside India and China. He had seen the evil of it in Australia. In Melbourne, in company with Colonel Barker, of the Salvation Army, he had seen numbers of English and colonial women in opium dens, the slaves of the drug. The vice was spreading. Not a few through it had been drawn into lives of shame.

*Opium.*

The part he had felt called upon to take in rebuking vice in high social and political circles in Victoria was next alluded to by Mr. Varley. He was not a popular man in Melbourne. No one would be popular who was a true preacher of righteousness—righteousness in Government; righteousness in Conferences; righteousness everywhere. He and his friend Alfred Dyer had had some experience together in this matter in dealing with the Government in England. The time needed men of grit. He was not sure that that Conference had acted wisely. During its proceedings, men had been kept from speaking that ought to have spoken. Had there been a vote that morning on the subject of education as a missionary agency, he thought there would have been a very large minority in opposition to the speaking in favour of education. He had been pained by some of the things he had seen. He counselled them not to submit to such tactics. The great curse of Christianity was its lukewarmness. He was afraid that many were meriting the condemnation of the words: "Because thou art lukewarm, and neither cold nor hot, I will spue thee out of my mouth."

*An unpopular man.*

## XXI.—WOMEN-WORKERS' UNION.

MONDAY, JANUARY 2ND, 1893.

SMALL HALL, AT 5.30 P. M.

FOURTH DAY. Besides the members of this Union all ladies interested in women's work were invited to this meeting. About one hundred assembled. After singing and prayer, it was decided to devote half an hour to each of the following subjects :—

### I.—CONVERTS' HOMES.

Mrs. SMALL, F. C. M., *in the Chair.*

A Home necessary.

Miss WAUTON, C. E. Z., Amritsar, said :—A Converts' Home is an essential part of every zenana mission. I was led to see the necessity for it about fourteen years ago when converts were beginning to be gathered in through God's blessing on the school and zenana teaching in Amritsar. We tried the plan first of placing them in Christian boarding schools, but the companionship of those who had been in contact with heathenism was not good for Christian girls, nor was the routine of school life suitable for grown up women. After one or two other experiments we found that the simplest plan was to build a row of small houses in our own compound. This is enclosed by a wall with a gate which is locked at night. Each inmate has her own separate house, and cooks her own food. A kind motherly Christian woman is in charge, living by herself in one of the houses, and the whole is overlooked by the zenana mission house which is only a few yards off. So much for protection.

Support.

*Support* is one of the greatest difficulties. Our general plan is to give a fixed allowance of from 4 to 6 rupees according to the status of the convert, and let her earn whatever more is needed for clothing and etceteras by her own exertions.

Women from the sweeper caste have been trained as ayahs *Fourth Day.*
or nurses, those from a higher class as teachers and Bible-
women; plain needlework is a resource for others. We have
now a needlework class open daily, to which friends give a
small subscription of one or two rupees a month, and send us
plain work and mendings to do, suited to the capacities of
the women.

We do not think it desirable to keep the converts always in a
Home of this kind. We look upon it as a nursery necessary
for the infant stage of the convert's life. But in course of
time, wherever possible, we try to place them out in some
sphere where they can live a more rational and independent
life.

The question was asked—" How many women had passed out *Questions.*
of this Home?" *Ans.*—" I cannot quite remember, but probably
about twenty."

*Question.*—" Do you admit women of questionable character?"
*Ans.*—" No. As there is a refuge in another branch of the
mission, this is not necessary."

*Question.*—" Would you admit any one not a Christian, nor a
professed enquirer, but who might apply for admission?" *Ans.*
—" We have never had such a case. I do not know what I
should do. It would depend so much upon the circumstances
and the probable motive in the applicant."

*Question.*—" Would you admit a woman whose husband
wished to cast her off?" *Ans.*—" There is danger in this, and
it should only be done in very exceptional circumstances, lest it
should encourage men to desert their wives. I should
never do so, unless the woman were actually deserted and in
danger of being cast out on the streets."

The subject of the *training* of the women referred to above
was considered to be of great importance; the zenana mission- *Personal*
aries should learn to know each convert personally, and care- *knowledge.*
fully avoid reducing them to one level, as they possibly differ
one from the other considerably.

## II.—VISITING AMONG WOMEN OF DOUBTFUL CHARACTER.

Miss Abbott, A. B. T. M., Bombay, *in the chair.*

Miss Ward, A. U. Z. M., Cawnpur, opened the
discussion by a reference to the urgent needs of these

FOURTH DAY. women, and also to the embarrassments and perplexities of any work in their behalf. Miss Ward said:—

"My interest in this unfortunate class dates back twenty-two years, when I was one day accosted on the street by a sad-faced young woman, who said she wished to forsake the life she was leading.

Hindu society.

Owing to the evil customs of Hindu society many women seem to be forced into houses where they ought not to be, and certainly it is the duty of a missionary to carry the Gospel to "all the world," hence to these, but it is not our duty to educate and to render them more attractive. I would emphasize this, and that only old and experienced workers should be allowed to visit such houses.

Often we find those to whom such a life is wholly distasteful; by all means let us save such.

Not properly married.

Sometimes after we have visited a zenana long time, we find the woman has not been truly married to the man with whom she is living, and at Cawnpur we have been able to snatch a few of these as "brands from the burning."

One case that comes to mind is where a young girl was enticed away by a neighbour's son, and when we found her she had been living with this man for about thirty years. Probably we should never have discovered this was the case, had not the truth of Christ's teaching pierced her conscience, so that she confessed it.

Question.

*Question.*—" Would you teach dancing-girls in a school?" *Ans.*—" No, for I think such teaching would only make them more attractive, and their influence on the girls from pure homes might be for evil."

Dancing-girls.

Though some ladies decidedly negative the advisability of admitting dancing-girls into mission day schools, others quite as emphatically state their belief to be that the *little harm* of their influence was in so many cases overpowered by the beneficial influence of the Gospel-teaching they received day by day in the schools.

Mrs. WILDER, of Sholapur, gave an interesting account of the admission of a young dancing-girl into the mission school, which resulted in very much blessing to the child.

Mrs. HARDING, of Sholapur, agreed with the undesirability of the ordinary zenana visitor teaching such girls and women— more especially for Bible-women—to include such houses in their ordinary work.

The general consensus of the meeting was that *only* the Bible should be taught to women of doubtful character, and that by missionaries of experience.

### III.—BAPTISM OF WOMEN IN ZENANAS.

Miss CRITALL, I. F. N. S., Bombay, *in the chair.*

Miss A. N. BUDDEN, M. E. C., of Pithorgarh, Kumaon, in opening the discussion, said:—

When asked to open this subject to-day I declined for three reasons: first, that I felt there were others here who could do it much better than I could; secondly, because our work in the hills is so different from that in the plains; and thirdly, because my own particular station is so remote and lies so entirely amongst an agricultural class of people that unless I tell you something of my surroundings you will not know the reasons for my conclusions.

When my sister and I first began work in Pithorgarh, she used to go to the women in the villages, and they gathered together to hear her sing and talk. But in order to get closer to them we decided to have what in England are called "Mothers' Meetings"—sewing classes where cloth is sold cheap and the women taught to make their own garments. We sold the cloth at two-thirds the real price, and after sewing for an hour and a half they had a Bible lesson for half an hour. Thus we got to hear much of their homes and private lives, and when my sister urged one and another to give up their evil ways, they always responded that it was impossible for them to do so unless they could leave their evil surroundings. They asked for land to cultivate, and when my sister presented their claim at Conference the ladies agreed to buy land and build houses and start a self-supporting farm for those women who had no means of earning a respectable livelihood. More than a hundred women have been in the Home during the twelve years of its existence, and at the present time there are nearly sixty. Applications for admittance were made by several members of the sewing class whose husbands were able and willing to keep them, but these we steadily refused to take. First, because morality is so low on this point amongst the people—the marriage tie is so easily broken—that we felt we were bound to set a different example,

*[margin: FOURTH DAY.]*
*[margin: Mothers' meetings.]*

**Fourth Day.**

*Scriptural teaching.*

and our Home must in no way seem to countenance a woman's forsaking husband and children simply because she chose to do so. And, secondly, because on Scriptural grounds it seemed to me that a woman was not expected to accept Christ in this way, where it says, "He that forsaketh father and mother, wife and children for My name's sake," and in all equivalent passages the word husband does not occur. I wondered, therefore, whether this was not in accordance with so much else in Scripture which shews that a woman can best please and glorify God by faithfulness to her home ties. So we always discouraged those of our women from being baptized whose husbands were unwilling to part with them. Lately, however, I have come to feel differently. First, because when the husbands of some of these women died and we told them that now they were free to do as they desired and urged them to come we found the wish had died out and they obstinately refused to yield to our persuasion. Secondly, because during the last three years I have had a Sunday school class of about twenty-five Hindu men who have taught me much. Several of them have been as near to accepting Christ as it is possible to be without actually doing so. One thing and another has held them back from the final step, generally the claims of father or mother, wife or children, and I have been tempted to hope that their heart service would be acceptable to the Master, and perhaps they too were not called on to break up the family by a public confession. To my horror I have found that residence in a heathen home *necessitates* participation in heathen rites and ceremonies, and so they continually sear their own consciences by doing what they know to be wrong. This has revealed to me the reason why so many who try to serve the Lord Jesus, while they remain in their heathen homes, finally fall away and cease to love Him. If men, who are the heads of their own families, find public feeling too strong for them and are obliged to conform to heathen practices, how much more impossible must it be for wives and daughters-in-law to be able to refuse to do what is required of them? I have therefore come to the conclusion that if any woman has learnt to believe in the Lord Jesus Christ it is our duty to urge her to confess her faith by baptism, and then, in accordance with Corinthians vii. 13, 15, if her husband is willing that she should live with him, it will

*Duty of home ties.*

*Men's S. S. class.*

*Duty of confessing Christ.*

certainly be her duty to do so; but if he refuses, the blame of separation rests with him and not with her. Without baptism she is in no way cut off from heathenism, but once baptized she would be expected to refuse to join in heathen rites and ceremonies, and could faithfully serve and glorify her Master even in a heathen home.

The discussion that followed shewed considerable difference of opinion and practice among zenana workers.

Before the close of the meeting a suggestion was made that all Christian women-workers in India should be linked together into one general society of the Christian Women Workers' Union. There was no time for the discussion of this matter, as it was simply laid before the assembly, and the meeting was closed with the Doxology.

FOURTH DAY.

## XXII.—TRANSMIGRATION.

MONDAY, *January* 2nd, 1893.

LARGE HALL, AT 8-30 P.M.

### LECTURE UPON "THE DOCTRINE OF HINDU TRANSMIGRATION.

BY

Rev. W. HOOPER, D.D., C. M. S., Jabalpur.

*Chairman:* Rev. R. SCOTT, Wilson College, Bombay.

The lecturer said:—I have been asked for a lecture whose main object shall be the information of the Christian world on the subject of Hinduism. It is evident that a single lecture of such a kind can attain its object only by being strictly confined to one particular aspect of, or element in, that astonishingly complex and many-sided system, or system of systems, which we call Hinduism. Among the many aspects competing for notice, I have been led to select one belonging to *orthodox* Hinduism rather than the modern modifications of Hinduism which contact with Christian thought has produced, because I think there is a danger of our attention being drawn off by the far greater showiness and (to most minds) interestingness of the latter, to the comparative neglect of the former, which however is still the creed of $\frac{99}{100}$ of those who call themselves Hindus. And among the many elements of orthodox Hinduism which might have been selected, I have chosen "Transmigration" for the following reasons:—

1. To the ordinary Western mind, it contains something so grotesque, that it is very difficult to approach it seriously, and, as a matter of fact, I believe very few Europeans and Americans realise the exceeding force of the passive resistance which it offers to the influence and spread of the Gospel.

2. Though no part of the original religion of the Aryas, there being only one sentence in the whole Veda, and that in its later Brahmana portion, which can even be twisted into teaching this doctrine, yet by the time the philosophical systems were elaborated, it had sunk so into the consciousness of the people, that they all assume it without a doubt, and proceed to argue, not for it, but on its basis. The even approximate date of this marvellous transformation of the religious ideas of a vast people

cannot, of course, be ascertained in a land without a history: but the fact that Gautama Buddha, whose *latest* date proposed by scholars is 400 B. C., perverted the doctrine into something meaningless, proves incontestably, it seems to me, that the Aryas must have adopted it, to say the least, *many* hundred years before Christ. And to this day it remains, interwoven in the mental nature of the people, imbibed as it were with their mothers' milk, so that the mass of them cannot imagine a state of things in which it should not be true. Hence the absolute necessity, in the case of those who would replace Hinduism by Christianity, of understanding and appreciating it.

3. Though there can be no doubt that those who have received a Western education, and even others also who are brought into close contact with them, do not regard it as a point of such vital importance as the mass of the people do—I was surprised as well as pleased the other day, on giving a lecture on "Transmigration" in a very provincial town, to find that the leading men quite consented to treat it as an open question, and that no disturbance whatever was raised by my remarks—yet the degree to which it is considered essential to Hinduism may be gauged by two facts—

(*a*) The Arya Samaj, while professing to found their system on the Veda alone, have not dared—perhaps have not wished—to throw "Transmigration" overboard, proving thereby, perhaps more than by anything else, the inconsistency and insincerity of their movement.

(*b*) Those Europeans and Americans who have in these days attempted to reinvigorate Hinduism and Buddhism, and both to urge them and to lead them to resist the onset of Christianity, always make a special point of "Transmigration" and teach that specially in *this* respect those systems are superior to Christianity. True, the doctrine of Transmigration which they preach is not the Hindu one, and is still further from being the Buddhist one, as I hope to make clear further on; but, whether from ignorance or from malice against the Gospel, they endeavour to make Hindus and Buddhists, and their own countrymen, too, believe, that they are striving for the victory of a doctrine which *is* believed by the millions of India and neighbouring countries. This is the cause of the fact that "Transmigration" has latterly been brought to the front in Western literature, to an extent unapproached before; and this fact seems to me to constitute, along with the other reasons above given, a sufficient reason for seeking to enlighten the non-missionary Christian world, and the young-missionary world also, on the real nature of the Hindu doctrine of "Transmigration."

A few words will, I hope, suffice for an explanation of what this doctrine is. Imagine the whole universe, other than the impersonal, unconscious, imperceptible, indescribable, unchangeable substratum of it, commonly called "Brahma" (neuter), suddenly turned into a vast anthill. The universe is in Sanskrit (and modern languages derived therefrom) called by two words indicative of perpetual, aimless *motion*. The universe consists of two ingredients, *viz.*, innumerable souls and innumerable bodies. The bodies are of all kinds, mineral, vegetable, and animal; human, divine, and demonic. In the case of minerals—by which I mean whatever we call inanimate—it is not said where one body ends and another begins; but, for all that, they are, somehow, all bodies, *i.e.*, they are all possessed by souls; in other words, there is nothing really inanimate. Well, then, while the bodies are stationary, there is a perpetual movement going on among the souls. Souls are leaving their bodies and seeking other bodies somewhere in what we call the scale of creation; some are rising in that scale, some falling, some mounting to the highest Divine forms, others sinking to the lowest in hell; some moving across, on the same level, one way, and some the other way. And yet, in all this apparent confusion, there is really, as in the anthill, the most perfect order, the completest reign of *law*. That law is the law of *merit*. The amount of balance, on the one side or the other, of good works over bad works or the reverse,—the balance arising not only from the works done in the immediately preceding body, but from the aggregate of *all* previous ones, so far as they have not been already worked off by enjoyment or suffering—this balance determines, with absolute precision, both the body which the soul shall, at any given change occurring, inhabit, and also the more or less happy or unhappy life which it shall live in that body. There is thus no natural limit or end to transmigration; for in every body the soul is not only working off its old scores, but also laying up, by its inevitable working, stores of merit or demerit which will *necessitate* its being reborn in order to enjoy or suffer the fruit of its works; and so the balance is ever being adjusted, and yet ever being disturbed, and a new account, so to speak, opened. I have said there is no *natural* end to Transmigration; and yet Hindus believe one method by which it *will* be, and another in which it *may* be terminated. *All* transmigration is, after fabulously long intervals, brought to an end by the Pralaya, or Dissolution of all things, in which the whole ever-moving universe is for a while absorbed into Brahma; and *any* soul, which has been lucky enough not only to reach a human body, but also to study Sanskrit philosophy, may put a final end to all its wanderings by convincing itself of the profound lie, that itself and Brahma are identical; in which case all merit and demerit, previously acquired, are burnt up, and the rest of life is spent in works which have no moral character at all, and then, at death, it goes at once into that state which is the *summum bonum* of the Hindus, absorption into the formless, unknowing and unknowable Brahma, never again to be born, to act, to enjoy, or to suffer.

Now it may be conceded at once that there are two, or perhaps three, great excellences in this system.

1. It is a mighty bulwark against materialism. A person who believes, without a doubt, that himself is so far independent of his body, that he once inhabited other bodies, and will again inhabit still others, in the same sense that he now inhabits his present body, is not likely to come to regard the spirit as a mere function of the brain. And here we see what an enormous deterioration there is in Buddha's supposed reformation of Hindu doctrine. True, Buddha limits transmigration to things which have, in one sense of the word, some sort of life, and so far he avoids difficulties which, with modern science at least, would be insoluble; but this gain is far more than compensated by the tremendous loss involved in his rank materialism. There is in Buddhism no transmigration of souls, for there are no souls to transmigrate. What transmigrates is only the Karma, the result of the works done, the merit or demerit acquired; and also the desire to live. Buddhism is thus grossly materialistic; but Hinduism is, so far as this matter is concerned, spiritualistic; and we cannot exaggerate the advantage this is in dealing with its professors.

2. It is an equally strong support to the instinct of justice which is innate in human nature, and yet may so easily be overridden by false opinions. Indeed, it seems to me clear that it was this which originated the doctrine in question. The inequalities and apparent unfairness in the distribution of pleasure and pain in the present life are so glaring, that any theory which professed to redress them was acceptable; and to the sages of ancient, though not *most* ancient, India the theory of transmigration seemed to redress them most completely, and therefore it was accepted. According to it, every action, whatever its seeming importance, and whatever its moral character, must inevitably meet with a reward exactly corresponding, and exactly proportionate, to it; and whether the reward come sooner or later, come it infallibly must, and not a particle of it be lost on the way, or pass without being enjoyed or suffered by the doer of the action. The Buddhist transmigration involves the most manifest *in*justice; for the effect of my deeds in the present life will, according to it, be experienced *not* by me, but by some other being; but

the Hindu theory seems the very embodiment of perfect justice. Certainly, in my own experience it is as embodying such justice, and as alone capable of embodying such justice, that it is defended by Hindus; I do not mean so much by those who are arguing to maintain a thesis, as by those who are expressing their constant convictions. Indeed, so rooted in the Hindu mind is the idea of justice as at the bottom of transmigration, that the two atheistic systems of orthodox Hindu philosophy, the Sānkhya and the Pūrva Mimānsā, maintain it as stoutly as the rest. The others rightly contend, that the precisely correct allotment of bodies, and of condition in them, to the innumerable souls of the whole universe, according to the merits or demerits of each, or the exact balance of merit over demerit, or the reverse, in each case, demands a being of vast, practically infinite, intelligence and power; and it is to meet this evident want that they postulate that Ishwara or Governor, whose name Christians in North India have adopted as the Indian word for God. The two above-named systems, however, deny this want, maintaining that works produce their fruits by their own inherent tendency, and therefore require no Controller to ensure those results. But both parties are alike in this, that the world is ruled, down to the minutest detail, by the strictest, most undeviating, most inexorable *justice*. " Whatsoever a man "—or any other thing— " soweth, that *shall* he also reap."

3. The third advantage which I referred to, somewhat doubtfully, as lying in this doctrine is that it assumes, that embodiment is necessary for the soul to receive the due reward of its deeds. Like the Gospel, it teaches that we must all " receive the things done *in the body*, whether good or evil " and receive them *in a body*, too. It is thus opposed to that excessive spiritualism of the Greek philosophers, which made it so hard for them to receive the Christian doctrines of the Incarnation and the Resurrection, because to them the body was a cage, in which they could not imagine the virtuous or the pious being imprisoned after this life. But while this is an advantage so far as it goes, it becomes a disadvantage to the Christian advocate, because it satisfies that need, which the hope of the Resurrection is intended to satisfy. The Hindu does not ridicule the Resurrection as the Greek did; but he looks on it as a clumsy attempt to solve a problem, which his own wise men have ages ago solved in a far completer fashion. Still, for all this, the doctrine of Transmigration *does* offer a *point d'appui*, which the skilful Christian teacher may sometimes succeed in using as a basis for a belief in the Resurrection.

Having thus conceded, and that cheerfully and thankfully, all that I think may fairly be urged in favour of this doctrine, I proceed to point out what appear to me to be its defects—defects which far, very far outweigh all the advantages which it may possess. Let it be understood that I am dealing with the *Hindu* doctrine of Transmigration and with no other, though I may refer to modern theories of our would-be orientalising Westerns.

1. The defect which meets us on the threshold of our enquiry is, that the doctrine in question is both unproven and unprovable. No one professes to remember the actions, or any of the circumstances, of his former lives. True, this remembrance is said to have been a distinguishing feature of the semi-divine Rishis of former ages; and one of the powers which the practice of Yoga (or bodily mortification) is said, in the system called by that name, to procure is this same remembrance; and the law-giver Manu declares that the study of the Veda, and abstinence from hurting living things, produces this power; and consequently some maintain that it is only the decay of true Hindu practice which has caused its loss; but while all these are mere assertions and theories, the fact above stated remains, that no one in these days, however good and strict and pious as a Hindu, and imbued with Sanskrit philosophy, pretends to have the slightest remembrance of his former lives. Now this, of itself, would not, of course, disprove a theory; nor would it avail at all against a clear and strong proof of that theory; but, in the absence of such proof, it is fatal to it. It throws the *onus probandi* on him who defends the theory; and all that the defender of this theory can say is, that without it he cannot see how the world can be said to be governed by justice. So that if we can prove, as I hope to do presently, that the theory of Transmigration does *not* really conserve the interests of justice, and if in addition we can also prove, as all Christian advocates ought to je able to do, that the gospel doctrines of the Resurrection and of eternal udgment conserve those interests far more truly,—then the fact that Transmigration rests on no experience, but is only a theory, is sufficient to condemn it.

2. In dealing with Hindus, it may be well to dwell on the fact, that this doctrine is opposed, in its natural tendency, to other doctrines or practices which are as generally, if not as universally, considered essential to Hinduism as this is. I say "the natural tendency," for I do not mean to accuse Hindus of any insincerity in holding Transmigration along with the other points alluded to. All I mean is, that these various tenets, *if thought out*, would be seen to clash with each other; and if

thought out without prejudice, would be seen to be not reconcilable by the various devices which Pandits have invented of reconciling them.

(a) For one thing, Transmigration is opposed to that Pantheism, which is not only the one thoroughly orthodox system of Hindu philosophy (the other five, so far as incompatible with Pantheism, being regarded as only semi-orthodox), but is also a theory of the world as instinctively believed, apparently, by the mass of the people as Transmigration itself is. And yet, if the individual soul is really identical with the One Supreme Soul, and its apparent distinction from it, and consequently also the apparent distinction between different individual souls, are only the result of Māyā, or Illusion, then Transmigration itself is all an illusion; and where remains the advantage of contending for the belief that each separate soul pursues its own way through countless bodies, meeting in every one with the exact reward of its own works and no others, when all souls are really but one, with one another and with Brahma?

(b) For another thing, Transmigration is opposed to the doctrine of the eternity of souls. The former presupposes a vastly long chain, in which every link has two elements, Work and Fruit; each link being connected with previous ones by containing the fruit of their activities, and also with future ones by containing the work, which shall bear fruit in them. But this chain cannot, in the nature of things, be endless. There must have been a first link, in which there was only work, and no fruit. There must have been a first action in some body, determining the next body. But if so, souls cannot be eternal *à parte ante*, as Hindus maintain. God and Brahma *can* be, because Brahma does not work, enjoy, or suffer at all; and God, *i.e.*, Ishwara, works without enjoyment or suffering, being invented only to see that other workers enjoy or suffer rightly; but others, whose very *raison d'être* is both work and enjoyment or suffering, cannot be eternal.

(c) Again, Transmigration is opposed in its natural tendency to the Hindu system of caste, which, more perhaps than either it or Pantheism, rules the Hindu mind. For the whole system of caste is grounded on the idea, that what entereth into the mouth, or otherwise affecteth the body, *doth* defile the inner man; in other words, that the body dominates the soul, and the state of the former determines that of the latter. But Transmigration proceeds on the exactly contrary supposition, *viz.*, that the soul dominates the body, and by its conduct in one body determines what shall be its next body.

(d) Equally is Transmigration opposed to the ancient doctrines and practices connected with the worship of ancestors, and funeral ceremonies, which some Westerns maintain (paradoxically, it appears to me) to be the essential element in Hinduism. It is evident, that these arose from an exaggerated idea of the family, or tribe, as a living unit extending through the generations; the same idea, though exhibited in a very different way, as we see in the Old Testament, particularly in the patriarchal times, when the idea of a man's living in his posterity was very real and practical. But if transmigration is the right theory of life then it matters very little indeed who a man's ancestors or posterity is. The body which he last inhabited is of far more consequence than his father is; and the body which he will next inhabit is of far more consequence than his son is. Why, then, should he be so careful to perform the prescribed duties, and offerings, to his father? and why is the begetting of a son among his most bounden duties, and necessary, in fact, to his welfare in the next world? Here, as in the other cases, there is no formal contradiction between the two; but they proceed on totally opposite theories of life, and if each was carried to its logical results, they would conflict.

(e) There is another Hindu doctrine opposed to Transmigration, which is as Christian as it is Hindu; indeed, it is not a product of Hindu philosophy at all, but of the human heart under all systems, and revolting against many systems, and set on a solid foundation by the Gospel alone. I allude to *belief in the mercy* of God, or of gods. Mercy seems to me the sole *raison d'être* of the 33 crores of gods, and 9 crores of goddesses, acknowledged by the Hindus. I am not speaking of them as mere results of tradition or speculation, but as living in the lives and hearts of the people. There is absolutely no room, as we have seen, for mercy in the system of Transmigration. According to it, the universe is dominated, in every part and every detail, by one idea alone, that of justice; and, such is the completeness of the system, there is nowhere a loophole by which the poor sinner can hope for even the slightest mitigation of the due reward of his deeds. Nor can Ishwara, though personal, help in the matter; he exists solely to carry out this inexorable, inflexible justice; mercy is no prerogative of his. It was necessary, therefore, for the convicted human conscience to posit some *other* divine being or beings, lest it should be reduced to utter despair. And, though it often seems as if the Hindus had no conscience, but were dominated by intellect and by system alone, yet they really *have* consciences, and sometimes those consciences can be got at, and then it is seen that there are more things in their heaven and earth than are dreamed of in their philosophy. And here we have, it seems to me, a foothold for the gospel. Though we must oppose polytheism on the one hand, and that hope of Divine mercy off-hand, *i.e.*, without justice, on the other, which is so natural to human nature everywhere, yet we must welcome the inconsistency which refuses to bind up everything to inexorable justice alone, and show them, for one thing, how much better is one Lord of mercy than numberless independent ones, and for another thing, what a wondrously worthy scheme is that, by which the claims of justice and mercy are fully and finally reconciled and blended.

3. I think the practically strongest argument against Transmigration is this, that its claim to moral power and value breaks down in practice, and instead thereof only an *immoral* effect is produced by it. To a foreigner, knowing the doctrine in question only from books, one can easily understand the attractiveness of the system. And Col. Olcott must certainly be reckoned among such, in spite of his travels and speeches throughout India, for he does not, I understand, know any vernacular. I once heard him descant with almost burning eloquence on the moral effect of believing Transmigration, as far greater than that of Christianity. What, he asked, could possibly prove a greater deterrent from sin, or incentive to virtue, than the belief that the former will inevitably produce a series of miserable lives, and the latter a number of happy ones? Yet converse with the *people*, and see whether their belief in this doctrine, which is firm indeed if any one's is, has any such effect at all. Talk to a Hindu in trouble, and find out what he is thinking about. He will tell you he is very unlucky, fate is clearly against him; and why? because the effect of the sin of past lives is *inevitable*. He does not reproach himself with that sin, it does not affect his *conscience* at all; it survives with him only in the form of *ill-luck*. So thoroughly is this the case that the same words are constantly used by the people for luck, good or bad, and the effect, good or bad, of the actions of past lives. This effect is supposed to be written invisibly on the forehead of each person; and, what is there written, is always spoken of as *fate*. But it is evident that, whenever happiness or misery are regarded as *luck*, they cease to have any moral value, any effect on the conscience, at all.

But is this result of the doctrine of Transmigration inevitable? May it not be an accidental coincidence? No, it is only according to the laws of the human mind. Conscience cannot work where there is neither memory, nor the possibility of memory. It does not accuse us, or commend us, for acts done so early in life that we could know nothing of them but for information given by others. Words uttered in deep sleep might indeed be put down to our merit or demerit, because they might indicate what our thoughts *had* been when we were awake, and which we *can* remember;

but if we could not by any possibility remember anything which could give rise to what we uttered in sleep, then conscience would have nothing whatever to say to such utterances. If, therefore, we could remember the actions of our previous lives, and could consequently really believe that we should, in coming lives, remember those of this present life, then belief in Transmigration would surely do us moral good, by deterring us from sin, and inciting us to virtue. But how can suffering in the present life do us good by being believed to be the fruit of sin which we cannot by any possibility remember? and how can the happiness which we believe we shall, in a future life, enjoy as the reward of present virtue do us good, when we shall not then remember our present virtue? The truth is, that belief in Transmigration not only fails to do the moral good which is claimed for it, but it does positive moral harm by making people believe in the existence of sin where conscience cannot work. The bare belief of sin, without the conscience of sin, is a soul-destroying belief, as can easily be seen. And any one familiar with Hindus can soon see that the self-attribution of sin, where there can be no conscience of sin, is a terrible hindrance to the work of conscience where it *can* work, i.e., with regard to the sins of the *present* life. Conscience, being unable to work where sin has been mostly attributed to oneself, is too paralysed to work properly where sin ought to be attributed to oneself. Suffering is, practically, ill-luck; no wonder, then, that its real causes, which are easily preventible, are not discerned, and even when pointed out to them are not removed. What the Musalman attributes to the will of Allah, the Hindu attributes to sins which he cannot, and could never, remember; both causes are equally independent of themselves, and the belief of both equally tends to deaden the conscience. What makes the Christian pause, and ask, and think what special message there is to him from his heavenly Father in the suffering which, perhaps, he finds he has brought on himself by a course of conduct which he can well remember and blame himself for, or, it may be, is sent him, without any special fault of his own, to draw his heart upwards—that makes the Hindu only bewail his hard fate; and, as we know, suffering which does not soften, only hardens. Of course, I do not mean that suffering never does moral good to Hindus; most of us, I suppose, know cases in which it has eventually brought them to Jesus; but this is *in spite* of their belief of Transmigration, and would not have been possible without a happy inconsistency.

4. But the evil of this belief is nowhere more clearly seen, than in the conduct which it induces towards *others* in sorrow. Most of us are familiar with what the Hindus call consolation—the pouring vinegar into the

heart's wound by assuring the sufferer that his suffering was inevitable, being the remorseless fate produced by the sins of his former lives. But this is only negatively evil;—what shall we say, then, of the cruelty to widows, because they are regarded as the causes of that bereavement, which is their lifelong cup of woe, and *theirs* more than any one's besides? O, if there were no other charge to be laid at the door of the doctrine of Transmigration, the unpitied tears and sighs of 21 millions of Indian widows, and the sin and degradation to which many of them are almost driven by the treatment they receive, would be enough to damn it utterly and for ever in the minds of all right-thinking people!

5. A less practical, perhaps, but a more fundamental objection to the doctrine is that it presupposes, and therefore confirms, radically false conceptions of the relation between soul and body. If the soul of a man and that of a spider can exchange tenements with no more inconvenience than might be involved in two people exchanging houses, then it is plain that bodies bear no necessary, or even natural, relation to the souls that occupy them. According to the doctrine in question, nothing is really human, or equine, or bovine, or belonging to any other species, except the *body* in each case. To talk of human duty, and human virtue, and human intellect, has no meaning at all except so far as these qualities are regarded as essentially material, being the result of the body inhabited for the time being. As a matter of fact, Hindus *do* so regard them; and thus the pure spiritualism, which at first sight the doctrine of Transmigration seemed to conserve, is found to give place to a degrading materialism. The merit and demerit which, as being purely spiritual qualities, the soul is supposed to carry with itself from body to body, are found to be the result after all, not of the soul's own activity, but of the influence of each body upon it; and thus the Hindu doctrine is seen to be practically, neither much more spiritualistic nor much more preservative of justice than the Buddhist. I know that the comparison of the body to a house, and of the soul to its tenant, is common among ourselves, and in our Scriptures, as a popular figure of speech; but what does no harm when thus used may do infinite harm when received as a matter of faith. One would have thought that the fact that, with only such exceptions as prove the rule, no kind of shell-fish can inhabit the shell of another species would have sufficed to cast doubt on the universally received hypothesis, that a soul can inhabit the body of another kind as easily as its own. The fact, as we all know, is that the body is only a term for the aggregate of material particles which may at any moment happen to be in vital connection with the soul; and is consequently changing every-

moment, while the soul remains the same. Otherwise put, the body is only the *expression in matter* of the soul; and each soul has its own expression, which it can no more exchange for that of another soul of even the same species, not to speak of those of other species, than one star can exchange its own effulgence, which surrounds it, with that of another star. This truth is not taught in our Scriptures, except so far as it may be implied in the figure of the seed and the plant employed by the Apostle; but certainly our Scriptures contain nothing against it. In Hinduism, on the other hand, no one can receive it without throwing overboard that doctrine of Transmigration which has for 2,500 years been an essential part of Hinduism.

6. I have said that these strictures apply to the doctrine of Transmigration as held by *Hindus*, not as elaborated from the brains of Europeans and Americans. Those who have read Sir Edwin Arnold's "Light of Asia" must have been struck by the exceedingly beautiful thoughts which he puts into Gautama's mouth in the closing sermon. The system of Transmigration is there pictured as a universal system of *moral and spiritual improvement.* Souls are represented as gradually rising from lower to higher species; or, if there be a fall, it is only temporary, and followed by a greater and steadier rise afterwards. As the soul ascends in the scale, it gradually loses whatever is low and debasing which clings to it, and becomes purer and more ethereal, and more and more worthy of that Parinirvana, in which the desire to cease to exist is finally and for ever gratified. Now, as I have said, this picture is a very beautiful one, but it exists only in the brains of certain Europeans. I have mentioned that Buddhist Transmigration is not really of *souls;* but I am not referring to that now, for Buddhists, with a delightful inconsistency, *do* teach a transmigration of those souls, whose existence they theoretically deny. What I am anxious to make plain is, that neither in Buddhist nor in Hindu Transmigration is there any notion at all of moral or spiritual improvement. It is simply a vast engine for securing that merit and demerit receive their due *rewards.* The notion, right or wrong, is an *old-world* notion. It has nothing in common with the modern tendency (itself a one-sided effect of Christianity) to look at *character* rather than merit, and therefore to think of the various states through which the soul passes as preparations for those to follow. Buddhism itself (though inconsistently as I have said above) utterly contradicts its would-be Western interpreters, when it maintains that he, who appeared in the world as Gautama, had once been a frog, twice a thief, once a gamester, ten times a lion, four times as a serpent, and so on; not by any means in any order of gradually ascending

superiority, but in the most delightfully chaotic arrangement, or disarrangement, as regards priority and posteriority. And so it is with Hindu notions; the gradual improvement of souls is certainly a *conceivable* theory of Transmigration, but it is as foreign to Hindu belief as Christianity itself is.

These remarks have been suggested to me by the last objection which I have against Transmigration as believed by Hindus. It is, that its direct tendency is to make its adherents *worldly-minded*. A very conceivable theory of transmigration would be, that virtue was its own reward; that the result of the cultivation of continence, and patience, and contentment, and integrity in the present life would be that in the next life we should find ourselves *more* self-restrained, and gentle, and contented, and straightforward than we are here. Such a theory would do good, in spite of the absence of any effect of it on conscience. But that is *not* the Hindu theory, or the Buddhist either. They believe that the reward of virtue is *earthly* prosperity and happiness. It is of those who have plenty of money, and servants, and equipage, and show, and large families of sons, and obtain positions of authority over others, that they infer great virtue and piety in a previous state of existence; *not* of those who are *now* very virtuous or pious, as such. I do not mean that the Hindus do not value that peace of mind, which we believe to be the chief reward of goodness; on the contrary, they make a great deal of it; but it is with them the *work*, which requires the reward, and not the reward of other work. Now, any one can see that those who believe that moral excellence leads only to outward happiness must, so far as they are affected by that belief, tend to put outward happiness above moral excellence, and to value the latter only as a means, or the means, to the former; in one word, to become worldly-minded. And, as a matter of fact, this *is* the state of the vast majority of Hindus. So it is, it may be truly said, of the vast majority of people everywhere; and, moreover, it cannot be denied that there are some Hindus who are in this respect, as in others, better than their creed; but professing Christians, who are worldly-minded, are so in spite of their creed, as would be acknowledged even by unbelievers; whereas Hindus are worldly-minded *by reason of*, and in logical consistency with, their belief of Transmigration. Whether the same effect would be produced if they did not hold this doctrine it is idle to speculate; but those who know them intimately can plainly see that their worldly-mindedness is, to a very great extent, indeed, the direct result of their belief of the Doctrine of Transmigration.

I have now finished my account of the charges which I think may be justly brought against the Doctrine as actually held, for millenniums past as well as now, by the vast majority of the 200 millions of Hindus, our fellow-creatures, and nearly all of them our fellow-subjects. In conclusion, I can only express the hope, that any mistake in fact of which I may have been guilty may be brought to my notice, any want of candour or tenderness may be forgiven, and whatever I have said that is true and good may be used by Him Who uses our poor efforts, and overrules our errors, for His own glory, to the overthrow of untruth, and the establishment of His Truth throughout this land.

## XXIII.—CONFERENCE SERMON

Delivered by the

Rev. G. Kerry, B. M. S., Calcutta,

on

Sunday, *January* 1st, 1893,

in the large hall, at 3 p. m.

---

*Acts xxviii.* 15—"*He thanked God and took courage.*"

These words are spoken of the Apostle Paul when he had reached the vicinity of the city of Rome. He had now come to the end of one period of his life and ministry and was about to begin another. He looked back on his past—his travels, his perils, his persecutions, his danger only recently passed of shipwreck—upon the manifestation of God's grace and power in all his past labours; and he thanked God, God had been true and faithful, the grace of the Lord Jesus had been sufficient for him according to the promise. And he looked forward. It was natural that he should do so. We all try to do so—often in vain, for the future is dark to mortals. In the usual sense it was as dark to the Apostle as to others, but for light which shone on his way as it shines on the way of faithful and loyal servants of the Master. The light came from the past, it was lighted by his thankfulness, as he thanked God for all the past, and for the present cheering of his heart in the meeting with the brethren who had come out to greet him from the city of Rome. He could look into the future—he did not know much—but he could see something, and he took courage. He knew there was still work to be done, toil to be endured, dangers to be met, but he could not be dismayed. The same God who had helped in the past would help him in the future. If God were for him what cause had he to fear?

We have been speaking of this year as the Centenary of Modern Missions, that is, of Protestant Missions—of Protestant Missions as carried on by British and American churches—and this seems a fitting time for us to look back and to look forward even as the Apostle Paul did, to look back with thankfulness, and to look forward with courage. This I ask you to do.

1   Let us look back and see what cause we have for thankfulness to God.

A hundred years ago the British churches were doing nothing to give the light of the Gospel to the nations of the earth. They were busy largely about their own concerns, which no doubt demanded earnest and constant watchfulness and care. Many of them were sinking into an almost lifeless condition. The large divine purpose of God in giving the Gospel of His Son had been lost sight of. The people of God cared for themselves and not for others. But God had not forgotten His purpose and He wrought a change in the hearts of His people. It is interesting to note some of the preparatory steps leading to the stirring of Christian hearts with something of missionary enthusiasm. Of course, we think of what took place in 1792; but the Spirit of God was working before that time. The missionary spirit is largely aroused by hymns. Now, years before the formation of the Missionary Society, some of our most stimulating missionary hymns were written by men whom I think God taught, and their words express the beginning of indistinct but true desire for the extension of Christ's Kingdom among men.

In 1696 Tate and Brady sung and taught the saints of the Church of England to sing—

"Let differing nations join
 To celebrate Thy fame,
 Let all the world, O Lord, combine
 To praise Thy glorious name."

Then in 1768 Mr. Bruce wrote with glad hope—

"Behold the mountain of the Lord
 In latter days shall rise,
 On mountain tops above the hills,
 And draw the wondering eyes."

And in 1772 was written the hymn beginning—

"O'er the gloomy hills of darkness
 Look my soul, be still and gaze;
 All the promises do travail
 With a glorious day of grace,
  Blessed Jubilee!
 Let thy glorious morning dawn."

These and similar devout utterances shew how the Spirit of God was working in many minds, teaching them to understand more fully the divine will. Then in 1784 the celebrated Jonathan Edwards sent forth to the churches of America and Great Britain his memorable call to prayer for the extension of the Kingdom of Christ; this call led to the establishment of the monthly missionary prayer meeting which continues to this day among many of the churches of the home lands.

It was at about this time that there began, what Andrew Fuller called, "the workings of brother Carey's mind" which bore fruit in the establishment of the Baptist Missionary Society. Missionary work, so far as our English churches are concerned began with William Carey. And in this there is to be noticed the wonderful choice of God, of whom the Apostle says (I. Cor. i. 27 and following verses):—"God hath chosen the weak things of the world, and the base things of the world, and the things which are despised hath God chosen, that no flesh might glory in His presence." *God made choice of William Carey.* Think of that poor, hardworking, shoemaking lad, starting life with but an elementary education, bound down to grinding poverty for years. He was a quiet gentle well-behaved lad, with nothing striking to ordinary observers about him. He was from the first curious about many subjects, observant, studious and thoughtful. The grace of God touched him when yet a youth, moved him, renewed him, and he became devout, prayerful and earnest as a believer in Jesus. He soon began to preach in cottages and small village chapels to people with as little education as himself, many of whom were simple God-fearing men who appreciated his humble ministry.

He still makes shoes and preaches the Gospel; this preaching stimulates his mental nature and he becomes more studious than before, especially of God's Word, and strives to fit himself for the work of preaching. Hence he tries to learn Greek and Hebrew that he may read the Word in the original for himself. There is one department of knowledge which had a special attraction for him, that is, what we term geography. The school manuals of to-day were not in existence, and he had few helps, but such as came in his way he took advantage of; books of travel had a great charm for him. That which interested him chiefly was not the physical features of the countries of which he read, their mountains and valleys and plains, the rivers and lakes, nor even the varied productions of these countries, but he considered the people, their condition of civilization and their religions. He had learnt to do the ordinary work of stitching mechanically, and found that he could, by fixing the book in front of the seat on which he sat, read and work at the same time. Then he prepared for himself a map of the world and placed that before him. Thus there was brought home to his mind a vivid representation of the varied languages of the world and of the ignorance and sin of its people, and at the same time there was borne in upon him a revelation of the far-reaching cove of God, and that the Gospel which saved and gladdened his heart was for the world. And the momentous question arose in his heart, "Ought not Christians to do something to make known the Gospel among those who are ignorant of it?" This question he answered for himself in the affirmative, and then he propounded it to his brethren. To his question he received many answers; some had doubts, others had objections, and some met his question with a scornful "No?" But he persisted in putting his question. A fire was burning in his heart, a Divine fire, which could not be quenched. This fire spread, some other hearts kindled and burnt also. He had meantime attained the position of a recognised minister of a Church of Baptised believers, and thus commanded a little more attention to his proposals. He then published as a pamphlet his remarkable treatise entitled "An enquiry into the obligations of Christians to use means for the conversion of the heathens." Soon after, he preached his memorable sermon before many of his ministerial brethren and other Christians with the two heads of his discourse, which read to-day like the inspired words of God—"Expect great things for God, and attempt great things for God." Six months after the preaching of this sermon twelve men met in a private house at Kettering, and, after prayer and gifts, formed the first Missionary Society in the British Isles.

The beginning was small, the first subscription amounting to £13-2-6. Just then Dr. John Thomas, who had been to India in the service of the East India Company, appeared on the scene. God had been speaking to him also. And his heart was moved with compassion for those who knew not the way of salvation. After some delay he and Carey started together for India: the mission thus became an accomplished fact.

Andrew Fuller, the first Secretary of the new society and others, travelled among the churches of England and Scotland, urging the claims of the nations of the earth on all Christian hearts, and met with a liberal response from many Christian men and women of all denominations. Yet to many, even good men, this idea of missions to the heathen seemed Utopian. Good men held back and hesitated. Politicians had fears and apprehensions of trouble in India as the result of efforts to convert the people of this land. The East India Company was opposed to the enterprise. The literary classes, when they condescended to give heed to what a few feeble Christians proposed to do, wrote and spoke strongly against the mission. One spoke of Carey as "the consecrated cobbler," and thought he had said a smart thing. Some of those who followed were designated as "apostates from the anvil and the loom." But this thing was of God; neither the scorn and contempt of worldly men, nor the coldness and doubt of Christian men, nor the opposition of rulers, could hinder its progress.

Soon other denominations of Christians caught the holy enthusiasm. The London Missionary Society was formed, then the Church Missionary Society, and one after another the other churches organised their plans and sent forth their messengers with the glad tidings of God's salvation through Christ for the nations. And now the churches of America and of Australia are rivalling British churches in their labours of love for the people who know not the Saviour.

Keeping pace with the growing zeal of the churches God's providence worked in a marvellous way, for when Christian missions in this era began, the world was almost closed against the Gospel. China, Africa, the islands of the sea, and India itself were sealed against the entrance of the missionary. But the seals have been broken. The doors are now wide open and cannot be shut.

Then in the past hundred years think of the grand succession of Apostolic men whom God has raised up for this work. Every church has on its roll the names of men who counted not their lives dear unto themselves so that they might make known the Saviour's name among the nations. We to-day here are surrounded by a new cloud of witnesses. Time would fail to tell of Serjent and Fenn, of Lacroix and Mullens, of Duff and Wilson and Anderson, of Judson and Boardman, of Morrison and Newton and Butler, and of hundreds more, who through faith did their work, and whose names remain as an inspiration to us and to the young Christian life of the churches from which we come.

Then, God is giving to the mission a marvellous additional power for diffusing His Gospel by the enlistment of holy women in this great undertaking. In the zenana missions God is giving back to His Churches a ministry of mighty power which, in this country, is becoming not only a ministry to women, but also to youths and young men. What consecrated enthusiasm these women are shewing and bringing to the work of evangelisation, and they come by scores and hundreds, and God is blessing their work. The women of India, long neglected, ignorant, superstitious, and, till within a recent period, inaccessible, are now hearing the wonderful, the old, and the ever new story of the love of Christ, of Him Who was born of a Woman that He might bring peace and salvation to women's hearts.

And what great things have been accomplished in the past century. The Word of God translated; a Christian literature being developed; the Press used, to spread the truth abroad; the Church of Christ planted; people by hundreds of thousands gathered to the Good Shepherd; heaven enriched by the redeemed from India; additions made to the great multitude gathered from all nations and tribes and people and tongues, who stand before the

Lamb clothed in white robes, and palms in their hands, saying "Salvation to our God Who sitteth on the throne, and to the Lamb." All this and much more has been accomplished in face of contempt and scorn, which have not yet ceased. We can afford to disregard it all. In a marvellous figure of speech the psalmist of old said, "He that sitteth in the heavens shall laugh, the Lord shall have them in derision." We too can smile at the contempt and opposition of men of the world and even of men of the Church.

Looking thus backward, and hastily and imperfectly scanning the past of missions, surely we may thank God to-day.

II. But we have to look forward. We are beginning a new era of missions. We cannot yet rest though we be thankful as we are. Toil is before us; there is yet much land to be possessed. We have to enter on the labours of our predecessors. It will not be well for us to-day to congratulate ourselves on the achievements of the past and there let the matter end. The glories of the past are to stimulate us to renewed activity and zeal. In the days of our Lord there were men who passed for very pious Jews, who looked back with pride to the prophets of a past age—heroic men who had been slain for their faithfulness to God's truth. These pious Jews built the tombs of the departed worthies and honoured them much. Notwithstanding our Lord calls them the children of those who slew the prophets, for they had the same disposition which their fathers had, and proved this by afterwards killing the Prince of Glory. We are not to look back in a self-satisfied and dreamy fashion which brings no sense of personal responsibility and duty. What we see in the past is but a trumpet call to more earnest works for the Lord.

The Apostle "took courage." The word shews that he realised new perils and dangers, but that he was not dismayed at them. We too need to take courage. Courage, faithfulness and hope are needed by us to-day as much as they were needed by our forefathers. The difficulties and dangers are not all surmounted. New difficulties and questions will arise. In the new century we shall meet with new conditions of work and new perplexities; some of these are already coming to the front. We shall need all the grace and wisdom our God has promised to give us. God will fulfil His promise, so that as we thank God we may well take courage. Take courage, brethren and sisters, God will not fail us. His promise is sure. Jesus lives and He has all power in heaven and in earth, and lo! He is with us always.

I wish to emphasize this—*take courage*. When the eye of faith is dim and the heart of love cold, or cooling, it is not an uncommon thing for missionaries to become despondent. One could easily mention a hundred things which to human eyes seem to forbid hope of the full triumph of our work. But we may remember with thankfulness what God has done already, and may find safe anchorage in the revealed purpose of God. The vision is for an appointed time, and though it tarries it comes, it *will* come and will *not* tarry. The sword of the Spirit, which is the Word of God, is still keen-edged, sharper than any two-edged sword, it needs no sharpening; it has only to be wielded with faith and prayer and the slain of the Lord will be many. It is not our duty to look for discouragements, they will appear without our search. It is on the other hand our duty and privilege to look at the encouragements, and thank God they are not far to seek. Whilst we have to-day the same resources of Divine grace and power, which our fathers had we have more means of another kind of reaching the people than have in any former age been in the possession of God's servants. We have the Press, schools, the means of rapid travel, and personal safety. Then we are permitted to see a wonderful weakening of prejudice in the minds of the people; enmity and misunderstanding is weakening also. Christian ideas of thought and speech are spreading in many places, there is a perceptible drift towards Christ. The new era has verily begun, bringing to us its own calls for patient work and unfailing courage.

There are two ways of looking at the new conditions of our work. We may be dismayed by them and regard them as the working of Satanic power and a sign of our own weakness and ultimate failure; but then we may regard them as the movements of human thought and feeling, under Divine and gracious guidance, a portion of the process of mysterious working by which Christ is subduing all things to Himself. By the one way of looking at these things we shall be moved to despondency, but by the other our courage will become bolder and more daring. Thus there is the spreading scepticism of the day as it affects the minds of the educated classes of the Indian people. Without doubt it is a sad thing to see men turning from the light of life and sinking into deeper darkness: but what if the usual and natural order of things be, that men who have been beguiled and deceived by a false religion should as by a rebound go to the opposite extreme, from super-belief to no belief at all? The scepticism then, instead of being a sign of failure, is a sign of progress; it is a mark showing that something has been accomplished; it is only disappointing if the advance stops there with unbelief. But we are not to believe that it will stop there. The Lord is accustomed to lead the blind by a way that they know not.

Then again some of our number have been filled with something like consternation by a threatening flood of nominal Christians of whom possibly only a small percentage may be genuine Christians. We think what a caricature of the Christian name and life will be given to the non-Christians. We ask how these numbers are to be instructed and elevated. How are scorners to be silenced? But I would say— What if this small movement of the mind towards Christ be a part of God's plan of raising people to a state of hallowed communion with Himself? What if this partial recognition of Christ as the Redeemer of men be the springing blade indicating the beginning of spiritual life? Are we to trample it down, and to fight against God? There will be only disappointment if a mass movement towards Christ stops short, if the *ear* is not developed from the blade and if there be no sign of the full corn in the ear.

Then following and accompanying this increase in the number of those who call themselves Christians, I think I see signs of a greater independence of thought and action and speech among Indian Christians. Some have already broken somewhat away from our missionary and ecclesiastical organization. In Calcutta certainly this has happened, and I think we shall see more of this. Possibly it will be attended by some evils which we shall deplore. Hitherto our converts have been bound to the missions with which they are connected, in a large degree by monetary bonds with the more intelligent of them, also by the natural dependence of new converts upon those from whom they have received the Gospel; but as years roll on these bonds will weaken and there may be a drifting away from missionary guidance and control. Hitherto the dependence of the converts on the missionary has been productive of one good thing, they have received what is held by us all to be the essential verities of the Christian faith. So far as I know no heresy of false doctrine has raised its head among the churches of Christ in India. The only unorthodox teacher who came from America, a Unitarian missionary of singular earnestness and zeal, made no impression on our converts where he laboured, and little on the Hindu and Brahmo Somaj community. But the growing independence and freedom of thought and opinion among some sections of the Indian Christian community may, and I think will, lead to a stir and commotion which may bring out ideas contrary to the truth as it is in Jesus. It will not be surprising if the next century should witness a resuscitation of errors and doctrines and practices of which we read in early Church History. And we shall have to deal with such circumstances as God may help us. For this we shall need courage as well as wisdom.

There is one thing which strikes me as remarkable about our Indian Christians, and that is the little regard they have for the church organizations introduced from the West by us missionaries. The converts can pass from one mission and one church to the other with the greatest ease. Generally speaking they have no special reverence for Episcopacy or the Presbytery, or for Independency. They have received Christ more or less intelligently, and ecclesiastical arrangements are to them but minor and accidental circumstances which have not taken hold of their minds. It seems to me that this state of things will not continue with a large part of the converts. There is a yearning in many Indian hearts for an Indian church—a longing to be free from leading strings. This desire is becoming more pronounced year by year, and in the near future we may be called to deal with it. It will be disappointing to some of us, but I think we should be ready to help and guide it if we may. We may remember that the Lord rules and will care for His own; and from what we may regard as disaster and may feel as a disappointment He will bring forth His glory.

Brethren, what we specially need is courage, the courage of hopefulness, of daring, of bold enterprise; courage quickened in us by God's Holy Spirit; stimulated by the remembrance of what God has done and of what He declares He will yet do; courage which perceives the dangers around us, which understands human weakness and impotence, but which realises the Divine power and presence. The history of God's doings in the past hundred years may well excite us to thankfulness and courage. It seems to me that in no age previous to the present century has God more fully manifested Himself to build up and extend the Kingdom of His Son than He is doing to-day. Christ's people on earth are making the Saviour's prayer their own, "Father, glorify Thy Name;" and the answer still comes from heaven with solemn voice, "I have both glorified it, and will glorify it again." The multitude to-day, as when the first answer was given, understand not the answer. The people then said that it thundered, and to-day they say, the answer we hear and know is a delusion. But it has been given to us to know the Scripture and the power of God. We believe, because we believe we are and ought to be full of the courage of hope, and of assured victory.

I rejoice to think that many hearts are filled with expectation of seeing greater things yet in connection with the coming power and glory of our Lord Jesus. The hope is expressed in different ways by God's people who are to-day waiting for the consolation of Israel. There is to be a glorious appearing of the great God our Saviour Jesus Christ. He is coming to take His Kingdom. There are signs that lead many to think this is near at hand. And we may expect, we may watch for, the rising of the Morning Star. It is not for me to say here whether that appearing of our Lord will be what some call a "personal appearing," or whether it will be by a new fulfilment of the words of the prophet Joel whose words had a fulfilment on the day of Pentecost, "It shall come to pass in the last days saith God that I will pour out of My Spirit on all flesh; and your sons and your daughters shall prophesy and your young men shall dream dreams; yea and on My servants and on My hand-maidens I will pour out in those days of My Spirit and they shall prophesy, and I will shew wonders in heaven above, and signs in the earth beneath, blood and fire and vapour of smoke. And it shall come to pass, that whosoever shall call on the Name of the Lord shall be saved."

It is not easy for us to read the signs of the times, but we may read them in part, and as I read them I think that I see, that God's time of blessing for the world is drawing nigh. The salvation of God is at hand and we may see it and our children shall see it. Wherefore, brethren, let us thank God to-day and take courage.

## XXIV.—MISSIONARY STATISTICS.

SIXTH DAY.

By the Rev. J. W. THOMAS, Baptist Mission Press, Calcutta.

Introduction. During the long process of compiling the Statistical Tables recently issued, the compiler was again and again made to feel that he had to work under tremendous disadvantages which seriously militated against the efficiency of the work. Several months before there was any thought of submitting the subject for the consideration of the Bombay Conference, it was decided, in consultation with the Statistical Committee, that a pamphlet should be issued, after the publication of the Tables, embodying their views, and making sundry suggestions for the guidance of others who might subsequently be engaged in similar work. When it was suggested by the Provisional Committee that a paper should be prepared for the Decennial Conference, the writer recognised the superior advantages of the plan and unhesitatingly acceded to the request.

Had the original plan been adopted he would have had the advantage of the help and advice of the Committee with whom he had been working for upwards of a year, and who would probably have shared the responsibility of the publication of the pamphlet; that Committee has, however, practically dispersed, two members being at the present time in Europe, so that the writer of this paper has to accept the sole responsibility for its contents. As he will have to refer largely to his personal experience in the compilation of the Statistical Tables, he having had most to do with their preparation, and as the suggestions he has to make are all the result of his own experience in connection with that work, he must request permission, at the risk of appearing egotistical, to write in the first person, the nature of the subject being such that any other course would seem pedantic and stilted.

Importance of the subject. It will not be necessary to devote much space to enforce the importance of the subject; this is generally admitted. There are some who are on principle opposed to the "numbering of the people," but these are comparatively few. Of the hundreds of schedules sent out, only *one* was returned through the post, "refused," and though, owing to some unexplained causes, there was considerable delay in getting in many of the returns, when the forms *did* reach those for whom they were intended, for the most part, the replies were prompt and cordial.

The number of copies of the Tables subscribed for, and the numerous enquiries made, when the publication was unfortunately delayed, show that a good many in the mission field are interested in the Decennial collection of statistics. It cannot be denied that not a few take but little personal interest in tables of figures, still most missionaries are aware of, and accede to, the demand for returns, called for by Home Committees, and those who support mission work, and it is believed that most men will recognise the advantage of a periodical review of the entire field, and systematic arrangement of the results, such as is provided for in the Decennial Tables of Statistics. To be of any value, however, it will be at once admitted that such statistics should be complete and reliable, and the purpose of my paper is to suggest some means for ensuring accuracy as far as it is attainable.

Most missions which publish reports put in Tables of figures, but these are all on such totally different lines that it is impossible to make much use of them for the purpose of preparing *comparative* Tables, such as those which have been published for the past five decades; of this any one may convince himself if he will only take the trouble to compare any half dozen reports that may fall into his hands.

It is perhaps premature to expect Missionary Societies to agree to any radical change in the form in which their statistics shall be presented to their constituents, or indeed any such change as shall obviate the necessity of collecting special Decennial statistics or very materially lessen the labour of collating them; still, if the matter be fairly brought to their notice, some modification and mutual approximation of the present divergent plans, may be found not impracticable. This question will be reverted to later on, there are other preliminary points which need to be first settled before we can even enter on a discussion of it.

The subject of my paper as given in the provisional programme was "A Plan of Uniform Missionary Statistics:" this is a

*(marginal notes: Sixth Day. / Title of Paper)*

**Sixth Day.**

**Co-operation.**

**Central Committees.**

wider subject than I propose treating of in this paper; I intend that all my remarks and suggestions should lead up to it, but in the limited space allowed to me I must, for the most part, confine myself to what from the first I contemplated—improved methods of collecting missionary statistics—and I wish it to be understood that, for the present at least, I limit the term to Decennial statistics, though later on I shall have something to say on the subject of the publication of Tables of figures in Annual Reports.

The first step towards acquiring improved methods of collecting statistics, and through them any plan of Uniform Missionary Statistics, will be to ensure the hearty co-operation of all interested in the results sought. When I was considering the form of the Title Page of the present Tables, I naturally turned to the former Tables for 1880, and there found it stated that they had been prepared "with the concurrence of the Madras and Bombay Conferences." I do not know what may have been involved in this, but as I was not aware of any such co-operation in the preparation of these Tables, I was compelled to leave out that line from the Title Page.

This want, which I keenly felt from the first, presented the most serious difficulty with which I had to contend in the task imposed on me, and I should wish to emphasize as strongly as I can the utmost, nay, absolute need, for co-operation the most thorough, in any future attempt to collect missionary statistics.

I would suggest that the matter be taken in hand *at once*, without waiting till another eight or nine years have passed, and that a Standing Committee be appointed at each of the three presidency towns to take all necessary steps for the proper collection of statistics when the time for so doing shall arrive, each Committee to undertake the collection of returns for its own district; the request for returns will come with more force if it is known to come with the combined authority of the Missionary Conferences at the presidency towns, and, still more so, if this Decennial Conference will strengthen that authority with its own imprimature. These Central Committees would decide on the form of the schedules to be issued, and on the jurisdiction of each, so that no part of the field should be overlooked; they would also collect the schedules when returned, and check them by previously prepared lists, to ascertain if any are missing; it would also be necessary for them to arrange the returns in the order in which they should be published; whether they should do anything more would be a minor detail which could be determined by consultation subsequently.

*Sixth Day.*

It will probably be found helpful to secure the co-operation of local Conferences, such as those at Allahabad, Lahore, Bangalore, &c., throughout the country, the essential point being to awaken such an interest in the work as that it may be taken up earnestly and with business-like promptness everywhere.

So far I have contemplated the continent of India only, but I assume that Ceylon and Burma will unite in the proposed collection of statistics; it would be necessary for the missionaries in these two countries to appoint their own Committees to undertake the duties of the Central Committees as above described.

*Ceylon and Burma.*

One very important point to be considered by the Standing Committees will be the fittest time to collect the statistics. It is a patent fact that the supplying of statistics is a most uncongenial task for most men; I have heard of one missionary who never supplies, even his own mission, with figures for their report; the statement may be exaggerated, but there is no doubt that the call for statistics is unwelcome to, perhaps, the majority of men, and one they would gladly dispense with, if possible. I have myself met with remonstrances from some, who resented the trouble of collecting figures for the Decennial statistics, when they had only recently gone through the labour of collecting them for their own mission. I would here repeat the suggestion already made in the Introduction to the Statistical Tables, that efforts should be made to supply each missionary with the Decennial schedules at the time when he would be engaged in collecting similar returns for his own report, so that the labour entailed on him may be reduced to a minimum. The Central Committees might ascertain from local secretaries when statistics are collected for their missions, and the requisite forms supplied accordingly.

*Time for collecting statistics.*

It may seem to some that it ought not to be very difficult for any one who has recently supplied figures for his own report to fill up a schedule that will only require a little different arrangement of the figures; in the case of a mission which gives pretty full returns in its reports, and where a local Secretary is

SIXTH DAY.

intimately familiar with the various stations in the district, he would probably be able, with no great expenditure of time or trouble, to fill in the schedules required for the Decennial statistics. I believe the late Mr. Badley supplied the returns for most of the stations belonging to the American Episcopal Methodist Mission in the N.-W. Provinces, and probably there was no one better fitted for the task; but for some missions it would not be so easy to obtain similar results.

When the original schedules were sent out, it was requested that with the forms, when filled up, a report of the mission for the year 1890 should be supplied; the intention of this may have been for purposes of reference in cases of doubt, and I certainly found these reports invaluable in many cases to supply omissions.

Deficiencies of reports.

In not a few instances reports were sent in *in lieu* of the schedules, accompanied sometimes with a very courteous note, to the effect that the writer was sure I should find everything I required in the report. Those who thus failed to fill in the forms, in order to save themselves some trouble, little knew the amount of labour they were imposing on the compiler. What would probably have taken any one an hour or so to do, who was familiar with the report and with the work at the station, involved many an hour of weary work—in one or two cases the whole of three evenings were devoted to the study of *one* report, and after all the result was not satisfactory to myself. Would it be deemed impertinent on my part to hint that a good many reports might be vastly improved in this matter of statistics? The tables in use were probably drawn up many years ago, and have not grown with the growth of the work, and in the case of others which have indubitably grown and attained a luxuriance which must delight the heart of such as revel in figures, perhaps some slight modification, or addition, would render them more serviceable for the purpose of comparison with returns from other missions.

I should like to be permitted to refer to a few of the reports I have had to wade through in the course of my labour, that I may point out some of the special difficulties I have met with. Let me premise that if I criticise, I do so in no unfriendly spirit, and solely in the hope that the subject may be taken up by others interested.

I shall commence with the report of the society to which I have the honour to belong, the Baptist Missionary Society. In the matter of schools, the number of schools is not stated, and though the numbers of boys and girls are given, the day-school teachers are grouped in one column, the respective numbers of each sex not being given; an additional column or two would be very desirable. One very noticeable feature of this report is, that the wives of missionaries are quite ignored, and, except for incidental references in the body of the work, it might almost be concluded that it was a mission of celebates. <sub>Sixth Day.</sub> <sub>Bap. Miss. Soc.</sub>

In the report of the B. Z. M., while pretty full returns are given at the head of each station, the various stations are arranged in no sort of order that is easily intelligible to the uninitiated, making it a somewhat difficult task to collect the returns in tabulated form; several of the stations either gave incomplete returns, or none at all, giving the impression that the returns are not drawn up on any uniform plan. A tabulated list at the end of the report would greatly add to its value.

In the London Missionary Society's report the number of teachers engaged in the various schools reported is not given. <sub>Lond. Miss. Soc.</sub>

The Church Missionary Society's report gives the number of boys and girls separately, but lumps together all the schools, so that it is not possible to ascertain how many there are for each sex; and as to teachers, we are merely told how many Christian teachers there are and how many non-Christian, a very important item of information by-the-bye, but how many of these are women, we have no means of knowing. Sunday schools are totally ignored, a serious omission in the present day of special activity in this branch of mission work. <sub>Church Miss. Soc.</sub>

This last remark applies equally to the report of the C. Z. M., and indeed to most of the reports for 1890 that fell into my hands.

The Wesleyan Missionary Society's report gives the number of attendants on public worship, and these I have had to assume as the total number in the Christian Community in cases where I had to appeal to the report for information; I felt, however, considerable doubts as to whether this met the need, as the heading states that the column includes scholars as well as members, and I could not be sure that a good many of these scholars may not have been heathen children, who attended the schools and were willing to attend Christian services. <sub>Wes. Miss. Soc.</sub>

**Sixth Day.** The number of Sabbath schools is given with the number attending, also the total of day schools, and the total attendance, including boys and girls, the numbers of each are not reported, nor is it stated how many of the teachers are men and how many women.

There is one column in this report which may serve an important purpose in the economy of the Wesleyan Mission, the bearing of which is not very clear to an outsider. It is headed, "Total number of scholars who attend *either* Sabbath or week-day schools;" it is evidently intended to show the full scope of mission work among the young, and I do not mention it for the sake of criticising it, but in order that I may make a suggestion which may serve as a hint to Dr. Phillips when he next tries to get in statistics for his own department of work. It might be interesting to know how many of those who attend Sabbath schools *also* attend day schools; and it would not be very difficult for teachers to obtain this information, and for Superintendents to enter it in their returns called for by the S. S. Union.

I need not add to the list, sufficient has been given to show what difficulties any one has to contend with who attempts to draw up comparative tables with the help of reports alone. As I have already said, we can hardly expect the various societies to adopt any radical change in the form in which their statistics are given to the public, and even if the small defects pointed out above were remedied, it would still go a very little way towards the filling up of the schedules required for the Decennial Statistical Tables. These are necessarily more elaborate than are required for ordinary purposes, and few reports give returns as full as those published by the American Episcopal Methodists, in dealing with which, indeed, my especial difficulty lay in the bewildering multiplicity of details.

**A suggestion.** It would vastly help in the work of collating the Decennial statistics if all the Missionary Societies would agree to print in their own reports the form of tables adopted by the Statistical Committee, *in addition* to any others they may require for their own purposes. If some such course were followed, the work of collecting Decennial statistics would be rendered a comparatively easy task, and the expense would be very considerably reduced, by being to a large extent distributed over the different Missionary Societies. [Sixth Day.]

As it is hardly likely that any such plan will be, for the present at least, very generally adopted, we have to fall back on the plan that has been followed for half a century, and collect the statistics at the close of each decade. I would here repeat the hope I have already expressed, that arrangements may be set on foot at once for the carrying out of this object. In the introduction to the tables recently published, a suggestion has been made which I wish to emphasise, as I regard it of considerable importance. When any new country has to be surveyed, the usual plan is to take a general survey of all the more striking features, and subsequent surveys fill in the details some such plan I would urge on any who may undertake the work of collecting Decennial statistics in the future. A full year before the time let reports be collected from all Missionary Societies, labouring in India, Burma and Ceylon; from these supplemented by all local information available, full lists of stations and mission agents might be prepared, which should later on be submitted to local Secretaries, and their co-operation sought in revising the lists, and bringing them up to date, supplying omissions, and indicating changes that may have taken place during the year. [Work to be put in hand early.]

These revised lists might be sent with the requisite number of schedules, to such local Secretaries, or to any who would be willing to assist in the distribution and collection of the papers; should any delay or neglect occur the Central Committees could more easily ascertain the fact and take steps to remedy the omission, than any one at a distance could possibly do. If some such plan were adopted, and all joined in hearty co-operation in the work, the Statistical Tables of 1900 will undoubtedly be the fullest and the most reliable of any that have ever been issued.

There is one more point that I cannot overlook; whatever plan be adopted, whether the one I have sketched out in these pages, or any modification of it, the carrying of it out will necessarily involve considerable expense, for which provision will have to be made. It is hardly likely, after the experience connected with the Tables of 1881 and 1890, that any Publishers will undertake the expense and risk of bringing out another set [Fund to meet initial expenses.]

SIXTH DAY. of similar Tables, without some guarantee against loss, nor would it be fair to expect that they should. The trouble and expense connected with the preparation of these Tables is considerable, nor is the demand for them such as to make it a paying speculation. The work is one in which most missions have direct interest, and all Missionary Societies, particularly the larger ones, should join to meet the initial expenses which will be inevitably heavy, and which are increasing each decade with the increased complexity and magnitude of missionary operations.

The suggestion I would offer is that each Missionary Society should be asked to contribute Rs. 20, or 50, or 100, according to the extent of its operations, or if it is decided to begin operations at once, each might be asked to contribute Rs. 5 or 10 a year towards the initial expenses, half of this sum to be refunded in copies of the Tables, when issued, for the use of the Home Committees.

I must now leave the subject to others to discuss, and I trust to bring to a practical issue. I shall be quite content if my suggestions shall prove in any measure helpful towards improving the methods adopted for the collection of Missionary Statistics, and still more so if they should lead to any Uniform Plan of Statistics being ultimately adopted.

## XXV.—HOW CAN OUR EDUCATIONAL WORK BE MADE MORE EFFECTIVE AS AN EVANGELISTIC AGENCY?*

By The Rev. M. Phillips, L. M. S., Madras.

This topic suggests three things : (1) that the work of missionaries in India is to evangelise the people ; (2) that education is an agency used for that purpose ; (3) that there is room for making it more effective.

I. There can be no two opinions among Christian people that the *sole* work of missionaries in India is to evangelise the Hindus. They are the messengers of the churches of Europe and America sent out for this express purpose. They are 'ambassadors for Christ, beseeching the heathen to be reconciled to God.' They are therefore bound to do all in their power to commend the Gospel to the people. Their chief and only aim should be to *convert* souls, to found churches and place Native Pastors over them ; and so to build up a strong Christian community that they may both sustain the Gospel among themselves and propagate it among their countrymen. The motto of every missionary should be "India for Christ," and every mission agency should be directed and made subservient to the accomplishment of this great end.

II. Among the mission agencies used to bring the Hindus to a living knowledge of Christ, education occupies a high and honourble position. Missionary Education includes schools of all grades, from A. B. to B. A., and also Industrial Schools. I suppose, however, that the latter do not necessarily come within the scope of this paper, and therefore I shall pass them by.

It must not be supposed for a moment that it is the function of missionary societies to educate the Hindus as a *nation*. This gigantic work can only be done by the Government and the people themselves ; and it is gratifying to note that both the Government and the people are waking up to a sense of their duty, and are putting forth increasing efforts every year to cover the

---

* The Provisional Committee asked Mr. Phillips first of all to write a paper on this subject, but at a later date, when drawing up the final programme and when some rearrangement was necessary, it was thought best to ask him to prepare a paper on Work among the Educated Classes in which work he is chiefly engaged. However, Mr. Phillips had already prepared the paper on the first subject, and in consideration of this the Committee gladly consented to print it at the end of the Report.—Ed.

land with schools. The question, therefore, that I have to consider is not, "How can missionary societies extend their educational agency so as to overtake the education of the *masses?*" or, "Whether they should *compete* with the Government and the people so as to counteract the influence of the non-religious education of the former and the anti-Christian education of the latter?"; but *simply* "*How can they use the limited means at their disposal for education so as to make it more effective as an evangelistic agency?*"

This can be done only by using their educational means for the *sole purpose* of building up and extending the influence of the Indian Church. Thank God, we have now a Church in India, gathered principally by the preaching of the Gospel to the people in their own tongue. It is small when compared with millions who are still in heathenism, but large enough for missionaries to make it the *base* of their operation against Hinduism. No one can doubt that India must be converted by means of her own sons and daughters. Foreign missionaries have *now* arrived at such a stage in their work as to make it their *paramount duty* to direct energies towards the consolidation and extension of the Indian Church. Hence all their educational work should be carried on for the promotion of this object.

But it may be contended, "Just so, that is the principle on which we carry on our educational work at present." That is true to a certain extent, for all missionary education is *intended* to evangelise the people and so to *increase* the number of the Indian Church. The difference between what is advocated here and the principle on which missionary education is carried on at present is this. Most, if not all, of our schools and colleges have been established and are being carried on, *irrespective of the needs of the Indian Christians* with the view of giving Christian education to non-Christian Hindus. The *chief object* is the education of the heathen as the means of evangelising them, and not of the Christians as the means of elevating them. What is maintained here is *that the process should be reversed*, and our educational work carried on *chiefly with the view of benefitting the Christians*, and so to make the Indian Church learned, strong, and capable of influencing the heathen far more extensively and powerfully than at present.

III. The adoption of this principle is what is suggested in this paper as the best method of making our "educational work more effective as an evangelistic agency." What does this principle imply?

1. That no school should be established by missionaries except as an auxiliary to the efficiency and immediate extension of the Indian Church.

I know that this will be regarded by not a few as a short-sighted policy, as 'walking by sight and not by faith,' but I am content to be in the company of the Apostle Paul, who in all his efforts among the Gentiles expected " some fruit." To establish schools among the heathen with the hope that they may be the means of bringing them some day to the church is of little value, as experience has abundantly proved. But when a village, or some families in a village, embrace Christianity, or express a sincere desire to embrace it, a day-school should be established to teach the children, and a night-school to teach as many of the illiterate adults as can be induced to attend. The school-room should be made the centre of evangelistic work in the village. The people should be invited to assemble there on week days and Sundays for prayer, Bible-teaching and public worship. Hindu children may be admitted to be taught with the Christian children, should there be sufficient room and teaching power.

In such a village, under such circumstances, an elementary school *only* would be necessary. But should the Christian children of a town or village be such as to require a middle class school, it should be provided. And in a district worked by a society, where there are a large number of Christian youths requiring a higher education than that afforded in a middle school, a high school should be established. It is a waste of time and resources, however, to place a foreign missionary in such a school. Every high school should be put in charge of a competent Christian graduate, and as many heathen boys should be admitted as can be accommodated without incurring extra expense.

Mission colleges should be established and conducted on precisely the same principle. One fully developed Christian College in each of the three presidencies would probably meet all the higher educational wants of the Indian Christians at present. These colleges need not belong to one missionary society, but may be the joint property of all missionary societies. Every society labouring in India should contribute its share towards their support. They should be Christian Colleges in the sense that they are *expressly for Christians*, non-Christians being allowed to attend as far as space and teaching power will admit. As the Scotch missionaries have a peculiar aptitude for this kind of work, and as they have a fully developed college in each of the three Presidency towns, would it not be well for all Protestant societies to entrust the higher education of Indian Christians to them? For the accommodation of pupils from a distance, hostels could be provided in connection with every college and placed under the direct supervision of missionaries. Every college should also have a chapel where the students can meet for prayer and worship. Missionaries of the different societies which support the college may be asked to help the Professors to conduct worship in the college chapel on Sundays.

If this plan were adopted, the large sums of money now expended by different societies in carrying on their colleges could, after deducting the amounts allotted to the joint colleges, be expended on scholarships to enable the children of poor Christians to pursue the higher education. A large number of missionaries could be set at liberty to preach the Gospel who are now chiefly engaged in secular education-work. Our colleges would be placed on a permanent footing in the estimation of the people, for they would know that their continuance does not depend on their patronage; and educational missionaries would feel that conversions need not endanger the existence of institutions in which they feel deep interest. The people themselves would estimate Christian education far more highly than they do at present, when under the impression that our schools are only nets to catch their children. Lastly, the adoption of this plan would be the means of raising the Indian Christian community intellectually and socially—a consummation to be most earnestly sought after, as being far-reaching in its influence on the ultimate evangelisation of India.

To carry on the higher education as at present for the sake of the higher classes with the hope of converting them to Christianity is almost a waste of money; for, as a matter of fact, our colleges are the means of producing scarcely any converts *now*! It is true that the first missionaries, who gave such an undue impetus to this method of mission work, had a few converts from the higher castes. But, notwithstanding their zeal and earnestness, we cannot view the history of Indian missions for the last fifty years without having the conviction forced upon us that they greatly erred in judgment by departing from Apostolic methods, and were the unconscious instruments of inflicting a severe blow on the work dearest to their heart, which has greatly retarded the progress of the Gospel in India.

For their plan, having been largely adopted by all missionary societies has been the means of diverting very considerably the stream of missionary energy from the work of vernacular preaching to the masses. It is very much as if the Apostle Paul had settled down in Jerusalem and gathered around him a few of the Scribes, Pharisees and Sadducees, to teach them Hebrew literature and philosophy, with the hope of *indirectly* convincing them of the truth of Christianity. Or, as if the eloquent Apollos had opened a school in Corinth to teach the Epicureans and Stoics rhetoric, with the hope of saturating their minds with the sayings and doings of Jesus by selecting passages from the Gospel for reading and reciting. How much poorer the world would have been to-day had the Apostles adopted this plan! Aye! and is not India much poorer spiritually to-day than it would have been had the Christian Church not deviated from Apostolic methods? For the past fifty years the direct work of missions has been crippled by the diversion of its energy to a wrong channel. And even now the stream is only beginning to turn backwards. In the presidency towns educational missionaries predominate out of all proportion. In Madras there are about fifteen as against two who preach in Tamil, the language of the people. Had the men and money expended on schools and colleges been thrown into the Apostolic method of preaching the Gospel everywhere, the number of Indian Christians would probably be much larger than it is at present. The history of the triumphs of Christianity in the past ought to teach us that the *divine method* of converting the world is *from the lower to the higher*, and not *vice versâ*. In India this is a pre-eminently wise Providence, for had the caste-keeping Hindus embraced Christianity *first*, there is every probability that they would retain their caste distinctions in the church. But as the lower classes have no caste properly so-called, in proportion as they rise in the intellectual and social scale to an equality with the caste-keeping classes, they will be able to receive the latter to the church on equal footing with themselves, and caste will quietly disappear.

A contrast is often drawn between the success of the first educational missionaries in gaining converts and the failure of those who are now engaged in the same work. This is both unfair and misleading. It is a reflection upon a number of hardworking brethren whose devotion and earnestness are beyond suspicion. How is it, then, that they do not gain converts like their predecessors? Partly because preparation for University examinations, which the students now consider the "be-all and end-all," so absorbs their time and thought that they are unable to give the same attention to religious instruction as students in former days; and partly because missionaries *now* are not so ready to support converts as they were *then*. Many high caste youths come to me every year and offer to receive baptism on condition that I keep them in college till they take their degree. Educational missionaries could easily lay their hands on such and many more if they felt justified in baptizing them on this condition.

But it is maintained that the education given in missionary colleges facilitates the work of conversion. All English education, which is saturated with Bible truths, does this more or less. It clears away superstitious weeds from the mind and prepares it for something higher and purer. But there is no reason to believe that mission college education does this much more effectually than any other college education. Certainly, the serious commotion, amounting to a mutiny, which shook the Madras Christian College to its foundation (the best institution of its kind in India) four years ago, because one of its sudents expressed a wish to be baptised, does not bear out the contention that missionary education facilitates conversion. The students, numbering about 400, held public meetings to express their "horror and dread" at the idea of one of their number embracing Christianity. They visited the would-be convert in the house of the missionary who sheltered him, and used every means at their disposal to dissuade him from being baptised, and with the aid of his relatives they succeeded. Had that student belonged either to a Government or Hindu College, there is no probability whatever that any such commotion or mutiny would have taken place. Indeed, there was no commotion among the students of the Maharajah of Vizianagram's College when one of its students was lately baptized.

Let us, then, give up the fallacy that these institutions are agencies for converting in any but a very vague sense of the term; and *let our colleges be kept up for the sake of the Indian Christians.* Let them be used primarily for educating our Pastors, Evangelists and Teachers of the higher grades, and for qualifying Christian youths for the learned professions. I know few things more conducive to the welfare and enlargement of the Indian church than the occupying of responsible positions in the Government Service, in the Medical Profession, at the Bar, and in Banks and Mercantile Houses, by Indian Christians. If we spend as much money on them as we spend on Brahmans, there is no reason why, in a short time, they should not occupy the same positions of influence and emolument which are now almost exclusively held by Brahmans. At any rate, it is the *first duty* of missionaries to do all in their power, by means of the higher education, to bring them forward to that goal.

And we have every encouragement to set about the task, for there is no lack of ability in the lower classes from which the majority of our Christians are drawn. Ethnologically they are the same people as the middle classes, who rank next to Brahmans. There are only two distinct races among the Hindus, viz., the Aryans and the Aborigines. The former are represented by the Brahmans of to-day, who form but a small percentage of the inhabitants of India, and the latter by the middle and lower classes.* The difference between the lower and the middle classes is of the same nature as that between the peasants of England and the great middle class population. When Christianised and educated, therefore, they are quite capable of holding their own, not only against the middle classes, but against the Brahmans also.†

But we are told that the higher education is the *only means* of bringing the Gospel to bear on the higher classes, and that if we withdraw

---

\* See Professor Oppert's Bharatavarsa.
† At the last Madras examinations of the Optional Branches of the B. A. degree, Native Christians passed 71·4 per cent., Brahmins 66·9 per cent., and non-Brahmin Sudras 52·4 per cent.

from it as an evangelistic agency, we abandon the most important part of the Hindu population. This is not so. People of all castes listen to the preaching of the Gospel in their own tongue every day, and among them a good sprinkling of women. Educated Hindus, as a class, cannot be so well reached by this method; but they can be reached by English Lectures, Literature, and House Visitation.

There is no fear that English education will suffer in case missionaries withdraw from it as is often asserted. It is the means of getting on in the world, and Hindus are shrewd enough to get it, even though missionaries and Government were to withdraw from it.

One thing is certain and cannot be too strongly emphasized, *viz., that should our schools and colleges be the means of bringing any number to a public profession of Christianity, they would be hopelessly emptied!* This is placed beyond a doubt by the conduct of the Christian college students, already referred to, and by the nascent spirit of patriotism which finds expression in many good things, but which is antagonistic to the adoption of what is considered a "foreign religion."

But it may be answered, "The schools of Duff, Anderson, Wilson and others were often emptied on account of baptisms but were soon filled again." Granted; but circumstances have changed since their time. There were no rival colleges in their day where pupils could pursue English education which alone pays at competitive examinations for Government service. Now, however, there are plenty ready and willing to absorb all students from missionary institutions. And if there were not, the people themselves would soon provide them.

2. It follows from the principle advocated in this paper that, *as a rule*, no teacher who is not a Christian should be employed in mission schools and colleges. I say, *as a rule*, for there may be circumstances in which non-Christians may be advantageously employed, but in no case should they predominate as is often the case at present. This proposition will probably be met with—"Yes, it would be much better to employ Christian teachers, but they are not forthcoming." True, and who is responsible for this? Is it not missionary societies which expend money on the education of the higher and richer classes at the expense of neglecting the education of the Christians who are too poor to avail themselves of *unaided* college education? Consequently, we have not a sufficient number qualified for our work. Better by far to prepare teachers first and then open schools and colleges with assistants in sympathy with our work, than to call in the aid of heathen teachers who, if not aggressively opposed, are by their example and influence stumbling-blocks in the way of the progress of our *real* work. That a few

heathen teachers are not far from the Kingdom, I am convinced, but that the great majority of them, though they speak glibly and write eloquently of the blessings of Christian education, are nothing better than designing hypocrites who laugh at the credulity of their employers, I am equally convinced. When religious lectures are delivered to educated Hindus, they are generally conspicuous by their absence.

3. No books should be taught in mission schools except such as are thoroughly Christian. The curricula appointed for Government and University examinations must unfortunately be adopted. But in all *other* classes Government books should be discarded and only Christian books taught. Great prominence should be given to the Bible; it should occupy the first hour in every school and college and never be relegated to the afternoon; nor should the number of hours for teaching it be curtailed when the time of examination is drawing nigh.

The Bible should be taught by converted, earnest men, who are anxious to bring others to a living knowledge of its truths. Perfunctory teaching of the Bible by dead-alive Christian teachers, though nominally an evangelistic work, is really of no use. What is wanted is the living and faithful pressing home of the teaching and life of Christ. It is as necessary to employ only converted men for this kind of work as for the work of preaching.

4. The principle laid down in this paper involves, if carried to its logical conclusion, the giving up of Government grants. For the taking of Government money does undoubtedly hamper us in the internal arrangements of our schools. Government looks to *head and brain* qualifications; we must look to *heart* as well. Government will not give grants to teachers who have not passed certain prescribed examinations. An earnest Christian man who is fully capable of teaching a class, but who has not passed the prescribed examinations, must be set aside in favour of one whose heart is stone-cold, or who is a heathen, simply because he is a passed candidate. I do not object to recognised examinations, but when we consider our educational institutions *in the light of spiritual agencies, we ought not to give the first place to mere intellectual attainments*. And here it is that the bondage of taking Government grants comes in. I am not prepared, however, to suggest that we should give up Government grants. What I suggest is that *we lose no time in setting about qualifying our Christian youths for all the requirements of our educational work*. This will take some time. Meanwhile, we must go on as before till we can man our educational institutions with scholastically and spiritually qualified teachers.

## Female Education an Exception.

The time has not yet come when girls' schools among non-Christians can be conducted on the principle advocated here.

1. Because female education is not so firmly rooted in India as to dispense with the aid and stimulus of missionaries. It will be a great work done if we can so create a desire for female education as to induce the people to carry it on of their own accord. And we are in a fair way of doing this. To teach the girls to read, write, and to do needle-work is a source of great comfort and joy to them when they settle down as wives and mothers. And as they are more impressionable than men, the religious knowledge which they acquire will not be forgotten; and if not the means of their conversion, will open their eyes to the folly of idolatry, and be the means of inducing them to promote the same knowledge among their children, and thus gradually break down heathenism in the home. When education, however, has reached the same point of progress among them as among the other sex, the principle advocated here may be applied.

2. Because girls' schools facilitate the work of zenana missionaries. The children in the mission school will be able, as a rule, to introduce the lady in whose charge the school is to the house of their parents. And when the girls become wives and mothers themselves, they will be glad to welcome her to their own homes, and so the good work commenced in school will be continued, the good impressions deepened and the women gradually redeemed from the power of darkness. Zenana ladies should be careful not to spend too much time in secular teaching. Educated Hindus like English ladies to teach their wives and daughters music and English literature; but this temptation they should resist, and keep to such teaching *only* as shall enable the women to appreciate books in their own language. Let every lady remember that she is sent out to win India's daughters for Christ.

In conclusion, I may be allowed to state that too much stress cannot be laid on the necessity of conducting Sunday schools in connection with *all* our educational institutions.

## Appendix A.
# SOCIETIES.

| Abbreviation. | Name in full. | No. of members present. |
|---|---|---|
| A. A. M. | American Arcot Mission of the Reformed Church. | 7 |
| A. B. M. | American Baptist Missionary Union ... ... | 13 |
| A. B. F. M. | American Board of Commissioners for Foreign Missions ... ... ... ... ... | 34 |
| A. F. B. M. | American Free Baptist Missionary Society ... | 5 |
| A. P. M. | American Presbyterian Mission. ... ... ... | 29 |
| A. L. M. | American Lutheran Mission ... ... ... | 8 |
| A. U. P. M. | American United Presbyterian Mission ... ... | 7 |
| A. U. Z. M. | American Union Zenana Mission ... ... | 9 |
| B. F. B. S. | British and Foreign Bible Society ... ... | 2 |
| B. M. S. | Baptist Missionary Society and Zenana Mission.. | 24 |
| Bas. M. | Basel German Evangelical Mission ... ... | 5 |
| C. B. M. | Canadian Baptist Mission ... ... ... | 8 |
| C. E. Z. | Church of England Zenana Mission ... ... | 8 |
| C. L. S. | Christian Literature Society ... ... ... | 2 |
| C. M. S. | Church Missionary Society ... ... ... | 75 |
| C. P. M. | Canadian Presbyterian Mission ... ... ... | 13 |
| Chr. M. | Christian Mission ... ... ... ... | 10 |
| D. L. M. | Danish Lutheran Mission... ... ... ... | 4 |
| E. C. S. | Established Church of Scotland and Zenana Mission ... ... ... ... ... ... | 13 |
| F. C. M. | Free Church of Scotland and Ladies' Society ... | 55 |
| F. M. A. | Friends' Foreign Mission Association ... ... | 9 |
| I. F. N. S. | Indian Female Normal School Society ... ... | 12 |
| I. M. A. | International Missionary Alliance ... ... | 10 |
| I. P. M. | Irish Presbyterian Mission ... ... ... | 11 |
| L. M. S. | London Missionary Society ... ... ... | 27 |
| M. E. C. | Methodist Episcopal Church of America ... | 127 |
| N. Z. B. M. | New Zealand Baptist Missionary Society ... | 2 |
| Raj. Pr. M. | Rajputana Presbyterian Mission ... ... ... | 2 |
| S. A. B. M. | South Australian Baptist Mission ... ... | 3 |
| S. E. L. M. | Swedish Evangelical Lutheran Mission ... ... | 4 |
| S. F. E. | Society for Promoting Female Education in the East ... ... ... ... ... ... | 1 |
| U. P. M. | United Presbyterian Church of Scotland ... | 3 |
| W. M. S. | Wesleyan Missionary Society ... ... . | 40 |
| Y. M. C. A. | Young Men's Christian Association ... ... | 3 |
| Y. W. C. A. | Young Women's Christian Association ... ... | 1 |
| | Independent or Smaller Mission ... ... ... | 34 |
| | Total... | 620 |

# Appendix B.

## LIST OF MEMBERS.

The following is as complete a list of Missionaries who attended the Conference as it has been possible to compile. No pains have been spared to obtain the names of all, but it is feared that many have been omitted. Under the heading "Address," the abbreviations are :—B., Bombay ; Bg., Bengal ; M., Madras ; N.-W. P., North-West Provinces ; P., Panjab ; T., Travancore.

| Name. | Society. | Town or District. | Year of Entrance on Mission Work. | Work in which engaged. | Attended Allahabad or Calcutta. |
|---|---|---|---|---|---|
| Abbott, Miss A. | A. B. F. M. | Bombay | 1888 | General. | |
| Aberley, M. A., Rev. J. | A. L. M. | Guntur, M. | 1890 | District. | |
| Abraham, Mr. L. | F. C. M. | Tanah, B. | | Medical. | |
| Do. Mrs. L. | Ib. | Do. | | | |
| Adams, M. A., Rev. A. J. French. | C. M. S. | Kotayam, T. | 1890 | Educ. | |
| Adams, Mrs. A. J. French. | Ib. | Do. | 1890 | | |
| Aitken, Miss A. S. | I. F. N. S. | Lahore | 1882 | General. | |
| Alexander, M. A., M. D., Rev. W. M. | F. C. M. | Bombay | 1885 | Ed. & Med. | |
| Alexander, Mrs. W. M. | Ib. | Do. | 1889 | S. S. | |
| Ambalavanar, Rev. C. W. | W. M. S. | Madras | 1885 | Pastoral. | |
| Anantam, B.A., Rev. D. | C. M. S. | Bezwada, M. | 1871 | Evang. | |
| Anderson, Rev. H. | B. M. S. | Calcutta | 1886 | Vernacular. | |
| Andrew, Rev. A. | F. C. M. | Chingleput, M. | 1879 | Ev. and Ed. | C. |
| Do. Mrs. A. | Ib. | Do. | 1879 | Zenana | C. |
| Andrews, M. A., Rev. H. M. | A. P. M. | Mainpuri, N.-W. P. | 1890 | General. | |
| Andrews, Miss A. M. | S. F. E. | Ludhiana, P. | 1669 | ,, | |
| Angus, Miss I. M. | B. M. S. | Bhiwani, P. | 1882 | ,, | |
| Arlikatti, Mr. S. | L. M. S. | Belgaum | 1889 | Evang. | |
| Archer, Miss A. | S. A. B. M. | Furreedpore, Bg. | 1892 | Zenana. | |
| Arnold, Miss E. | Ib. | Iubna, Bg. | 1882 | General | C. |
| Ashcroft, M.A., Rev. F. | Raj. Pr. M. | Ajmere | 1884 | ,, | |
| Bacon, Mrs. E. M. | A. U. Z. M. | Lalitpur, N.-W.P. | 1889 | ,, | |
| Baily, Rev. Y. | B. M. S. | Cuttack | 1861 | ,, | |
| Baker, Rev. A. H. | M. E. C. | Bangalore | 1881 | Eng. & Vern. | C. |
| Do. Mrs. A. H. | Ib. | Do. | 1881 | ,, | |
| Baker, Mr. S. | F. M. A. | Hoshangabad, C. P. | 1878 | General | C. |
| Baldwin, M. D., Miss O. A. | Dis. M. | Bilaspur, C. P. | 1888 | Medical. | |
| Ballantine, Rev. W. O. | A. B. F. M. | Ahmednagar, B. | 1875 | Med. & Ev. | |
| Banerjee, Rev. C. N. | L. M. S. | Bhowanipore, C. | 1860 | Ev. & Lit. | A. |

APPENDIX B.    827

| Name. | Society. | Town or District. | Year of Entrance on Mission Work. | Work in which engaged. | Attended Allahabad or Calcutta. |
|---|---|---|---|---|---|
| Banurji, M.A., B.I., Mr. K. C. | Ch. Samaj | Calcutta | ...... | Evang. | C. |
| Barker, Rev. J. | M. E. C. | Naini Tal, N.-W. P. | 1890 | General. | |
| Barrell, Mr. H. E. | B. M. S. | Byculla, B. | 1891 | Eng. & Vern | |
| Basu, M.A., Mr. Kasi N. | C. M. S. | Jabalpur, C. P. | 1881 | Educ. | C. |
| Bates, Miss C. B. | I. M. A. | Khamgaon, Berar | ...... | Evang. | |
| Bateson, Rev. Y. H. | A. T. A. | Simla | 1886 | Secty. | |
| Beatty, B.A., Rev. W. | I. P. M. | Surat | 1865 | General | C. |
| Begg, B.A., Rev. A. P. | L. M. S. | Bhowanipur, C. | 1884 | Educ. | |
| Belchambers, Miss N. | A. U. Z. M. | Cawnpur | ...... | Zenana. | |
| Benjamin, Mr. Luke | M. E. C. | Mysore | 1884 | Evang. | |
| Do.   Mr. S. | Ib. | Khandwa, C. P. | ...... | ,, | |
| Bernard, Miss El. | E. C. S. | Poona | 1875 | General. | |
| Do.   Miss Em. | Ib. | Do. | 1878 | Educ. | |
| Bethell, Miss B. | Vict. B. M. | Mymensing, Bg. | 1890 | Zen. & Med. | |
| Bewley, Miss A. | F. M. A. | Bhopal | 1891 | Zenana. | |
| Bickford, B.A., Miss E. S. | I. M. A. | Berar | 1892 | Evang. | |
| Birkett, M.A., Rev. A. I. | C. M. S. | Lucknow | 1888 | General. | |
| Bishop, B.A., Rev. J. H. | Ib. | Malabar | 1867 | Evang. | |
| Do.   Mrs. J. H. | Ib. | Do. | 1868 | Educ. | |
| Bissell, Rev. H. G. | A. B. F. M. | Ahmednagar, B. | ...... | General. | |
| Biswas, Rev. K. C. | C. M. S. | ...... | ...... | | |
| Do.   Rev. P. T. | Ib. | Calcutta | 1868 | Theo. Sem. | |
| Blackmar, Miss L. E. | M. E. C. | Hyderabad, D. | 1873 | Zen. & Ed. | C. |
| Blackstock, M.A., Rev. J. | M. E. C. | Shahjehanpur | 1875 | Educ. | C. |
| Blackwell, Miss F. | B. M. S. | Agra | 1889 | Zenana. | |
| Blair, Miss K. A. | M. E. C. | Calcutta | 1888 | Lit. and V. | |
| Boggess, Rev. Wheeler | A. B. M. | Ramapatam, M. | 1892 | ...... | |
| Boggs, D. D., Rev. W. B. | Ib. | Do. | 1874 | Educ. | C. |
| Do., B.A., Mr. W. E. | Ib. | Kurnool, M. | 1891 | Evang. | |
| Bose, B.A., B.L., Rev. M. N. | Ind. M. | Gopalgunj, Bg. | 1874 | ,, | A. C. |
| Bonnsall, Miss L. M. | L. M. S. | Coimbatore, M. | 1877 | General | C. |
| Bowman, M.A., Rev. A.H. | C. M. S. | Bombay | 1889 | English. | |
| Do.   Mrs. A.H. | Ib. | Do. | 1889 | ,, | |
| Boyd, B.A., Rev. R. | I. P. M. | Guzarat | 1884 | ,, | |
| Do.   Mrs. R. | Ib. | Do. | 1886 | ,, | |
| Do.   Miss A. | Chr. M. | Bilaspur, C. P. | 1882 | Zenana. | |
| Brandon, Miss J. P. | C. E. Z. | Masulipatam | 1875 | General. | |
| Bremner, Mr. J. | F. C. M. | Nagpur, C. P. | 1885 | Educ. | |
| Broadhead, Rev. J. R. | W. M. S. | Dum Dum, Bg. | 1876 | Eng. & Ver. | C. |
| Brock, Rev. G. H. | A. B. M. | Nellore | 1892 | Evang. | |
| Brown, Rev. J. | W.M.S. | Calcutta | 1866 | General | C. |
| Do.   M. A., Rev. J. A. | Raj. Pr.M. | Rajputana. | 1884 | Educ. | |
| Do.   B. A., Rev. J. G. | C. B. M. | Vuyyuru, M | 1889 | Evang. | |
| Do.   M. B., Miss | B. M. S. | Delhi | 1891 | Medical. | |
| Browne, Miss I. | A.U.Z.M. | Cawnpore | ...... | Zenana. | |
| Bruce, B.A., Rev. H. J. | A.B.F.M. | Satara | 1863 | General. | |
| Do.   Miss H. L. | Ib. | Do. | ...... | Ed. & Zen. | |
| Bruere, Rev. W. W. | M. E. C. | Poona | 1880 | Educ. | C. |

# APPENDIX B.

| Name. | Society. | Town or District. | Year of Entrance on Mission Work. | Work in which engaged. | Attended Allahabad or Calcutta. |
|---|---|---|---|---|---|
| Bruere, Mrs. W. W. ... | M. E. C. | Poona ... ... ... | 1885 | Educ. | |
| Buchanan, Rev. Dr. J. ... | C. P. M. | Ujjain... ... ... | 1888 | Medical. | |
| Do. Mrs. Dr. J. ... | Ib. | Do. ... ... ... | ...... | ,, | |
| Buck, M. A., Rev. P. M. | M. E. C. | Mussoorie ... ... | 1867 | Ed. and Ev. | A. C. |
| Budden, Miss A. N. ... | Ib. | Kumaon ... ... | 1866 | General. | |
| Do. Miss M. ... ... | L. M. S. | Almora, N.-W. P. ... | 1887 | ,, | |
| Bulloch, Rev. G. McC. ... | L. M. S. | Do. ... ... | 1874 | ,, | |
| Burditt, B. A., Rev. J. F. | A. B. M. | Narsaravupet, M. ... | 1881 | ,, | |
| Burnet, Rev. A. ... ... | W. M. S. | Bangalore ... ... | 1882 | English. | |
| Butcher, Rev. J. C. ... | M. E. C. | Moradabad, N.-W.-P. | 1885 | General. | |
| Butler, Rev. E. T. ... | C. M. S. | Krishnagar, Bg. ... | 1887 | ,, | |
| Butterfield, Rev. H. W. ... | M. E. C. | Narsinghpur, C. P. ... | 1891 | Educ. | |
| Do. Mrs. H. W.... | Ib. | Do. ... ... | 1891 | ,, | |
| Buttrick, Rev. J. B. ... | Ib. | Bangalore ... ... | 1888 | Evang. | |
| Do. Mrs. J. B. ... | Ib. | Do. ... ... | 1888 | ,, | |
| Butts, Miss E. M. ... | A. F. B.M. | Midnapore, Bg. ... | 1887 | Educ. | |
| Campbell, Rev. A. ... | F. C. M. | Manbhum ... ... | 1871 | General. | |
| Do. Rev. J. F. ... | C. P. M. | Rutlam, C. I. ... | 1876 | Ev. & Lit. | |
| Do. Mrs. J. F. ... | Ib. | Do. ... ... | 1877 | ...... | |
| Do. M.A., B.D., Mr. W. H. | L. M. S. | Cuddapah, M. ... | 1884 | Ev. & Past. | |
| Do. Miss A. ... | I. F. N. S. | Bombay ... ... | 1874 | Ed. & Zen. | |
| Do. Miss M. J. ... | A. U. P.M. | Zaferwal, P. ... ... | 1885 | Zenana. | |
| Canaran, Mrs. S. T. ... | A. B. F. M. | Bombay ... ... | ...... | Educ. | |
| Carey, Rev. W. ... ... | B. M. S. | Barisal, Bg. ... | 1885 | General. | |
| Carlsson, Rev. P. ... | S. E. L. M. | Betul, C. P. ... ... | 1881 | Ed. & Ev. | |
| Carpenter, M.A., Rev. J. N. | C. M. S. | Agra ... ... ... | 1890 | Educ. | |
| Carroll, Miss M. E. ... | M. E. C. | Bombay ... ... | 1889 | General. | |
| Carter, Miss A. F. ... | Ind. M. | Do. ... ... | 1892 | Rescue. | |
| Chamberlain M.A., M.D., D.D., Rev. J. | A. A. M. | Madanapalle, M. ... | 1859 | General. | |
| Chandy, Rev. J. ... | C. M. S. | Cottayam, T. ... | 1875 | Pastoral. | |
| Charlesworth, Rev. W. ... | W. M. S. | Ceylon ... ... | 1887 | Evang. | |
| Charlton. M.A., Rev. I. W. | C. M. S. | Nuddea, Bg. ... ... | 1889 | General. | |
| Do. Mrs. I. W. ... | Ib. | Do. ... ... | 1889 | ,, | |
| Chatterjea, Rev. T. P. ... | L. M. S. | Calcutta ... ... | 1854 | Ev. & Past. | C. |
| Chatterjee, Rev. K. C. ... | A. P. M. | Hoshyarpur, P. ... | 1861 | General ... | C. |
| Chatterji, Rev. T.... ... | L. M. S. | Calcutta ... ... | 1879 | Pastoral ... | C. |
| Clancy, Rev. R. ... ... | M. E. C. | Allahabad ... ... | 1884 | Eng. & Vern. | |
| Do. Mrs. R. ... ... | Ib. | Do. ... ... | 1892 | ,, | |
| Clark, M.D., C.M., M. H. | C. M. S. | Amritsar ... ... | 1882 | Medical. | |
| Clarke, Miss A. M. ... | Ind. M. | Kollegal, M. ... | 1890 | Evang. | |
| Clifford, M.A., Rev. A. ... | C. M. S. | Allahabad ... ... | 1874 | Bp. Desig... | C. |
| Do. Mrs. A. ... ... | Ib. | Do. ... ... | 1883 | ...... | |
| Cole, Rev. F. T. ... ... | Ib. | Santal, N. I. ... | 1871 | General. | |
| Colton, Rev. J. ... ... | A. B. F. M. | Dindigul ... ... | 1848 | Pastoral. | |
| Conklin, Rev. C. G. ... | M. E. C. | Calcutta ... .. | 1885 | Literary. | |
| Cook, Rev. A. E. ... | Ib. | Secunderabad ... | ...... | English. | |

APPENDIX B.

| Name. | Society. | Town or District. | Year of Entrance on Mission Work. | Work in which engaged. | Attended Allahabad or Calcutta. |
|---|---|---|---|---|---|
| Cook, Mrs. A. E. | M. E. C. | Secunderabad | | English. | |
| Cooke, Mr. J. E. | Open Br. | Calcutta | | ,, | |
| Cooling, B.A., Rev. J. | W. M. S. | Royapettah, M. | 1876 | Ed. & Secty. | |
| Core, B. D., Rev. L. A. | M. E. C. | Moradabad, N.-W. P. | 1890 | General. | |
| Craig, B.A., Rev. J. | C. B. M. | Godavari | 1878 | Evang. | C. |
| Do. Mrs. J. | Ib. | Do. | 1885 | Educ. | |
| Do. Miss | M. E. S. | Calcutta | | | |
| Crane, M.A., Rev. H. A. | Ib. | Bombay | 1892 | English. | |
| Do. Mrs. H. A. | Ib. | Do. | 1892 | ,, | |
| Craven, M.A., B.D., Rev. T. | Ib. | Lucknow | 1870 | Literary. | |
| Crawford, Miss | F. C. M. | Bombay | 1886 | Educ. | |
| David, Rev. J. | A. P. M. | Allahabad | | B. & R. T. S. | |
| Davis, B.A., Rev. J. E. | C. B. M. | Coconada, M. | 1887 | General. | |
| Dawbarn, Miss E. Y. | B. M. S. | Delhi | | Eng. & Vern. | |
| Day, B.A., Miss M. E. | M. E. C. | Moradabad | 1889 | Educ. | |
| Do. Miss M. M. | A. B. M. | Tondiarpetta, M. | 1878 | Zenana. | |
| Deimler, Rev. J. G. | C. M. S. | Bombay | 1858 | Vern. | |
| Do. Mrs. J. G. | Ib. | Do. | | ,, | |
| Day, Miss | Ib. | Do. | 1892 | ,, | |
| DeLine, Miss S. M. | M. E. C. | Do. | 1884 | Zenana. | |
| Denning, M.A., Rev. J. O. | Ib. | Narsinghpur, C. P. | 1891 | Evang. | |
| Do. Mrs. J. O. | Ib. | Do. | | ,, | |
| De St. Dalmas, Rev. H. G. E. | N. Z. B. M. | Tippera, Bg. | 1872 | Ev. & Gen. | A. |
| Do. Mrs. H. G. E. | Ib. | Do. | 1882 | Zenana. | |
| Dence, Miss E. | M. E. C. | Baroda | 1888 | ,, | |
| Dey, Rev. K. C. | C. M. S. | Nuddea, Bg. | 1882 | Pastoral. | |
| Dhalwani, Rev. K. M. | A. B. F. M. | Satara, B. | 1856 | Evang. | |
| Diez, Rev. C. A. E. | Bas. M. | Canara | 1851 | General. | |
| Donaldson, Miss E. | A. P. M. | Dehra Doon, N. I. | | Educ. | |
| Doss, Rev. M. L. | L. M. S. | Calcutta | 1864 | Ed. & Ev. | C. |
| Do. Mrs. M. L. | Ib. | Do. | 1864 | Evang. | |
| Douglas, M.A., Rev. J. | F. C. M. | Nagpur, C. P. | 1878 | Evang. | |
| Do. Mrs. J. | Ib. | Do. | 1879 | | |
| Drake, Rev. J. | Ind. M. | Berar | | Ev. & Ed. | |
| Dryden, Miss F. M. | A. L. M. | Guntur, M. | 1883 | Educ. | |
| Dunkill, Miss H. | W. M. S. | Bangalore | 1885 | Zenana & Ed. | |
| Dunlop, Miss J. | A. P. M. | Saharanpur | 1889 | ,, | |
| Durand, Dr. C. S. | Chr. M. | Harda, C. P. | 1889 | Med, and Gen. | |
| Do. Mrs. C. S. | Ib. | Do. | | General | C. |
| Durrant, M.A., Rev. G. B. | C. M. S. | Allahabad | 1876 | Secty. | |
| Do. Mrs. G. B. | Ib. | Do. | 1888 | | |
| Duthie, Rev. J. | L. M. S. | Nagercoil, F. | 1856 | Educ. | |
| Dutt, Mr. G. C. | Ib. | Calcutta | 1867 | Evang. | |
| Dutton, Mr. T. E. | I. M. A. | Akola, Berar | 1892 | ,, | |
| Dyer, Mr. A. S. | Ind. M. | Bombay | 1889 | Literary. | |
| Do. Miss M. E. | Ib. | Do. | 1889 | Lit. & Ev. | |

# APPENDIX B.

| Name. | Society. | Town or District. | Year of Entrance on Mission Work. | Work in which engaged. | Attended Allahabad or Calcutta. |
|---|---|---|---|---|---|
| Easton, Miss S. | A.U.Z.M. | Calcutta | 1886 | Zenana | C. |
| Edwards, Rev. T. R. | B. M. S. | Serampore, Bg. | 1879 | Educ. | |
| Ekholm, Mr. F. G. | S. F. M. | Betul, C. P. | 1884 | Evang. | |
| Ellis, Rev. J. R. | W. M. S. | Madras | 1883 | Eng. & Ver. | |
| Ellwood, Rev. J. P. | C. M. S. | Meerut, N.-W. P. | 1871 | Ev. & Ed. | |
| Elsam, Rev. C. G. | M. E. C. | Kampti, C. P. | 1888 | Ver. & Eng. | |
| Embleton, Miss M. M. | A. P. M. | Sialkot, P. | 1891 | Zenana. | |
| Erickson, Rev. C. | I. M. A. | Berar | 1892 | Evang. | |
| Ernsberger, M. D., Miss I. | M. E. C. | Baroda | | Medical. | |
| Ernst, M.D., Miss A. | A.U.Z.M. | Calcutta | 1890 | ,, | |
| Ewart, Miss M. | C. E. Z. | Bangalore | | Zenana. | |
| Ewing, D.D., Rev. J.C.R. | A. P. M. | Lahore | 1879 | Educ. | C. |
| Fairbank, B.A., B.D., Rev. H. | A.B.F.M. | Amednagar | 1886 | Ev. & Ed. | |
| Do. M.A., D. D., Rev. S. B. | Ib. | Bombay | 1846 | General. | |
| Farrar, M.B., B. S., Miss E. M. | B. M. S. | Bhiwani, P. | 1891 | Medical. | |
| Faye, M.D., Miss T. | A. B. M. | Nellore | 1891 | Med. & Zen. | |
| Ferries, Miss C. J. | Fr. Meth. | Berar | | Evang. | |
| Ferris, Rev. G. H. | A. P. M. | Kolhapur, S. M. C. | 1879 | ,, | |
| Findlay, M. A., Rev. W. H. | W. M. S. | Tanjore | 1882 | General. | |
| Fletcher, Miss G. M. | B. M. S. | Gurgaon, P. | 1885 | ,, | |
| Folsom, Miss E. A. | C. B. M. | Cocanada, M. | | Eng. Ed. | |
| Foote, M.A., Rev. F. W. | M. E. C. | Naini Tal, N.-W. P. | 1884 | Educ. | |
| Forman, Rev. J. N. | A. P. M. | Fatehgarh, N.-W. P. | 1882 | Evang. | |
| Fox, M.A., B.D., Rev. D.O. | M. E. C. | Poona | 1872 | ,, | C. |
| Do. M.A., Ph.D., Mrs. D.O. | Ib. | Do. | 1881 | ,, | C. |
| Do. Miss M. | B. M. S. | Delhi | 1891 | Zenana. | |
| Frankland, Miss E. | F. M. A. | Sohagpur | | Ed. & Zen. | |
| Frater, Rev. W. D. | W. M. S. | Faizabad, O. | 1887 | Evang. | |
| Do. Mrs. W. D. | Ib. | Do. | | Ev. & Ed. | |
| Freuse, Rev. E. F. | M. E. C. | Baroda | 1888 | General. | |
| Fritchley, Mrs. R. N. G. | Ib. | Bombay | | Zenana. | |
| Frohnmeyer, Rev. L. J. | Bas. M. | Malabar | 1876 | Ed. & Past. | |
| Fuller, M.A., B.D., Rev. M. B. | I. M. A. | Berar | 1882 | Ev. & Ed. | |
| Gange, Miss A. | B. M. S. | Delhi | | Educ. | |
| Garden, Rev. J. H. | M. E. C. | Hyderabad, Deccan | 1884 | Evang. | |
| Do. Mrs. J. H. | Ib. | Do. | | ,, | |
| Gardner, Miss H. | F. C. M. | Bombay | 1885 | Educ. | |
| Do. Miss S. J. | A.U.Z.M. | Calcutta | 1879 | Secty. | C. |
| Garside, B.A., Rev. R. | C. B. M. | Tani, M. | 1888 | Evang. | |
| Do. Mrs. R. | Ib. | Do. | | Educ. | |
| Gates, Rev. L. S. | A.B.F.M. | Sholapur, B. | 1875 | Evang. | |
| Do. Mrs. L. S. | Ib. | Do. | 1875 | | |
| Geisinger, Miss H. | A. P. M. | Dehra Doon, N. I. | | Zenana. | |
| Giddings, Miss C. C. | Ib. | Mussoorie | | Educ. | |
| Gilbert, Miss M. I. | Ans. B. M. | Calcutta | 1882 | General | C. |

| Name. | Society. | Town or District. | Year of Entrance on Mission Work. | Work in which engaged. | Attended Allahabad or Calcutta. |
|---|---|---|---|---|---|
| Gilchrist, Miss J. | F. C. M. | Giridih, E. I. R. | 1890 | Educ. | |
| Do. Miss M. S. | Ib. | Do. | 1890 | Evang. | |
| Gilder, Rev. G. K. | M. E. C. | Hyderabad, Deccan | 1874 | Eng. & Ver. | |
| Gill, Rev. C. H. | C. M. S. | Jubbulpore | 1887 | General. | |
| Do. Miss A. E. | L. M. S. | Benares | 1887 | Ed. & Zen. | |
| Gladwin, Rev. W. J. | Ind. M. | Bombay | 1871 | Literary | A. |
| Goheen, Rev. J. M. | A. P. M. | Kolhapur | 1875 | Ed. & Ev. | |
| Goldsmith, M.A., Rev. H. D. | C. M. S. | Madras | 1879 | Div. Sch. | C. |
| Goray, Mr. M. | Ib. | Bombay | | Pastoral. | |
| Gordon, Mr. E. M. | Chr. M. | Mungeli, C. P. | 1891 | Evang. | |
| Do. Miss J. P. | A. B. F.M. | Satara | 1890 | Ed. & Zen. | |
| Gow, Miss J. | U. P. M. | Rajputana | 1888 | Zenana. | |
| Graham, M.A., Rev. J. A. | E. C. S. | Darjeeling | 1889 | General. | |
| Do. Rev. J. P. | A. P. M. | Saugli, S. M. C. | 1875 | Evang. | |
| Gray, B.A., Rev. J. S. | C. M. S. | Lucknow | 1891 | ,, | |
| Do. M.A., Rev. R. M. | F. C. M. | Bombay | | English. | |
| Grenon, Rev. W. H. | M. E. C. | Nagpur, C. P. | 1885 | Eng.&Vern. | |
| Griffin, Rev. Z. F. | A.F. B.M. | Orissa | 1883 | | |
| Gulliford, Rev. H. | W. M. S. | Bangalore | 1877 | Ed. & Lit. | |
| Hahn, Rev. C. H. P. F. | Goss. M. | Chota-Nagpur | 1868 | General. | |
| Haigh, Rev. H. | W. M. S. | Mysore | 1874 | Ev. & Lit. | |
| Hanson, Rev. N. P. | D. L. M. | S. Arcot | 1889 | Evang. | |
| Hannay, Miss M. R. | C. E. Z. | Krishnagar, Bg. | 1886 | ,, | |
| Harding, M.A., Rev. C. | A. B.F.M. | Sholapur, B. | 1857 | General | A. |
| Do. Mrs. C. | Ib. | Do. | 1869 | ,, | |
| Harriss, M.A., Rev. J. A. | C. M. S. | Poona | 1886 | Div. Sch. | |
| Do. Mrs. J. A. | Ib. | Do. | 1891 | General. | |
| Hart, Miss D. | M. E. C. | Baroda | 1889 | Zenana. | |
| Haskew, M.D., Miss J. | I. F. N. S. | Lucknow | 1888 | Medical. | |
| Hawker, Rev. J. G. | L. M. S. | Belgaum | 1865 | Evang. | |
| Hazen, Rev. A. | A. B. F.M. | Sholapur, B. | 1847 | General. | |
| Hoafer, Miss L. | M. E. C. | Hyderabad, D. | | Eng. Ed. | |
| Haythornthwaite, M.A., Rev. J. | C. M. S. | Agra | 1890 | Educ. | |
| Heinricks, Rev. J. | A. B. M. | Kistna | 1889 | Evang. | |
| Henderson, M.A., Rev. R. | I. P. M. | Broach | 1890 | Past. & Ev. | |
| Do. Mrs. R. | Ib. | Do. | 1890 | Evang. | |
| Do. M.D., Miss A. E. | F. C. M. | Nagpur, C. P. | 1890 | Medical. | |
| Hewes, Rev. G. C. | M. E. C. | Lucknow | 1891 | Educ. | |
| Hill, Mr. C. B. | Ib. | Poona | | ,, | |
| Hoch, Rev. M. | Bas. M. | Mangalore | 1876 | ,, | |
| Hocken, Rev. C. H. | W. M. S. | Bangalore | 1872 | Vern. & Ed. | |
| Holdsworth, M.A., Rev. W. W. | Ib. | Mysore | 1864 | Educ. | |
| Holliday, A.M., Rev. T. E. | A. U. P.M. | Gurdaspur | 1889 | Evang. | |
| Hollister, Rev. W. H. | M. E. C. | Mysore | 1888 | Ed. & Past. | |
| Do. Mrs. W. H. | Ib. | Do. | | Zen. & Orph. | |
| Holmes, Miss E. L. | I. M. A. | Berar | 1892 | Evang. | |
| Holten, Rev. E. P. | A. B.F.M. | Madura | | ,, | |

APPENDIX B.

| Name. | Society. | Town or District. | Year of Entrance on Mission Work. | Work in which engaged. | Attended Allahabad or Calcutta. |
|---|---|---|---|---|---|
| Hooper, D.D., Rev. W... | C. M. S. | Jubbulpore, C. P. | 1861 | Lit. & Ev.... | C. |
| Do. Mrs. W. ... | Ib. | Do. | 1883 | | |
| Hopkins, M.A., Rev. G. F. | M. E. C. | Jubbulpore, C. P. | 1888 | Eng. | |
| Hoskins, M.A., Ph.D., Rev. R. | Ib. | Cawnpore | 1868 | General | C. |
| Do. Mrs. R. ... | Ib. | Do. | 1868 | ,, | |
| Hudson, B.A., Rev. J... | W. M. S. | Bangalore | 1864 | | |
| Hume, M.A., Rev. R. A. | A. B. F. M. | Ahmednagar, B. | 1874 | Theol. Sem. | C. |
| Do. Mrs. R. A. ... | Ib. | Do. | 1882 | Gen. & Lit. | |
| Hunt, Miss E. A. ... | C. E. Z. | Calcutta | 1882 | General. | |
| Husband, F.R.C.S., &c., Rev. J. | U. P. M. | Ajmere | 1870 | Medical. | |
| Do. Mrs. J. ... | Ib. | Do. | 1870 | General. | |
| Hutchison, Miss C. ... | A. P. M. | Mussoorie | | Educ. | |
| Irwin, Rev. J. M. ... | Ib. | Kolhapore, S. M. C. | 1890 | ,, | |
| Do. Miss R. ... | Ib. | Do. | | ,, | |
| Jack, M.A., Mr. J. ... | F. C. M. | Bombay | 1885 | ,, | |
| Jackson, Mr. J. ... | C. M. S. | Bombay | 1867 | ,, | |
| James, Rev. W. B. ... | B. M. S. | Jalpaiguri, Bg. | 1878 | Evang. | C. |
| Jamieson, Rev. W. J. ... | C. P. M. | Neemuch, C. T. | 1890 | Ev. & Ed. | |
| Do. Miss M. ... | Ib. | Do. | 1888 | Zen. & Ed. | |
| Jervis, Mr. G. S. ... | I. P. M. | Surat | 1879 | Educ. | |
| Jigajinee, Rev. P. S. ... | L. M. S. | Belgaum | 1861 | General. | |
| John, Rev. S. ... | C. M. S. | Madras | 1856 | Evang. | |
| Johnson, M.D., Rev. T. S. | M. E. C. | Jubbulpore, C. P. | 1862 | General | A. |
| Do. Mrs. T. S. ... | Ib. | Do. | 1862 | Eng. & Ver. | |
| Jolly, Mr. J. ... | A. P. M. | Sangli, S. M. C. | 1891 | Industr. | |
| Do. Mrs. J. ... | Ib. | Do. | 1891 | Educ. | |
| Jones, Rev. D. ... | B. M. S. | Patna | 1874 | General | C. |
| Do. M. A., Rev. J. P. | A. B. F. M. | Madura | 1878 | Theol. Sem. | C. |
| Do. M.A., Rev. P. Ireland. | C. M. S. | Calcutta | 1885 | Secty. | |
| Kale, Rev. G. ... | M. E. C. | Bombay | 1888 | Pastoral. | |
| Kealley, Miss L. ... | S. A. B. M. | Pulua, Bg. | | Zenana. | |
| Keeler, Miss A. C. ... | M. E. C. | Rangoon | | Educ. | |
| Kellett, M.A., Rev. F.W. | W. M. S. | Madras | 1892 | ,, | |
| Kember, Rev. T. ... | C. M. S. | Palamcottah | 1865 | Theol. Sem. | |
| Kemper, Miss H. L. ... | M. E. C. | Moradabad, N.-W. P. | 1892 | Educ. | |
| Kennedy, Miss M. R. ... | Ib. | Bombay | 1891 | ,, | |
| Kerry, Rev. G. ... | B. M. S. | Calcutta | 1856 | Secty. ... | A. C. |
| Khandaji, Rev. G. ... | M. E. C. | Igatpuri, B. ... | 1877 | Pastoral ... | C. |
| Kiellman, Rev. A. ... | Ib. | Calcutta | | Evang. | |
| King, B.D., Rev. W. L... | Ib. | Vepery, M. | 1888 | Lit. & Ev. | |
| Kingsbury, Miss M. ... | Chr. M. | Bilaspur, C. P. | 1882 | Educ. | |
| Kistler, Miss S. R. ... | A. L. M. | Guntur, M. | 1888 | Ed. & Ev. | |
| Knott, Rev. A. E. ... | W. M. S. | Bombay | 1891 | English. | |
| Kugler, M.D., Miss A. S. | A. L. M. | Guntur, M. | 1883 | Medical. | |
| Kullman, A. B., Rev. A. | M. E. C. | Calcutta | 1893 | Evang. | |
| Kyle, Miss T. J. ... | Ib. | Bareilly, N.-W. P. | 1886 | Educ. | |

APPENDIX B.   833

| Name. | Society. | Town or District. | Year of Entrance on Mission Work. | Work in which engaged. | Attended Allahabad or Calcutta. |
|---|---|---|---|---|---|
| Laker, Mr. J. | M. E. C. | Mhow, C. I. | ...... | Evang. | |
| Lamb, Rev. J. | E. C. S. | Calcutta | ...... | Educ. | |
| Lash, Rev. A. H. | C. M. S. | Kotayam, T. | 1867 | Theol. Sem. | |
| Lauck, B. A., Miss A. J. | M. E. C. | Cawnpore | 1893 | Educ. | |
| Lawson, Rev. J. C. | Ib. | Sitalpur, O. | 1881 | Evang. Ed. | C. |
| Do. Mrs. J. C. | Ib. | Do. | 1881 | Bdg. Sch. | C. |
| Do. M.A., Miss A. E. | Ib. | Bareilly, N.-W. P. | 1886 | Zen. and Ed. | |
| Do. Miss C. H. | Ib. | Bombay | ...... | Zenana. | |
| Lay, B.A., B.D., Rev. C. W. | A.B.F.M. | Ahmednagar | 1890 | General. | |
| Do. Mrs. C. W. | Ib. | Do. | 1890 | Educ. | |
| Lazarus, B. A., Rev. J. | D. L. M. | Madras | 1881 | General. | |
| Do. Mrs. J. | Ib. | Do. | 1885 | Zen. and Ed. | |
| Lee, Mr. S. G. | W. M. S. | Colombo | 1887 | Educ. | |
| Le Feuvre, Mr. A. | C. M. S. | Nuddea, Bg. | 1889 | Evang. | |
| Le Quesne, Rev. W. R. | L. M. S. | Calcutta | 1886 | ,, | |
| Do. Mrs. W. R. | Ib. | Do. | 1889 | ,, | |
| Levering, M. D., Mr. F. H. | A. B. M. | Nellore | 1892 | ...... | |
| Lewis, Mr. M. | M. E. C. | Mysore | 1886 | Evang. | |
| Little, Rev. T. | W. M. S. | Madras | 1879 | ,, | |
| Lloyd, Miss | T. F. N. S. | Bombay | 1888 | Zenana. | |
| Longhurst, Mrs. M. A. | E. C. S. | Madras | 1882 | General. | |
| Loshrudya, Mr. N. | M. E. C. | Kolar, M. | ... | Evang. | |
| Luke, Rev. T. | W. M. S | Tunkur | ... | Pastoral. | |
| Lundborg, Rev. N. E. | S. E. L. M. | Saugor, C. P. | 1879 | Scety. | |
| Lyon, Rev. J. | M. E. C. | Ajmere | 1879 | Eng. & Ver. | |
| Macdonald, Rev. J. A. D. J. | C. L. S. | Calcutta | 1878 | Literary | C. |
| Mackichan, M.A., D.D., Rev. D. | F. C. M. | Bombay | 1875 | Educ. | |
| Do. Mrs. D. | Ib. | Do. | ... | General. | |
| Do. Miss M. | E. C. S. | Gujrat, P. | 1893 | Zenana Ed. | |
| Macmillan, Miss H. M. | Ind. M. | Bombay | 1892 | Rescue. | |
| Macphail, M.A., M.B., C. M., Mr. J. M. | F. C. M. | Chakai, Bg. | 1889 | Medical. | |
| Do. L.R.C.S., &c, Miss A. M. | Ib. | Royapuram, M. | 1888 | ,, | |
| Malhar, Rev. D. G. | Ib. | Poona | 1885 | Past. & Ev. | |
| Do. Mrs. D. G. | Ib. | Do. | 1885 | General. | |
| Mansell, M.A., B.D., D.D., Rev. H. | M. E. C. | Mussoorie | 1862 | ,, | |
| Do. M.A., M.D., Mrs. H. | Ib. | Do. | 1873 | ,, | |
| Do. M.A., B.D., Rev. W. A. | Ib. | Lucknow | 1889 | Educ. | |
| Manley, M.A., Rev. W. R. | A. B. M. | Nellore | 1879 | Evang. | |
| Manwaring, Rev. A. | C. M. S. | Bombay | 1879 | General. | |
| Martin, M.A., Rev. J. H. | A. U. P. M. | Gujranwala | 1888 | Evang. | |
| Masaji, Rev. S. | A. P. M. | Kolhapur, S. M. C. | 1881 | Pastoral. | |
| McBurnir, Miss S. | M. E. C. | Cawnpore | 1888 | Eng. Ed. | |

105

# APPENDIX B.

| Name. | Society. | Town or District. | Year of Entrance on Mission Work. | Work in which engaged. | Attended Allahabad or Calcutta. |
|---|---|---|---|---|---|
| McCahon, Miss E.... | A. U. P. M. | Sialkot P. ... | 1875 | Educ. | |
| McCann, Mr. R. ... | Y. M. C. A. | Bombay ... | 1892 | Y. M. C. A. | |
| McConaughy, M.A., Mr. D. | Ib. | Madras ... | 1889 | ,, | |
| McGavran, B.A., Rev. J. G. | Chr. M. | Harda, C. P. ... | 1891 | Educ. | |
| McGregor, Rev. J. ... | M. E. C. | Jabalpur ... | ... | Evang. | |
| McLaurin, D.D., Rev. J. | A. B. M. | Bangalore ... | 1870 | Literary. ... | C. |
| McMahon, B.A., Rev. J. T. | M. E. C. | Kumaon ... | 1871 | Evang. ... | A. C. |
| Mevill, M.D., Miss A. ... | Chr. M. | Bilaspur, C. P. ... | 1889 | Medical. | |
| Millara, Miss A. ... | A. B. F. M. | Bombay ... | 1887 | Educ. | |
| Miller, Rev. A. ... | F. C. M. | Scotland ... | 1859 | Comtee. | |
| Do. LL.D., C. I. E., Rev. W. | Ib. | Madras ... | 1862 | Educ. ... | A. C. |
| Do. Miss I. ... | Ib. | Nagpur, C. P. ... | ... | Zenana. | |
| Do. Miss R. ... | F. C. M. | Bombay ... | ... | ,, | |
| Millett, Miss H. M. ... | Ind. M. | Bombay ... | ... | Evang. | |
| Modak, Mr. S. ... | A.B.F.M. | Ahmednagar, B. ... | ... | ,, | |
| Do. Mrs. S. ... | Ib. | Do. ... | 1886 | Educ. | |
| Mody, Rev. M. H. ... | Ind. M. | Bombay ... | 1878 | Evang. | |
| Do. L. L. A., Mrs. M. H. | Ib. | Do. ... | 1878 | Ed. and Ev. | |
| Moffat, M. A., B.Sc., Mr. A. | F. C. M. | Madras ... | 1892 | Educ. | |
| Moore, Rev. W. A. | Ind. M. | Berar ... | ... | Evang. | |
| Morrison, M. A., Rev. W. J. P. | A. P. M. | Dehra Dun, N.-W. P. | 1866 | Eng. & Vern. | A. |
| Mortimer, Rev. E. ... | W. M. S. | Bombay ... | 1883 | English. | |
| Do. Mrs. E. ... | Ib. | Do. ... | ... | ,, | |
| Morton, Rev. T. E. F. ... | M. E. C. | Hurda, C. P. ... | 1874 | ,, ... | C. |
| Do. Mrs. T. E. F. ... | Ib. | Do. ... | 1881 | ,, | |
| Moses, Miss L. ... | F. C. M. | Poona ... | ... | Hosp. | |
| Muller, Rev. M. O. A. ... | Ind. M. | Berar ... | 1892 | General. | |
| Mulvaney, Miss S. L. ... | C. E. Z. | Calcutta ... | 1876 | Evang. ... | C. |
| Murdock, LL.D., Mr. John | C. L. S. | Madras ... | 1844 | Literary ... | A. |
| Nash, Miss A. ... | M. E. C. | Narsingpore, C. P. ... | ... | Zenana. | |
| Nath, Rev. P. C. ... | W. M. S. | Calcutta ... | ... | Past.and Ev. | |
| Nathoji, Rev. T. ... | A.B.F.M. | Bombay ... | ... | Pastoral. | |
| Do. Mrs. T. ... | Ib. | Do. ... | ... | ...... | |
| Navalkar, Rev. G. ... | F. C. M. | Alibag, B. ... | 1856 | General. | |
| Neelam, Mr. R. ... | A. L. M. | Guntur ... | ... | Educ. | |
| Neeld, B. D., Rev. F. L. | M. E. C. | Bareily, N.-W. P. ... | 1881 | Theol. Sem. | |
| Do. Mrs. F. L. ... | Ib. | Do. ... | 1881 | Educ. | |
| Neele, Miss E. ... | C. M. S. | Calcutta ... | 1892 | ,, | |
| Do. Miss H. J. ... | Ib. | Do. ... | 1865 | ,, ... | C. |
| Newson, A.M., B.D., Rev. J. E. | M. E. C. | Cawnpore ... | 1891 | English. | |
| Nisbet, Miss H. ... | Y.W.C.A. | Calcutta ... | 1892 | Y.W.C.A. | |
| Nowroji, Rev. D. | F. C. M. | Bombay ... | 1847 | General ... | A. |

APPENDIX B. 835

| Name. | Society. | Town or District. | Year of Entrance on Mission Work. | Work in which engaged. | Attended Allahabad or Calcutta. |
|---|---|---|---|---|---|
| Nowroji, Mrs. D. | F. C. M. | Bombay | | | |
| Do. Miss I. | Ib. | Do. | 1886 | Zenana. | |
| Do. Miss L. | Ib. | Do. | 1886 | ,, | |
| Oakley, Rev. E. S. | L. M. S. | Almora, N.-W. P. | | Educ. | |
| O'Brien, B.A., Mr. G. | F. M. A. | Hoshangabad, C.P. | 1891 | Educ. | |
| Oliver, M.D., Miss M. | C. P. M. | Indore, C. I. | | Medical. | |
| Olver, Rev. G. W. | W. M. S. | London | | Secty. | |
| Orbison, Miss A. | A. P. M. | Saharanpur | 1890 | Zenana. | |
| Organe, Rev. S. W. | B.F.B.S. | Madras | 1867 | Secty. | |
| Osborne, Rev. D. | M. E. C. | Mussoorie | 1873 | General | A. C. |
| Padfield, B.D., Rev. J. E. | C. M. S. | Masulipatam | 1868 | Theol. Sem. | |
| Padmanji, Rev. B. | F. C. M. | Bombay | 1867 | Literary. | |
| Panes, Rev. J. B. | C. M. S. | Khammamett | 1883 | Ev. & Past. | |
| Park, Mr. G. W. | M. E. C. | Bombay | | Evang. | |
| Parker, Rev. A. | L. M. S. | Benares | 1887 | Ed. & Ev. | |
| Do. Mrs. A. | Ib. | Do. | 1888 | Zen. & Ed. | |
| Do. D.D., Rev. E. W. | M. E. C. | Lucknow | 1859 | General | A. C. |
| Do. Mrs. E. W. | Ib. | Do. | 1859 | Evang. | |
| Parks, Miss M. C. | A.U.P.M. | Sialkot, P. | 1892 | Zenana. | |
| Parson, Rev. J. | W. M. S. | Lucknow | 1882 | Theol. Sem. | |
| Parsons, Rev. G. H. | C. M. S. | Calcutta | 1879 | Evang. | C. |
| Paul, Rev. S. | Ib. | Tinnevelly | 1874 | Pastoral. | |
| Paxton, Miss J. | F. C. M. | Poona | | Educ. | |
| Peattie, M.A., Rev. J. C. | Ib. | Madras | 1884 | Secty. | |
| Peel, Rev. W. G. | C. M. S. | Bombay | 1880 | ,, | C. |
| Do. Mrs. W. G. | Ib. | Do. | 1880 | | C. |
| Penn, M.A., Rev. W. C. | Ib. | Masulipatam | 1892 | Educ. | |
| Perkins, Miss M. R. | A.B.F.M. | Madura, M. | | Ed. & Zen. | |
| Perrine, B.A., Miss F. M. | M. E. C. | Lucknow | 1889 | Educ. | |
| Peter, Rev. D. A. | C. M. S. | Madras | 1885 | Pastoral. | |
| Peters, Mr. R. J. | C. P. M. | Indore | | Educ. | |
| Phillips, M.A., M.D., LL.B., Mr. J. L. | S. S. U. | Calcutta | 1865 | S. Sch. | C. |
| Do. Rev. M. | L. M. S. | Madras | 1862 | General | C. |
| Do. Miss H. P. | A.F.B.M. | Orissa | 1878 | Zen. & Ed. | |
| Do. Miss N. M. | Ib. | Do. | 1881 | ,, | C. |
| Pickard, Miss E. | A.U.Z.M. | Cawnpore | | Zenana. | |
| Do. Miss L. | Ib. | Do. | | ,, | |
| Pike, Miss S. R. | F. M. A. | Hoshangabad, C. P. | | ,, | |
| Plumb, Miss T. | E. C. S. | Sialkot | 1883 | Zen. and Ed. | |
| Plunkett, Miss L. | F. C. M. | Poona | | ,, | |
| Poynter, Miss E. S. | I. F. N. S. | Allahabad | | Zenana. | |
| Prautch, Rev. A. W. | M. E. C. | Thana, B. | 1884 | Evang. | |
| Do. Mrs. A. W. | Ib. | Do. | 1890 | General. | |
| Prentice, Miss S. B. G. | I. F. N. S. | Bombay | 1892 | Educ. | |
| Rahator, Rev. S. | W. M. S. | Bombay | | Pastoral. | |
| Rambo, Mr. W. E. | Chr. M. | Bilaspur, C. P. | | Evang. | |
| Ramsay, Mr. W. J. | I. M. A. | Berar | 1881 | ,, | |
| Reade, Miss F. M. | Ind. M. | Arcot | 1875 | General. | |
| Redman, Rev. J. | C. M. S. | Hyderabad, S. | 1880 | Ed. & Ev. | |

| Name. | Society. | Town or District. | Year of Entrance on Mission Work. | Work in which engaged. | Attended Allahabad or Calcutta. |
|---|---|---|---|---|---|
| Redman, Mrs. J. ... | C. M. S. | Hyderabad S. | 1880 | Ed. & Zen. | |
| Rees, Rev. D. A. ... | W. M. S. | Mysore | 1876 | Evang. | |
| Reid, M.A., B.D., Rev. D. | F. C. M. | Calcutta | 1891 | English. | |
| Do. Miss C. A. | E. C. S. | Darjeeling | 1884 | Zenana. | |
| Rensaa, Rev. M. ... | S. E. L.M. | Betul, C. P. ... | 1889 | Evang. | |
| Revie, M.B., C.M., Rev. D. | F. C. M. | Wardha, C. P. | 1889 | Medical. | |
| Rice, Rev. H. | E. C. S. | Madras | 1869 | General | C. |
| Richards, M.A, Rev. I. A. | M. E. C. | Mysore | 1879 | Past. & Ev. | C. |
| Do. Rev. W. J. | C. M. S. | Allepy, T. | 1871 | Evang. | |
| Ritter, Rev. G. | Bas. M. | Udapi, M. | 1869 | Pastoral. | |
| Roberts, M.A., Rev. W. A. | C. M. S. | Nasik ... | 1869 | General | C. |
| Do. Miss S. ... | I. P. M. | Gujerat | 1883 | Medical. | |
| Robertson, M.B., M. C., Rev. A. | F. C. M. | Nagpur, C. P. | 1885 | Med. & Ed. | |
| Do. Miss I. | Ib. | Do. | 1889 | ...... | |
| Robinson, Rev. J. E. | M. E. C. | Poona ... | 1874 | General. | |
| Do. Mrs. J. E. | Ib. | Do. ... | ...... | English. | |
| Rocke, Miss N. | B. M. S. | Delhi ... | 1890 | Zen. & Ed. | |
| Rockey, B.A., M.A., Rev. N. L. | M. E. C. | Shahjahanpur | 1885 | Evang. | |
| Do. M.A., Mrs. N. L. | Ib. | Do. | 1885 | Educ. | |
| Rooke, Miss A. E. | B. M. S. | Delhi ... | 1883 | Zen. & Ed. | |
| Rouse, M.A., LL.B., Rev. G. H. | Ib. | Calcutta | 1862 | General | A. C. |
| Do. Mrs. G. H. | Ib. | Do. | 1869 | Zenana. | |
| Row, Rev. I. J. ... | A. I. E. S. | Poona ... | 1876 | Secy. & Ev. | C. |
| Do. Mrs. T. J. ... | Ib. | Do. ... | 1876 | ...... | |
| Royle, Miss E. ... | I. M. A. | Berar ... | 1892 | Evang. | |
| Russell, M.A., Rev. J. M. | F. C. M. | Madras | 1887 | Educ. | |
| Do. B.A., Rev. N. H. | C. P. M. | Mhow, C. T. ... | 1891 | Ev. & Ed. | |
| Do. Mrs. N. H. | Ib. | Do. ... | 1892 | " | |
| Ruthquist, Mr. J. | S. E. L. M. | Chhindwara, C. P. ... | 1885 | Evang. | |
| Sadtler, Miss A. L. | A. L. M. | Guntur, M. ... | 1890 | Educ. | |
| Sanders, Rev. C. M. | A. B.F.M | Jaffna, C. | ...... | Pastoral. | |
| Sandilands, M.A., M.B., C.M., Rev. J. | F. C. M. | Bhandara, C. P. | 1888 | Medical. | |
| Sangle, Mr. A. M. | A. B.F.M. | Bombay | ...... | Literary. | |
| Do. Miss S. ... | Ib. | Ahmednagar, B. | ...... | Zenana. | |
| Saptal, Rev. D. | Ib. | Do. ... | ...... | Pastoral. | |
| Sarkar, Mr. C. P. K. | C. M. S. | Nuddea, Bg. ... | ...... | Educ. | |
| Sawday, Rev. G. W. | W. M. S. | Tunkur, M. | 1876 | Evang. | |
| Scott, M.A., B.D., Ph.D., Rev. J. E. | M. E. C. | Muttra, N.-W. P. | 1873 | Vern. & Eng. | C. |
| Do. Rev. R. ... | F. C. M. | Bombay | 1879 | Educ. | C. |
| Do. Mrs. R. | Ib. | Do. ... | ...... | ...... | |
| Do. M.A., D.D., Rev. T. J. | M. E. C. | Bareilly, N.-W. P. | 1863 | Theol. Sem. | A.C. |
| Do. Mrs. T. J. ... | Ib. | Do. | 1863 | Educ. | |
| Do. Miss F. A.... | Ib. | Lucknow | 1890 | Zenana. | |
| Scudder, M.A., Rev. E. C. | A. A. M. | North Arcot | 1882 | Ev. & Ed. | |

APPENDIX B. 837

| Name. | Society. | Town or District. | Year of Entrance on Mission Work. | Work in which engaged. | Attended Allahabad or Calcutta. |
|---|---|---|---|---|---|
| Scudder, Mrs. E. C. | A. A. M. | North Arcot | 1889 | Zen. & Ed. | |
| Do. M.D., Rev. L. R. | Ib. | Ranipet, M. | 1888 | Medical. | |
| Do. Mrs. L. R. | Ib. | Do. | | | |
| Do. B.A., Mr. H. J. | Ib. | Do. | 1890 | Educ. | |
| Do. Miss T. S. | Ib. | North Arcot | 1870 | Ed. & Zen. | |
| Sectal, F.A., Rev. W. | C. M. S. | Agra | 1869 | Pastoral | A. |
| Sell, B.D., Rev. E. | Ib. | Madras | 1865 | Secty. | |
| Sellers, Miss R. | M. E. C. | Naini Tal, N.-W. P. | | Eng. Ed. | |
| Shaw, Rev. F. | Ib. | Karachi | 1883 | Eng. & Vern. | |
| Do. Mrs. F. | Ib. | Do. | | Zenana. | |
| Sheldon, Miss M. A. | Ib. | Muttra, N.-W. P. | 1888 | Med. & Zen. | |
| Shikela, Rev. T. S. | F. C. M. | Amraoti | | General. | |
| Shillidy, M.A., Rev. J. | I. P. M. | Surat | 1874 | ,, | C. |
| Shome, M.A., B.L., Rev. J. G. | Ch. Smj. | Calcutta | 1861 | Literary | C. |
| Sibley, Mrs. M. | A.B.F.M. | Satara | 1878 | Ed. & Zen. | |
| Simeon, Mr. J. | | Allahabad | 1869 | | A. |
| Simpson, Rev. W. B. | W. M. S. | Chinglepat, M. | 1883 | General. | |
| Sinclair, Miss J. | C. P. M. | Indore, C. I. | | Educ. | |
| Singh, Rev. P. | M. E. C. | Godawara | 1890 | Evang. | |
| Do. B.A., Rev. S. N. | C. M. S. | Allahabad | 1873 | Theol. Sem. | |
| Slade, Miss B. L. | A. B. M. | Nellore, M. | | Medical. | |
| Small, Rev. J. | F. C. M. | Poona | 1863 | General | A. |
| Smith, Rev. J. | B. M. S. | Simla | 1842 | Evang. | A. C. |
| Do. Mrs. J. | Ib. | Do. | 1864 | Zenana. | |
| Do. Rev. T. S. | A. B. F. M. | Jaffana, C. | 1871 | Ev. & Ed. | C. |
| Do. Mrs. T. S. | Ib. | Do. | | ,, | |
| Do. Mrs. D. F. | A. F. B. M. | Orissa | 1853 | Educ. | C. |
| Soper, Rev. W. H. | W. M. S. | Hyderabad | 1886 | Evang. | |
| Sorabji, Rev. K. | C. M. S. | Poona | 1842 | General. | |
| Do. Mrs. F. | I. F. N. S. | Do. | 1853 | Ed. & Ev. | |
| Do. Miss L. | Ib. | Do. | 1879 | Educ. | |
| Do. Miss S. | Ib. | Do. | 1880 | ,, | |
| Spink, Rev. W. | W. M. S. | Barrackpore | 1884 | | |
| Stagg, Rev. W. T. | M. E. C. | Calcutta | | Evang. | |
| Stahl, Miss J. | Ib. | Do. | | Educ. | |
| Stanley, Mr. R. S. M. | I. M. A. | Berar | 1892 | Evang. | |
| Steele, M.A., Rev. J. F. | I. P. M. | Anand, B. | 1883 | ,, | |
| Do. Mrs. J. F. | Ib. | Do. | 1882 | Ev. & Ed. | |
| Stephens, Rev. W. H. | M. E. C. | Bombay | 1880 | Evang. | |
| Do. Mrs. W. H. | Ib. | Do. | | ,, | |
| Do. Miss G. | Ib. | Madras | 1889 | Zen. & Ed. | |
| Stephenson, Miss H. B. | E. C. S. | Gujrat, P. | | Zenana. | |
| Stock, Mr. E. | C. M. S. | London | | Secty | Y. |
| Stone, Rev. G. I. | M. E. C. | Kurrachee | 1879 | General | C. |
| Do. Mrs. G. I. | Ib. | Do. | 1879 | | |
| Do. Rev. J. | C. M. S. | Kistna | 1876 | Evang. | |
| Stunty, M. A., Rev. H. C. | M. E. C. | Naini Tal, N.-W. P. | 1887 | English. | |
| Sullivan, Miss L. W. | Ib. | Lucknow | 1888 | Zenana. | |
| Sutherland, Rev. W. S. | E. C. S. | Darjeeling | 1880 | Theol. Sem. | |

## APPENDIX B.

| Name. | Society. | Town or District. | Year of Entrance on Mission Work | Work in which engaged. | Attended Allahabad or Calcutta. |
|---|---|---|---|---|---|
| Sutherland, Miss A. G. | I. F. N. S. | Lahore | 1891 | Educ. | |
| Tanner, M.A., Rev. H. J. | C. M. S. | Masulipatam | 1887 | ,, | |
| Taylor, M.A., B.D., Rev. G. P. | I. P. M. | Ahmedabad | 1877 | ...... | C. |
| Do. Mr. J. | F. M. A. | Malwa, C. P. | 1889 | General. | |
| Do. Mrs. J. | Ib. | Do. | 1889 | Zenana. | |
| Do. Miss L. | F. C. M. | Poona | 1884 | Educ. | |
| Tebb, Rev. R. | W. M. S. | Galle, C. | 1869 | General. | |
| Do. Mrs. R. | Ib. | Do. | 1875 | ,, | |
| Tedford, Rev. L. | A. P. M. | Ratnagiri | 1880 | Evang. | |
| Terrel, Mr. C. D. | F. M. A. | Bhopal | 1889 | Ev. & Ed. | |
| Theobold, Rev. H. H. | L. M. S. | Benares | 1892 | Evang. | |
| Do. Miss R. M. | Ib. | Do. | | Zen. & Ev. | |
| Thoburn, D.D., Bishop J. M. | M. E. C. | Calcutta | 1859 | Suptd. | A. C. |
| Do. Miss J. M. | Ib. | Lucknow | 1870 | Educ. | A. C. |
| Thomas, Rev. A. A. | W. M. S. | Trichinopoly | 1885 | General. | |
| Do. Rev. S. S. | B. M. S. | Delhi | 1885 | Theol. Sem. | |
| Thompson, Rev. C. S. | C. M. S. | Oodeypore | 1880 | Evang. | |
| Do. M.A., Rev. J. | Ib. | Kotayam, T. | 1888 | Theol. Sem. | |
| Do. Miss A. M. | M. E. C. | Baroda | 1888 | Ed. & Zen. | |
| Do. Miss M. | Chr. M. | Hurda | 1892 | Evang. | |
| Thomson, Rev. J. A. | B. F. B. S. | Allahabad | 1889 | Secty. | |
| Thorn, Miss B. | B. M. S. | Delhi | 1875 | Zen. & Med. | |
| Thwaites, Rev. W. | C. M. S. | Peshawar | 1871 | Evang. | |
| Do. Mrs. W. | Ib. | Do. | | ...... | |
| Tomary, M.A., Rev. A. | F. C. M. | Calcutta | 1887 | Educ. | |
| Torrance, Rev. J. | Ib. | Poona | | Evang. | |
| Tracy, M.A., Rev. T. | A. P. M. | Mainpuri, N.-W. P. | 1869 | ,, | A. |
| Trott, Miss S. | L. F. N. S. | Bombay | 1874 | Ed. & Zen. | |
| Turton, Mr. J. G. | M. E. C. | Bangalore | | Evang. | |
| Uhl, Ph.D., Rev. L. L. | A. L. M. | Guntur, M. | 1873 | General | C. |
| Ullah, Rev. I. | C. M. S. | Sialkot, P. | | Evang. | |
| Vanes, B.A., Rev. J. A. | W. M. S. | Bangalore | 1876 | General. | |
| Vardon, Rev. A. S. E. | M. E. C. | Khandwa, C. P. | 1881 | Evang. | |
| Do. Mrs. A. E. | Ib. | Do. | | ...... | |
| Vines, Miss S. C. | C. M. S. | Tinnevelly | | Educ. | |
| Visuvasam, Mr. S. | D. L. M. | S. Arcot | | Evang. | |
| Wade, B.D., Rev. T. R. | C. M. S. | Amritsar | 1863 | General. | |
| Wadleigh, Mr. T. B. | Ind. M. | Poona | | Eng. | |
| Waitt, Miss A. | L. M. S. | Mirzapur, N.-W. P. | 1888 | General. | |
| Walker, Rev. J. A. K. | C. B. M. | Godavari | 1889 | Evang. | |
| Wanless, M.D., Mr. W. J. | A. P. M. | Miraj, S. M. C. | 1889 | Medical. | |
| Do. Mrs. W. J. | Ib. | Do. | 1889 | Zenana. | |
| Wann, B.D., Rev. A. B. | E. C. S. | Calcutta | 1886 | Educ. | |
| Ward, Rev. C. B. | M. E. C. | Yellandu | | Ev. & Indns. | |
| Do. Rev. R. J. | L. M. S. | Madras | 1893 | Eng. | |
| Do. Miss C. H. | C. E. Z. | Ellore | | Zenana. | |
| Do. Miss G. R. | A. U. Z. M. | Cawnpore | 1870 | Zen. & Ed. | C. |
| Warrack, Miss M. E. | F. C. M. | Calcutta | 1880 | Zenana | C. |

APPENDIX B.

| Name. | Society. | Town or District. | Year of Entrance on Mission Work | Work in which engaged. | Attended Allahabad or Calcutta. |
|---|---|---|---|---|---|
| Watson, Rev. E. W. | L. M. S. | Madras | | Educ. | |
| Wauton, Miss E. | C. E. Z. | Amritsar | 1872 | Ed. & Zen. | |
| Wayte, Miss J. E. | A. B. M. | Nellore | 1884 | Ed. & Zen. | |
| Webb, Miss K. | C. E. Z. | Hyderabad, S. | 1890 | Medical. | |
| Webster, Rev. E. | W. M. S. | Negapatam, M. | 1887 | Educ. | |
| Weitbrecht, Ph.D., Rev. H. U. | C. M. S. | Batala, P. | 1876 | General | C. |
| Wells, Miss A. F. | I. F. N. S. | Lahore | | Evang. | |
| West, A.M., B.D., Rev. J. N. | M. E. C. | Madras | 1892 | Eng. & Vern. | |
| Do. Mrs. J. N. | Ib. | Do. | 1892 | ,, | |
| Wharton, Mr. G. L. | Chr. M. | Bilaspur | 1882 | Evang. | |
| Whitamore, Rev. T. H. | W. M. S. | Madras | 1872 | Eng. | |
| White, B.A., Rev. W. E. | F. C. M. | Chantoli | 1890 | ,, | |
| Do. Miss E. | Ib. | Calcutta | 1882 | Educ. | |
| Do. Miss J. | A. U. P. M. | Gujranwala, P. | 1884 | Zenana. | |
| Whitton, Rev. D. | F. C. M. | Nagpore, C. P. | 1869 | Educ. | A. |
| Do. Mrs. D. | Ib. | Do. | | ,, | |
| Wilder, M.A., Mr. R. P. | A. P. M. | Kolhapur | 1892 | Evang. | |
| Do. Mrs. R. D. | Ib. | Do. | 1892 | ,, | |
| Do. Mrs. R. G. | Ib. | Do. | | Zen. & Ed. | |
| Do. Miss G. E. | Ib. | Do. | 1888 | | |
| Wilkie, M. A., Rev. J. | C. P. M. | Indore, C. P. | 1879 | General. | |
| Do. Mrs. J. | Ib. | Do. | | ,, | |
| Williams, Mr. J. H. | F. M. A. | Sohagpur, C. P. | 1878 | Evang. | |
| Williamson, M. A., Rev. H. D. | C. M. S. | Mandla, C. P. | 1878 | ,, | C. |
| Do. Mrs. H. D. | Ib. | Do. | 1878 | ,, | |
| Wilson, M.A., B.D., M.D., Rev. P. T. | M. E. C. | Budaun, N.-W. P. | 1863 | Gen. & Med. | A. |
| Do. Mrs. P. T. | Ib. | Do. | 1879 | ,, | C. |
| Do. Miss M. E. | Ib. | Bareilly, N.-W. P. | 1890 | Educ. | |
| Winston, Rev. W. R. | W. M. C. | Mandalay | 1873 | General. | |
| Do. Mrs. W. R. | Ib. | Do. | 1876 | | |
| Wolf, M.A., Rev. L. B. | A. L. M. | Guntur, M. | 1883 | Educ. | |
| Wood, Mr. F. H. | Y.M.C.A. | Madras | | Secty. | |
| Do. Mr. M. D. | I. M. A. | Berar | 1892 | Evang. | |
| Do. Miss C. | M. E. C. | Hyderabad, D. | | Educ. | |
| Woodhouse, Miss M. | E. S. C. | Madras | | Zenana. | |
| Yardi, Rev. A. B. | C. M. S. | Poona | 1845 | Pastoral. | |
| Young, Miss S. A. | A. U.P.M. | Pasrur, P. | 1893 | Zenana. | |
| Ziegler, Rev. F. | Bas. M. | Dharwar | 1862 | Ed. & Lit. | |

## Appendix C.

*Receipts.*

|  | Rs. | a. | p. |
|---|---|---|---|
| By Sale of Tickets | 759 | 0 | 0 |
| ,, Collections | 403 | 14 | 10 |
| ,, Missionary Societies | 600 | 0 | 0 |
| ,, Individuals | 972 | 0 | 0 |
| ,, Amounts promised | 377 | 0 | 0 |
| ,, Deficit | 548 | 13 | 7 |
| Total......Rs. | 3,660 | 12 | 5 |

*Expenditure.*\*

|  | Rs. | a. | p. |
|---|---|---|---|
| To Cost of Encampment at Chowpatty, about | 2,800 | 0 | 0 |
| ,, Printing, Advertisements, &c. | 171 | 8 | 0 |
| ,, Hire of Furniture, Sanitary expenses | 245 | 4 | 0 |
| ,, Hire of Framjee Hall Reporters | 135 | 8 | 5 |
| ,, Expenses incurred by Provisional Committee | 176 | 0 | 0 |
| ,, Postage and Stationary in Bombay, and Sundries | 132 | 8 | 0 |
| Total......Rs. | 3,660 | 12 | 5 |

\* The Treasurer, the Rev. W. G. Peel, had not been able to close his accounts at the time of going to Press, so the above is only approximate.

## Appendix D.

### SUBSCRIPTIONS.

|  | Rs. | a. | p. |
|---|---:|---:|---:|
| Sale of Tickets | 759 | 0 | 0 |
| Collections | 403 | 14 | 10 |
| Church Missionary Society | 170 | 0 | 0 |
| Irish Presbyterian Mission | 50 | 0 | 0 |
| Lutheran Mission, Guntoor | 50 | 0 | 0 |
| Wesleyan Missionary Society | 100 | 0 | 0 |
| American Mission, Ahmednugar | 30 | 0 | 0 |
| Baptist Missionary Society | 100 | 0 | 0 |
| Bombay Missionary Conference | 100 | 0 | 0 |
| Through the Rev. J. Pusell | 20 | 0 | 0 |
| ,,   ,,   ,,   J. Small, Poona | 75 | 0 | 0 |
| ,,   ,,   ,,   H. Rice, Madras | 193 | 0 | 0 |
| Dr. J. M. M. Phail | 50 | 0 | 0 |
| Rev. J. F. Gardner | 100 | 0 | 0 |
| H. Conder, Esq. | 50 | 0 | 0 |
| Rev. Morrison, Calcutta | 20 | 0 | 0 |
| Rev. Paton Begg | 20 | 0 | 0 |
| Dr. Fairbank | 50 | 0 | 0 |
| Rev. J. H. Bruce | 10 | 0 | 0 |
| ,, J. Small | 30 | 0 | 0 |
| C. E. G. Crawford, Esq. | 10 | 0 | 0 |
| Mr. Kelner, Lahore | 10 | 0 | 0 |
| Rev. R. M. Gray | 50 | 0 | 0 |
| Miss Patterson | 10 | 0 | 0 |
| Rev. R. Scott | 50 | 0 | 0 |
| Rev. H. E. Barrell | 10 | 0 | 0 |
| J. Jackson, Esq. | 10 | 0 | 0 |
| L. J. K. | 10 | 0 | 0 |
| A. Tomlinson, Esq. | 10 | 0 | 0 |
| B. Phillips, Esq. | 10 | 0 | 0 |
| J. Morris, Esq. | 50 | 0 | 0 |
| E. H. A. | 20 | 0 | 0 |
| Miss Smith | 10 | 0 | 0 |
| Rev. Torrance | 11 | 0 | 0 |
| Dr. Alexander | 10 | 0 | 0 |
| W. Lee-Warner, Esq. | 20 | 0 | 0 |
| Rev. G. Kerry | 10 | 0 | 0 |
| Sums under Rs. 10 | 43 | 0 | 0 |
|  | 2,734 | 14 | 10 |

Promised :—

|  | Rs. | a. | p. |
|---|---:|---:|---:|
| C. M. S. (Bombay) | 50 | 0 | 0 |
| Rev. W. G. Peel | 15 | 0 | 0 |
| Dr. March | 30 | 0 | 0 |
| J. Jack, Esq. | 50 | 0 | 0 |
| Miss Bernard | 72 | 0 | 0 |
| Miss Abbott | 10 | 0 | 0 |
| Rev. T. H. Greig | 50 | 0 | 0 |
| Methodist Episcopal Mission | 100 | 0 | 0 |
|  | 377 | 0 | 0 |
| Total ... Rs. | 3,111 | 14 | 10 |

# COMPLETE INDEX

## TO VOLUMES I. AND II.

|  | PAGE |
|---|---|
| ACKERMANN, Miss J., Speech by | 754 |
| A. I. E. Society, Nature of Work | 653-7 |
| ,, ,, Work in Assam | 653 |
| Almora, Leper Work at... | 112-3, 116 |
| A. L. O. E., Reference to | 681, 736 |
| Anantam, Rev. D., Speech by | 470 |
| Anderson, Rev. H., Speech by | 207 |
| Andrew, Rev. A., Speech by | 574 |
| Andrews, Miss A. M., Speech by | 662 |
| Anglo-Indians and Eurasians, and Work among— | |
| ,, A Missionary subject | 637-8, 654-5, 658, 663 |
| ,, Catholic influence among | 643, 657 |
| ,, Character of the people | 638, 641, 646, 659 |
| ,, Character of work desirable | 641, 644, 646-50, 660 |
| ,, Difficulty of the work | 639, 644 |
| ,, Importance ,, | 637, 638, 645, 658 |
| ,, Lack of Protestant Schools among | 658, 661 |
| ,, Predjudice regarding | 611, 660 |
| ,, Producing Missionaries | 639, 651 |
| ,, Work as carried on | 642-3 |
| Anti-Christian Literature | 277 |
| Apostle's Creed, References to | 20, 37, 40, 43, 46, 47, 50, 54, 124 |
| Appaji Bapuji, Rev., Speech by | 75 |
| Appeal by Decennial Conference | 744-6 |
| Appendices | 825-41 |
| Arcot Mission, Reference to | 132 |
| Arnold, Sir E., Reference to | 793 |
| Aryra-Somaj, Reference to | 300 |
| Ashcroft, Rev. F., Speech by | 407, 614 |
| Augustine, St., Reference to | 158 |
| Aurungabad, Work at | 48 |
| BAILEY, W. C., Esq., Paper by | 96 |
| ,, Reference to | 115 |
| Baker, Mr. S., Speech by | 160 |
| Baldwin, Dr., Quotation from | 654 |
| Banerjea, Rev. C. N., Speech by | 49, 311 |

|   | PAGE |
|---|---|
| Banurji, K. C., Esq., Paper by | 121 |
| ,,   Speech by ... ... ... 87, 171, 303, 409, 461, 538, 763 | |
| Baptism, Questions relating thereto, 89, 92, 180, 351-5, 362-3, 366-7 | |
|   446, 468, 570, 583, 586, 588, 614, 779-781 | |
| Basel Mission Work ... ... ... ... 168, 479-93, 505, 710 | |
| Bateson, Rev. J. H., Speech by | 748 |
| Beatty, Rev. W., Speech by | 120 |
| Begg, Rev. A. P., Speech by | 525, 540 |
| Benares, Maharajah of, on Marriage Law | 62 |
| Bernard, Miss, Paper by | 315 |
| ,,   Speech by | 366 |
| Bestall, Rev. A. H., Quotation from | 103 |
| ,,  ,,  Work of | 117 |
| Bible, Commentaries and Paraphrases ... ... 667-8, 727 | |
| ,, Depôts ... ... ... ... ... 692-3, 738 | |
| ,, Free Distribution of (see also Bible Society B. and F., Finance) ... 732-3 | |
| ,, Society, *British and Foreign*— | |
| ,, ,, Colportage in connection with 693-5, 697-8, 725 | |
| ,, ,, Finance and Free Grants ... 691-2, 695, 731, 738 | |
| ,, ,, Future Demands upon ... ... ... 695-6, 738 | |
| ,, ,, Letter from ... ... ... ... 698 | |
| ,, ,, Revision Committees ... ... ... ... 690 | |
| ,, ,, Style and size of Bibles ... ... ... ... 691 | |
| ,, ,, Suggestions to Translators ... ... 689, 729 | |
| ,, ,, Tasks involved in Translations ... ... ... 688-9 | |
| ,, ,, Translations, Number of ... ... ... ... 687 | |
| ,, ,, Work in India ... ... ... ... 688, 737 | |
| Bible Translations (see also Bible Society B. and F.) ... ... 666, 726 | |
| ,, Women, their Work and Training ... ... ... 322-3, 342 | |
| Bissell, Mrs., Paper by | 319 |
| Blackstock, Rev. J., Speech by | 506 |
| Blind, Work among the | 580 |
| Boggs, Rev. W. B., Speech by | 406 |
| Bose, Rev. M. N., Speech by | 220 |
| Bounsall, Miss, Speech by | 364 |
| Brahmo-Somaj, policy and support of | 402 |
| Brahmoism, Reference to | 269, 280 |
| Braille, System of teaching | 566, 580 |
| Brown, Rev. J., Speech by | 178 |
| Bruce, Rev. H. J., Speech by | 90, 732 |
| Budden, Miss A. N., Speech by | 779 |
| Budden, Rev. J. H., Reference to | 116 |
| Bullock, Rev. G. M., Letter from | 103 |
| ,,   Speech by | 111 |
| Burditt, Rev. J. F., Paper by | 5 |

# INDEX. 845

| | PAGE |
|---|---|
| Burmah, LeperWork at ... | 116 |
| Business arrangements ... | 741 |
| ,, Committees and Resolutions (see also Standing Committee | 2, 747 |
| Butler, Mrs. Josephine, Letter from ... | 774 |
| CALCUTTA, Duff College at ... | 307 |
| Calvin, Reference to ... | 228 |
| Cambridge Mission, The, Reference to ... | 272, 300 |
| Campbell, Rev. A., Speech by ... | 36 |
| Campbell, Rev. J. F., Speech by ... | 537 |
| Campbell, Mr. W. H., Speech by ... | 39, 89, 408, 575 |
| Carey, Wm., Reference to ... | 745, 768, 797-9 |
| Caste Difficulties ... | 331, 428-31 |
| Centenary of Modern Missions ... | |
| Chamberlain, Rev. Dr., Speech by ... | 46, 173, 500, 726 |
| ,, ,, Paper by ... | 127 |
| Charlton, Rev. J. W., Speech by ... | 534 |
| Chatterjee, Rev. K. C., Speech by ... | 78, 403 |
| Children (see under Training of the Young.)— | |
| Chota Nagpur, R. Catholic Work at ... | 246, 254 |
| Christaram, Hymn by ... | 104 |
| Christian Literature— | |
| ,, Character desirable ... | 288, 669, 671, 703, 727 |
| ,, Children's Books required ... | 210 |
| ,, Christian Newspapers ... | 670-1 |
| ,, Christian Literary Society, one for all India | 673-4 |
| ,, Circulation, difficulties of ... | 712, 720-4, 730 |
| ,, ,, Methods of | 706, 732-4, 705 |
| ,, Colporteurs required ... | 713, 730, 734 |
| ,, English Literature ... | 674-700, 702 |
| ,, ,, ,, its importance ... | 675, 711, 716 |
| ,, Financial Questions of ... | 703-5, 708-10, 714-5, 718, 731 |
| ,, Free Distribution of ... | 705 |
| ,, Increased needs, and how to meet (see C. L. S. letter) ... | 683-6, 739 |
| ,, Missionaries required (Literary) ... | 672-3, 682 |
| ,, Present description of ... | 665, 670, 682, 739 |
| ,, Publications by— | |
| ,, ,, American Meth. Publishers | 676, 678 |
| ,, ,, Calcutta "Oxford" Mission | 678 |
| ,, ,, Christian L. Society | 678 |
| ,, ,, Gujarat Tract Society | 701 |
| ,, ,, Madras Christian College... | 679 |
| ,, ,, Religious Tract Society | 676-7 |
| ,, ,, Surat Mission Press | 703, 706 |
| ,, School Books required ... | 680, 728 |
| ,, Tract Society Statistics ... | 676, 737 |

# 846 INDEX.

|  | PAGE |
|---|---|
| Christian Translation Work | 666 |
| ,, Women's Work in connection with | 736-7 |
| ,, Literature Society, Letter by | 683 |
| Christo-Somaj, Reference to | 160 |
| Chumba, Leper Asylum at | 118 |
| Church History, Reference to | 377 |
| Chuhras, Work among the | 45 |
| Clark, Dr. H. M., Speech by | 242, 256. 307 |
| Clifford, Rev. A., Paper by | 590 |
| ,, ,, Speech by | 630 |
| Clough, Dr., Work begun by | 9 |
| Colportage (see under Christian Literature and B. and F. B. Society)— | |
| Condon, Rev. Dr., Speech by | 778 |
| Conference, Resolutions, Adopted by | 744-1 |
| Conference Sermon | 796-807 |
| Conklin, Rev. C. G., Speech by | 535 |
| Constantine, Reference to | 243, 529 |
| Cousland, Dr. C. B., Work among Lepers | 108 |
| Crosthwaite, Sir Charles, on Leper Work | 116 |
| | |
| St. Dalmas, Rev. H. G. E., Speech by | 538 |
| Davis, Rev. J. E., Speech by | 576 |
| DeSouza, Rev. C. W., Letter from | 103 |
| Deceased Wife's Sister, Marriage of | 82 |
| Depressed Classes (see under Lower Classes.) | |
| Diez, Rev. C. A. E., Paper by | 227 |
| ,, ,, Speech by | 168, 256, 657 |
| Din, Rev. Imadud, Reference to | 717, 761 |
| Divorce (see also "Marriage") | 65, 83, 85, 86, 89, 90 |
| Duff, Dr., Reference to | 261, 680 |
| Dufferin Fund, Reference to | 350 |
| Duthie, Rev. J., Speech by | 51, 175, 305, 471, 509, 734 |
| Dyer, Mr. A. S., Speech by | 773 |
| | |
| Educated Classes— | |
| ,, Attitude of the | 266, 279, 301, 303, 309-12 |
| ,, Christian Influence among the | 267, 278 |
| ,, Duty towards the | 277 |
| ,, Influence of | 258, 274-5, 310 |
| ,, Lectures among the | 271, 286, 304 |
| ,, Methods of Work among the | 285, 290, 302, 306, 308, 311 |
| ,, Necessity of Work among the | 276, 283, 306 |
| ,, Work among the | 258-313 |
| Education and the University (see also Government Grants) | 434, 444, 450, 463 |

| | PAGE |
|---|---|
| ducation as a Missionary Agency | 183, 413-77 |
| ,, Influence of | 437, 445, 447, 452, 465, 470 |
| ,, Interest in | 415, 425 |
| ,, Importance and Necessity of. | 415-6, 422, 428-9, 441-2, 448, 451, 454, 455-6, 463-4 |
| ,, Nature of | 417, 424-7, 439-41, 449, 457, 462, 465-7, 471, 473-4 |
| ,, Opinions regarding | 241, 413, 454-7, 459-60, 462, 468, 472 |
| ,, Outside Testimony to | 466 |
| ,, Present position of | 431-2, 438, 446, 451, 462-4, 472 |
| ,, Progress of | 430, 433-4 |
| ,, Qualification for | 438, 449 |
| ,, Results of | 264, 294, 452-3, 461-2, 464, 468-9, 471 |
| ,, How to be made more effective | 815-23 |
| Education among women | 320, 339, 348, 350, 359 |
| Educational Statistics | 262, 273-4 |
| Elsam, Rev. E. G., Speech by | 536 |
| English Literature (see under Christian Literature). | |
| Epworth Leagues, Reference to | 35, 217 |
| Europeans and Eurasians (see also Anglo-Indians and Eurasians) | 241, 358, 364 |
| Evangelists (Native), Questions relating thereto—(see also under Native Preacher) | 318, 379 |
| Ewing, Rev. Dr., Speech by | 300, 448, 748 |
| | |
| FAIRBANK, Rev. Dr., Speech by | 498 |
| Findlay, Rev. W. H., Paper by | 414 |
| Free Thought Depôts | 676 |
| Frohnmeyer, Rev. L. J., Paper by | 479 |
| ,, ,, Speech by | 509 |
| Fuller, Rev. M. B., Speech by | 504, 772 |
| | |
| GARDNER, Miss S. F., Paper by | 178 |
| Gladstone, the Hon'ble W. E., Quotation from | 531 |
| Gladwin, Mr. W. J., Speech by | 252 |
| Goldsmith, Rev. H. D., Speech by | 391 |
| Gordon, Miss, Speech by | 540 |
| Goldsmith, Rev. H., Paper by | 638 |
| Government Grants, Reference to | 364, 368, 434, 444, 463 |
| ,, Schools ,, | 219, 220 |
| ,, Universities | 294, 434-5 |
| Graham, Rev. J. A., Speech by | 161, 585 |
| Gray, Rev. J. S., Speech by | 538 |
| Greenfield, Miss, Speech by | 351 |
| Gregory VIII., H. H. Pope, Reference to | 230 |
| Grubb, Rev. C., Mission by, Reference to | 656 |
| Guilford, Rev. E., Quotation from | 105 |

|  | PAGE |
|---|---|
| Guilford, Rev. E., Work of | 117 |
| Gulliford, Rev. H., Speech by | 617 |
| Gujarat Tract Society | 701 |
| | |
| Hahn, Rev. C. N. P. F., Speech by | 147, 254 |
| Hahn, Rev. F., Work among Lepers | 107 |
| Haigh, Rev. H., Paper by | 664 |
| ,,   ,,   Speech by | 303, 735 |
| Harding, Rev. C., Speech by | 314 |
| Harding, Mrs., Speech by | 778 |
| Haskew, Miss, Speech by | 364 |
| Hawker, Rev. J. G., Speech by | 164, 463 |
| Haythornthwaite, Rev. I., Speech by | 465 |
| Heinrichs, Rev. J., Speech by | 563, 589 |
| High Schools (embraced under "Educational Work"). | |
| Hindu Tract Society | 302, 310 |
| Hinduism purified | 281 |
| Holkar, H. H. the Maharajah, Reference to | 769 |
| Hong Kong, Letter from Christian Churches at | 771 |
| Hooper, Rev. Dr., Lecture by | 782 |
| ,,   ,,   Paper by | 371 |
| ,,   ,,   Speech by | 409, 413, 629 |
| Hugenots, The, Reference to | 234 |
| Hunter, Sir W., Opinion of | 49, 582 |
| Hume, Rev. R. A., Paper by | 56 |
| ,,   ,,   Speech by | 92, 305, 627 |
| Husband, Rev. J., Speech by | 96 |
| | |
| Indore, Work at | 769 |
| Industrial Homes | 343 |
| Industrial Work and all questions thereto relating... | 478-510 |
| | |
| Jaffna, Industrial Work at | 493 |
| Jesuitism and R. Catholicism | 227-256 |
| John, Rev. S., Speech by | 309 |
| Johnson, Rev. T. S., Speech by | 154, 628 |
| Johnson, Rev. W. F., Letter from | 103 |
| ,,   ,,   Speech by | 719 |
| Jones, Rev. J. P., Paper by | 362 |
| ,,   ,,   Speech by | 89, 411, 629 |
| Jones, Rev. V. L., Speech by | 159 |
| Justyn Martyr, Reference to | 528 |
| | |
| Kerry, Rev. G., Sermon by | 796 |
| Khan, Dr. B., Testimony re Leper Work | 101 |

|  | PAGE |
|---|---|
| Kols, Work among the | 147 |
| Kugler, Miss A. S., Paper by | 326 |
|   ,,   ,, Speech by | 366 |
| La Trobe, Bishop, Quotation from | 98 |
| Lash, Rev. A. H., Speech by | 302 |
| Lay, Rev. C. W., Speech by | 503 |
| Lazarus, Rev. J., Speech by | 53, 162, 172, 393 |
| Leitners, The, Work among Lepers | 97 |

Lepers—
| ,, Children of | 113 |
|---|---|
| ,, European | 110, 118 |
| ,, Government attitude towards | 110 |
| ,, Government Commission on | 15 |
| ,, Medical Advice concerning | 119 |
| ,, Moravian Stations among the | 101 |
| ,, Number of | 111 |
| ,, Remedies for | 115 |
| ,, Segregation of | 115-6, 117 |
| ,, Separate Organisation for | 109 |
| ,, Work among | 96-119 |
| Literature (see under "Christian Literature.") | |
| Literature found in the Homes | 675 |
| ,, General | 681 |
| Longhurst, Mrs., Speech by | 354 |
| Lord's Day Act Memorial of Calcutta | 512, 516, 518, 522 |
| Lord's Day Act Repeal, Reference to | 512, 529, 539 |

Lord's Day Observance in India—
| ,, European attitude towards | 513, 514, 532-3, 535 |
|---|---|
| ,, Government attitude towards | 514-5, 517 |
| ,, Importance of | 512, 535, 537 |
| ,, Its Scriptural Basis and Moral Aspect, | 519-20, 523-4, 526-8, 534, 536-7 |
| ,, Native Observance of | 516, 529, 538 |
| ,, Relation of, to Native Church | 512, 535 |
| ,, Testimony concerning the | 530-1 |
| Lord's Day Union for India | 518, 521-2, 522, 539-40 |

Lower Classes—
| ,, Attitude towards Christianity | 549-50, 556, 567 |
|---|---|
| ,, Government attitude towards the | 547-8, 564, 575, 579 |
| ,, How to aid the | 546, 549, 553, 561-3, 565, 572-3, 576, 579, 585 |
| ,, Mass Movements among the | 556-60, 562, 567, 569, 573 |
| ,, M. E. C., Work among the | 28, 766 |
| ,, ,, Intellectual condition of | 54 |
| ,, Pariahs, Moral condition of | 545, 552, 554, 572, 584 |
| ,, ,, Social condition of | 544-5, 551, 552, 571, 575, 581, 584 |
| ,, Prospects of Work among the | 14, 555, 566, 573, 764 |

850                           INDEX.

| | | PAGE |
|---|---|---|
| Lower Classes— | | |
| ,, Results of Work among the | ... ... ... ... ... | 769 |
| ,, Social condition of the | ... ... ... ... ... | 541, 564, 589 |
| ,, Who comprise the | ... ... ... ...544, 550-1, 563, | 567-8, 581 |
| ,, Work among the... | ... ... ... ... | ...5, 8, 766, 769 |
| Loyala Ignatius,'Reference to ... | ... ... ... ... | 228, 229 |
| Lundborg, Rev. N. F., Speech by | ... ... ... ... 218, | 506, 578, 624 |
| Luther, Martyn, Reference to ... | ... ... ... ... ... | 228, 234 |
| | | |
| MACDONALD, REV. DR. K. S., on Marriage Law | ... ... ... ... | 62 |
| ,, ,, on School Literature ... | ... ... ... | 680 |
| Macdonald, Rev. J. A., Speech by | ... ... ... ... ... | 529, 728 |
| Mackichan, Rev. Dr., Opening Speech by | ... ... ... ... ... | 1 |
| ,, ,, Paper by | ... ... ... ... ... | 424 |
| ,, ,, Speech by | ... ... ... ... ... | 298, 475 |
| Madras Christian College, Reference to | ... ... ... ... | 261, 673 |
| ,, ,, Magazine... | ... ... ... ... ... | 679 |
| ,, Conference Pariah Memorial... | ... ... ... ... ... | 546 |
| ,, Women's Work at | ... ... ... ... ... | 355, 357 |
| Maine, Sir W., Quotation from .. | ... ... ... ... ... | 84 |
| Malas, Work among the | ... ... ... ... ... | 39 |
| Malhar, Rev. D. G., Speech by | ... ... ... ... ... | 161 |
| Manley, Rev. W. R., Speech by | ... ... ... ... ... | 52 |
| Mansell, Rev. Dr., Speech by ... | ... ... ... ... ... | 306 |
| Mansell, Rev. W. A., Speech by | ... ... ... ... ... | 464 |
| Martin, Rev. Dr., Paper by | ... ... ... ... ... | 18 |
| Marriage and Divorce ... | ... ... ... ... ... | 56-95 |
| ,, Fees ... ... ... | ... ... ... ... ... | 150 |
| ,, Indian Christian Act... | ... ... ... ... ... | 94 |
| | | |
| Mass Movements.— | | |
| ,, ,, Converts or not? | ... ... ... 560, 569, | 586, 588, 589 |
| ,, ,, Danger of ... | ... ... ... 558, 559, 569, | 574, 588 |
| ,, ,, Referred to ... | ... ... 556, 558, 560, 562, 567, | 573, 586 |
| McAfee, Mrs. F. L., Speech by | ... ... ... ... ... | 660 |
| McCann, Mr. R., Speech by ... | ... ... ... ... ... | 222 |
| McConaughy, Mr. D., Speech by | ... ... ... ... ... | 185, 222 |
| McLaurin, Rev. Dr., Speech by | ... ... ... ... | 165, 289, 586 |
| McMahon, Rev. J. T., Speech by | ... ... ... ... ... | 118 |
| Medical Mission, Reference to ... | ... ... ... ... 305, | 307, 316, 324 |
| ,, ,, Women's | ... ... ... ... 326, | 335, 365, 366 |
| Miller, Rev. W., Speech by ... | ... ... ... ... ... | 258, 472 |
| Missionary Comity, its present policy and suggested alterations ... | | 590-636 |
| ,, Encouragements and Prospects | ... ... ... ... | 759-770 |
| ,, Public Meeting ... | ... ... ... ... ... | 759-770 |
| ,, Statistics ... ... | ... ... ... ... ... | 806-814 |
| Modak, S. R., Esq., Speech by | ... ... ... ... ... | 291 |

# INDEX.

|  | PAGE |
|---|---|
| Mody, Rev. M. H., Speech by | 252, 731 |
| Moravians, Work of, among Lepers | 97 |
| Morris, Jas., Esq., Speech by | 478 |
| Morrison, Rev. W. J. P., Speech by | 211 |
| Muhammadan Women, Work among | 336 |
| Muir, Sir W., Letter by | 73 |
| Mulvaney, Miss S. L., Paper by | 335 |
| ,, ,, Speech by | 367 |
| Murdoch, Dr. J., Paper by | 674 |
| ,, ,, Speech by | 736 |
| | |
| NARSINGPUR, Work at | 219 |
| Nasik Industrial Home | 501 |
| Native Christians, Education of | 435-6, 475 |
| Native Church, the | 120-177, 370, 412 |
| ,, Conception of | 121, 124 |
| ,, Conference concerning | 141 |
| ,, Opposition to | 128 |
| ,, Organisation of | 123-4, 127, 130, 166 |
| ,, Property of | 150 |
| ,, Responsibility of | 170 |
| ,, Self-Government of | 163, 170 |
| ,, Self-Support of, 51, 125, 143, 148, 156, 163-7, 170, 173-179, | |
| | 374, 387-8, 392, 403, 408, 410-1 |
| Native Preachers, Qualification of, 148, 150, 371, 383, 385, 392, 395, 399- | |
| | 400, 402, 403, 407, 409, 412 |
| Responsibility of | 389, 400, 403 |
| Training of | 370, 373, 378-9, 383-6, 395, 400-10, 412 |
| Navalkar, Rev. G., Speech by | 48, 293 |
| Newsom, Rev. J. E., Speech by | 661 |
| Newton, Dr. John, Reference to | 100 |
| Noble College, Reference to the | 470 |
| North India Bible Society, Reference to the | 710 |
| Nowroji, Rev. Dhanjibhai, Speech by | 370 |
| Nowroji, Rev. Ruttonji, Work of | 48 |
| | |
| OPENING SPEECH | 1 |
| Opium Question, Discussion upon | 771-775 |
| Organe, Rev. S. W., Paper by | 687 |
| ,, ,, Speech by | 658, 737 |
| Osborne, Rev. D., Speech by | 645 |
| Oxford Brotherhood, The | 272, 300, 678 |
| | |
| PADFIELD, REV. J. E., Speech by | 91, 175, 249, 404, 582, 730 |
| Panjab, R. Catholic, Work in the | 216 |
| Pantheism, doctrine of, Reference to | 266, 276 |

|  | PAGE |
|---|---|
| Pariah Classes (see under "Lower Classes")— | |
| Parker, Rev. A., Speech by | 755 |
| Parker, Rev. Dr., Paper by | 26 |
| ,, ,, Speech by | 54, 217 |
| Parson, Rev. J., Speech by | 581 |
| Pentecost, Rev. Dr., Reference to | 287, 291, 307, 356 |
| Perkins, Rev. H. E., Paper by | 67 |
| Pestonji, the late Rev. H., Reference to | 707 |
| Phillips, Rev. J. L., Paper by | 195 |
| ,, ,, Speech by | 115, 163, 223, 580, 627, 662, 725 |
| Phillips, Rev. M., Paper by | 815 |
| ,, ,, Speech by | 51, 301, 462 |
| Phillips, Rev. W. B., Paper by | 511 |
| Polygamy, Reference to | 64 |
| Prautch, Rev. A. W., Speech by | 252, 538, 707 |
| Press, The, Reference to | 232, 235, 288 |
| Press, Free Ch. Printing, at Poona | 499 |
| Public Morals in India | 771, 775 |
| Pulayans, Work among the | 42 |
| | |
| RAMBO, REV. W. E., Speech by | 50 |
| Ramsay, Hon'ble Sir H., Reference to | 99 |
| Ramsey, General, Reference to | 116 |
| Reid, Rev. Dr., Speech by | 659 |
| Religious Tract Society, Work of | 673, 676-7 |
| ,, (see also under "Christian Literature"). | |
| Richards, Rev. W. J., Speech by | 42, 114, 734 |
| Roberts, Rev. N. A., Speech by | 46 |
| Roman Catholicism, discussed | 227, 256 |
| Rouse, Rev. G. H., Speech by | 165, 251, 630, 729 |
| Row, Dewan Raganath, on Marriage Law | 61 |
| Row, Rev. I., Speech by | 653 |
| | |
| SANTALS, Work among the | 36 |
| Satthianadhan, Mr. S., Speech by | 260 |
| Septicism, Reference to | 266 |
| Schools— | |
| ,, Day Schools (see also under "Education") | 181, 184, 219 |
| ,, High Schools ( ,, ,, ,, ) | |
| ,, Low Caste Schools | 821 |
| ,, Sunday Schools (see below) | |
| Scoble, Sir Andrew, Quotation from | 544, 646 |
| Scott, Rev. Dr. T. J., Speech by | 45, 221, 402, 637, 732 |
| Scott, Rev. J. S., Speech by | 764 |
| Scott, Rev. R., Speech by | 467 |

|                                                          |                                      |
| -------------------------------------------------------- | ------------------------------------ |
|                                                          | PAGE                                 |
| Scudder, Rev. J., Speech by                              | 544                                  |
| Selwyn, Bishop, Quotation from                           | 131                                  |
| Shahjanpore, Industrial Work at                          | 506                                  |
| Shillidy, Rev. J., Speech by                             | 166, 468, 621                        |
| Shome, Rev. J. G., Speech by                             | 157, 401, 511                        |
| Simeon, Mr. J., Speech by                                | 88                                   |
| Simpson, Rev. W. R., Speech by                           | 584                                  |
| Slater, Rev. T. E., Paper by                             | 272                                  |
| Small, Rev. J., Speech by                                | 169, 226, 499                        |
| Smith, Rev. J., Speech by                                | 86, 541                              |
| Smith, Rev. T. S., Paper by                              | 493                                  |
| Social Purity Question                                   | 774                                  |
| Society of Christian Endeavour                           | 134, 208, 211, 213                   |
| Somerville, the late Dr. A., Reference to                | 291                                  |
| Sorabji Kharshetji, Rev., Speech by                      | 85, 501                              |
| ,,         ,,       Mrs., Speech by                      | 213, 658                             |
| Standing Committee for Decennial Conference, 1903        | 747                                  |
| Stone, Rev. J., Speech by                                | 571                                  |
| Stuntz, Rev. H. C., Speech by                            | 235, 658                             |
| Sunday School Journal                                    | 201, 209                             |
| Sunday School Teachers                                   | 182, 200, 204-7, 209, 212, 215       |
| Sunday School Union                                      | 195, 199, 224                        |
| Sunday School Work    12, 51, 134, 181, 184, 195, 204, 209, 241, 321, 663 |                  |
| Surat Mission Press                                      | 703, 706                             |
| Syrian Church, The, Reference to                         | 734                                  |
|                                                          |                                      |
| Tanna, R. Catholic Work at                               | 252                                  |
| Tarn Taran, Leper Work at                                | 105, 117                             |
| Taylor, Rev. G. P., Paper by                             | 701                                  |
| ,,       ,,     Speech by                                | 738                                  |
| Tebb, Rev. R., Paper by                                  | 139                                  |
| ,,      ,,    Speech by                                  | 173, 399                             |
| Telegu Country, Work in the                              | 50                                   |
| Temperance Appeal                                        | 757, 759                             |
| ,,    Work among Civilians, Soldiers and Natives         | 748, 759                             |
| Thoburn, Bishop, Closing Speech by                       | 741                                  |
| ,,       ,,    Paper by                                  | 601                                  |
| ,,       ,,    Speech by                                 | 43, 167, 458, 631                    |
| Thoburn, Miss, Paper by                                  | 345                                  |
| Thomas, Rev. J. W., Paper by                             | 806                                  |
| Thompson, Rev. J. A., Speech by                          | 711                                  |
| Thompson, Rev. J., Speech by                             | 42                                   |
| "Times of India." The, Quotation from                    | 547                                  |
| Tomory, Rev. A., Speech by                               | 307                                  |
| Tract Societies (see under " Christian Literature ")     |                                      |

                                                                                          PAGE
Training Institutions ... ... ... ... ... ... ...   493-509
Translation Work (see under "Christian Literature and B. F. B. S.").
Transmigration, Hindu Doctrine of ... ... ... ... ...   782, 795
Twing, Mrs., Speech by ... ... ... ... ... ... ... ...   365


UFFMANN, REV. H., Letter from ... ... ... ... ... ...   102
Uhl, Rev. Dr., Paper by ... ... ... ... ... ... ...   550
   ,,    ,,    Speech by ... ... ... ... ... ... 50, 587, 626
Unity of the Church in India ... ... ... ... ... 157, 165, 169, 171
VARLEY, Mr. H., Speech by ... ... ... ... ... ... ...   775
WADE, REV. T. R., Speech by ... ... ... ... ... ...   117, 760
Wai, Appeal for legal rights at ... ... ... ... ... ...   91
Wann, Rev. A. B., Paper by ... ... ... ... ... ... ...   426
   ,,       ,,    Speech by ... ... ... ... ... ... ...   477
Ward, Miss, Speech by ... ... ... ... ... ... ... ...   777
Ward, Rev. C. B., Speech by ... ... ... ... ... ... ...   581
Warne, Rev. F. W., Speech by ... ... ... ... ... ... ...   519
Warrack, Miss, Speech by ... ... ... ... ... ... ...   361
Wauton, Miss, Speech by ... ... ... ... ... ... ...   677
Weitbrecht, Rev. Dr., Speech by ... ... ... 45, 299, 508, 579, 716
Wesley, Rev. John, Reference to ... ... ... ... ... ...   155
Wilder, Rev. R. P., Speech by ... ... ... ... ... ... ...   218
Wilding, Mrs., Speech by ... ... ... ... ... ... ...   778
Wilkie, Rev. J., Speech by ... ... ... ... ... ... 170, 767
Williams, Sir Monier, Quotation from ... ... ... ... ...   271
Winston, Rev. W. R., Speech by ... ... ... ... ... ...   116
Wolf, Rev. L. B., Speech by ... ... ... ... ... ... 308, 454
Women, Baptism of ... ... ... ... ... ... ... 779-781
   ,,   Converts' Homes for ... ... ... ... ... ... ...   776
   ,,   Work among ... ... ... ... ... ... 314, 369, 776-781
   ,,   Work, Method of ... ... ... ... ... ... 315-317, 320
Women's Worker's Union, Desirability of ... ... ... ... ...   781
World's Women's Christian Temperance Union ... ... ... ...   754


XAVIER, ST. FRANCIS, Reference to ... ... ... ... 245, 250, 252, 253


Y. M. C. A., Paper upon the ... ... ... ... ... ...   185, 195
   ,,      References to ... 135, 208, 211, 216, 222, 223, 241, 271, 288, 291
Young, Training of the ... ... ... ... ... ... 178, 196, 225, 360
Y. W. C. A., References to ... ... 135, 216, 223, 211, 291, 341, 342, 356


ZENANA WORK ... ... ... ... ... ... 314, 316, 322, 344, 357, 360, 361
   ,,   (see also "Women, Work amongst") ... ... ...


*FINIS.*

ERRATA.

Page 148, line 1, for "among 50 times as many people" *read* "among so many people."

Page 148, lines 2/3, *read* " to feed 50 times as many thousand of heathen Kols with the Bread of Life."

www.ingramcontent.com/pod-product-compliance
Lightning Source LLC
Chambersburg PA
CBHW022138300426
44115CB00006B/245